About the author

Dr Robert Muggah is the Research
Director of the Geneva-based Small Arms
Survey. Previously, he was a Global Security
and Cooperation Professional Fellow
(SSRC) at the Refugee Studies Centre,
Queen Elizabeth House, University of
Oxford. Muggah received a PhD at Oxford
University and his MPhil in Development
Studies at the Institute for Development
Studies, University of Sussex.

Relocation failures in Sri Lanka

A short history of internal displacement and resettlement

Robert Muggah

Zed Books

LONDON | NEW YORK

Relocation failures in Sri Lanka: a short history of internal displacement and resettlement was first published in 2008 by Zed Books Ltd, 7 Cynthia Street, London N1 9JF, UK and Room 400, 175 Fifth Avenue, New York, NY 10010, USA

www.zedbooks.co.uk

Cover designed by Andrew Corbett
Set in OurType Arnhem and Futura Bold by Ewan Smith, London
Index: ed.emery@thefreeuniversity.net
Printed and bound in the UK by the Charlesworth Group.

Distributed in the USA exclusively by Palgrave Macmillan, a division of St Martin's Press, LLC, 175 Fifth Avenue, New York, NY 10010.

A catalogue record for this book is available from the British Library.
Library of Congress cataloging in publication data are available.

ISBN 978 1 84813 045 6 hb
ISBN 978 1 84813 046 3 pb

Contents

Tables, figures and maps

Acknowledgements

This volume was prepared during a time of immense political volatility in Sri Lanka and global affairs more generally. Field research began immediately after a 2002 ceasefire temporarily ended almost two decades of civil conflict between the Sri Lankan government and the Liberation Tigers of Tamil Eelam (LTTE). In the event, the agreement was short-lived and only temporarily stayed a return to extreme violence. A few months after a devastating tsunami struck the island in December 2004, the country started its inexorable return to dirty war. The ceasefire was pronounced dead in 2008 and the appalling costs of war began to be felt from Jaffna, Trincomalee and Batticaloa to Colombo. Meanwhile, international attention and engagement in Sri Lanka began to stall. Wars and natural disasters in Afghanistan (2002) and Iraq (2003), Sudan (2003), Haiti (2004), Bangladesh (2007) and Burma (2008) superseded Sri Lanka in geopolitical importance.

There are literally hundreds of experts and lay people who patiently guided me in my attempts to better understand the highly politicised landscapes of Sri Lanka. They helped me navigate a vast array of historical, economic and political fault-lines and the fiendishly complex names of places and people I visited between 2001 and 2008. Spanning several continents, I could fill volumes in naming them individually. It will be to the reader's relief, then, that I confine my thanks to a small selection. At the outset, I extend deepest gratitude to my family – all of them. Each member played an instrumental role in keeping my spirits high during the inevitable lows of preparing this volume. Likewise, colleagues at the Graduate Institute of International and Development Studies in Geneva and my own organisation, the Small Arms Survey, also gave generously of their time and allowed me a measure of flexibility to research an issue about which I am deeply passionate. The government of Switzerland, particularly the Swiss Development Cooperation (SDC), and the US-based Social Science Research Council (SSRC) must be specially credited for providing generous support to see this research process through.

New and old friends in Sri Lanka, Switzerland, Canada, the United Kingdom and the United States offered relentless encouragement. In particular, colleagues affiliated with the Colombo-based International Centre for Ethnic Studies (ICES), the UN High Commissioner for Refugees (UNHCR), the World Bank and the Asian Development Bank provided constructive insight and practical logistical support – particularly Sunil Bastian, Radhika Coomeraswamy, Ponnudarai Thambirajah, Bradman Weerakoon, Neill Wright, Phil Esmond and my dear colleague Michael Cernea. A host of internationally recognised scholars and academics working with the University of Colombo, the University of Peradeniya, the University of the East and various research centres from Jaffna and Trincomalee to Kandy and Colombo gave liberally of their time, listened to long-winded lectures and commented on early drafts.

I am grateful to colleagues at Oxford University who supplied steady counsel during periods of high anxiety, particularly Professors Stephen Castles and Dawn Chatty. Others helping to steer the volume to the finish-line version include Richard Black, Gil Loescher, Ed Benson, Clifford Spence, David Gelnder, Nick Van Hear, Norman Uphoff and Eric Mooney. Colleagues commenting directly on specific chapters include Bob Picciotto, Simon Bagshaw, Peter Batchelor, Jesse Bernstein, Francis Deng, Conrad Detissera, David Evans, Rajat Ganguly, Timmo Gaasbeek, Ayman Gharaibeh, Katarzyna Grabska, Cristina Hoyos, Tania Inowlocki, Keith Krause, Jay Maheswaran, Lyla Mehta, Aninia Nadig, Sarah Nouwen, Aruvasi Patel, Bryan Pfaffenberger, Bob Rae, Charan Rainford, Ambika Satkunanathan, Tad Scudder, Jagath Seneratne, Timothy Shaw, Rajesh Venugopal and Tod Wassel. Also thanks to an anonymous reader, who supplied thoughtful and pointed comments on an earlier draft, and to my father, who issued blunt, but excellent, editorial comments.

There are many others to whom I am thankful after more than half a decade of research in Colombo, Mullaitivu, Trincomalee, Batticaloa and Ampara, as well as visits to Washington DC, New York, Delhi, Manila, Geneva and elsewhere. These include translators, enumerators and mapping specialists – particularly Chandreenie Kariyawasan, Upekha Chanduka, Amir Kamirthalingam, Prasadi Indrawimala, Regunanthan Umapathy, Jillie Luff and Mil Illangasinghe – without whom I literally would have been lost. Appreciation must also be extended to my surrogate family in Colombo – the Jayatilikas, Samanayakes and their relatives – who taught me much about the history of the island and the hospitality of its people. Finally, I am indebted to the many people who told me their stories, openly and in confidence – particularly resettled communities, government officials and aid workers in northern and eastern Sri Lanka. Indeed, the tragedy of Sri Lanka is that many of them cannot be thanked publicly and must remain anonymous, a reality that one hopes will change soon. This volume is a tribute to these nameless men, women and children – many of whom are living and bringing up families in the face of horrendous suffering.

Acronyms

ADB	Asian Development Bank
AfDB	African Development Bank
ARN	Authority for Rebuilding the Nation
AU	African Union
AusAid	Australian Aid Department
CAP	consolidated inter-agency appeals process
CCD	Coastline Conservation Department
CCSC	Central Committee for Swedish Cooperation
CEA	Central Environmental Authority
CEDMHR	Commission for the Elimination of Discrimination and Monitoring of Human Rights
CERF	Central Emergency Revolving Fund
CFA	ceasefire agreement
CGES	Commissioner General for Essential Services
CHA	Consortium of Humanitarian Agencies
CIDA	Canadian International Development Agency
CIDR	conflict-induced internal displacement and resettlement
CNO	Centre for National Operations
COHRE	Centre on Housing Rights and Evictions
CPA	Centre for Policy Alternatives
CPP	Council for Public Policy
DANIDA	Danish Development Agency
DfID	UK Department for International Development
DHA	Department of Humanitarian Affairs
DIDR	development-induced internal displacement and resettlement
ECHO	European Community Humanitarian Office
ECOSOC	UN Economic and Social Council
ECOWAS	Economic Community of West African States
EEC	European Economic Community
ERRP	emergency reconciliation and rehabilitation programme
ESCR	UN Covenant on Economic, Social and Cultural Rights
EU	European Union
EXCOM	Executive Committee for UNHCR
FAO	Food and Agricultural Organization
FDL	forward defence line
GDP	gross domestic product

GIS	geographic information system
HRC	Human Rights Commission
HRTF	Human Rights Task Force
HSZ	high security zones
IADB	Inter-American Development Bank
IASC	UN Inter-Agency Standing Committee
IASFM	International Association for the Study of Forced Migration
IBRD	International Bank for Reconstruction and Development
ICC	International Criminal Court
ICCPR	UN International Covenant on Civil and Political Rights
ICES	International Centre for Ethnic Studies
ICIHI	Independent Commission on International Humanitarian Issues
ICISS	International Commission on Intervention and State Sovereignty
ICRC	International Committee of the Red Cross
IDD	Internal Displacement Division
IDMC	Internal Displacement Monitoring Centre
IDP	internally displaced person
IFC	International Finance Corporation
IFRC	International Federation of the Red Cross/Crescent/Crystal
IGAD	Intergovernmental Authority on Development
IMF	International Monetary Fund
IPKF	Indian peace-keeping force
JBIC	Japan Bank for International Cooperation
JICA	Japan International Cooperation Agency
JOSSOP	Joint Security Services Operation
JVP	Janatha Vimukthi Peramuna (People's Liberation Front)
LST	Law and Society Trust
LTTE	Liberation Tigers of Tamil Eelam
MDB	Mahaweli Development Board
MDIP	Mahaweli Development and Irrigation Programme
MDTF	multi-donor trust fund
MEA	Mahaweli Economic Agency
MECA	Mahaweli Engineering and Construction Agency
MP	Member of Parliament
NCP	North Central Province
NECORD	North East Community Restoration and Development
NEDECO	Netherlands Engineering Consultants
NEERP	North East Emergency Rehabilitation Project
NEIP	North East Irrigated Agriculture Project
NEPC	North East Provincial Council

NERF	North East Reconstruction Fund
NGO	non-governmental organisation
NHDA	National Housing and Development Authority
NIDR	natural disaster-induced internal displacement and resettlement
NIRP	National Involuntary Resettlement Policy
NLC	National Land Commission
NRP	National Resettlement Plan
OAU	Organisation of African Unity
OCHA	Office for the Coordination of Humanitarian Affairs
ODA	Overseas Development Administration
OECD	Organisation for Economic Co-operation and Development
OED	Operations Evaluation Department
OMS	Operational Manual Statement
OPN	Operations Policy Note
ORC	open relief centres
OSCE	Organization for Security and Co-operation in Europe
PAP	project-affected person
PLOTE	People's Liberation Organisation of Tamil Eelam
PMU	Programme Monitoring Unit
PRA	participatory rural appraisal
PRSP	Poverty Reduction Strategy Paper
PTOMS	Post Tsunami Operational Management Structure
QIP	quick impact projects
QUNO	United Nations Quakers Office
R2P	responsibility to protect
RADA	Reconstruction and Development Agency
RAP	resettlement action plan
RAW	Research and Analysis Wing
RPPA	Rehabilitation of Persons and Property Authority
RRAN	Resettlement and Rehabilitation Authority of the North
RRR	relief, rehabilitation and reconstruction
RRTG	relief and rehabilitation thematic group
RSC	Refugee Studies Centre
SADC	Southern African Development Community
SAHR	South Asians for Human Rights
SCF	Save the Children Fund
SDN	subcommittee on de-escalation and normalisation
SIDA	Swedish International Development Agency
SIHRN	subcommittee on immediate humanitarian and rehabilitation needs

SLFP	Sri Lankan Freedom Party
SLMM	Sri Lanka Monitoring Mission
TAFLOL	Task Force for Logistics and Law and Order
TAFOR	Task Force for Relief
TAFREN	Task Force to Rebuild the Nation
TAFRER	Task Force for Rescue and Relief
TEC	Tsunami Evaluation Coalition
TELO	Tamil Eelam Liberation Organisation
THRU	Tsunami Housing and Reconstruction Unit
TRO	Tamil Rehabilitation Organisation
TULF	Tamil United Liberation Front
TVA	Tennessee Valley Authority
UAS	unified assistance scheme
UDA	Urban Development Authority
UDHR	Universal Declaration of Human Rights
UN	United Nations
UNCHR	United Nations Commission on Human Rights
UNDAF	United Nations Development Assistance Framework
UNDP	United Nations Development Programme
UNDRO	United Nations Disaster Relief Coordinator
UNEP	United Nations Environment Programme
UNESCO	United Nations Educational, Scientific and Cultural Organization
UNGA	United Nations General Assembly
UNHCR	United Nations High Commissioner for Refugees
UNICEF	United Nations Children's Fund
UNITAR	United Nations Institute for Training and Research
UNP	United National Party
UNSC	United Nations Security Council
USAID	United States Agency for International Development
USCR	United States Committee for Refugees
UTHR	University Teachers for Human Rights
VRC	village rehabilitation committee
WFP	World Food Programme
WHO	World Health Organization

To Henry and Betty
and the grounded men and women
who came before them

Introduction

Millions of people are internally displaced and relocated around the world each year to make way for dam and urban renewal projects and in the wake of wars, cyclones and floods. Meanwhile, a global coalition of activists and policymakers are advocating for, and implementing, policies and programmes to safely return or resettle them. Owing to the multiple causes and consequences of population dislocation, the range of governmental and non-state entities involved in resettling them and the variety of conceptual and disciplinary approaches to framing these issues, resettlement is typically described as a totalising phenomenon and an extreme form of spatial socialisation.

This book is principally concerned with understanding why the resettlement of internally displaced people so often fails. It necessarily begins with an exploration of how states, multilateral agencies, non-governmental organisations and scholars conceptualise issues such as internal displacement and resettlement. Then it seeks to explain their rationale and motivation in providing protection and durable solutions for different categories of populations internally displaced in the context of development, war and natural disasters. In focusing on Sri Lanka's many decades of experience with displacement and population resettlement, the volume appraises why and how such interventions were pursued and proposes an explanation for relocation failure. The book applies a unitary approach to understanding and researching the phenomenology of internal displacement and resettlement. Such a perspective is by definition *comparative* and examines otherwise exclusive categories of internal displacement and resettlement arising from development, armed conflict and natural disasters. A unitary approach is inherently *multi-disciplinary* and consciously borrows from a range of social science disciplines and methodologies. The volume therefore seeks, where possible, to balance theoretical and empirical findings generated by anthropologists, ethnographers, sociologists and human geographers with insights from international relations and political science theory, law and political economy.

Volume structure

Chapter 1 critically assesses the theory and labels used to explain internal displacement and resettlement processes. It challenges the impulse among policymakers and planners to standardise and categorise forced migrants. An analysis of how labels are constructed and deployed reveals the 'political in the seemingly apolitical arena of bureaucratic practices' (Zetter 2007: 184). It is also essential in order to lay out the discursive foundations of subsequent chapters. Crucially, the chapter unpacks assumptions nurtured by forced migration specialists that displacement consists of involuntary, temporally and geographically specific processes. It then introduces a definition of resettlement as a planned and involuntary process entailing the permanent relocation of an individual, family or household from one's place of origin to another place. It is important to distinguish this definition from 'third-country' resettlement as described in the 1951 Refugee Convention and 1967 Protocol, which entails planned and voluntary movement across an international border. In mobilising the work of Zetter (1991, 2007), Oliver-Smith (2004), Castles (2002, 2003), Hyndman (2000) and Malkki (1995) in particular, the chapter considers the attendant difficulties of labelling populations on the move and the ways in which compartmentalised forms of knowledge production inform international norm-setting and policymaking. The chapter then traces out the conceptual evolution of three separate categories of internal displacement and resettlement since the middle of the twentieth century. These categories were conspicuously structured according to the attributed causes of displacement – whether development, conflict or natural disasters.

Chapter 2 compares and contrasts state and non-state understandings of – and bureaucratic responses to – internal displacement and resettlement through the prism of international regimes. Drawing from rationalist and constructivist traditions, the chapter describes how an array of governmental and non-governmental actors with different ideational problem-sets fostered and created loose institutional arrangements to enhance predictability, reduce transaction costs and promote cooperation in situations where they might otherwise compete. It reviews the origin and shape of these international regimes and how they are (expected to be) actualised at the national and sub-national level.[1] The chapter shows how these regimes were themselves fostered by an international network of academics, practitioners, organisations and state representatives. Taken together, they include (transnational) advocacy coalitions and public policy networks – veritable 'capillaries of power' – bent on forging consensus and support for three separate regimes composed of overlapping principles, norms, rules and decision-making procedures. Oriented towards different categories of internal displacement and resettlement, these three regimes appear to be as distinct from the so-called refugee regime as they are from each other.

Regimes for different categories of internal displacement and resettlement are more declarative than performative. While introduced from above, they are nevertheless expected to influence state and non-state understandings of particular issues, their behaviour and ultimately outcomes from below. In different ways, the three regimes are expected to contain, protect and promote durable solutions for those internally displaced and resettled by development, conflict and natural disasters. While the practical expression of protection and durable solutions differs subtly between regimes, they embody progressive universalising standards as reflected in international law and good practice. It is seen that the evolution of these regimes into more robust (enforceable) arrangements is hampered by endogenous constraints, including narrow interpretations of state sovereignty (as non-interference) and challenges with overcoming collective action dilemmas among regime proponents. The chapter considers how these regimes are also inadvertently blind to a range of historical and political processes associated with state-building and ethnic nationalism in ways that can make their prescriptions potentially counter-productive.

Chapter 3 reviews the chronology of settlement and resettlement patterns in Sri Lanka from the late nineteenth to the early twenty-first century. It also traces out a number of exogenous factors influencing the three regimes. The chapter documents the evolution of so-called colonisation (settlement) schemes from the late 1800s to independence in 1948. It finds that while state-sponsored settlement and resettlement initiatives continued into the post-colonial era, they were harnessed by an emerging indigenous elite to a new political purpose. Rather than be driven by the imperatives of colonial plantation economics, settlement and resettlement were soon inextricably hitched to modernist nation-building paradigms, ethnic nationalism and the state's assertion of control over land. Population relocation served to consolidate state (Sinhalese) hegemony over non-state-controlled areas and, combined with discriminatory religious and language legislation, triggered a (Tamil) secessionist project. The parallel introduction of universalising international regimes designed to permanently resettle internally displaced populations potentially entrenched ethnic and spatial segregation between the south on the one side and the north and east on the other.

Chapter 4 focuses on the relationships between the international regime for development-induced internal displacement and resettlement (DIDR) and a controversial multi-purpose dam, irrigation and 'settlement' initiative. One of the largest rural integrated development schemes in the world at the time, the Mahaweli Development and Irrigation Programme

3

(MDIP) was formally launched in the late 1960s and subsequently accelerated in the late 1970s by a newly elected government. Drawing primarily from archival records and short site visits, the chapter considers the outcomes of two specific 'Systems' of the MDIP straddling ethnically heterogeneous areas of several northern and eastern districts during the 1980s and 1990s. It highlights how the establishment of these Systems contributed to the (planned and unplanned) internal displacement of tens of thousands of Sri Lankan Tamil 'encroachers' and the settlement and resettlement of many more Sinhalese 'peasants'. The resulting purpose-built 'colony units' formed a new spatial boundary that segmented and en-claved minority communities and led to heightened militarisation in the north-east. Proponents of the nascent DIDR regime unintentionally sanc-tioned and entrenched state-led demographic and politico-administrative transformation while simultaneously contributing to the real and relative impoverishment of successive generations of resettling households.

Chapter 5 considers the international regime for conflict-induced internal displacement and resettlement (CIDR) within the context of protracted armed conflict waged primarily in northern and eastern Sri Lanka. Since the early 1980s, the country's civil war pitted the armed forces and their auxiliaries against an array of militarised groups, in-cluding the LTTE, the self-declared representatives of the Sri Lankan Tamil community. The UNHCR, a key proponent of the CIDR regime that also includes bilateral and multilateral donors and non-governmental agencies, was invited to the island by the Sri Lankan government in 1987. The agency initially oriented its activities towards repatriating Sri Lankan refugees from India and promoting protection in-country to contain 'would-be' refugees. By the early 1990s, however, UNHCR pro-moted durable solutions for IDPs. Based on field research conducted in the north and east of the country, the chapter considers the evolution of conceptual and bureaucratic responses to CIDR since independence. With support from regime proponents, such as UNHCR and the World Bank, the state established and managed so-called 'welfare centres' and 'relocation villages', composed primarily of resettled Sri Lankan Tamil and Muslim populations internally displaced from areas of conflict. In order to highlight the outcomes of state-sanctioned resettlement, the chapter focuses on the experiences and livelihoods of several relocation villages in Trincomalee and Batticaloa involving both Sinhalese and Sri Lankan Tamil resettlers. It finds that regime proponents, while seeking to promote protection and durable solutions, unintentionally reinforced the demographic and politico-military imperatives of the state and the LTTE.

Chapter 6 reviews the sudden emergence and influence of a regime for natural disaster-induced internal displacement and resettlement (NIDR) in the context of the tsunami. It examines the manner in which vulnerable coastal populations composed primarily of Sri Lankan Tamils and Muslims in the north and east (as well as Sinhalese in the south) were affected by a massive wave that struck the island in late 2004. The chapter considers the role of the nascent NIDR regime in encouraging durable solutions: these consisted primarily of 'transitional' and 'permanent' housing schemes for internally displaced populations. As predicted in Chapter 2, regime proponents encountered considerable exogenous challenges owing to the state's (temporary) application of restrictive 'buffers' to coastal areas and the limited access to appropriate land, as well as a host of strategic barriers introduced by the government, the armed forces and the LTTE. It is too early to discern the influence of the NIDR regime in relation to protection and durable solutions. Nevertheless, Chapter 6 considers preliminary findings generated by site visits with tsunami-affected households living in permanent houses in northern and eastern districts such as Trincomalee, Batticaloa and Ampara.

'Conclusions' distils the basic commonalities and distinguishing characteristics of all three categories of internal displacement and resettlement. It compares the inter-related determinants, shared bureaucratic logic and common impoverishment effects of DIDR, CIDR and NIDR in Sri Lanka, and elsewhere. The chapter also examines the prospects for enhanced cross-fertilisation between epistemic communities and the potential for regime convergence in the twenty-first century. It detects an increasingly prolific rights-based discourse that emphasises complementarity and equality in the promotion of protection and durable solutions. The chapter also traces out a shift in discourse of state sovereignty away from a traditional focus on non-interference to one that emphasises responsibility with attendant obligations to protect civilians from extreme violence.[2]

In spite of contemporary geopolitical developments – in Iraq, Afghanistan and Sudan, the preference for unilateral over multilateral humanitarian intervention and the reordering of global order in light of the rise of China and India, the principle of state sovereignty as responsibility is increasingly accepted by international institutions such as the United Nations Security Council (Deng 2007; Evans 2007). In Sri Lanka, however, the 'responsibility to protect' concept remains contentious and a source of considerable tension and acrimony. Perhaps more optimistically, the conclusion observes a gradual tendency towards increasing centralisation of accountability for internally displaced people within specific institutions and organisations – including multilateral and bilateral aid agencies and the Sri Lankan state – a trend that hints at the potential of overcoming collective action dilemmas in the long term. Whether these transformations ultimately yield improved protection and durable solutions in Sri Lanka or elsewhere remains to be seen.

Methodological considerations

The phenomena of internal displacement and resettlement defy the application of a single disciplinary lens. Nevertheless, ethnographic, anthropological, sociological and psycho-social approaches tend to dominate forced migration studies. Consequently, scholarship highlights the 'lived experiences' of internally displaced and resettled populations, including their patterns of vulnerability, coping strategies and social interactions with host communities. There is comparatively less exploration of the normative or policy environment in which such processes are conceived and framed, much less the ways in which specific policies and practices yield positive (or negative) outcomes (Weiss and Korn 2006). In consciously adopting an inter-disciplinary approach that includes international relations theory, political geography, history and development studies, this volume considers the wider cluster of norms, institutions and agents shaping the process and outcomes of internal displacement and resettlement.

Such an approach is typically described as 'grounded'. It is grounded because it builds theory directly from the field and assumes that the processes of data collection, analysis and theory building proceed simultaneously rather than sequentially. Field research is thus undertaken to accumulate broadly comparable data from which a range of specific categories and their associated properties can subsequently be isolated and the relationships between them identified (Glaser 1992). By definition, a grounded methodology also requires the researcher to apply a combination of qualitative and quantitative instruments and to triangulate findings appropriately (Mason 2004; Read and Marsh 2002; Strauss 1987). These methods can range from key informant interviews and participant observation to participatory focus groups and analysis of sizeable demographic datasets. A grounded approach typically tailors research design, selection of field sites, sampling techniques, local recruitment strategies and specialised research tools to the particularities of the local context (Hyndman and de Alwis 2000; Savolainen 1994; Welch 1975).

As noted above, a primary objective of the volume is to generate a comparative assessment of international regimes designed to protect and promote durable solutions for internally displaced people, including their influence on shaping resettlement outcomes in a single country. Sri Lanka offers a compelling, albeit complex and unstable, environment in which to test these propositions. On the 'positive' side of the ledger, Sri Lanka experienced all three forms of internal displacement and resettlement – often concurrently – before and after the negotiated ceasefire agreement (CFA) between the government and the LTTE in 2002. It is not unique in this respect: countries such as Sudan, Uganda, Ethiopia, the Democratic Republic of Congo, Haiti, Colombia, Nepal, the Philippines, Solomon Islands and Indonesia also experienced mass population relocation as a result of development, conflict and natural disasters.[3] The CFA also generated a measure of (temporal and physical) space to conduct field-work – an environment unlike any other witnessed in the previous two decades. Indeed the substance and methods of the research were initially welcomed and encouraged by international and national authorities and representatives of the LTTE. But with the resumption and intensification of conflict, the mood soured.

A major constraint to analysing forced migration in Sri Lanka relates to both the politicisation, and the poor state, of descriptive statistics in the country. Discussed at length in Chapters 3, 4, 5 and 6, data are highly biased, poorly collated and thus only tentative estimates of longitudinal and spatial trends can be rendered. Though the country boasts a credible national surveillance infrastructure in relation to monitoring population health and socio-economic well-being, statistics on sensitive topics such as displacement and resettlement are frequently restricted, selective and of dubious quality. For example, the Mahaweli Authority reportedly 'lost' all socio-economic data for more than 250,000 settler and resettler families affected by DIDR between 1970 and 2000. Although UNHCR's Sri Lankan Colombo office maintained disaggregated demographic data on certain temporal and geographic aspects of CIDR, they were isolated to specific years and districts and seldom demographically disaggregated until after the 2002 ceasefire.[4] Similarly, the Reconstruction and Development Agency (RADA), UN-HABITAT and the UN Office for the Coordination of Humanitarian Affairs (OCHA) collated statistics on NIDR – including transitional shelters and permanent housing – but data were often out of date, sporadic and widely dispersed. As a result, an imperfect profile was reconstructed by the author from the backrooms of district government agent offices, *land kacheri* buildings and NGO warehouses in Sri Lanka and triangulated with 'official' data presented by government and various UN agencies.

Although official public and non-governmental statistics are often manipulated for political economy reasons, it is possible to render an order of magnitude estimate of the scale and ethnic distribution of internal displacement. For example, more than one million Sinhalese were (involuntarily) resettled as a result of the MDIP since the late 1970s. At least another million more Sri Lankan Tamils and Muslims were (forcibly) displaced, returned or resettled during various periods of the armed conflict since the early 1980s, with rates increasing again since 2005. Almost half a million Sri Lankan Tamils, Muslims and Sinhalese were internally displaced following the tsunami in late 2004.

The administration of field research while different forms of internal displacement and resettlement were occurring concurrently generated both opportunities and dilemmas. While it allowed for access to actually occurring phenomena and personal exposure to the actors and agents at the coal face, it also impinged on the author's potential for dispassionate analysis and the accumulated wisdom born of hindsight. In many cases, the only way to 'do' research in otherwise inaccessible areas was to participate in the relief effort itself.[5]

One of the goals of this volume is to test the association between nascent international regimes for development-, conflict- and natural disaster-induced internal displacement and resettlement (independent variables) on state behaviour and ultimately resettlement outcomes (dependent variables). This entailed extensive investigation of the real and perceived policies and practices of state and non-state institutions and of the experiences of relocated populations before and after the 'resettlement' intervention. Of course, public and non-governmental authorities and resettled populations do not necessarily describe their situation in relation to neatly defined categories or external interventions. To the contrary, the experience of displacement and relocation is described by respondents as a messy sequence of events explicitly informed by their lived experiences. A major challenge then, relates to the reliable and representative framing of the policies and practices characterised by the aforementioned regimes. In order to do this, ideas and concepts were repeatedly tested with key informants. Likewise, early drafts of certain chapters were sent to senior analysts affiliated with multilateral institutions such as the World Bank, UNHCR and IFRC and Sri Lankan government and non-governmental entities in order to test candidate theories.

The ability to test the relationships between international regimes and local outcomes such as protection and durable solutions requires a clear definition of 'regimes'. As Chapter 2 makes clear, regime theorists have long struggled with 'measurability' partly due to the lack of consensus over what exactly constitutes a regime. Most approaches therefore opt for an interpretive methodology. In such cases, scholars examine the communicative processes (verbal and written statements) of government leaders, public servants and non-governmental actors in order to discern evidence of emerging principles, norms, rules and decision-making procedures (Finnemore 2003; Klotz 1995; Kratochwil and Ruggie 1986). The conceptual parameters of separate regimes emerge from interviews with (and a review of the statements made by) key representatives of international institutions such as bilateral donors, multilateral, financial and bilateral agencies, senior government decision-makers and policy researchers from London, Geneva, New York and Washington DC to Delhi, Manila, Colombo and Trincomalee.

This volume constitutes the first systematic attempt to compare and contrast different cases of *internal* displacement and resettlement, though previous studies have examined refugees and development 'oustees' (Cernea and McDowell 2000). It also offers an original effort to test the influence and outcomes of three regimes in a single country, something that has not been attempted in Sri Lanka or elsewhere to the best of the author's knowledge. In order to control for variations across time and space and to compare categories of forced migration, individual resettlement schemes were selected from broadly comparable geographic and ethnic districts in the country.[6]

A case study approach does not stand alone and should be considered within a family of comparable case studies. The intrinsic value of comparative research on forced migration is acknowledged by Turton (2003) and Richmond (1994) who, on the basis of multiple case studies, developed typologies of different categories of migrants, forced or otherwise. Moreover, the selection of a single country with multiple cases concurs with Eckstein's (1975: 175) claim that a single crucial case to test candidate theories can score a knock-out blow over more theoretical deductive approaches. Thus, the case study approach advanced in Chapters 4, 5 and 6 is therefore widely accepted in the social sciences (King and Murray 2002). In presenting evidence on the themes laid out above, the three case study chapters are not symmetrical. Certain cases highlight particular themes more than others. The individual cases and their narratives are introduced more as a way of developing the central arguments than as equal blocks of evidence.

A host of methods were employed to analyse the influence of international regimes on state behaviour, the constitutive features of bureaucratic institutions and the spatial distribution of resettlement schemes. These included an archival review of parliamentary records (Hansard), government bills and land legislation[7] since the nineteenth century. As noted above, primary data were also collected from semi-structured interviews with a wide array of respondents. In all, more than 125 key informant interviews were administered in the capital Colombo and in district and divisional capitals and rural areas with active and retired government agents, district secretaries, municipal public servants, development practitioners and researchers.[8] Other approaches included the geo-referencing of past and current resettlement schemes using geographic information system (GIS) software with data drawn from a combination of ministries, authorities and UN agencies.

In order to examine the extent to which international regimes contributed to de facto protection and durable solutions, participatory focus groups were held with purposefully selected samples of resettled populations in six 'resettlement schemes'. The process entailed the gathering together of a representative sample of between ten and twenty resettled men, women and youth through locally recruited Sinhalese, Tamil and Muslim intermediaries for short sessions with repeat visits over several intervals. Special dispensations were made to ensure that sessions were undertaken in deference to the requirements of labourers and household routines. Given the sensitivities of the topic, consent was agreed beforehand and the names of participants were stripped from all physical outputs to avoid them from being misused.[9] As noted by Hyndman and de Alwis (2000):

> PRA [participatory rural appraisal] ... involves the collection of household data ... and includes family names and a 'social map' of who lives where, with whom and owns what. Such information in the hands of the LTTE for the purposes of monitoring the current military training and recruitment campaign could be disastrous. In the hands of the armed forces it could also be dangerous.

Participatory methods were introduced in order to assess whether displaced and resettled populations themselves determined that they had realised a durable solution. Building on research undertaken by the author in other conflict zones, they provided an inclusive platform for a selection of resettlers to express their view 'from below'.[10] Ultimately, the effectiveness of the regimes in relation to protection and durable solutions must be assessed according to objective and subjective criteria.[11] As noted above, specific districts were purposefully selected not just because they experienced disproportionately high rates of forced migration, but because they exhibited comparatively higher levels of ethnic diversity than more ethnically homogeneous southern and northern districts.

The decision to focus on common districts for all categories of internal displacement and resettlement was taken to minimise the risk of omitted variable biases – the (causal) influence of non-accounted-for independent variables influencing resettlement outcomes.

Ethics in forced migration research

An underlying motivation for undertaking comparative research on internal displacement and resettlement is the potential to learn across competing epistemic communities and to deepen and strengthen awareness, understanding and international and domestic policy responses across sectors. This is consistent with the aspirations of forced migration to enact positive change. Research on forced migrants was described by Davis (1992) as the 'anthropology of suffering', focusing as it does on violence, dislocation and its effects. Oliver-Smith (2004), Colson (2003) and Turton (1996) observe that research on refugees and other forced migrants is only justified when it contributes meaningfully to alleviating such suffering. Hathaway (2006: 2) observes that 'whatever else forced migration scholars are, we have always been linked by our determination to be a community of engaged scholars, that is, persons who do what we do with a view to improving the lot of those whose lives we study'.

Practical research on displacement and resettlement invariably generates a number of ethical tensions. A threefold imperative confronts forced migration researchers and scholars. Jacobsen and Landau (2003) emphasise the first as the retention of high academic standards and the second as the commitment to creating and disseminating knowledge that actively contributes to enhanced protection, influences state and non-governmental agency behaviour and reduces human misery. They argue that researchers must avoid the temptation to undertake 'advocacy research' and to overstate claims if they are going to contribute meaningfully to policy and programming and generate credible impetus for (positive) change. A third imperative is – as the Hippocratic oath recommends – doing no intentional harm. There is a very real risk that research aggravates tensions and insecurity: displacement and resettlement processes, particularly in contexts of acute violence, are inherently volatile.

A number of these ethical dilemmas can be offset with careful preparation. For example, confidentiality lapses can be mitigated by acquiring informed consent and guaranteeing anonymity for respondents. The majority of key informants consulted during the preparation of this study requested that their names not be cited in the final document.[12] The 'protection' of informants and focus group respondents can potentially be enhanced by (physical) presence, though this does not necessarily ensure that harm is avoided over the longer term (Smythe and Robinson 2001; Anderson 1999; Mooney 1995). Reactivity – wherein the presence of an outsider influences the behaviour of respondents – can be offset through the transparent communication of the aims and expectations of the research, triangulation, continuous dialogue with respondents and, where appropriate, the passing on of expressed grievances to responsible authorities (Betts 2005; Goodhand 2000). Where administered appropriately, participatory research allows for immediate triangulation and analysis with participants themselves and thus minimises potential reactivity (Skinner 2005).[13]

The deteriorating security environment profoundly shaped the possibilities for meaningful field research in northern and eastern Sri Lanka (Muggah 2008b). In some instances, resettlement schemes established in the 1980s and 1990s were literally swept away by disasters and war a decade later. Owing to the increased deployment of armed forces personnel and the LTTE in the north and east, the ratcheting up of counter-insurgency efforts by the government, the (unsolved) massacres of aid agency staff[14] and progressively hostile attitudes towards foreigners, access to certain areas of the country were progressively more uncertain. Sustained visits to certain resettlement schemes required official clearance. By 2006 the issues of internal displacement and resettlement in north and eastern Sri Lanka were considered so politically charged that certain interviews were postponed or denied outright. Even secondary data on displacement and resettlement previously made public by government authorities and non-governmental agencies were later withdrawn or altered *post hoc*. Throughout the preparation of this volume, the exposure of the author to real risks obviously paled in comparison to the routine dangers facing civilians. Nevertheless, research on social suffering at times requires assuming informed risks and making sacrifices. Persistence is warranted on the grounds that the suffering arising from internal displacement and resettlement can be carefully documented and eventually reversed.

1 | A unified approach to displacement and resettlement

The forced migration studies literature is rife with conceptual tension. It is precisely because of the field's many disciplinary and ideological fault-lines that foundational concepts and terminology must be revisited. While specialists acknowledge the centrality of power asymmetries and co-ercion, there are still fundamental disagreements over basic parameters: whether displacement and resettlement is voluntary or involuntary, when these processes begin and end and whether they are restricted to physical movement or include other non-spatial forms of dislocation. While this debate potentially signals a healthy intellectual state of affairs, lingering disputes over rudimentary concepts are a major obstacle to building theory, refining and habituating norms, and ultimately refining practice (Finnemore and Sikkink 1998). Consensus continues to be hindered by narrow agendas demanding standardisation together with epistemic fault-lines dividing the many disciplines that comprise the forced migration field.

This chapter considers the ways distinct policymakers and researchers coalesced around separate categories of internal displacement and resettlement. It finds that the specialisation of knowledge and expertise in each domain reinforced unnecessary barriers between groups of scholars and practitioners. It traces the evolution of academic-practitioner networks engaged on various categories and how they constituted more or less unitary *epistemic communities* sharing knowledge about cause–effect relationships in specific policy arenas and adopting shared sets of normative and principled beliefs (Haas 1992: 3). These communities include adversarial *advocacy coalitions* and more collaborative *public-policy networks* that transmit and promote normative and ontological axioms across policy arenas. While discourse and practice associated with development, conflict and natural disaster-induced internal displacement and resettlement are epistemologically and bureaucratically compartmentalised, a unified perspective reveals that they have more in common than often assumed.

A critical review of core concepts in forced migration studies is essential to establishing a coherent and consistent nomenclature for the remainder of this volume. Despite their shared characteristics, different categories of forced migration are conceptually segmented and seldom compared, either in Sri Lanka or elsewhere. The particular framing of specific categories inevitably leads to specific forms of policy and practice. Many of the basic assumptions underpinning these framings play a crucial role in shaping specific regimes for categories of internal displacement and resettlement. In revealing the basic tensions in fundamental concepts of forced migration, the chapter demonstrates how more nuanced and comparative study could lead to very different judgements and conclusions relating to protection and durable solutions.

Definitions and labels

Definitions and labels matter. The representation of conditions and experiences in certain ways serves specific interests and is an inescapable element of public policymaking, its bureaucracies and its discourse. How, by and for whom a concept or phenomenon is defined and labelled frames debates, the design and implementation of interventions and valuations of success or failure. Labelling is neither neutral nor benign. In the case of the refugee label, Zetter (2007: 188) traces out the ways in which it is 'formed, transformed and "normalised" in policy discourse by bureaucratic practices which seem necessary, appropriate and even benign'. But the highly politicised dynamics of these processes are concealed. Labels affect the balance of power as a result of their capacity to reinforce or deny identity and guarantee conditionality, differentiation, inclusion and exclusion. Labels are therefore an essential feature of stereotyping and social control.

There is a compelling theoretical and moral case for enhanced clarity and interrogation of labels in the forced migration field. Certain refugee studies specialists actively critique the political interests that inform the labelling of refugees and the terminological opacity of their field (Zetter 1991, 2007; Turton 2003). Hathaway (2006: 2) believes that forced migration scholars have 'an ethical responsibility not to adopt categorical distinctions which, while perhaps administratively convenient, fail to reflect true substantive differences'. If arbitrary labels are uncritically accepted and academic contributions reinforce the absorption of these labels into policy 'then we acquiesce in and perhaps even support that arbitrariness' (ibid.).

Labels are iteratively transmitted between theory and practice. In the case of forced migration studies, as in other sectors relating to development or international law, the divide between the academic and practitioner community is blurred. For example, many labels regularly deployed in contemporary academic discourse featured prominently in the development, humanitarian, post-conflict recovery and natural disaster management sectors since at least the mid-twentieth century (Zolberg et al. 1989; Wood 1985; Drabek and Boggs 1968; White, G. F. 1964). Likewise, a sizeable number of the anthropologists and sociologists making seminal contributions to the forced migration field in the 1970s and 1980s were simultaneously employed by organisations involved in 'managing' displacement and resettlement, thus hastening an iterative exchange between theoreticians and practitioners. Since the 1970s, labels were simultaneously refined and cognitively transmitted between academia and various policy arenas through specialist journals, public forums, training courses and universities (Dwivedi 2002).[1]

It is not surprising that the forced migration field exhibits so many contested labels. The literature itself comprises a diverse collection of scholarly and policy writings on subjects ranging from refugee law, economic and labour migration to people-trafficking, transhumance, colonisation and frontier settlement. Given such intrinsic disciplinary heterogeneity, the proliferation of different labels was inevitable. Zetter (1991) describes these competing labels as akin to 'currencies' with fluctuating values and exchange rates. But without a fixed exchange rate, consensus on core concepts and definitions remained elusive. There are also a wide range of bureaucratic interests that condition the application of specific labels. Labels are harnessed by a public policy discourse, whether security-oriented, developmental or humanitarian and used to apportion out assistance and codify entitlements. Sending and Neumann (2006) and Rosenau (2002) describe the instrumentalist use of labels as an extension of governmental rationality or 'governmentality'. Voutira (1997) described the fusion of bureaucratic interests with labelling as a form of 'policy logic': a calculated set of discourses and practices designed to control and regulate populations. While they may project neutrality and impartiality, they are only seldom critically interrogated. Although bureaucratically expedient, they (unintentionally) contribute to the denial of difference, particularly the experiences and attributes of affected populations or acts of (legitimate) resistance.

Labels are instruments of power because they assign differences in beneficiary rights (Zetter 1991, 2007). How a population group is labelled and defined and the distinctions between those who qualify for a particular right and those who do not, informs state and non-governmental obligations, budgeting, intervention strategies and associated entitlements. Shacknove (1985) observed how for the wide array of forced migrants facing acute vulnerability 'refugee status' is a privileged position. In contrast to others who may be worse-off or destitute, refugees are entitled to many forms of international assistance.[2] Both refugee and IDP

15

labels can also unintentionally promote social and economic exclusion by reinforcing latent and revealed prejudices among those who are not similarly categorised. According to Zetter (2007: 184) 'these new, and often pejorative labels, are created and embedded in political discourse, policy and practice'. They can generate stereotypes and essentialist understandings, whereby being a 'refugee', 'IDP', 'illegal asylum seeker', 'trafficked migrant' or 'economic refugee' overshadows other axes of identity, whether gender, ethnicity, class or caste. The social anthropologist Catherine Brun (2003: 377) noted in her study of internally displaced Muslims in Puttalum, western Sri Lanka, that the IDP category ascribed benefits and stigmas that affected the behaviour of resettled populations and host communities: the label constituted 'a social category and identity on the ground ... [leading to] discrimination instead of preventing it'.

Defining displacement

Despite their many ideological and disciplinary differences, forced migration scholars agree that displacement exhibits a range of characteristics distinguishing it from migration.[3] These characteristics inform state and non-governmental discourse, policy and the bureaucracies associated with promoting protection and durable solutions. Displacement is conventionally accorded three core features by academics and practitioners, including involuntariness, temporariness and physical dislocation. By way of contrast, migration is characterised as voluntary, even if it is temporally and spatially varied.[4] When held up to closer scrutiny, even these three fundamental axioms of displacement are on shaky ground.

Voluntary or involuntary Migration is conventionally attributed to voluntary decision-making while displacement is regularly described as 'involuntary' (Castles and Miller 2003; Ghosh 2000; van Hear 1998). Displacement is generally conceived as dichotomous to economic or labour migration: intra-urban and rural–urban population migrations associated with regional imbalances in supply and demand for labour are seldom characterised as displacement. Likewise, mass displacements generated by reservoir development, internecine conflict and earthquakes are distinct from large-scale migrations. Goodwin-Gill (2000: 164) argued that migration should be considered broad enough to include irregular or undocumented migrants, but not 'refugees, exiles, or others *compelled* to leave their homes' (italics added). Though migration can and often does take place before and after displacement it is generally conceded that they are not synonymous.

Certain scholars challenge the presumption that migration and dis-

TABLE 1.1 Labelling migrants and displaced persons

Migrant	Displaced
economic migrant	displaced person
migrant worker	refugee
encroacher	IDP
squatter	de-housed
seasonal migrant	evacuee
economic refugee	environmental refugee
labour migrant	oustee

placement can be readily distinguished on the basis of a voluntary–involuntary dichotomy (Hathaway 2006; Castles 2003; Zolberg et al. 1989). They argue that the determination of 'involuntariness' depends on whether a choice to remain is in fact available. Discerning whether or not a choice is freely exercised is invariably subjective. Referring to the case of villagisation in Ethiopia, Gebre (2002: 270–1) problematised the binary classification and added new sub-categories or degrees of 'intent': voluntary, induced–voluntary, compulsory voluntary and involuntary. Critics of the voluntary–involuntary dichotomy contend that it presupposes a level (or lack) of agency: it artificially reduces displacement to situations where there are no viable alternatives other than self- or household-preservation. But who defines viable alternatives and self-preservation? Is choice exercised exclusively by an individual, by the family or a larger collective? What is the threshold that constitutes a threat to personal or household survival? These questions are inherently subjective and tricky to measure, as asylum claimants and immigration officials regularly attest.

A tipping point distinguishing the phenomenon of voluntary migration from involuntary displacement is real and implied coercion. Whether in the context of poverty or affluence, the practice of migration reflects a deliberate pursuit of new and better opportunities free of external encumbrance. An Intergovernmental Working Group of Experts established by the UN Commission on Human Rights (UN 1997a: 15) confirmed that migration occurs in 'all cases where the decision (to migrate) is taken *freely* by the individual concerned, for reason of *personal convenience* and *without intervention* of an external compelling factor' (italics added). By contrast, displacement is most likely to occur where choices are restricted and where an individual or an individual's family faces more physical and psychological risks than opportunities by staying in their place of residence (Muggah 2003; Hyndman 2000). While overt violence

A unified approach

may trigger displacement, there are more subtle forms of coercion that also shape or restrict choices. As Penz (2003) observed, whatever the attributed real or perceived causes leading to population movement, 'if it is voluntary, it is not displacement'.

Even where displacement is assumed to be taking place, the label is often at odds with the actually occurring phenomena. As will be demonstrated in the case study sections of this volume, circumstances cast by policymakers and bureaucrats as voluntary migration (e.g. whether labour-related or as part of a colonisation scheme) can, on closer inspection, entail involuntariness such as forced evictions and evacuations. Likewise, interventions that generate displacement and resettlement, including dam and reservoir construction or the relocation of populations into emergency camps during wars, may trigger an influx of ostensibly voluntary encroachers, squatters, landless peasants and assisted migrants (Partridge 1993; Hansen and Oliver-Smith 1982, table 1). It is important to recall that settlement and resettlement programmes labelled as 'voluntary' or 'involuntary' may be accompanied by degrees of coercion or no implied threat at all.

Temporary or permanent The categorisation of different types of displacement converges around their attributed causes. For example, displacement is typically causally linked to a discernible external shock. These shocks range from urban renewal or village expansion to dams or mining projects, armed conflicts, ethnic cleansing and natural disasters such as tidal waves, cyclones, floods or mud-slides. With the attribution of a cause, it follows that displacement can be traced to a clearly demarcated starting point. But internal displacement can also begin *well before* the alleged triggering event(s). For example, the alienation and annexation of land that precedes urban renewal or a large-scale dam-building project may require planned 'evacuations' well before physical assets are appropriated, compensated for, or destroyed (Cernea 2003). Depending on informational asymmetries and the relative vulnerability of households, displacement may also begin long before a specific (life-threatening) attack or major climatic event – in which case population movement may, confusingly, be cast by outsiders as migration.

There is a persistent belief among forced migration scholars that displacement usually constitutes a *temporary* disequilibrium. As a short-term aberration, it follows that displacement can be 'normalised' with the introduction of 'protective measures' and ended with the provision of so-called durable solutions. There is an underlying compulsion among scholars and policymakers to redress displacement with the return of the displaced to either their original 'place' following their (voluntary) 'return' or 'resettlement' to a new place to resume an otherwise 'normal' existence. Pedersen (2003: 4) argues that this perspective is based on deeply embedded political and cultural values prevalent in the forced migration field (and others) that suppose a 'natural' link between people, identity and territory. Likewise, Malkki (1995) describes the instinctive attachment to sedentarism as part of the *national* order of things' (italics added). In practice, displacement is rarely temporally fixed, much less temporary. Depending on the situation, displacement ranges from nocturnal flight to protracted situations – and instances of varying periods of displacement can occur side by side as in northern Uganda, Colombia, Nepal or Sri Lanka (Muggah 2000a, 2005b, 2006).

A lingering question among certain forced migration scholars is the determination of when displacement ends. There is virtually no consensus on when internal displacement ends, much less who decides. As Mooney (2002a: 4) makes clear, 'decisions on when internal displacement ends are made, if at all, on an *ad hoc* and arbitrary basis'.[5] Most often the 'end' of displacement is constructed as a set of legal and bureaucratic exit-strategies independent of whether the political and social factors that gave rise to dislocation persist. In the case of development projects, displacement ends when resettlement is said by project planners to have taken place, irrespective of whether first-, second- or third-generation households integrated into designated schemes or not. Conflict and natural disaster-induced displacement ends when a specified quantity of relief aid and shelter is provided, the conditions for return or resettlement are considered 'safe' and individuals are sent to 'voluntarily' relocate. A growing cadre of forced migration scholars also emphasise the use of subjective criteria to measure when internal displacement ends: affected populations themselves must decide whether they are displaced (or not) even if this approach is susceptible to manipulation (Castles 2002; Frelick 2001; Demusz 2000).

A number of international research institutes elaborated typologies for determining when displacement ends. The Brookings-SAIS project, for example, outlined 'cause-based' criteria drawn by analogy from the concept of 'cessation' in refugee studies, where the *absence of the attributed cause* (e.g. a large-scale dam or the well-founded fear of persecution) is grounds for ending the classification of internal displacement.[6] Also noted are 'solutions-based' criteria, wherein displacement is claimed to end when the *possibility of a durable solution* – whether 'local integration', 'return' or 'resettlement' – exists. Thus, after a designated period of time, those not availing themselves of the opportunity are determined to have spontaneously settled on their own. A third possibility includes a 'needs-based' criterion which considers displacement to have ended when affected *populations no longer register unmet needs or requirements for protection* and assistance. Some practitioners argue that arbitrary and externally determined cut-off points could put the lives of such populations in jeopardy (Frelick 2001).

Physical or extra-geographic Policymakers and practitioners often assume that the *physical movement* of individuals and households (with or without their assets) is a core criterion of displacement. As such, displacement entails a geographic relocation from legally or customarily owned, rented or borrowed land and property to another place. 'De-territorialisation' is frequently held as a necessary condition of displacement such that proof (e.g. formal or informal documentation including deeds and title or oral testimony) is required by authorities in order for the displaced to claim entitlements and access to a durable solution. Physical dislocation is also expected to generate a number of pathologies depending on the profile of the displaced individual or household. Research since the 1970s detected a number of outcomes associated with physical dislocation ranging from the loss of physical home and property to reduced income-earning potential and productivity.[7] Sutton (1977: 284) observed in many instances of displacement that resettlers adopted a 'bi-polarised' attitude to their predicament: at one extreme there emerged 'a high degree of activity and self-help combined with individualism ... at the other a high degree of inactivity and apathy combined with dependent attitudes'.

The fundamental expectation of physical or geographic movement as a core feature of displacement raises tricky conceptual and ethical questions. For example, what is the metric of physical dislocation? Can it be limited to a few metres from one's original place or must it extend to the neighbouring home, village, district or country? What constitutes an original place? Should those lacking formal or customary rights to a fixed territory or who are non-property owners be excluded? What happens to pastoral or nomadic populations who are without a 'formal' home to begin with? These questions are frequently glossed over in the rush to provide assistance. They inevitably resurface in the process of planning and executing durable solutions.

Certain scholars accept that displacement should not and cannot be restricted to physical dislocation alone. Many of them are exploring the extra-geographic or non-spatial manifestations of displacement in relation to the dispossession of assets, entitlements and lost opportunities before and after a displacement event (Cernea 1999). In their view, displacement encompasses more than the physical movement of individuals and households. For example, Cernea (2003) describes how upstream development projects can affect water quality, salinisation, pasture land and cash-crop production in designated catchments, potentially contributing to the 'displacement' of livelihoods and leading to suffering that may or may not ultimately contribute to physical displacement.[8] Jacobsen (2001) demonstrates how food security, access to public services and markets and social networks can be 'displaced' as a result of armed conflicts even if affected populations are not physically dislocated. The debate over whether displacement entails physical movement is not esoteric or purely semantic. In some cases, the extra-physical outcomes of displacement are explicitly accounted and compensated for even if these in turn raise more questions about what is *not* displacement and how to prioritise and budget for possible durable solutions. It is to one of these durable solutions – resettlement – that this chapter now turns.

Parameters of resettlement

Like displacement, resettlement is a diffuse and misunderstood concept. Writing on settlement and resettlement in Africa, Sutton (1977: 219) lamented the 'inability of research to draw meaningful generalisations from the disparate literature on settlement and resettlement schemes'. While Palmer (1974) initially saw the virtues in possibly comparing different forms of relocation arising from development, war and overpopulation, Chambers (1969: 12) condemned resettlement studies to an 'academic no man's land ... [wherein] no single science or study has yet established its claims and each has its limitations'. At its most basic, resettlement entails the planned and controlled relocation of populations from one physical place to another. It involves the relocation of individuals and even entire communities to a new place which distinguishes it from 'return' to one's place of origin. Though frequently conflated with other forms of migration, resettlement can occur only when the choice to remain in one's original place is fundamentally constrained by real or perceived coercion. As noted by Scudder (1973), the compulsory nature of resettlement is crucial: resettlement schemes are an expression of coercion.

Resettlement as social engineering While there may be no natural category of resettlement, there are relatively clear boundaries to the debate. As one scholar on resettlement observed in the late 1960s, resettlement consists of 'planned social change that necessarily entails population movement, population selection and most probably population control' (Chambers

21

1969: 5). Resettlement therefore incorporates a strong spatial element and a high degree of social control. Since at least the middle of the twentieth century, urban planners, civil engineers and certain social scientists presumed that resettlement followed a predictable and mechanical sequence which, with adequate planning and management, could account for and minimise the risks and vulnerabilities that accompanied physical dislocation (Cernea 1990; Scudder and Colson 1982; Colson 1971). More recently, a number of scholars and practitioners have also endorsed the instrumental use of resettlement as a vehicle for development.

Resettlement has long been construed as a platform for social engineering and an opportunity to enact far-reaching political, economic, social and demographic transformation. Since the 1950s it constituted an important pillar of modernisation theory and, inevitably, attracted considerable contoversy and subaltern opposition.[9] Chambers (1969: 34) described resettlement schemes as 'experiments in nation-building in miniature', while Scudder (1973) introduced the concept of 'ecological imperialism' to highlight the ways in which resettlement schemes represented an extension of the international economic system – command- or capitalist-driven – into new domains. Whatever paradigm is ultimately invoked to explain resettlement, most scholars arrived at similar conclusions regarding its outcomes: resettlement had immense destructive potential in relation to human lives and livelihoods. Both Sutton (1977) and Scudder (1973) observed that resettlement often faltered precisely because it was not initiated 'from within' but rather by (outside) social actors who negated complexity and embraced technical solutions. They attributed poor returns to the inability of resettlement planners to reconcile modern and 'traditional' value-systems.

Resettlement was expected to harness modernist management procedures to transform (civilise) 'backward', 'primitive' and otherwise dislocated populations. Considerable faith was vested in the technical machinery of resettlement, including an efficient administrative bureaucracy, the resources of international agencies and donors and the innovative spatial morphology of the schemes themselves. Reacting to the high modernist aspirations of the resettlement enterprise was an eclectic opposition movement comprised of actors within 'civil society'.[10] They actively resisted hegemonic and frequently elite-driven resettlement interventions. Likewise, forced migration scholars critically examined the (negative) effects of resettlement – particularly on minority and indigenous groups and in some cases identified strategies to mitigate and reverse the pathologies that frequently accompanied the process.

Despite repeated and documented failures of resettlement to create durable solutions for those involved – whether in terms of self-reliant and productive communities or livelihoods restored to (or above) pre-displacement levels – faith in its potential was unshakeable. The World Bank (2000), ADB (2001) and others anticipated that carefully planned and managed resettlement could side-step impoverishment of those ousted by development projects. The yardstick of successful resettlement included criteria such as income restoration and land-for-land compensation (Cernea 1999, Cernea and Mathur 2008). Although less optimistic than the World Bank, the UN (1998) was also convinced that successful resettlement of conflict- and disaster-affected populations could be administered in such a way as to be equitable and free of discrimination, accounting for the safety and dignity of the 'beneficiaries', ensuring fair compensation for lost land, income and assets and involving the 'full participation of the [internally] displaced in public affairs'.[11] These criteria, they also argued, formed the basis of durable solutions.

Labelling resettlement Resettlement is persistently confused with other, related processes. Sutton (1977) observed a bewildering variety of 'origins, sizes and objectives' of resettlement schemes, making it difficult to generalise across cases but also leading to confusion about what was and what was not resettlement. For example, the expression is often used interchangeably with 'settlement' and 'colonisation' (Kibreab 1989; Colson 1971; Chambers 1969). Unlike these latter concepts, resettlement is *involuntary*. Whether or not settlement and colonisation processes coincide with development programmes or ethnic cleansing, the incidence of coercion distinguishes resettlement from otherwise voluntary population relocation. Resettlement is distinct from 'assisted migration', a process that also includes an element of state planning and involves the relocation of individuals – ideally 'enterprising' young men – and the clearing, development and (re)population of otherwise uninhabited areas (Table 1.2). Dunham (1982, 1983) described how settlement schemes and colonisation processes from Sri Lanka's southern districts to the north were purposefully described as economic and labour migration, thus ensuring benign – if subtly hegemonic – connotations.

Additional concepts are often substituted with resettlement and further complicate a coherent and unified understanding. For example, 'return', 'repatriation', 'reintegration' and 'integration' are all expressions frequently invoked as synonyms of resettlement by policymakers and practitioners (Kibreab 1989, 1996a). Depending on who invokes them, the expressions 'return' and 'repatriation' carry precise legal meanings and refer to the relocation of displaced populations either across an

TABLE 1.2 Labelling settlers and resettlers

Settlement	Resettlement
(spontaneous) settler	resettler
coloniser	reintegratee
assisted migrant	relocate
pioneer	project-affected person
encroacher	project-dislocated
slum dweller	integratee

international frontier or back to their original place of residence. 'Reinsertion', 'reintegration' and 'integration' are concepts that refer more generally to the restoration of living standards and the rearticulation of social, cultural and economic networks with host communities. They may accompany resettlement or they may or not (Muggah 2008a; Jacobsen 2001; Kibreab 2000). Although certain scholars and practitioners contend that they represent constitutive features of resettlement, others are adamant that one or all may take place independently.

A wide range of labels exists to classify resettled populations and to compartmentalise assistance strategies (Tables 1.2 and 1.3). These labels are seldom consistently applied and can generate new contradictions on the ground. In Sri Lanka, people resettled in the wake of conflict and natural disasters are referred to alternately as 'refugees', 'internal refugees', 'evacuees', 'inmates', 'unsettled', 'IDPs', 'de-housed', 'homeless', 'rehoused' and 'settlers'. Those resettled following development projects are described as, *inter alia*, 'oustees', 'project-affected persons' (PAPs), 'resettlers', 'pioneers' and 'colonisers'. Although certain expressions may

TABLE 1.3 Forced migration terminology in Sri Lanka

Cause	Displacement	Resettlement
Development	oustee, evictee, PAP, de-housed, settlers, resettler coloniser	colony units, settlement schemes and resettlement schemes
Conflict	refugee, internal refugees, evacuees, inmates, IDPs, conflict-displaced	refugee camps, transit centres, welfare centres and relocation villages
Natural disasters	disaster refugees, IDPs and tsunami IDPs	temporary shelters, transitional shelters, donor-driven housing and owner-driven housing

be deployed as rhetorical devices in order to draw attention to a specific population group or experience, the lack of consensus on labels can disguise the causes of their relocation. In the 1990s, for example, the Sinhala media labelled development-induced displaced and resettled as *jalasayata yatawena*, which can be roughly translated as 'people who were getting inundated'. Similarly, those internally displaced and resettled by war during the early 1980s were labelled alternately as refugees or *anatha* – 'orphans' or 'lacking a lord or master'.[12] Later classified as 'victims' (and later 'survivors') by international aid agencies, they were soon derided and stigmatised in welfare centres and relocation villages owing to their alleged involvement in the war (Brun 2003).

Resettlement as permanence If displacement is perceived to be temporary, resettlement is envisioned as a *permanent* process of relocation. In the case of development-induced displacement and resettlement, schemes are ordinarily prepared as a sub-component of a larger enterprise, whether dam and reservoir project, road-building initiative, urban renewal or parkland development. Provisions for resettlement, where they are incorporated at all, are anticipated to begin before and extend far beyond the life-span of the intervention giving rise to relocation in the first instance. Meanwhile, planned relocation arising from conflict and natural disaster-induced internal displacement and resettlement is often designed in such a way as to ensure a permanent (e.g. *durable* in the vernacular) solution. But actual experience frequently deviates from expectations.

Resettlement is conceptualised and designed in such a way as to catalyse self-sustaining or self-reliant communities. Resettlement schemes typically offer 'modern' housing designs and materials and are schematically ordered and laid out in a grid-pattern. The compactness and proximity of the new housing schemes often contrasts with the more dispersed and organic village clusters from where resettlers hailed. Despite the unfamiliar (social and geographic) layout of the new schemes and surrounding area, resettlement planners expect that they can result in durable solutions if prepared adequately in advance and in consultation with affected populations. Paradoxically, planned resettlement schemes are often prematurely abandoned by project implementers and resettlers a short time after they are established. To paraphrase Jane Jacobs (1961), while much may be known about what a broken community looks like, comparatively less is known about how to bring about a functional community.

The following sections consider the emergence of three separate epistemic communities, focusing alternately on development-, conflict- and disaster-induced internal displacement and resettlement. Separate communities preoccupied with forced migration – themselves composed of advocacy coalitions and public policy networks – emerged in the latter half of the twentieth century. Though struggling to define the conceptual boundaries of the debate and often working on multiple forms of displacement and resettlement, they were instrumental to the development of the basic ideational parameters of the regimes described in Chapter 2. Often characterised and studied as discrete phenomena, this chapter reveals that there are many more synergies between different types of displacement and resettlement than commonly assumed.

Development-induced displacement and resettlement Research on DIDR exhibits a comparatively long and distinguished pedigree. In the 1940s urban planners in the United States generated critical insights into the more ruinous outcomes of the Tennessee Valley Authority (TVA) project, including longitudinal evidence of the consequences of large-scale hydro-electric power generation systems on the livelihoods of hundreds of resettled households.[13] But few scholars loom larger in the early debates on DIDR than Brokensha and Scudder (1968), Chambers (1969) and Colson (1971). From the beginning of their academic careers, these researchers worked as consultants to major multilateral and bilateral agencies, governments and private sector corporations. As such, their research and findings were not immune to policy imperatives. While generating empirical contributions, they simultaneously aimed to influence the protocols and practices of their patrons.

Early research on DIDR shared a number of methodological features. Many studies transferred anthropological and sociological models of social change and migration theory to the phenomenology of resettlement – focusing primarily on the stresses and responses of populations to relocation. Long-term and frequently ethnographic research and cohort surveys explored the experience of populations resettled by dams and infrastructure projects in Africa and South Asia (e.g. Zambia, Kenya, Ghana and Sri Lanka). Most of these early scholars held essentially common, if radical, positions on the overwhelmingly negative consequences arising from urban and rural development. Colson (1971: 1) wrote how 'massive technological development hurts … economic planners, technicians and political leaders … count the engineering cost but not the social costs'. Likewise, Scudder (1973) described how 'compulsory resettlement is a traumatic experience which precipitates stress and leads to a crisis of cultural identity'.

The dominant conceptual resettlement models emerging from this period were formulated by Chambers (1970, 1971) and Colson (1971). Each detected a series of trends and patterns of change (stresses) that characterised resettled communities across time and space. Colson expanded Chambers's multi-stage framework and formulated a four-staged linear model that began *before* the displacement event, anticipated a measure of risk adversity in the *immediate post-displacement period* and was followed by a comparatively smooth period of transition from *rehabilitation* to the *handing-over* phase. Though initially focusing on (voluntary) settlement in Zambia, her conceptual framework was later extended to the analysis of (involuntary) resettlement by Scudder and Colson (1979, 1982) and Eriksen (1999) in Africa. Many of these early contributors doubted whether resettlement, as with many instances of 'assisted migration', left people better off than those settling on their own. Criticism began to focus on the structure of resettlement management processes and the ways in which the process regularly deviated from a predictable chronological trajectory. Critics of the linear modelling of resettlement emerged in the late 1970s and throughout the 1980s (Hulme 1988; Sutton 1977). On the basis of a growing body of empirical evidence, much of it generated from prior evaluations of World Bank-financed projects, they determined that 'not all projects pass through all stages [described by Chambers or Colson]' and that 'a steady movement [through all four stages] is the exception rather than the rule' (Cernea 1997).

The next generation of DIDR scholars included, among others, Cernea (1991, 1996) and Harrell-Bond (1982, 1986). Despite holding divergent epistemological perspectives from their predecessors and each other they nevertheless embarked on a useful collaborative experiment to learn from one another. There were deep unacknowledged ideological fault-lines dividing scholars and practitioners working on DIDR in the 1980s and 1990s, and perhaps fewer areas of consensus than presumed. Their perspectives were neatly, controversially, summarised by Mathur (2000) and Dwivedi (2002) into contiguous camps: *applied* and *action researchers. Applied scholars* envision DIDR as an inevitable, if unintended, consequence of development. They contend that with effective planning and micromanagement, social pathologies can be avoided and that resettler livelihoods can be substantially improved.[14] *Action researchers* consider DIDR to be a failure of the development paradigm and an expression of deep power asymmetries. They focus on identifying the causes of dislocation, measuring the individual, communal and societal costs of the enterprise, the vested interests of elites, subaltern movements and identity-based politics shaping the resettlement and the dynamics of resistance.

Most contemporary resettlement specialists fall somewhere in between the two camps. Some reject interventions that lead to mass displacement in principle, though they are compelled to identify the opportunities afforded to some groups by the political and economic dynamics of social change. While working as a consultant to the World Bank, Partridge (1993) documented the ways in which certain indigenous northern Colombian populations resettled in the context of oil and hydro-electric projects in the 1970s and 1980s exhibited 'productive energy' and entrepreneurial spirit following their 'release' from culturally and socially embedded 'constraints'. Likewise, Kibreab (1996a) described the ways in which Ethiopians resettled as a result of villagisation schemes – particularly single female-headed households – availed themselves of new market-based opportunities when patriarchal (Tigrayan) systems of land and asset ownership broke down. The transformation of a pre-existing social order made possible by resettlement gave rise to new social, cultural and economic spaces in which to reconstitute radically changed identities and livelihoods. Despite this rapprochement, applied and action researchers speak to differentiated understandings of the fundamental purpose, values and principles of development.

In time, Cernea (1997) introduced a new conceptual approach to measuring and practically responding to DIDR. His 'impoverishment risk and livelihood reconstruction' framework was innovative precisely because it advanced a synchronic perspective to estimating and ultimately reversing the poverty-inducing risks associated with resettlement. In purposefully departing from linear modelling, the model proposed a typology to anticipate and mitigate impoverishment. The framework forced planners and researchers to consider a wider assortment of risks accompanying resettlement, including landlessness, joblessness, homelessness, social marginalisation, increased mortality and morbidity, food insecurity, loss of access to common property and social disarticulation. Other potential risks added (in the context of war-displaced) include reduced access to public and private services (i.e. education and health), political disenfranchisement and exposure to acute violence (Muggah 2000a, 2000b). The model was evidence-based, drawing as it did from a multi-project review of World Bank- (1994) and non-bank-financed resettlement schemes with an active reflection on past theoretical contributions. While the merits and limitations of the conceptual framework are widely debated, it acquired a considerable degree of legitimacy in the DIDR community and is widely in use in Africa, South Asia and Latin America (Cernea 2005, 2006).

Conflict-induced displacement and resettlement Theoretical innovations in relation to CIDR lagged behind those debated by DIDR scholars and practitioners. Unlike early practitioners working on dam-related displacement and resettlement, scholars examining displacement arising from war attached more importance to the immediate logistical imperatives of aid delivery than to sustained reflection and research. During the 1970s and 1980s grounded and long-term research in and around war zones was limited to only the most assiduous researchers (Crisp 1999; Harrell-Bond 1986). By the 1990s, empirical research on CIDR expanded dramatically. The focus of this nascent epistemic community was oriented towards the production and dissemination of the Guiding Principles on Internal Displacement (UN 1998), described in greater detail in Chapter 2. Most published outputs were noteworthy more for their rich advocacy potential than for their original theory development. Rather than drawing on inductive approaches, conceptual models for CIDR borrowed heavily from refugee studies.

That the study of CIDR stimulated comparatively limited academic engagement from the 1950s to the 1970s should come as little surprise to the discerning reader of Cold War era geo-politics. After all, it was refugees – not IDPs – who figured prominently in the contest between the United States and the then Soviet Union. In addition to serving as a valuable source of potential intelligence, refugees and asylum claimants were held up as a vindication of the failings of the other. By way of contrast, those unable to flee across borders were seldom enumerated, consigned instead to collateral damage arising from the proxy wars of the period. The drafters of the 1951 Refugee Convention and many of the relief agencies operating in and around war-affected areas since the 1960s were aware of these so-called internal refugees. But robust scholarly enquiry was constrained by intermittent access and marginal political and popular interest. Many felt it was simply too difficult to fit the phenomenon into contemporary discourse or legal doctrine associated with war, peace and development. The truth is that internal displacement did not really matter. There were few obvious normative or political gains to drive the agenda and, in any case, attention was focused on bolstering the emerging refugee regime (Chapter 2).

By the late 1980s and early 1990s a dedicated literature on CIDR was emerging. It was accompanied and even stimulated as in the case of DIDR, by persistent advocacy and lobbying from a transnational movement composed of non-governmental entities. Prominent among them were the United Nations Quakers Office (QUNO) and the American Friends Associations who, together with certain humanitarian and development practitioners, were placing a premium on (human) rights and need-driven relief assistance. Although the management and response to internal displacement was initially cast as distinct from the protection and permanent solutions endowed to refugees, CIDR discourse and practice borrowed liberally from the refugee field (Hathaway 2006). Early analysts spoke of protecting and providing assistance for internally displaced people, of preparing systems to ensure 'care and maintenance' and facilitating 'durable solutions' such as local integration, return and resettlement.

Even though the internal displacement issue presented a conundrum to their mandate, UNHCR, together with a host of research institutions, played a seminal role in building the conceptual scaffolding of CIDR. Throughout the early 1990s the UNHCR, alongside the UN Commission on Human Rights (UNCHR) and the United Nations General Assembly, issued a series of resolutions, declarations, statements and guidelines on the subject of 'in-country flight alternatives', return and resettlement – often at the insistence of a core group of donor states and advocacy groups noted above (UNGA 1993a, 1993b, 1995). Although not statutorily mandated to advocate on behalf of the internally displaced, the UNHCR mobilised support for them, supported inter-institutional capacities within the UN to respond to their needs and took the lead to protect and assist them in certain circumstances – usually on the grounds that they were preventing new refugee flows or extending their reach to 'others of concern' where programmes already supported refugees. The Brookings Project on Internal Displacement (renamed the SAIS/CUNY-Brookings Project) also provided an institutional platform for a UN Special Representative on Internal Displacement to carry out his mandate to elaborate Guiding Principles (Chapter 2).

The conceptualisation of CIDR drew from UNHCR's evolving experience with local (re)settlement of refugees. In the first few decades of its existence, UNHCR, with the backing of UN member states, promoted third-country resettlement of refugees, particularly where options for repatriation were unavailable (Pitterman 1997).[15] 'Internment' or 'refugee' camps were comparatively rare during this period and resorted to only as an interim measure (Wigley 2002; Black 1998; van Damme 1995). The strategy of permanent third-country resettlement for refugees soon gave way to two other durable solutions: (voluntary) *repatriation* and *local (re)-settlement*. Because of their relatively low political and economic cost to donor states, repatriation and local (re)settlement emerged as the preferred durable solution for refugees in developing countries from the late 1970s onwards (Roberts, A. 1998).

By the 1980s in-country settlement of refugees became widespread – primarily in Africa. The expansion of 'local' (re)settlement can be attributed to two key factors: first, the steadily diminishing interest of Western states to process refugees from underdeveloped countries and second the prominence of a modernisation ideology calling for increased agriculture-led development through cheap labour. Notwithstanding the fact that most countries hosting large refugee caseloads already displayed a massive labour surplus, so-called local durable solutions were frequently preferred by refugees themselves, many of whom anticipated swift repatriation. Local (re)settlement came to be modelled after two prototypes: the refugee *camp* and the rural *(re)settlement scheme*.

Bakhet (1987) traced the refugee camp model to the early 1960s where it emerged in East Africa – particularly Uganda, Tanzania and Kenya.[16] According to Black (1998: 2), camps then as now were 'large ... overcrowded sites that are ... dependent on assistance'. Camps were frequently characterised as holding tanks, remote from line-service functions and (intentionally) isolated to keep (foreign) refugees separated and distinguishable from the local populace. They were distinct from the 'small open settlements where refugees have been able to maintain a village atmosphere' that Black (ibid.) and, later, Schmidt (2003) described as 'settlements' or 'village schemes'. Key characteristics of camps included the active promotion of self-reliance coupled with centralised and heavily managed systems of control. Early approaches to the design and management of camps were analogous to the settlement schemes examined by Colson (1971) and others in the case of DIDR. Their design drew consciously on predictable linear models that anticipated an *emergency phase*; a *self-support and transition phase*; an *integrated settlement phase*; and, the eventual possibility of a transfer or *handing-over of services* to refugees themselves. Owing to early successes with local (re)settlement in Africa, the camp approach began to spread, often replicating assumptions and lessons derived from the African context to new and challenging environments.

It was not until the late 1980s and early 1990s that the social consequences of camps came under scrutiny and the issue of 'protracted refugee situations' emerged as a concern to the donor community (Crisp 2002; van Damme 1995). The camp model for refugees and IDPs came under withering criticism. A persistent objection was that camps unnecessarily prolonged displacement and failed to offer concrete durable solutions. Camps allowed policymakers to side-step hard choices associated with repatriation and third-country resettlement in favour of uncontroversial technocratic interventions. By publicly exhibiting suffering they served as a magnet or a visible vector for aid. But critics began to recognise that the core aspirations of camps, whether defined as self-sufficiency, self-reliance or community viability, were seldom realised on the ground.

One popular narrative was that the failures of camps were somehow internal to the populations that inhabited them. Because the least resilient and most vulnerable people frequently relocate to camps and resettlement schemes, particularly the extreme poor, single-parent households, children and the elderly, their evolution into functional communities was unlikely. By contrast, the wealthier and socially connected spontaneously relocated elsewhere, joining an international diaspora, in some cases housing their extended families in camps until they could be relocated.[17] Another narrative attributed camp failures to paternalistic and top-down regulatory structures and systems of management and control that deprived camp residents of alternative livelihoods or kept them from drawing on or creating organic social and economic networks (Hyndman 2000; Harrell-Bond 1998).

The rural (re)settlement scheme emerged as a de facto response to the inherent challenges of accounting for and physically controlling mass refugee influxes in the 1970s and 1980s. Early operational reactions to refugee movements depended less on externally planned and administered camps then on the hospitality and absorptive capacity of hosting communities. Where there were shared ethnic, religious, linguistic or socio-cultural characteristics between host communities and refugees, (rural) resettlement schemes appeared to be more easily administered than large camps (Wolde-Selassie 2000; Kibreab 1996a, 1996b; Hansen 1981). These localised resettlement schemes therefore tended to adopt fewer systems of centralised control than was the case in camps and advocated complementary, rather than parallel, social services for both refugee and hosting populations.

Resettlement schemes were readily distinguishable from refugee camps. The former put a premium on self-sufficiency in agricultural production, the granting of tenancy rights, an expansion in cash-cropping and in certain cases, permanent integration. According to Neldner (1979: 33), from the earliest days the aim of such planned resettlement schemes was to bring refugees into 'self-support through agricultural production' even if on inhospitable, unproductive and marginal land. This particular feature was not lost on many host governments, which recognised the opportunities of bringing peripheral land into cultivation, or even of the potential for refugee camps to serve as frontier 'buffers' against hostile neighbouring states. Nor was the logic of these schemes missed by many locally resettled refugees who saw in these actions evidence that international support for their 'cause' and eventual repatriation was waning (Malkki 1995).

The debate over the advantages and disadvantages of camps and re-settlement options for *internally* displaced populations (as compared to refugees) endured into the late 1990s. So-called safe havens were formally authorised by the UN Security Council for the first time in northern Iraq during the first US-led Gulf War in 1991. Over the next decade, dozens of camp-like settlements for IDPs – managed primarily by UN agencies and other relief and development organisations – rapidly emerged from Angola and Bosnia and Herzegovina to Somalia and Sri Lanka. Although the limitations of these de facto camps as durable solutions were widely acknowledged, they offered a new and unprecedented form of 'in-country protection' – particularly in situations of war and insecurity. Camps were attractive because they allowed internally displaced populations to be controlled and monitored: they served as a means to regulate population movements and as bargaining chips during inter-state negotiations.

Acceptance of the Guiding Principles on Internal Displacement by UN member states in the 1990s revealed a nascent commitment to the principle of protecting and achieving durable solutions – including re-settlement – for internally displaced populations. The Principles them-selves laid out a conceptual and normative framework for advocating, monitoring and promoting (human) rights on their behalf. While the Principles were described by their proponents as the bedrock of an incipi-ent regime for CIDR, critics claimed that they added 'virtually nothing to the pre-existing corpus of already binding international human rights law' (Hathaway 2006: 8). Even so, the Principles issued for the first time a definition of internally displaced that included 'all those who have left their homes and places of habitual residence involuntarily, whatever the circumstances and have not crossed an international frontier'. They pre-scribed a set of rights and affirmed the obligation of competent national authorities to assume responsibility to provide and ensure access to basic assistance, regardless of whether IDPs were living in camps or dispersed in cities. Crucially, they set out the fundamental standards for return and resettlement – or durable solutions – in line with international human rights and refugee law.

Natural disaster-induced displacement and resettlement More people are forced to leave their homes owing to natural or environmental 'dis-asters' than development or war (IFRC 2008). But the effects of these disasters are variable: similar disaster types tend to exhibit differentiated impacts depending on the 'development' context.[18] Davis and Seitz (1982:

557) noted that natural disasters, while not necessarily more frequent in developing countries, are disproportionately more severe (measured as a function of mortality, morbidity and displacement). Irrespective of where they emerge, disasters are heterogeneous: they arise in an immense variety of ways. They are also generally understood in relation to their social context: disasters are measured as a function of their 'effects on human settlements rather than [their] effect on sparsely populated or unpopulated environments' (Committee on International Disaster Assistance 1979: 26).[19]

The experience of NIDR (natural disaster-induced displacement and resettlement) occurs at the interface of environmental, social and technological change. In spite of its monumental (and apparently expanding) scale, there is virtually no empirical research on NIDR. One major impediment to the elaboration of a robust theoretical framework for researching the phenomenon is the difficulty in defining what is actually meant by a 'natural disaster'. As noted by Britton (1986), disasters tend to be more easily recognised than studied. Connoting a complex process with (usually) dramatic ecological consequences, the concept is often narrowly conceived as a single uncontrolled 'pathogen' or set of interlocking 'hazards' – whether a hurricane, earthquake or flood. Natural disasters are frequently treated as one-off events rather than processes mediated by interrelationships between natural (meteorological or ecological) phenomena and society (Davis and Seitz 1982; White and Haas 1975).

The study of disasters as a distinct field of enquiry stretches back to the early twentieth century. Early pioneers include physical geographers such as Barrows (1923) and G. F. White (1945). They defined natural disasters as causal agents (vectors) that contributed to a sudden and unexpected shock or disruption to an otherwise 'normal' social and geophysical arrangement. In projecting a linear trajectory between a natural disaster on the one hand and social consequences on the other, they explicitly link a specific event with a clear outcome. The disaster-centric approach emphasises the event and its physical consequences rather than the relationships of the event to a broader social universe. Omitted from these early characterisations of natural disasters were the socio-cultural constructions, relationships and vulnerabilities of socio-economically and culturally stratified communities, households and individuals. Natural disasters were neatly detached from those affected, including the internally displaced.

Deterministic and mono-causal understandings of natural disasters came under scrutiny in the 1960s and 1970s. For one, the attribution of disasters and their consequences to fate – god or geography – were discredited. Acceptance of alternative explanations emerged incrementally. Most experts accepted that physical location and topography played a role in relation to exposure though disagreed on the 'human element' (Glantz 1976; Baker and Chapman 1962). Owing to pressure from social scientists, disaster specialists began to recognise that the resilience of a given society's social and economic institutions and endowments were critical factors to take into account when modelling the risks and impacts of ostensibly ecological events.

Several disciplinary approaches to studying natural disasters and hazards emerged in the 1970s, ranging from geographic to anthropological, sociological, developmental, public health-oriented and engineering-based. For arguably the first time, Hewitt (1983) analysed the relationships between natural events and pre-existing structural social conditions, rather than focusing exclusively on the causes or intensity of the disaster itself. Contemporary disaster specialists – including ecologists, meteorologists, human geographers, sociologists and anthropologists – soon began examining the relationships between the vector, the environment and the agent as a complex 'system' (Benthal 1993). Natural disasters were no longer envisioned as temporary and abrupt disruptions to a stable system, but more importantly as an index of 'the success or failure of a society to adapt ... to certain features of its natural and socially constructed environment in a sustained fashion' (Oliver-Smith 2002, cf. 2006).

The specific ways in which natural disasters were conceived influenced contemporary approaches to NIDR. For example, analysts working in the natural sciences often interpreted disasters as discrete environmental or ecological events amenable to preventive intervention. Because natural disasters precipitated and aggravated certain forms of risk, they counselled for the preparation of early-warning systems, specialised interventions (such as reinforced break walls and structural enhancements to tenements) and responses focused on comprehensively rehabilitating the built environment. Other approaches drawing from sociology and human geography were more proactive and conceptualised disasters as clusters of interconnected hazards mediated by pre-existing human (social and political) structural conditions in society. The latter perspective advocated measures to enhance community resilience, so-called protective factors, social networks and longer-term restoration. By the 1980s as a result of a growing acceptance of multi-disciplinary approaches to natural disaster reduction, approaches to NIDR began for the first time to combine efforts to limit biophysical and environmental risks with efforts to enhance political, economic and social capital. This expanding approach to conceiving disasters also resulted in a corollary expansion of labelling. The variability of disaster labels contributed to both over- and under-identification (Davis and Seitz 1982).

As in the case of CIDR, few scholars examined the causes, approaches to and consequences of NIDR until the 1980s. The most widely recognised include anthropologist Oliver-Smith (1979, 1986; Hansen and Oliver-Smith 1982) and sociologists such as Hewitt (1983) and Drabek (1986). As with applied researchers undertaking ethnographic and policy-oriented assessments of DIDR and CIDR, these scholar-practitioners generated a stylised continuum to describe the various stages of NIDR. Drabek (ibid.), for example, described how NIDR began first with a planning and (early) warning stage *before* the displacement event which was then followed by evacuation, emergency restoration and reconstruction.[20] Others called for a less Hegelian approach, noting the ways in which bureaucratic responses waxed and waned depending on the context (Davis and Seitz 1982). Even so, the positioning of NIDR at the intersection of external shocks and dynamic social processes – including human agency, choice and behavioural responses – constituted an innovation that would have far-reaching implications for relief planning models more generally (Twigg 2004).

Research on NIDR qualitatively and quantitatively expanded in the 1990s. According to Oliver-Smith (1996) new contributions focused on behavioural and organisational responses to traumatic events and social change, the political economy of disaster relief and environmental restoration. A growing number of forced migration researchers began to include in this category not just people affected by ecological or meteorological shocks, but also those fleeing 'human-induced' environmental deterioration in their communities and cities. While not necessarily crossing an international border, *'environmental'* or *'climate refugees'* were alleged to have fled from floods and mud-slides in heavily eroded areas. They were also displaced due to unsustainable resource use, desertification and uncontrolled population growth and other forms of deterioration in their built environment (Black 1994). Environmental refugees were believed in some cases to have *caused* NIDR on account of their 'backward' agricultural practices and management of the commons. Though not *de jure* refugees, they faced analogous stigmas that reflected 'adversity in their homelands ... bio-indicators of environmental quality and national indicators of resource management competence' (El-Hinnawi 1985).

Notwithstanding the controversial causal assumptions underpinning the concept, the environmental refugee label is legally incongruous. The definition of a refugee is carefully articulated in the 1951 Refugee Convention and consciously eschews people forced to move as a result of environmental factors. There is mounting concern that ascribing the refugee label to all manner of displacement by advocates and academics

> potentially exposes groups and individuals to accusations of naivety and failing to produce a sound legal basis for their argument. Use of incorrect terminology gives governments grounds to disregard advocacy on behalf of the displaced. (Romer 2006: 26)

Likewise, Hathaway (2006) strongly resists the merging of *de jure* refugees with others in 'like' circumstances for fear of diluting the quality and quantity of refugee assistance. Romer (2006) herself proposed an alternative – 'environmentally displaced person' (EDP) – for the basis of advocacy and policy development.

The study of NIDR took on a new urgency in the 1990s as signs of massive environmental degradation and climate change began to emerge. Myers (1997), for example, asserted that desertification, deforestation and soil erosion compounded by natural and human-induced disasters could result in the NIDR of more than 50 million people each year by 2010. Evidence of large-scale internal displacement and relocation arising from deteriorating habitat was increasingly detected by mainstream forced migration scholars (Leiderman 1996; Forbes 1992). Although heavily criticised, the environmental refugee label took hold and was swiftly absorbed into policy discourse (Castles 2002; Black 2001b). According to Leiderman (1996: 12), environmental refugees included those fleeing

> toxic spills and dump sites, desertification, hydroelectric projects, strip mining, radon and other radiation exposure, severe logging, soil erosion, agricultural land abuse, disease epidemics, defoliation, land mines and other unwitting or intentional human activities.

Oliver-Smith and Button (2005: 5) continued to challenge this construct, arguing that it was misleading and out of step with evolutions in the NIDR field: by assuming 'single-agent' causality they felt the concept denied the political, social and economic complexities of NIDR. The attribution of (latent) resource degrading habits to so-called environmental refugees also stimulated fierce arguments over the legitimacy of the label (Leach and Fairhead 2000).

Undeterred, conflict and security studies specialists began to detect possible relationships between environmental calamities, NIDR and the potential for escalating resource-related conflict and contagion. Political scientists started to investigate the relationships between rapid environmental transformation and collapse, increased exposure and vulnerability to socio-natural hazards, communal tension and ultimately the incidence of armed conflict and ethnic cleansing (Homer-Dixon 1994, 2000). Although criticised for their reified treatment of the issue, they nevertheless began to identify explicit associations between different categories of displacement and resettlement, including NIDR and CIDR. These (comparative) perspectives introduced, for the first time, compelling ways of interpreting the causes of past and ongoing conflicts that were previously characterised as ethnic or religious in character, or motivated purely by profit and economic advantage.

By the end of the 1990s the pendulum swung back again as specialists renewed their focus on vulnerability as an exacerbating factor for NIDR (Twigg 2004). Vulnerability, according to Oliver-Smith and Button (2005: 2), referred to 'the totality of relationships in a given social situation producing the formation of a condition that, in combination with natural forces, produces a disaster'.[21] The scale and intensity of internal displacement in the context of disasters was contingent on pre-existing characteristics present in the community and household.[22] The focus on the vulnerability approach in the study of NIDR coincided with Cernea's (1997) impoverishment risks framework reviewed above. In adopting a vulnerability-first approach, the emphasis was less on the 'natural disaster' as a mono-causal agent than on the pre-existing patterns of risk or susceptibility (e.g. low income, inadequate health care, spatial location of homes and housing quality, poor education, access to markets, etc.) and the relative resilience (e.g. endowment sets and coping strategies) of those exposed.

The reorientation of focus on the agency of internally displaced and resettled populations in the context of natural disasters challenged prior assumptions of passivity and dependency-proneness. It was increasingly accepted that the emergence, consequences and responses to natural disasters had as much to do with pre-existing political, social and economic asymmetries as with the disaster or hazard 'events' themselves. The adoption of a human-centred approach to NIDR revealed how highly stratified communities affected by a common natural disaster such as a tsunami, could experience differentiated exposure and risks accorded with, *inter alia*, income, ethnicity, gender, age and even political persuasion.

Conclusions

The internal displacement and resettlement agenda was shaped by separate clusters of epistemic communities and sustained interaction between scholars, policymakers and practitioners. Consequently, many foundational concepts and labels used to describe the DIDR, CIDR and NIDR phenomena were informed by the bureaucratic imperatives of specific groups of international agencies and governments. Predictably, a lively debate persists among a multi-disciplinary network of forced migration scholars over the parameters of core concepts. The discourse and practice of internal displacement and resettlement are contested and often blurred. A basic level of consensus on core concepts is required if the forced migration field is to mature. As signalled by Ostrom (1986: 4) 'no scientific field can advance far if the participants do not share a common understanding of key terms'. Despite a rapprochement between certain policymakers, practitioners and academics working on DIDR, CIDR and NIDR and instinctive agreement on certain basic concepts, there is comparatively less evidence of a robust dialogue between specialists seized by different categories of internal displacement and resettlement. A self-conscious and critical application of terminology and a unitary approach to researching the issue is critical.

2 | Protection and durable solutions: regimes for internally displaced and resettled populations

There is growing optimism in certain development and humanitarian quarters that an international regime is emerging to promote and guarantee protection and durable solutions for IDPs. Human rights advocates are adamant that it is not so much an expansion of the existing refugee regime as something fundamentally different. They contend that the new regime was forged by multi-layered and polyarchic networks comprised of advocates and government representatives. The regime is manifest in the discursive and behavioural adaptations made by states, non-state actors, multilateral agencies and non-governmental agencies. Despite a rapid expansion of policy and action research on internal displacement and resettlement in the latter half of the twentieth century, there was less empirical consideration of the normative parameters of the nascent regime.

But can one really speak of a single overarching regime for protecting IDPs and promoting durable solutions? A growing coalition of UN agencies and scholars certainly believe so and are adamant that states take responsibility for internally displaced populations irrespective of the attributed cause (IASC 2005; UN 2005a). This chapter contends that there is not one, but instead three or more contiguous regimes focused on different categories of internally displaced persons: a DIDR regime, a CIDR regime and a NIDR regime. These regimes are expected to contribute to the state's protection of the internally displaced and encourage the promotion of durable solutions on their behalf. Protection extends beyond domestic legislation and entitlements to real and perceived security and well-being. Likewise, durable solutions refer to sustainable and equitable resettlement, and in the case of CIDR, local integration and return. Following a review of regime theory, this chapter reveals how these separate regimes were forged by prolonged exchange between states, multilateral agencies, advocacy coalitions and public policy networks. While sharing common ground, the chapter finds that they also exhibit distinctive features.

Regimes are by definition state-centric and designed to guide state behaviour and potentially influence the behaviour of non-state actors. Though non-state actors – international and non-governmental organisations, advocacy groups and transnational corporations – may contribute to their creation and play a role in executing key functions, national governments are the dominant power in forming, transforming and enacting regimes. Regimes are an instrument of 'governmentality' – they reveal how states work with, and independent of, non-state actors to advance certain objectives (Sending and Neumann 2006). Regimes are useful because they potentially explain why and how cooperation occurs on disparate problem sets.

Drawing from rationalist and constructivist perspectives, the chapter borrows from Krasner (1982, 1998) to define regimes as a cluster of implicit and explicit *principles, norms, rules* and *decision-making procedures* around which the expectations of diverse actors converge.[1] Regimes are not static but are inter-subjectively moulded by their proponents. Nor are they easily located or pinned down: they are embodied in an ensemble of treaties, conventions, declarations and exchanges.[2] An underlying contention of this chapter is that 'ideal type' regimes (in a Weberian sense) for internal displacement and resettlement are declarative, restorative and decentralised. These regimes are discursive rather than proscriptive, emphasise the restoration of rights and needs and are operationalised by a diverse and overlapping constellation of institutions and agencies. As noted by Duffield (2007: 10) even where norms and rules may be ignored 'they do not necessarily possess any evaluative or deontic content: no moral opprobrium is necessarily attached to their violation'.

These regimes exhibit intrinsic limitations. They tend to be universalising and are challenged to accommodate the many differentiated interests and agencies of states, non-state actors and the internally displaced with respect to protection and durable solutions. Because regimes are by definition top-down they only partially allow for the contestation of rights and are poorly equipped to account for agency (including resistance) from below. Regimes themselves do not exhibit agency and are unevenly applied and enforced by their proponents. Governments and non-governmental agencies may be unable to ensure adherence to regimes in spite of their efforts to promote conditionality and enforce compliance through inspections panels, domestic codification, guidelines and specialised financing arrangements. Vicissitudes in influence are internal to regimes themselves: states ensure that they are born weak and remain so. The chapter finds that endogenous factors inhibiting their influence include the persistence of sovereignty paradigms narrowly conceived in terms of non-interference and collective action dilemmas among multilateral and bilateral actors responsible for regime implementation.

Regimes and forced migration

The concept of regimes is a relatively well-established fixture of international relations. That said, it is commonly invoked in relation to environment, human rights and trade in order to predict how and why states cooperate on particular issues of international concern (Risse et al. 1999; Young 1989) rather than in describing state responses to forced migration. Since the early 1980s, political scientists have disagreed over what precisely constitutes a regime (Hasenclever et al. 1997; Keohane 1993; Strange 1988). Regime theorists themselves can be separated into two distinct camps reflecting clear and long-standing divisions in the rationalist and constructivist traditions. The rationalist school focuses on power and rational choice and interest-based explanations to explain *why* states behaved in particular ways (Axelrod and Keohane 1985; Krasner 1998). Constructivists draw more from inductive, subjective and knowledge-based or relativist perspectives to explain *how* states and non-state actors gave meaning to regimes (Wendt 1992; Haas 1989; Habermas 1987).

Despite their differences, rationalists and constructivists concede that a regime includes a principled element characterised by a degree of shared and inter-subjective understandings of an issue and reciprocal expectations held by states and other actors. Regimes also incorporate a normative and rule-based element encapsulated in multilateral agreements and prescriptive guidelines and adopt some form of 'decision-making structure' responsible for promoting, disseminating and, where possible, managing and enforcing associated norms and rules. The value of regime theory is that it explains how principles, norms, rules and decision-making procedures can shape state and non-state behaviour. Crucially, it permits a more structured and coherent appraisal of seemingly chaotic phenomena, highlighting the rationale behind specific forms of international action. While the actions of states, non-state actors and non-governmental agencies are potentially influenced by regimes, the process is also iterative (Zeender 2005). Indeed, support for and compliance with regimes can generate certain benefits such as positive recognition, visibility and reputation enhancement.

The principles, norms and rules that apportion out rights and duties are determined by more than (state) self-interest and a drive for self-help in a (rationalist) anarchic 'system'. Constructivist contributions to regime theory suggest that regime formation and compliance is also potentially motivated by a shared understanding of a common good (Hurrell 2002; Finnemore and Sikkink 1998). Thus, regimes are predicated to a certain extent on a common and dynamic moral consciousness of state representatives that can be engineered, adapted and shared by individuals within a moral community. Commenting on the refugee regime, Goodwin-Gill (2000: 2) observes that 'international solidarity and cooperation are key fixtures in a regime oriented to protection and solutions'.

Regime influence is often inhibited by both narrow interpretations of state sovereignty and collective action dilemmas. Weiss and Korn (2006) consider how narrow understandings of sovereignty (as non-interference) have persistently hampered more progressive approaches to protection for internally displaced populations. A. Betts (2005) also describes how in the case of the refugee regime, protection constitutes a collective or 'public' good. Despite the benefits accrued by all states regardless of who provides refugee asylum, he predicts that the prospects for cooperation and burden sharing are poor, owing to free-riders. For example, certain states may perceive the cost of non-participation to be low and then transfer responsibilities to other states or UNHCR. Collective action dilemmas are equally common among regime proponents in cases where decision-making mechanisms are not clearly defined.

An international refugee regime

Despite decades of policy research and action, there are still tremendous challenges to achieving protection and durable solutions for displaced populations. A 'comprehensive international regime for forced migrants ... [with] internally displaced persons at the centre' has yet to emerge (Loescher 2000: 210). Even in the case of the refugee regime wherein the UN Security Council, UNHCR and national immigration departments are technically accountable for protection and durable solutions, there are still profound disagreements over how to ensure that the full spectrum of rights and needs of refugees are addressed in sustainable and dignified ways (Muggah 2007a, 2007b).

The basic normative bedrock of the refugee regime consists of a combination of *principles* including *humanitarianism, non-discrimination* and *non-refoulement*, the right of refugees not to be returned by force to their country of origin (see Table 2.1). These principles were codified into a cluster of rights for refugees – rights that are supposed to be guaranteed by states in reciprocal arrangements. Gibney (1999: 177) describes *humanitarianism* as the principle 'affirming the existence of certain responsibilities owed by agents (individuals and states) to outsiders by virtue of their shared membership of a single human community'. It is codified in the Declaration of Human Rights and, to a lesser extent, the Geneva Conventions and Protocols. *Non-discrimination* emphasises essential equalities and is a central tenet of both human rights law and refugee law and articulated in Article 3 of the 1951 Refugee Convention

43

TABLE 2.1 Comparing forced migration regimes

Regime	Principles	Norms	Rules	Decision-making procedures
Refugee	Humanitarianism; non-discrimination; non-refoulement; protection; durable solutions	Refugee law; international humanitarian law; human rights law	1951 Refugee Convention; 1967 Protocol and regional refugee agreements; 1969 OAU (now African Union) Refugee Convention; 1948 Universal Declaration of Human Rights (UDHR); 1966 International Covenant on Civil and Political Rights (ICCPR); 1966 UN International Covenant on Economic, Social and Cultural Rights (ESCR)	UNHCR; EXCOM
DIDR	Minority and indigenous rights; right to compensation; durable solutions	International and national human rights law	1980/91 World Bank Involuntary Resettlement Guidelines and sister Bank guidelines; UDHR; ICCPR; ESCR; 1986 Declaration on the Right to Development; 1957/1989 ILO Indigenous and Tribal Peoples Convention	World Bank; ADB; IADB

CIDR	Preventive protection; non-discrimination; voluntariness; durable solutions	Refugee law; international humanitarian law; inter-national and national human rights law	1998 Guiding Principles for Internal Displacement and Regional IDP Agreements; UDHR, ICCPR and ESCR; 2006 Pinheiro Principles; 1965 International Convention on All Forms of Racial Discrimination; 1981 International Convention on the Elimination of All Forms of Discrimination Against Women; 1989 Convention on the Rights of the Child	UNHCR; OCHA-IDD; International Committee of the Red Cross (ICRC); UNCHR; UNGA; World Bank*
NIDR	Non-discrimination; vulnerability-reduction; needs-based; durable solutions	International and national human rights law	1997 SPHERE Standards; 2006 IASC Guidelines; 1996 IASC Operational Guidelines; UDHR; ICCPR; ESCR	IFRC; OCHA; UNDP; World Bank; UNHCR

Note: *The World Bank and UNHCR are both often practically engaged in elements of CIDR and NIDR even if absent from contemporary debates on the subject.

and the 1967 Protocol. Normative claims to 'protection' and 'asylum' are founded on the principle of *non-refoulement* which is also spelled out in the Refugee Convention and Article 3 of the 1984 Convention against Torture.

The refugee regime draws on a number of key *norms* and *rules* that are prescriptive and proscriptive on state action. For example, the 1948 Universal Declaration of Human Rights codifies the personal, legal, social, economic, cultural and political rights of civilians, including refugees (Stedman and Tanner 2003). The Refugee Convention, the Protocol and the Statute of UNHCR constitute the normative basis of the refugee regime.[3] Signatories to the Refugee Convention and the 1967 Protocol, as well as associated regional declarations and resolutions, are expected to abide by the norms and rules contained therein (Table 2.1). The Refugee Convention did not grant refugees the *right* of asylum, which remained a national prerogative. Even while sovereignty remains the dominant paradigm in which regimes operate, tensions persist over its interpretation, the character of specific interventions to uphold human rights and end international crimes against humanity and war crimes, or when core norms and rules are systematically violated (Evans 2007).

Certain rules set clear standards such as the equitable (legal) treatment of refugees in line with nationals. Others are more informative and entail various monitoring, reporting and in rare cases, verification arrangements.[4] Rules may also be introduced to support the transfer and sharing of information – ostensibly to promote transparency in relation to state compliance with higher-order rules and decisions. In best-case scenarios, regime rules are codified into national law and are thus directly responsible for stimulating changes in state behaviour.[5] These rules may lead to the formation and enhancement of human rights structures, ombudsmen and related commissions at the local level.

Though overseen by states, *decision-making* procedures of the refugee regime were vested in a separate organ, the UNHCR. National authorities are nevertheless the final arbiters of national refugee policy as expressed by immigration laws and the mandates and activities of relevant ministries and departments. Despite the relevance of discrete internationally mandated principles, norms, rules and decision-making procedures, state interpretation and engagement with the refugee regime is ultimately discretionary. While UNHCR plays a pivotal role in generating and sharing information, promoting and strengthening international and domestic norms and monitoring implementation,[6] its capacity to enforce compliance was intentionally circumscribed from the beginning. As a rule, UNHCR operates only in cases where (host) state consent or acquiescence is agreed. Thus the refugee regime generally monitors existing guidelines, promotes the transfer and exchange of information and provides assistance *at the request* of states, rather than acting autonomously.[7]

International relations theorists – whether rationalists or constructivists – concede that regimes are born weak (Hasenclever, Meyer and Rittburger 1997; Haggard and Simmons 1987). The refugee regime is no exception: it is in many ways a normatively strong but procedurally weak regime. It purposefully included a number of key exemptions. Since the 1950s, for example, internally displaced persons were consciously excluded (Loescher 2000; UN 1972). Reductions in asylum since the 1970s and the increase in UN Security Council-sanctioned interventions in the 1990s resulted in certain pressures on the regime to simultaneously extend the conceptual (as opposed to legal) definition of refugees and promote 'in-country' solutions. The expansion of UNHCR's mandate had the potential to open the door for interference in the affairs of refugee-producing states – a concern that did not go unnoticed (Martin, D. 1995: 422–3). Despite efforts within UNHCR to adopt a more proactive approach to 'protecting' refugees and internally displaced populations, many doubt whether the agency can do much more than it already does (Hathaway 2006).

International regimes created to secure the protection and durable solutions for internally displaced populations are comparatively new. As a cluster of practices – including principle-, norm- and rule-setting together with decision-making – they span a few decades. The following section considers the discrete origins and evolution of emerging regimes for DIDR, CIDR and NIDR. In outlining their conceptual parameters, this section elaborates a research agenda to examine their uneven transfer from international prescriptions to the Sri Lankan context. It is worth stressing that these regimes were developed in parallel with considerable displacement and resettlement experience in Sri Lanka and other places around the world. As universalising and standardising processes, international regimes tend to override existing local practices and experiences – including in many cases the interests and experiences of the displaced and resettled themselves – a critical shortcoming to which we will later return.

A regime for DIDR In the aftermath of the Second World War, the prevailing development paradigm was one of nation-building and modernisation. Planned interventions to promote social progress were frequently exercised by forceful, often authoritarian, state intervention (Gibson 2001; Scott 1998; Heilbroner 1962). By the late 1980s, an estimated 10 million people were being displaced and relocated each decade by massive infrastructure projects in just three sectors, hydro-power, urban renewal and transportation (Cernea 1991, 2004). The social costs were deemed to be tolerable: national industrialisation required certain sacrifices, even if these were to be experienced by the poorer and marginal segments of society at the periphery. Central planners and donors justified their ideologies and actions by claiming that backwardness could be reversed by large-scale development projects entailing extensive social and demographic transformation. These bold development projects included 'villagisation' of peasant farmers, the 'sedentarisation' of pastoral groups and 'transmigration' to rural areas. In countries as geographically diverse as Brazil, Canada, China, Ethiopia, India, Indonesia, Jordan, Sri Lanka, the United States and Zambia, massive dam-building, power-generation and irrigation schemes were in effect radical experiments in social, political and economic engineering.

Bilateral and multilateral donors promulgated ambitious projects in underdeveloped countries on the grounds that they might stimulate economic growth and strengthen geo-political alliances. Such interventions generated considerable returns on investment for contractors and construction firms. When viewed through a political economy lens, technological and capital transfers from rich to poor countries in support of trickle-down development promised positive-sum gains. They also allowed the international aid establishment to side-step sensitive impediments to development, such as agrarian reform, changes to property and land tenure systems and structural inequality. There was a generally agreed principle that development cooperation – including interventions contributing to DIDR – was highly discretionary. Bilateral and multilateral lenders were keen to avoid being accused of interfering in the affairs of borrowing states, many of which were recently independent. Even so, the growing political, economic and social costs of major infrastructure projects on the livelihoods of those forced to move were not lost on early researchers and activists.

By the mid-1970s there began a progressive diffusion and deepening of global principles and norms expected to mitigate the pernicious consequences of large-scale development projects on specific vulnerable groups. Despite the wariness of many in the international community of being cast as neo-imperialist, a rash of new norms emerged designed to protect and preserve human rights and the environment, especially the rights of first nations, indigenous and minority populations. The Universal Declaration of Human Rights (1948), the Indigenous and Tribal Populations Convention and Recommendation (1957), the International

Covenant on Economic, Social and Cultural Rights (1966) and the International Covenant on Civil and Political Rights (1966) offered a template for rights-based advocacy on behalf of marginalised peoples (Table 2.1). Growing interest in the promotion of equitable, bottom-up and sustainable development revealed a pattern of subaltern resistance from within civil society to aggressive or 'high' modernism.

By the 1980s, activist scholars and action researchers – many of them intensely engaged in the formulation and propagation of rights-based norms – began to openly criticise state-planned development that justified economic growth at the expense of both individual and collective rights (Scott 1998; Sachs, W. 1992). As noted in Chapter 1, a cadre of forced migration scholars began documenting and publicising the negative externalities of DIDR. Drawing lessons from a variety of failed resettlement schemes from Latin America to South and South-east Asia, they consciously advocated development alternatives that either abandoned DIDR altogether, or mitigated related pathologies through carefully prepared, decentralised and culturally sensitive interventions. The influence of their pioneering work on changing the behaviour of state authorities was initially meagre.

At the same time, a growing constituency of donor governments, aid agencies and activists galvanised themselves around a cluster of principles and norms advocating increased protections for the displaced and resettled. They expected to minimise the incidence and adverse consequences of DIDR through the protection of minority rights, promotion of compensation and investment in durable solutions. This advocacy coalition impressed upon policymakers and representatives of states, multilateral financial institutions and the private sector, the extensive and far-reaching (human) consequences of resettlement on particular groups. New evidence, combined with growing popular resistance to DIDR, stimulated awareness of and changes in states' understanding of the issue (Cernea 2005: 10; Collier 1984).[8] Innovations during this period included the emergence of norms condemning the arbitrary eviction of minorities and indigenous people, codified a decade later by the UNCHR.[9] More general rights to equitable development in the context of resettlement were also actively taken up at the World Social Summit in Copenhagen in 1995 and integrated into the Final Declaration and the Programme of Action on Poverty Eradication several years later (Sarfaty 2005).

The World Bank played a central role – as exponent and target – in DIDR regime formation. Advocating on behalf of communities independently resisting resettlement, advocacy coalitions targeted the World Bank, its sister banks and their shareholders in a bid to force them to alter the accepted rules and decision-making procedures associated with planned resettlement. The World Bank, the Inter-American Development Bank (IADB), the Asian Development Bank (ADB) and the African Development Bank (AfDB) were all heavily invested in various aspects of the resettlement enterprise. As their global portfolio and share in resettlement-inducing projects steadily dropped from the 1970s onwards (as developing countries began to identify alternative sources of capital with which to finance large-scale development projects), they began to recognise the reputational and strategic risks accompanying controversial investments and were determined to minimise them at all cost (*Economist* 2007; Hall 2005).

Responding to internal and external pressures, the World Bank drafted a set of *involuntary resettlement* guidelines during the 1980s to influence both donor and borrower practices. The agency's first concrete policy response – encapsulated as a set of rules – was Operational Manual Statement (OMS) 2.33 and tied resettlement planning to environmental impact assessments. The OMS required that 'each project should ensure a distinct treatment regime for this group, a "package" of special measures, to be described in a new instrument integral to the project: the "resettlement action plan" (RAP)' (Cernea 2005: 12). The first test of the guidelines occurred during an appraisal of India's Narmada Sardar Sarovar Dam project. Following an internal review by World Bank-appointed sociologists, the guidelines were acknowledged as an effective tool in shaping DIDR planning. After the subsequent release of a critical internal review of World Bank-assisted agriculture and hydro-electric projects (1979–85), senior managers updated the guidelines by way of Operations Policy Note (OPN) 10.98 in 1986 (World Bank 1986). By 1988, the World Bank integrated OMS and OPN into a single set of guidelines and disseminated them in multiple languages. Thus, Operational Directive 4.30: Guidelines on Involuntary Resettlement was introduced following the restructuring of the World Bank in 1990.

Indirectly sanctioned by the World Bank's shareholders, the revised Guidelines introduced transparent rules to instruct both lender and borrower behaviour and practice. The World Bank and its associated agencies assumed a decision-making function for the DIDR regime by default. In expanding the application of the Guidelines, the World Bank and its partners initiated a policy review and dialogue to support the (re)-formulation, codification and implementation of resettlement legislation in borrower countries. This extended to legislation pertaining to specific social and economic rights (such as the restitution of property and compensation for expropriation) as well as concrete proposals to ensure that certain needs were met, particularly with respect to economic livelihood restoration and transparent governance in resettlement planning. The 1990s witnessed a norm cascade, described by Cernea (2005) as 'ripple effects', as the DIDR regime began to take hold. Owing to the pressure applied by the World Bank and its sister agencies, but also growing unease with resistance to forcible relocation and controversy arising from negative publicity, the governments of Brazil, China, Colombia, Mexico, the Philippines, Uganda and Sri Lanka, among others, eventually adopted basic provisions of the Guidelines and began intensive processes to codify them into national law and policy directives.

The (non-legally binding) Guidelines reflected many of the principles demanded by advocacy coalitions. These included the minimisation of DIDR where possible, special safeguards for minority and indigenous rights and investment in, restoration of and *improvement* of living standards, earning and production capacities to pre-displacement levels (Table 2.1). These safeguards extended to the protection of specific economic, social and cultural rights and needs in the pursuit of durable solutions. The Guidelines also required that ousted populations be adequately consulted, relocated in groups and on a 'voluntary' basis, provided with compensation regardless of whether they held legal title or deeds and resettled as close as possible to their original land. Newly resettled communities were to be adequately equipped with social and economic infrastructure and services, host communities were to be assisted as part of an overall area-based approach and public sector resources were to be provided as part of an overall compensation package based on the clear and fair valuation of household and community assets (Cernea 1993a: 24–5). In order to enhance rule adherence, the World Bank actively disseminated the Guidelines among borrower governments *requiring* them to adapt their own national policy and legal frameworks to the new resettlement standards (Cernea 2005).[10]

The extent to which the emerging DIDR regime is enforced and sanctions are effective in shaping state behaviour and ultimately durable solutions is more difficult to measure. Representatives of the World Bank and associated advocacy coalitions discovered that the preparation and dissemination of guidelines did not guarantee their practical application, much less assurances that rights or livelihoods of resettled populations would be 'improved' (Grabska and Mehta 2008). Intervening variables such as the states capacity to implement resettlement frustrated the implementation of key regime rules. As noted by Shihata (1993):

> it is easy to understand that in complex situations such as those created by imposed relocations, weaknesses of the local systems and civil service

may distort the outcome of government programmes. This is why it is often necessary to strengthen the local legal instruments available for addressing resettlement matters.

After the World Bank established an Independent Inspection Panel in 1993 to monitor and enforce compliance more assertively,[11] certain borrowers began to turn to private capital and alternative lenders when they felt conditions were too stringent.[12] Although the World Bank revised the Guidelines in 2001 (Operational Policy 4.12), the concept of 'impoverishment risks' was criticised by advocacy coalitions for watering down earlier provisions (Downing 2002). Even so, the Guidelines represented an important step in relation to enhancing DIDR regime reach and influence. They also began to register inroads among private sector actors.[13] Cernea (2005) observed still more ripple effects extending to private lenders by the late 1990s, including investment banks, oil and gas companies and private creditors. According to Picciotto, a number of publicly registered firms subsequently requested that borrower countries introduce NRPs in their respective funding agreements.[14] Following meetings of the World Bank's lending arm for the private sector (IFC) with major European investment banks, a set of voluntary Equator Principles were adopted in 2003 (Lazarus 2004). These Principles expressed a commitment among enlightened private sector entities to adhering to strict environmental and social practice and, while certain to enhance their public image, constituted a watershed in DIDR regime expansion.

States and international agencies invested in the DIDR regime in order to advance their own interests but also in response to an (inter-subjective) commitment to principles espousing minority rights, sustainable development and durable solutions. Their record of success, as the case of Sri Lanka in Chapter 4 makes clear, is uneven. The conclusions of the World Commission on Dams (2000) emphasise the persistent weaknesses of the incipient DIDR regime regarding its capacity to induce fundamental changes in state behaviour – and the tendency of governments to simply ignore them. Likewise, with the reopening of the debate on involuntary resettlement 'safeguards' by the ADB in 2008, certain advocates fear that social and environmental standards may be diluted (ADB 2008). These limitations notwithstanding, the ultimate benchmark of regime existence and influence is not measured reservedly as a demonstrated change in state (and international agency) behaviour. Indeed, even when states do not abide by the prescriptions of regimes, basic principles, norms or rules must exist to account for the (external) determination of non-compliance and the resort to sanctions.

A regime for CIDR

Despite international engagement with displacement across five decades, an incipient regime for CIDR did not surface until the early 1990s. The international refugee regime was from the beginning considered an ideal framework to conceptually and practically situate the rights and needs of populations internally displaced, returned and resettled by war.[15] As early as 1949, the Greek government informed the UN General Assembly that populations displaced within their borders or made stateless should, like refugees, have access to international aid even if they could not be awarded 'international protection' (Weiss and Korn 2006). As noted above, the 1951 Convention already tentatively stretched the mandate to include 'others of concern'. Though not by design, these others of concern included millions of people internally displaced by partition between India and Pakistan in the 1950s, hundreds of thousands of civilians dislocated by a vicious conflict in Nigeria's Biafra region in the late 1960s and millions of people internally displaced from Africa's independence struggles (Goetz 2001).

As with the DIDR regime, developed and developing states were at first intensely wary of forging a separate regime for protecting and promoting durable solutions for people internally displaced by war. Fundamental tenets of the refugee regime are still considered contentious and interventionist by a number of states, including Sri Lanka, that refused to sign or ratify the 1951 Refugee Convention and 1967 Protocol. Nevertheless, precedents for the CIDR regime quietly emerged below the radar. A particularly important case occurred in 1972 following the approval by the UN Economic and Social Council (ECOSOC) and the UN General Assembly of UNHCR operations in southern Sudan to assist '[third-country] resettlement of refugees returning from abroad, as well as persons displaced within the country' – an initiative that later evolved into Operation Lifeline Sudan. A growing coalition of advocates began to engage the topic and UN member states gradually felt compelled to identify solutions for internally displaced people in Nigeria-Biafra (1967), Guinea-Bissau, Angola, Mozambique and Cyprus (1974) and Vietnam and Laos (1975).

From the mid-1970s, a number of UN General Assembly resolutions affirmed the role of the UNHCR and others to protect IDPs. The principles underpinning intervention were analogous to those featuring in the refugee regime. These interventions often hinged on Article 9 of UNHCR's Statute which observed that 'the High Commissioner shall engage in such additional activities ... as the General Assembly may determine within the limits of the resources placed at his disposal' (UNGA 1975). By the

53

late 1980s, the agency and its core donors were staging regular conferences on how to manage both refugee and internal displacement flows in Africa and enhance absorptive capacities in resettlement areas (UNHCR 2002a).[16] Concerns over what to do with the internally displaced were climbing up the international agenda in the late 1980s due to growing unease with refugee flows and because certain actors felt 'it was neither reasonable nor feasible to treat the two categories [refugees and IDPs] separately' (UNHCR 1994b: 5; ICIHI 1986).

A set of norms, rules and decision-making procedures underpinning state and non-governmental responses to CIDR gradually emerged in the late 1980s and early 1990s that remained essentially unchanged for the next two decades. UN Resolution 688 authorised safe havens for internally displaced Kurds in northern Iraq and was considered by advocates as a key operational precedent for protecting 'conflict IDPs' (UN 1991). The safe haven concept was eventually extended, with mixed results, to internally displaced populations in Bosnia and Herzegovina in the early 1990s and in Sri Lanka soon after the arrival of UNHCR in 1987 (Hyndman 2003). Indeed, the Balkan conflicts marked a critical turning point for the consolidation of the CIDR regime as western European countries pushed for the 'right to remain' of would-be refuges in the former Yugoslavia (Barutciski 1996; Hathaway 1995). By the mid-1990s, the accepted prerequisites for UNHCR intervention on behalf of IDPs included authorisation from the UN General Assembly, UN Secretary General, or another principal organ of the UN; consent of the concerned state; the relevance of UNHCR's operational experience *in situ*; and fiduciary capacities (UNHCR 1998a; UNGA 1993a).

The UNHCR adopted a working definition of internal displacement in 1992 and began formalising its approach on the issue.[17] Under the stewardship of former High Commissioner Sadako Ogata and with support from sympathetic US and northern European diplomats, the overall caseload 'of concern' to UNHCR began to *increase* in the 1990s from 17 to 21.1 million (from 1991 to 1998), many of whom included IDPs (UNHCR 2005a).[18] Before long less than half of the agency's overall population of concern consisted of refugees (UNHCR 2001a). Within a few short years the incipient CIDR regime appeared to be successfully achieving what proved to some critics to be its more invidious aim: the containment of prospective refugees (Hathaway 2006; Dubernet 2001).[19] Proponents of the refugee regime also began to publicly complain that the CIDR regime was beginning to draw international attention away from refugees (Goodwin-Gill 2000; Barutciski 1998, 1999). Owing to the clear potential for the CIDR regime to be construed as a form of Western interventionism or as detrimental to the interests of refugees, its development proceeded cautiously and in deference to state sovereignty.

Many of the core principles associated with the CIDR regime were formalised in the early 1990s. For example, the UN General Assembly repeatedly affirmed 'its support for the [UNHCR] High Commissioner's efforts ... to provide humanitarian assistance and protection to persons displaced within their own country in specific situations'.[20] UNHCR elaborated de facto principles to guide activities focusing not just on protection, but also 'ascertaining that return or resettlement is taking place voluntarily in conditions of safety and dignity; facilitating the actual return or resettlement movement process; monitoring the conditions of those who are returned/settled/resettled ... and assisting (re)integration' (UNHCR 2001a: 13). Like the World Bank, UNHCR emphasised that:

> [durable] solutions require the political commitment and full support of the government and the local community as well as specific commitments from relevant ministries in charge of providing the services required by the beneficiaries, such as housing, land, health services and education. (ibid.)

In order to assuage sensitivities among certain states regarding sovereignty, CIDR regime proponents actively promoted additional principles such as 'in-country' solutions and 'preventive protection' to prevent refugee flows (Cohen 1996). This emphasis on in-country solutions coincided with clear strategic shifts in the international priorities of certain North American and western European states. Refugees increasingly failed to capture the imagination of liberal Western democracies in the way they once had. Governments of industrialised countries claimed that they could broker comparatively little domestic support for (third-country) resettlement of large numbers of refugees from developing states and began to actively privilege a rights-based discourse to justify solutions closer to the site of displacement and a pragmatic strategy of preventing further flows by providing domestic 'flight alternatives'.

Industrialised countries were not alone in expressing reservations about core aspects of the refugee regime and the need for alternative approaches to dealing with internally displaced populations. A growing number of developing countries, once lauded for their hospitality towards refugees, were increasingly uneasy with hosting massive refugee caseloads – particularly as the (temporary) camps installed in the 1970s and 1980s were acquiring a more permanent character (UNHCR 2004a). Countries managing large refugee populations in Africa, Latin America, the Balkans and South-east Asia began raising uncomfortable questions

55

about 'burden sharing' and the double standards exhibited by North American and western European governments that actively restricted third-country resettlement throughout the 1990s (Loescher and Milner 2005). The CIDR regime began to be perceived by both sides as a suitable compromise solution.

With UNCHR serving as a forum for the normative expression and advancement of the CIDR regime, UNHCR was the natural focal point for practically taking the issue forward. During the early 1990s, the UN General Assembly agreed to 'support for the High Commissioner's efforts ... especially where such efforts could contribute to the prevention or solution of refugee problems' (UNGA 1993b). Likewise, members of UNHCR's Executive Committee (EXCOM) conceded publicly that the refugee regime – designed to accommodate the political and economic realities of western Europe during the post-Second World War era – was no longer commensurate with contemporary realities (UNHCR 1994b). In this way, EXCOM began to refine the agency's mandate and obligations with respect to CIDR (UNHCR 1997a). In 1993, the agency issued policy guidelines on the CIDR question and published an assessment of its 'Operational Experience with Displaced Persons'. By the end of 1997, UNHCR had operationalised elements of the CIDR regime.

Yet while the issue of internal displacement acquired growing inter-national notoriety throughout the 1990s, disagreements arose over the practicalities of implementing key tenets of the CIDR regime. Many wondered openly how UNHCR, already overburdened, might expand its role further still. Certain donors, forced migration experts and practi-tioners initially called for an extension of the refugee regime to include internally displaced who for all intents and purposes lived in refugee-like circumstances. These proposals were rejected by more orthodox refugee regime supporters, themselves legal experts closely allied with UNHCR (Barutciski 1998, 1999, 2000; Kingsley-Nyinah 1999; Rutinwa 1999). As with the controversies generated by the Guidelines within the World Bank, many in UNHCR were polarised over the dilemma posed by internal displacement to asylum: was a structured approach to protection and durable solutions for IDPs a bridge too far?

Even where couched in the principles of preventive protection and the right to remain, there were concerns among some UNHCR supporters that tampering with refugee law and the decision-making structures of the refugee regime could unintentionally undermine the asylum principle (Table 2.1). Certain scholars felt that while IDPs warranted attention, clear guarantees of international protection could only be made to those crossing state borders (Goodwin-Gill 2006; Hathaway 2006). Keeping the regimes separate was as much a legal issue as a practical and ethical one. The International Committee of the Red Cross (ICRC) expressed reservations about singling out assistance on the basis of presumed or a priori categories of need, rather than demonstrated vulnerability. Representatives of the ICRC claimed that this could unintentionally create a privileged sub-group and discriminate against others equally in need. A clear tension emerged between 'those who felt that existing law provided adequate coverage for the rights of the internally displaced and those who advocated a new regime' (Bagshaw 1998: 12).

The incubator of the incipient CIDR regime emerged from what Bagshaw (2000) describes as global public policy networks. Less adversarial than the advocacy coalitions shaping the DIDR regime, these networks were composed of scholars, activists and non-governmental agencies that worked together with like-minded diplomats and international bureaucrats – especially UNCHR.[21] As predicted by constructivists, these networks facilitated an iterative process of value formation and transposition of ideas across both institutional and sectoral boundaries. By embedding the issue of CIDR in an international forum, norm entrepreneurs such as QUNO together with Austrian and Norwegian diplomats managed to leverage a Special Representative on the topic in 1992. Following the appointment of former Sudanese Foreign Minister Francis Deng as the Special Representative on Internal Displacement by the UN Secretary General, a comprehensive study was submitted to the UNCHR in 1993. The 1993 report recommended that a compilation and analysis of existing principles, norms and rules be prepared to advance the issue.

Drafted by the Special Representative, Francis Deng and activist scholars such as Roberta Cohen and Walter Kälin, the Guiding Principles for Internal Displacement laid out the basic rules of the CIDR regime. A review of humanitarian, human rights and refugee law determined that while existing jurisprudence addressed many aspects of CIDR, an array of institutional and legal gaps remained where protection and durable solutions for IDPs were not sufficiently addressed. The 1994 compilation confirmed that there were few clearly articulated rules and no coherent decision-making mechanism within the UN with specific responsibility for CIDR. It further recommended that the issue either be added to the mandate of an existing agency or that the UN and its member states create an equivalent entity. Building on the previous debates concerning the right to remain and preventive protection, the compilation concluded that the legal basis for providing protection prior to displacement could be strengthened significantly by articulating a 'right not to be arbitrarily

57

displaced' (Baghsaw 2000: 14). The Guiding Principles were submitted to UNCHR in 1996 and formally adopted by consensus in 1998.

The Principles formalised a broad definition of internally displaced people and rearticulated the basic shared principles, norms and rules under which the protection, care and maintenance and durable solutions were to be undertaken (Table 2.1). As with the DIDR Guidelines, by virtue of being adopted in the UNCHR, the Principles indicated that a threshold was being breached whereby certain norms became institutionalised in a specific set of rules and organisations (Finnemore and Sikkink 1998). Regime proponents expected that the dissemination, codification and diffusion of the Principles into national legislation and non-governmental agency practice would enhance their potency. Various aspects of the Principles were also strengthened by additional subsidiary standards emerging several years later. For example, the UN Principles on Housing and Property Restitution for Refugees ('Pinheiro Principles') also draw from existing international, humanitarian and refugee law and are expected to ensure that 'the right to return' and 'rights to restitution' are understood and sanctioned by states and non-state actors. The Pinheiro Principles advocate for restitution (restoration to pre-loss condition) over compensation, with potentially important implications for CIDR and NIDR.

The UNHCR and other multilateral and non-governmental agencies, such as OCHA and the World Food Programme (WFP), formally endorsed the Guiding Principles and disseminated them as early as 1993, despite lingering disagreements concerning their practical application.[22] Owing in part to the absence of a clear decision-making structure to advance the Principles, criticisms were directed at their relevance and potential to influence state behaviour, much less generate genuine protection and durable solutions. Nevertheless, the basic rules issued by the Guiding Principles were rapidly endorsed by a number of states and institutions. For example, Angola, Azerbaijan, Burundi, Colombia, Georgia, Liberia, Nepal, Peru, the Philippines, Russia, Serbia and Montenegro, Sri Lanka, Turkey, Uganda and the United States made explicit references to the Principles in their national laws or relevant policies on internal displacement.[23] Reminiscent of the Equator Principles discussed above, the Guiding Principles were actively disseminated to armed non-state actors in conflict-affected areas of several countries (Zeender 2005). Some regional organisations also took them on board, including the African Union (AU) which adopted an official policy on CIDR in late 2006 (Beyani 2006).

Disagreements continued to simmer over the 'decision-making' apparatus of the CIDR regime. Certain donors and advocates called on UNHCR to assume a more muscular role in advancing the regime (Cohen and Deng 1998a). Others demanded that a new agency be created as advocated in the 1994 compilation, though key states (i.e. Russia and China) and certain multilateral agencies resisted the creation of a centralised international decision-making mechanism that could translate rules into practice. While explicitly recommended in the Principles and by influential exponents of the nascent regime such as former US ambassador to the UN Richard Holbrooke, it became apparent that a centralised entity was not politically feasible. UNHCR (2001g: 3–6) for its part maintained that minimum preconditions for protecting and overseeing durable solutions for IDPs included authorisation by the UN Secretary General, the consent or acquiescence of national authorities and voluntariness. Activities would therefore focus on creating optimum conditions conducive for return and resettlement, monitoring of such processes and assistance towards achieving reintegration. In spite of the agency's repeated efforts to clarify its role, there was still internal uncertainty about how far it should become involved (UNHCR 1998c, 2001g, 2005a, 2005b). In time, a collaborative approach emerged by default.

Despite calls by the UN General Assembly for 'an effective, accountable and predictable' approach to protection and durable solutions, unresolved challenges remain (UNHCR 2005a). Instead of working in a coordinated fashion to advance resettlement, agencies tend to adopt a 'pick and choose' approach on the basis of their mandates, resources and interests. The weaknesses of the collaborative approach were assumed to lie with its lack of leadership and resources, the absence of predictable standards as well as the highly competitive nature of relief and development assistance (Muggah 2007c; Bagshaw and Paul 2004). In recognition of these limitations, the UN developed a 'cluster approach' to programming dismissed by Hathaway (2006: 8) as 'an agreement among relevant UN agencies to "play nice" with each other'. Introduced in 2006, the cluster approach was intended to strengthen system-wide preparedness and technical capacities to respond to internal displacement in *both* conflict and natural disaster situations.[24] Cluster leads were assigned for emergency shelter, protection, health, nutrition, water, hygiene and sanitation, early recovery, logistics and emergency telecommunications. Though UNHCR's role was confined to 'shelter and camp management' and 'protection' it nevertheless retained a dominant role in putting the CIDR regime rules into practice (UNHCR 2005c).

There are indications that a more robust decision-making mechanism is emerging within the UN system. Building on a UN Inter-Agency Standing Committee (IASC) framework established in 1999,[25] by 2002, a specialised unit was created in OCHA (2000) – the Internal Displacement Division (IDD).[26] The IDD was expected to bolster voluntary compliance with regime rules, but was hampered from the beginning by limited authority and resources and considerable opposition from proponents of the CIDR regime, who felt it lacked clout. The UN Security Council and General Assembly also continued to agitate for more compliance among states and for better cooperation between non-governmental agencies.[27] Following a process of humanitarian reform within the UN beginning in 2004, UNHCR (2007a: 3) reported that it 'must reposition itself to provide protection and assistance to displaced people in need, regardless of whether they have crossed an international border'.

By 2007, UNHCR launched a corporate strategy and established an internal unit within the agency to advance a rights-based approach to CIDR. UNHCR (ibid.: 5) declared that 'all IDP activities and operations undertaken by the Office will incorporate the norms, standards and principles of international human rights and humanitarian law, as well as the United Nations Guiding Principles on Internal Displacement'. Further, the agency announced that 'UNHCR will ... advocate on behalf of these norms, standards and principles' (UNHCR (ibid.). The (re)-positioning of responsibility for IDPs in UNHCR and the gradual reduc-tion of OCHA responsibilities suggests that that the former is assuming tentative decision-making functions for the CIDR regime. Moreover, the expansion of the Guiding Principles into realms of development and natural disasters reveals increased potential for regime convergence in the twenty-first century.

In the case of the CIDR regime, states and international agencies are concerned with minimising refugee flows but also advancing principles associated with the right to remain, protection and durable solutions without discrimination. As in the case of the DIDR regime, an inter-national agency – in this case UNHCR – assumed a decision-making role that focused on standard setting, advising and monitoring. UNHCR faced structural limitations in relation to how far it could push the CIDR agenda owing to its non-political and humanitarian mandate as set out in paragraph 2 of its Statute. Apart from the rhetorical commitments made by states and agencies to core aspects of the CIDR regime, the extent to which norms and rules are adhered to remains difficult to discern. The case of Sri Lanka highlights how while certain objectives of the CIDR regime are met (i.e. diminished refugee flows), its promotion of protec-tion and durable solutions is constrained by narrow interpretations of sovereignty and ongoing collective action dilemmas (Chapter 5).

A regime for NIDR

Millions of people are internally displaced each year, directly and indirectly, by so-called environmental or natural disasters. According to the IFRC, one of the agencies most active in relation to NIDR, the total numbers *affected* by natural disasters tripled between 1990 and 2000 to more than two billion, or some 211 million directly affected per annum, though these numbers are difficult to verify. While dramatic and permanent changes to the physical and social environment arising from catastrophic events such as floods, volcanoes, cyclones and earthquakes have long been recognised as major contributors to protracted natural disaster-induced internal displacement and resettlement, a coherent regime was slow to emerge.

As observed in Chapter 1, the almost imperceptible evolution of an NIDR regime is due in part to disagreement over what is implied by a 'natural disaster'. Differences of opinion over what is and is not included in the definition of natural disasters and their relationships with human migration persisted for decades (Oliver-Smith 2005). Traditionally, disasters were considered to be a consequence of ecological or elemental forces independent of human agency. In the past three decades, owing in part to enhanced collaboration between the natural and social sciences, disaster specialists began to recognise the ways that geographies of the built environment were shaped by pre-existing patterns of social inequality. Social and political factors, then, were thereafter recognised as prominent risks in relation to the incidence and severity of internal displacement and resettlement associated with natural events (Black 2001b).

Because of the sheer variety of natural disasters and competing interpretations of how they were induced, policymakers and practitioners were loath to issue unified conceptual templates to guide operational responses to mitigate disaster risk in the 1950s and 1960s. Rather, early approaches were highly technical and capitalised on innovations in hydrology and geology. In many industrialised contexts, 'early warning' and 'disaster preparedness' systems were tested and disseminated (Cuny 1983). In some cases, interventions focused on 'vulnerability reduction' to prevent these natural hazards from affecting high-risk or disaster-prone areas – though they tended to focus on the physical rather than the social environment. Early interventions aimed at reinforcing physical safeguards and minimising exposure to disaster-related risks through, in some cases (preventive), population relocation. Technological know-how to enhance protection was the order of the day.

The genesis of an NIDR regime can be traced to the 1970s. As anthropologists, sociologists and human geographers were increasingly seized of the issue, attention was reoriented away from the events triggering disasters to latent and existing patterns of socio-economic vulnerability within human settlements. As in the case of the incipient CIDR regime, early contributors to the NIDR regime began to opportunistically identify an amalgam of principles and norms through which they might enhance the resilience of affected populations. An underlying expectation of these policymakers, practitioners and scholars was that the scale, speed and organisation of external responses to NIDR would reflect prevailing geo-political and bilateral interests – even if core principles associated with reducing vulnerability and promoting durable solutions were widely acknowledged. There was an understanding that states themselves affected by large-scale natural disasters would sanction external interventions according to their sovereign interests.

The disparateness of disasters is also apparent in the variety of agencies that deal with them and of groups studying them (Chapter 1). In the 1970s, for example, White and Haas (1975) counted more than twenty governmental agencies addressing natural disasters in the United States alone. The first bureaucratic expression of the international NIDR regime was the Office of the United Nations Disaster Relief Coordinator (UNDRO) in 1971. The agency was expected to coordinate the efforts of other multilateral agencies including the World Bank, UNDP, FAO, WFP, the UN Children's Fund (UNICEF), the UN Educational, Scientific and Cultural Organization (UNESCO), the UN Environment Programme (UNEP), the UN Institute for Training and Research (UNITAR) and the World Health Organization (WHO). Though not provided with resources per se, UNDRO was from the beginning expected to coordinate aid and services in the event of a major natural disaster.

UNDRO was designed to assist governments to prevent and mitigate disasters through contingency planning and information dissemination (UN Chronicle 1985; Davis and Seitz 1982). Between 1972 and 1987, for example, UNDRO reportedly coordinated or assisted relief efforts in more than 380 disasters (UN Chronicle 1991). As predicted above, it was circumscribed by states from assuming a more assertive role. Recognising the intrinsic limitations of UNDRO in the early 1990s, the UN General Assembly approved the creation of an Emergency Relief Coordinator (ERC) to consolidate the coordination process (UNGA 1991). By 1992, the Secretary General established a Department for Humanitarian Affairs (DHA), which in turn created the IASC to coordinate UN policy; the Central Emergency Revolving Fund (CERF) to disburse rapid emergency aid; and the consolidated inter-agency appeals process (CAP) that articulated the

UN's strategy on, among other priorities, NIDR. In the context of UN reforms and the International Decade for Natural Disaster Reduction (1990–2000),[28] DHA was eventually converted into OCHA in 1998.

In the early 1980s the nascent NIDR regime consisted of an assemblage of principles drawn explicitly from disaster relief more generally. While simultaneously conditioned by donor states concerned with preventing contagion and minimising political and economic disruption, the incipient regime accommodated basic needs commensurate with the requirements of survival and the minimisation of risks to women and children (Table 2.1). It advocated 'non-discrimination' and 'voluntariness' in all interventions intended to enhance protection and durable solutions. While reflecting certain established human rights norms (as in the case of DIDR and CIDR), it was to a large extent needs-driven. Only comparatively gradually did proponents of the NIDR regime begin to adopt a concerted 'rights-oriented' lens and promote 'parity' (with citizens, for example) for survivors of natural disasters. Kälin (2005a: 10) observed how 'violations of economic, social and cultural rights can become more entrenched the longer [natural disaster-induced] displacement lasts'.

Debates over the comparative advantages of rights- and needs-based approaches were ratcheted up in the 1990s. Proponents of the rights-based approach[29] reiterated norms such as, *inter alia*, the right to voluntary return, adequate housing and secure tenure, temporary and permanent housing and inheritance (Leckie 2005: 16). The Guiding Principles, a cornerstone of the CIDR regime, also highlighted the importance of ensuring the protection of disaster-induced displaced (Hedman 2005; Cohen and Deng 1998a). But despite the evolving importance attached to a human rights doctrine, the UNCHR and OCHA (2000) only recently began to articulate guidance towards promoting rights-based approaches in situations of natural disasters. Meanwhile, advocates of the so-called needs-based approach[30] such as the IFRC and national Red Cross and Red Crescent societies pushed for a more pragmatic approach emphasising basic needs and entitlements while reducing vulnerability. Specifically they focused on ensuring that provisions for health and sanitation were integrated into NIDR strategies, though they were frequently criticised for adopting a short-term and overtly humanitarian orientation. Predictably, champions of the rights-based approaches argued that such perspectives failed to stress the social, economic and cultural rights to which survivors were entitled (Twigg 2004).

Two clusters of rules were fundamental to the consolidation of the nascent regime. These included the Humanitarian Charter and Minimum Standards in Disaster Response (Standards) and the Guiding Principles on Internal Displacement (Principles). Though not legally binding, both the Standards and the Principles advance constitutive norms that aim to reconcile the dual imperatives of needs and rights (Table 2.1). Initiated in the mid-1990s by the UN Steering Committee for Humanitarian Response and InterAction, the Standards were an attempt to lay out the minimum conditions for emergency and recovery activities following a complex emergency.[31] While not exclusive to NIDR, the Standards played a pivotal role in setting benchmarks and targets for protection and durable solutions. Specifically, they issued minimum criteria for state and non-governmental agencies in relation to providing water, food, sanitation, health and shelter – all ostensible human rights. The Standards also included provisions to enhance compliance, including indicators to document and monitor implementation and to hold state and non-state actors accountable. Meanwhile, the Principles, backed up by the UN (2005a) and the IASC (2006b), articulated the obligations and responsibilities of governments and non-governmental organisations to facilitate voluntary return and resettlement.

Like the DIDR and CIDR regimes, the coherence and influence of the NIDR regime are inhibited by the extreme decentralisation of its decision-making mechanisms. Owing to the perception that disasters are contingent, there are few clear or predictable institutional approaches and defined mechanisms to promote protection and durable solutions. Short of massive investment to reduce vulnerability in areas susceptible to disaster, the international community – including donors, multilateral agencies and non-governmental organisations – are compelled to work with and through existing state institutions of affected countries which in turn are presumed to conscientiously support return and resettlement according to the prescriptions of the Standards and Principles. There is a modest selection of options for censure or proscription: where affected states fail to comply with declared rules, certain international actors may temporarily suspend, limit or redirect their assistance. Because a considerable proportion of the capital generated for natural disasters is itself derived from private donors and not official public aid departments, donor states exert comparatively limited leverage to ensure that recipients conform to regime rules.

The international community assembled a highly decentralised bureaucratic mechanism to coordinate responses to NIDR. In addition to the IFRC, which works through national societies, the UN assumed a key role in coordinating responses to populations affected by natural disasters, including internally displaced and resettled people. As noted above, UNDRO, DHA and eventually OCHA were mandated to monitor and enhance transparency and compliance with established principles and rules and coordinate funding as appropriate (UNDP 2004). In time Operational Guidelines were established to assist in the translation of core regime norms and rules into programmes (IASC 2006b).[32] These Guidelines drew explicitly from rights-based approaches:

> [the guidelines were] drafted with the consequences of natural disasters in mind ... [and are] informed by and draw on relevant international human rights, as well as existing standards and policies pertaining to humanitarian action and human rights guidelines on humanitarian standards in situations of natural disaster. (ibid.: 1)

In much the same way as the CIDR regime advocates a collaborative approach, the UN and non-governmental agencies such as the IFRC are expected to work closely together and jointly define activities to protect and promote durable solutions for the displaced. In most cases, the IFRC and its national societies are key agencies responsible for implementing interventions, with the UN playing a subsidiary role. Interventions are frequently criticised for falling short with respect to durable solutions. Ultimately, the scale and magnitude of activities are also strongly determined by the perceived severity of the hazards themselves, the relative vulnerability of the population and geo-political interests (Kälin 2005b; Uyangoda 2005).

The NIDR regime is motivated by fewer clear strategic interests than either the DIDR or CIDR regimes. Though drawing from established principles in human rights law and disaster relief, the human rights and humanitarian imperative appears to be a core driver, while a desire to maintain stability and reduce population outflows are others. The discretionary nature of international engagement and the decentralised parameters of regime decision-making procedures delimit a coherent and coordinated set of interventions. Moreover, as Chapter 6 makes clear in the case of Sri Lanka, collective action dilemmas that invariably arise in the case of NIDR threaten the integrity of the nascent regime itself. Depending on where a natural disaster occurs, there may be a massive array of international and national non-governmental, state and non-state actor agencies involved – as was the case with the 2004 tsunami affecting fifteen countries in Africa and South and South-east Asia.

Conclusions

The application of regime theory to understanding international responses to internal displacement and resettlement can help illuminate the underlying constellation of motivations and interests shaping state, non-state and non-governmental behaviour. By tracing out the parameters of three individuated regimes for different categories of internal displacement and resettlement, it becomes possible to compare and learn from them. In their points of convergence and divergence, such analysis reinforces the value of applying a unitary approach to appraising categories of forced migration. Regimes for DIDR, CIDR and NIDR emerged from a combination of adversarial and cooperative exchanges between clusters of states, academics and activists. These regimes exhibit occasionally overlapping principles, norms and rules that are expected to contain further displacement while simultaneously protecting and promoting durable solutions for the internally displaced.

Each regime exhibits strengths and weaknesses. In all cases regimes are highly discretionary and characterised by decentralised decision-making mechanisms that rely primarily on national authorities and non-governmental agencies. Regimes were intentionally constructed in such a way as to accommodate narrow interpretations of sovereignty. Despite efforts to enhance regime absorption at the national level, legislation and policy statements, regimes are dependent on voluntary compliance and are susceptible to collective action dilemmas. Indeed, there is a long way to go from the articulation of international regimes and their application in the national context where the interests of actors at local, sub-national and national level often compete and collide in complex ways. Whilst each regime varies in its capacity to influence state, non-governmental, non-state and private sector behaviour, their existence and relevance is not necessarily a function of demonstrated behavioural changes of these same actors. As observed by Puchala and Hopkins (1982: 247) a 'regime need not serve the common or separate interests of every participant very well or even at all ... most regimes function to the advantage of some participants and to the disadvantage of others'.

Although states play the decisive role in the design and administration of regimes, a major contribution to their evolution comes from transnational advocacy coalitions and public policy networks. They contributed to a cascade of norms and rules through a purposeful process of state–civil society bargaining. Although ideational flows are not unidirectional, this chapter detects a clear transference of concepts and values from research to policy. In certain cases, policymakers were former practitioners or academics and vice versa. In other cases, universities, training institutes and even practitioner journals expanded awareness on the issue. These networks recognised that a crucial feature of regime deepening and expansion included the generation and dissemination of shared understandings of complex problems, the nurturing of shared values and expectations and the generation and dissemination of information. Regime proponents also understood that rule generation and consolidation could be fostered through both formal and customary means.

Regimes are expected to enhance the predictability and coherence of state and non-state actions towards achieving protection and durable solutions for internally displaced populations. Regime proponents sought to encourage this by cementing and codifying relevant international commitments and obligations in multilateral resolutions, national legislation, informal guidelines and contracts and declarations and statements. Even where norms are codified and enshrined in national legislation, rules are not necessarily followed. There is a formidable range of challenges that confront the full realisation of the three regimes. The persistence of classical sovereignty paradigms presents a constraint to their full actualisation. The collective action problems plaguing multilateral agencies – their persistence due in part to the decentralised nature of regimes themselves – are core hurdles not easily surmounted in the short term.

Protection and durable solutions

3 | A short history of settlement and resettlement in Sri Lanka

International regimes do not emerge in *terrus nullius* but rather from fluid and contested debates. Chapter 2 signalled endogenous constraints embedded in regimes such as the interpretation of sovereignty by states as non-interference and collective action dilemmas among regime participants. This chapter turns to a range of exogenous factors that directly and indirectly shape the parameters and influence of international regimes formulated to protect and promote durable solutions at the local level. Drawing directly from the Sri Lankan experience, the chapter demonstrates that these factors are historically, politically and socially contingent. They are connected fundamentally to the political economy of development and nation-building and identity politics. Although international regimes advocate universalising principles, norms and rules, this chapter finds that they could also be construed as a-historical, ethnic-blind and non-responsive to the interests and lived experiences of displaced and resettled populations. The Sri Lankan case reveals how regimes crafted ostensibly to support the welfare of internally displaced and resettled populations can unintentionally entrench structural inequality and ethnic tension.

Sri Lanka features a long and comparatively well-documented record of planned population relocation.[1] Critical reflection on past experience can shed light on the interconnected causes of – and bureaucratic responses to – contemporary patterns of displacement and resettlement. This chapter describes how early settlement and resettlement schemes were an ineluctable feature of the colonial plantation economy and accompanied by experimental land tenure systems and the importation of foreign labour. In Sri Lanka, highly centralised and paternalistic approaches to population relocation persisted well after independence (1948), albeit harnessed to a new political purpose. Settlement and resettlement were thereafter intimately linked to the assertion of (strong) state control over land, political control of minority areas in the north and east and competing ethnic nationalisms. Under the pretext of development, counter-insurgency and disaster-response, the state engaged in what amounted to demographic engineering. Faced with these and other exogenous factors, international regimes faced sizeable challenges.

This chapter divides Sri Lanka's forced migration experience into five chronological phases. While overlapping, each period reveals subtle shifts in the rationale and practice of state-sanctioned resettlement. The first phase ends with the occupation and colonisation of then Ceylon[2] by Great Britain in the early nineteenth century. The second spans the expansion of the plantation economy, the growth of early nationalist movements and preliminary efforts to settle the so-called 'dry zone' (1815–1947). A third phase begins at independence, includes two massive integrated development projects and comes to a close during the prologue of an insurrection (1948–82). A fourth phase features protracted warfare (punctuated by intermittent ceasefires) between the state and a guerrilla movement (1983–present) while the fifth begins after a massive natural disaster (2004–present). Crucially, international regimes promoting protection and durable solutions did not materialise in earnest until the latter stages of the third phase.

Settling the past and present

Competing claims over who settled (or was resettled) where and when are among the defining controversies of twentieth- and twenty-first-century Sri Lankan politics and scholarship. They are central to the legitimacy of the so-called homeland debates and competing territorial claims of Sinhalese nationalists and Sri Lankan Tamil separatists who dominated the country's political landscape since independence.[3] While history is of course contested, certain Sri Lankan historians and archaeologists trace many of the first planned settlements to the fourth century BC. A key, albeit highly biased, chronicle of settlement patterns is the *Mahavamsa*.[4] The *Mahavamsa*'s legitimacy is intensely debated due to its Buddhist derivation and 'updates' by the Sinhalese government in the latter half of the twentieth century (Bond 1988; Gombrich and Obeyesekere 1988). Nevertheless, the *Mahavamsa* describes how population settlements were frequently constructed alongside reservoirs, temples (and *kovils*) and monuments. Spatially, these early population clusters were centrally planned and ordered with colonial administrators describing them as contiguous 'agricultural republics' each with their tank (reservoir) and field (Brohier 1934).

There are many fiercely waged and unresolved debates over the ethnicity of the island's early inhabitants. The 'original' islanders are described alternately as ethnically homogenous (Thornton and Nihthiyananthan 2001; Wilson 1988) or highly stratified, as in neighbouring India, according to ethnicity, class, lineage, clan, caste, occupation and political status (Gunawardana 1990). The British colonial authorities, not without prejudice, categorised the population according to indigenous 'Vedda', 'lowland' and 'Kandyan' Sinhalese who were Buddhist, 'Sri Lankan Tamils' who practised Hinduism, 'Sri Lankan Moors' who were Muslim, 'Malays', 'Burgher' and later, Hindu and Christian 'Indian' or 'estate Tamils' and Christian 'Europeans'. Before the arrival of Portuguese, Dutch and eventually British colonialists, land ownership was believed to be concentrated within the Sinhalese aristocratic and ecclesiastic classes. Early British colonial administrators wryly remarked that 'custom became prevalent of forming tanks with the pious intention of conferring the lands that enriched the Church' (Tennent 1977: 311). To their frustration, they found that the island's early aristocrats had long supplied land to the (Sinhalese) priest class to the extent that by the end of the nineteenth century, the Buddhist clergy owned up to one-third of the island's arable lands over which the Crown at the time exercised few rights of taxation.

A populist settlement narrative emerged in the twentieth century that stubbornly dominates empirical claims to the contrary. Spencer (1990b) characterises this as the 'Vijaya colonisation myth' – a fable describing the origins of the Sinhalese that resurfaces in contemporary political debates on identity and development (Bastian 1995; Tennekoon, S. 1988). The *Mahavamsa* describes how Vijaya, an exiled prince from northern India, arrived to the island and married a Yakka [Vedda] princess, one of the island's original inhabitants in the fifth century BC on the day of Buddha's death. Seven hundred followers of Vijaya, along with several thousand families from Indian service castes soon followed after being sent by the King of Madhura. Crucially, south Indian Tamils, described only pejoratively in later chapters as 'Chola invaders', arrived much later (Manogaran 1996). The Vijaya colonisation myth persists in populist discourse despite extensive evidence of intermarriage and heterogeneous settlement patterns over the past millennia.

Contemporary claims to land settlement on the basis of racial purity or ethnic precedent are eerily reminiscent of nineteenth- and twentieth-century German exceptionalism. The Vijaya myth was mobilised by Sinhalese nationalists in the early and mid-twentieth century (and today) to explain how they were descendants of an ancient race of Indo-Aryan settlers with distinct bloodlines from Sri Lankan Tamils. As noted above, British colonial administrators cemented these hitherto unacknowledged fault-lines by dividing the colony into three administrative regions, a Sri Lankan Tamil region in the north and two Sinhalese (upper and lower) in the centre and southern coastal areas. Not surprisingly, Sri Lankan Tamil nationalists and separatists by the mid-twentieth century elaborated a counter-narrative. Some claimed to register evidence of more than seven centuries of uninterrupted settlement and resettlement patterns marked out with Tamil names in specific areas of the north and east (Wilson 1988; Tambiah, S. J. 1986). These areas soon incorporated all districts in the north and east of the country and eventually assumed the name of *Eelam* or the 'homeland'.

In addition to enduring controversies over homelands is a fierce debate concerning the population size and the (national) ratios of specific ethnic groupings. The first official census (1871) estimated that roughly two-thirds of Ceylon's inhabitants were Sinhalese, one-fifth Sri Lankan Tamil and the rest divided between Muslims, Burgher, Malay, European and Vedda. While census records reveal a trend towards overall spatial and numerical dominance of the Sinhalese from the late 1800s onwards,[5] there is no consensus on the population size or ethnic distribution before then, much less the discrete ratios of different ethnic groups at the district level (Annex 1a–1d). Farmer (1957) observed presciently that efforts to predict pre-nineteenth-century population figures were 'difficult if not outright dangerous'.

The colonial epoch: 1815–1947

After being rebuffed on numerous occasions, the British formally conquered all of Sri Lanka in 1815 and retained possession until the country's independence in 1948, when it became a Dominion of the Commonwealth. From the nineteenth century to independence, planned settlement and resettlement schemes transformed the demography of Ceylon. Specifically, colonisation schemes featured prominently in the agrarian and economic policies of successive colonial administrations. In order to expand their powers of eminent domain and encourage the development of the plantation sector, aggressive land legislation was also progressively introduced. As such, the opening decades of British colonisation witnessed a surge in formal legislation associated with land appropriation and experimentation with different types of tenure systems and colonisation schemes.

The preparation of a robust land expropriation system was intended to stimulate export-oriented plantation development. Overseen by the island's governor, the Coolbrooke–Cameron Report (1830) laid out a rudimentary administrative and bureaucratic structure and land policy for the new colony. Administratively, the island was divided into five provinces and twenty-one separate districts.[6] A government agent was appointed by the governor to oversee each district and divisional affairs were managed by a newly introduced village headman (*grama niladari*), all public management devices imported from neighbouring India. The Coolbrooke–Cameron reforms established courts, taxation mechanisms and juridical procedures for drafting, promulgating and enforcing legislation. Specific policies designed to consolidate 'privately held' land rapidly followed. The Crown Land Ordinance (1840, 1851), Wasteland Ordinance (1850) and Temple and Devale Lands Registration Ordinance (1856) ensured that the state acquired land where ownership could not be proven. The Crown Land Ordinance in particular made specific provisions for the 'ejectment of any person, without probable claim or pretence to title, [who] was in possession of land claimed by the Crown, provided his possession did not extend to 30 years duration'.

The Coolbrooke–Cameron reforms precipitated far-reaching transformations in existing land holdings and related usufruct practices. They ensured that virtually all forest cover and unoccupied or otherwise uncultivated land was presumed to be held by the Crown. Proof of ownership included presentation of a legitimate deed by residents or unambiguous evidence of having paid tax in the two decades. The colonial administration was fully aware that local peasants were not in a position to take their cases to trial and harboured virtually no tradition of formalised (private) landownership. According to Peiris (1985), early judgments for those contesting the expropriation of their land revealed a strong presumption in favour of the Crown. By 1860 almost 40 per cent of the country's total surface area of an estimated 16 million acres was held by the British under the terms of the Crown Land Ordinance. Land reform effectively opened up the fertile highlands to European capitalists at low cost.[7]

The British pursued a highly centralised and paternalistic approach to population settlement and resettlement in Sri Lanka. The objective of land policy in the nineteenth and early twentieth centuries was to support the growth of the plantation economy through the creation of rigidly demarcated plots and the formalisation of property rights. It required the production of cadastral surveys, topographical maps and the identification of single owners with clear title for each parcel of surveyed land. With five separate legal systems in the country – Dutch Roman, Portuguese, Common, Muslim and Kandyan – the articulation of a functional property rights framework was of the utmost importance (Basnayake 1975). By clarifying property rights and making newly cleared land available to the upper and middle class, colonial administrators expected to eliminate certain domestic constraints to investment in (plantation) agriculture. Predictably, land policy was heavily weighted in favour of outside investors, especially those with ready access to capital and connections. As a result, land was gradually and inexorably prised away from the Buddhist clergy and local aristocracy in the Kandyan highlands and southern lowlands.

Colonial administrators were set on liberalising the economy and, to a lesser extent, mitigating monopolies in key agricultural sectors. Organised settlement was pursued in order to expand cinnamon, coffee, tea and rubber production between 1870 and 1890. These efforts were shaped in no small part by the nineteenth-century economic *zeitgeist*. Governor Coolbrooke was particularly enthused by the burgeoning free trade movement in Great Britain during the mid-1800s and made this a central component of his colonisation strategy (Brayne 1928). In order to attract more foreign and domestic capital, incentives were introduced ranging from favourable interest rates for bank deposits and liberal land grants to the comprehensive revision of traditional land allotments previously enshrined in the *rajakariya* – described then as the 'King's Duty, but [which] encompassed any service to the king, a lord, or temple in the Kandyan Kingdom' (de Silva, K. M. 1970: xiii).

These early colonisation schemes varied subtly in purpose and design. They included plantation colonies and resettlement schemes arising from village expansion and tank-renewal initiatives (Weeramunde 1982; Ratnaweera 1979; Tambiah, R. 1958). Plantation owners and colonial administrators experimented with a range of different protected land tenure arrangements with varying limitations on transfer, leasing and subdivision. Restrictive land tenure policies were intended to 'protect' tenants from predation by local middlemen and feckless moneylenders (*mudalalies*), but also to prevent reckless entrepreneurship and the fragmentation and non-occupation of holdings. Many of these tenure arrangements proved ineffective owing to the common local practice of pledging crops and land to *mudalalies* (rather than cash) and imposed restrictions on using land as collateral (Schickle 1960, 1970). Colonial administrators also launched a rash of cooperative and communal arrangements for peasants and specialised programmes tailored to the burgeoning middle class. These included 'divisional development council agricultural schemes' and 'land reform cooperative settlements' designed to harness collective labour (Ellman 1975; Ellman and Ranaweera 1974).

The British were confident that the combination of collective and individual incentives would lead to increased domestic productivity and investment. A government agent noted in the 1900s that 'when every villager has a piece of land – small though it may be – of his own, he is given a stake in the interests of law and order and feels that he is at least removed from the fear of urgent want' (Denham 1912). On the whole, these land reforms did not lead to the promised revolution in local productivity. Instead, according to Farmer (1957: 17), the Crown Land Ordinance generated 'far-reaching and negative effects ... [it was]

the prime cause of land hunger which later developed ... to which the pressure of population transfer and the establishment of the Dry Zone can be traced'. Many plantation owners also complained of 'dependency syndrome' and 'low productivity' arising from the planned colonisation and cooperative schemes. These complaints were not unlike memoranda issued by frustrated World Bank and UNHCR officials more than a century later.

The exigencies of a rapidly expanding plantation sector and the failure of colonisation schemes to achieve self-reliance compelled the administration to promote 'assisted migration' to meet their growing requirements. Despite access to steadily improving technology and the gradual reduction in demand for plantation labour, escalating international demand for tea and rubber stimulated the 'assisted migration' of foreign plantation managers and Indian (Tamil) labourers into the (Kandyan) Sinhalese-dominated central highland districts of the country. Colonial administrators and plantation owners actively encouraged foreign migration from India due to the apparent reluctance of Sinhalese to undertake wage labour and their comparatively low levels of productivity. Despite sporadic resistance from a fledgling Sinhalese nationalist movement, more than 500,000 Indian Tamils were relocated to then Ceylon, including approximately 208,000 in 1900 alone (Denham 1912: 40). Most Indian or 'estate' Tamils were settled into highland plantations while others later relocated to the dry zone and were (controversially) repatriated to India following independence.[8] A minority dispersed into the informal sectors of the capital, Colombo. Though the total number of repatriated estate Tamils is unknown, the Sri Lankan Department of Immigration and Emigration claimed that at least 313,000 were returned to India in the 1960s (Sri Lanka 1981: 24). Apart from the deplorable conditions in which they eked out an existence, the tragedy of the estate Tamils is that many became economically superfluous within a generation of their arrival: tea sector employment declined steadily from the 1940s onwards so that it became economically feasible to deport them in large numbers.

The dry zone and the peasant: 1815–1947

With the economy gradually diversifying, attention soon turned to overpopulation and the redoubled efforts to colonise the dry zone. Colonial authorities were preoccupied with what appeared to be rapid population growth and urbanisation in coastal wet zone areas of the south-west. The wet zone included Colombo and the arable south-western coast while the dry zone was malaria-infested, rural and thought to be generally underpopulated. The dry zone, an area described as such because of its limited

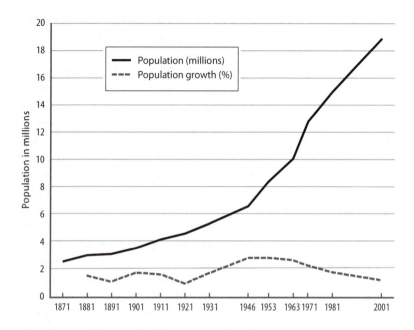

FIGURE 3.1 Population growth in Sri Lanka (1871–2001) *Source*: Reconstructed from the Department of Census and Statistics.

rainfall, spanned the districts of what are now Jaffna, Vavuniya, Mannar, Mullaitivu, Puttalam, Anuradhapura, Trincomalee, Ampara, Batticaloa, Moneregala and certain divisions of Hambantota. It accounted for less than one-quarter of the country's population and more than half its acreage in 1945. Census records from 1871 to the mid-twentieth century revealed disproportionate population growth in wet zone populations in relation to the dry zone. The wet zone in fact reached its peak population growth by the late 1940s and then began a steady decline (Figure 3.1).[9]

The settlement and resettlement of the dry zone occupied an important place in land-related debates during the early and middle twentieth century. Concern with dry zone settlement was set against a growing paranoia over the carrying-capacity of the southern wet zone. These concerns were tied to then popular theories that presumed a negative linear relationship between rising populations and the (diminishing) ability of land to provide for their needs. The presumption of a negative correlation between demographic pressure and environmental scarcity was originally proposed by Thomas Malthus in the late eighteenth century. Malthus theorised that where potential increases in food supply did not keep pace with population growth, and where humans did not exercise preventive checks (e.g. marriage and moral restraint), populations could experience dramatic reversals in size through so-called welfare checks (e.g. poverty, disease, famine and war).

Though few colonial administrators disputed the relevance of dry zone settlement and resettlement to solve the population issue, the practical challenges were immense. For one, the agricultural potential and absorptive capacity of the dry zone was comparatively meagre. Colonial officers decades earlier complained that in 'parts of the Dry Zone, the finishing touches to the process of decay and depopulation were added fairly recently ... the continuing absence of dense population also owed much to the repellent nature of the physical environment and the weakness of the autochthonous people' (Brayne 1928). The dry zone, Farmer (1957) argued, was an anomaly in South Asia – 'a region that makes up two thirds of the country but is sparsely populated'. Others doubted whether settlers could live there at all and were confounded by the ruins of long-abandoned settlements and tanks preceding arrival of European colonists (Ismail 1995; Peiris, G. H. 1996). Another major constraint to dry zone colonisation was malaria. There were a series of malarial outbreaks in Sri Lanka throughout the early twentieth century, with by far the worst occurring in 1934–35: 1.5 million of the country's 5 million inhabitants were affected (Jones 2000). Pervasive levels of poverty were identified as the catalyst for another massive malarial outbreak in the dry zone ten years later (1944–45) in which more than 100,000 people reportedly died. It was not until the introduction of DDT spraying in the mid-1940s that the dry zone was opened up in earnest.

From their inception, efforts to colonise the dry zone incorporated an ethnic dimension. Following comparatively unsuccessful experiments in settling estate Tamils from the plantations into the area, colonial administrators turned to other candidates including low-country Sinhalese from over-populated urban centres and villages in wet zone districts. Early colonial censuses revealed comparatively high growth rates in Sinhalese-dominated wet zone districts of Colombo, Kurunegala, Kegalle, Kandy, Chilaw, Kalutara, Ratnapura and Badulla (Denham 1912: 46–8). As centres of commerce and economic growth in the nineteenth and early twentieth centuries, these areas generated substantial pull-factors for rural–urban migration. Both colonial administrators and a rising elite Sinhalese land-holding class were preoccupied with the increasing delinquency among the poorer strata, together with the increased landlessness and attendant social problems presented by urban migration. Thus began a purposive process of constructing the 'peasantry' to settle the dry zone.

The interest in creating and preserving a peasant class coincided with the emergence of vocal Sinhalese nationalism in the 1920s and 1930s. Moore (1985, 1989, 1992), Pfaffenberger (1990), Samaraweera (1970) and K. M. de Silva (1970) describe how the social construction of the peasantry and welfarist interventions to assist them fit into a competitive discourse between entrepreneur landowners (foreigners) and indigenous nationalists. A central argument advanced by nationalists was that land should be held *in trust* by the Crown and *on behalf* of the colonised. They contended that this would not only solve the issue of landlessness triggered by the extension of a predominantly foreign-owned plantation sector but also ensure that land was transferred to Sinhalese landholders soon after independence. Sinhalese nationalists increasingly called on the colonial authorities to 'Ceylonise' the administrative machinery of governance to ensure 'a change on the complexion of the administration to effect the transfer of power to Ceylonese hands' (de Silva, K. M. 1970: 413–14).

Sinhalese nationalists were divided over the peasant question. The seeds of Sinhalese nationalism were planted following the introduction of a limited form of the elective principle by the British in 1910. Increasingly violent protests against restrictive colonial policies and labour discrimination flared shortly thereafter in 1912. The rise of nationalism led to a rupture between the two principal ethnic groups, the Sinhalese and the Sri Lankan Tamils. Although both groups cohabited,[10] the situation deteriorated in the early 1920s, whereafter Sinhalese nationalists began regarding themselves as a majority community (de Silva, K. M. 1981). In the meantime, colonial administrators and the Sinhalese elite rapidly crafted an economic rationale for colonising the dry zone. In their preparations for the First World War and its aftermath, the British were determined to achieve self-sufficiency (and a marketable surplus) in rice production so as not to drag on its war economy. Ceylon's primary comparative advantage was cheap labour: the allocation of land for peasant production and the settlement of poor peasants provided a neat economic argument for justifying large-scale resettlement of Sinhalese into the hinterland. A Land Commission set up in 1929 expected to 'preserve the peasantry as an institution', observing that 'no satisfactory substitute ... was yet found for the thrill of possession as a stimulus to agricultural activities' (ibid.).

Both the Land Commission and the newly established Donoughmore Commission (1927–31) attached a priority to agricultural self-sufficiency and advocated increased investment in settlement and resettlement. Likewise, the Donoughmore Commission sanctioned adult franchise and the formation of a unicameral State Council (de Silva, K. M. 1970; Weerawardena 1951). The Land Commission was subsequently converted into a Land Commissioner's Department to oversee the control and alienation of Crown land, as well as conditions for leasing of land and certain 'protections' for tenants. The condition of the peasantry was skilfully manipulated by nationalists and nationalist historiography in the 1920s and 1930s to expand Sinhalese settlement and resettlement schemes on Crown lands.[11]

Land settlement policy was increasingly politicised in the 1930s and 1940s. The onset of the global depression and a marked deterioration in the economy ensured that 'the cry was back to the land' (*Tropical Agriculturist* 1932: 253). Panic sales of land and plummeting socio-economic conditions raised the prospect of acute landlessness. Crucially, with the granting of universal adult suffrage by the 1931 Donoughmore Constitution and the promise of an expanded (Sinhalese) electoral base, settlement opportunities were offered as patronage. Aspiring politicians had a clear incentive to increase the electoral pool in what were supposedly 'uninhabited' areas. In order to quell growing discontent and civil unrest over newly imposed rationing systems, policymakers prepared the ground for ambitious new legislation.

A rash of new land, agriculture and irrigation ordinances was introduced in order to prepare for the large-scale relocations of Sinhalese 'peasants'. The Land Development Ordinance (1935) was one of the most influential.[12] This did not formally articulate provisions for compensation or restitution to those whose land, housing or agricultural assets were expropriated. Nor did it require executing agencies to avoid or minimise displacement, to compensate those without title, or consult affected populations as later prescribed by the DIDR regime. The Land Development Ordinance was nevertheless enthusiastically adopted by Sinhalese nationalists who envisioned the dry zone as the exclusive preserve of the Sinhalese. In a pamphlet entitled *Agriculture and Patriotism*, Dudley Senanayake (1935a) pronounced that 'migration from over-populated zones to less crowded areas was 'no longer a matter of choice, but of grim necessity'.

At independence in 1948, the nationalist elite successfully fused a chauvinistic pro-peasant policy with an economic agenda oriented around colonising the dry zone. According to Pfaffenberger (1990: 390) dry zone settlement and resettlement provided a symbolic link between the past and present. The zealous relocation of Sinhalese peasants into the dry zone can also be interpreted as a reaction to earlier colonial policies of importing foreign labour to work in the plantation sector. In dry zone colonisation the nationalist elite[13] championed an approach that resonated with an expanding and increasingly self-aware electorate.[14]

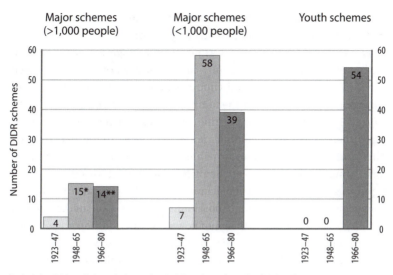

| Major schemes (>1,000 people) | Major schemes (<1,000 people) | Youth schemes |

* Includes Gal Oya which involved more than 80,000 settlers and resettlers (1948–52)
** Includes MDIP which involved more than 250,000 settlers and resettlers (1970–80) and many more thereafter

FIGURE 3.2 Large-scale settlement/resettlement schemes (1920–80)

Dry zone resettlement policies also fit into an emerging competitive discourse associated with Sinhalese control over the east, an area more densely populated by Sri Lankan Tamils and Muslims (Annexes 1a–1d).[15] That Sinhalese peasants were to be relocated into otherwise marginal and unforgiving districts evoked 'ethnic myths that idealise the prosperity and simple piety of the ancient Sinhalese [and] the hostility of the Tamils' (Peebles 1990: 32).

The ethnic bias in settlement and resettlement policy grew progressively sharper from independence onwards. Though not explicitly restricting Sri Lankan Tamils from participating in colonisation schemes, nationalist Members of Parliament (MPs) demanded that estate Tamils were excluded from owning Crown land. High- and low-country Sinhalese speculators from landholding families were keen to promote schemes free from multiple land claims (Roberts, M. 2001; Moore 1985). The bias towards Sinhalese settlers was evident in the targeting of Sinhalese landless and the uniquely Buddhist rituals that accompanied the opening of new sites (Peebles 1990; Tennekoon, S. 1988). Though official state policy allowed for the allocation of land to Sinhalese and Tamils in proportion to existing *national* ethnic ratios (as opposed to district or divisional ratios) this nevertheless created 'large Sinhalese constituencies in the Northern and Eastern Province ... areas claimed by Tamils as their traditional homelands' (Pfaffenberger 1990: 391).

Eminent domain legislation was made increasingly robust in the post-independence period. The Land Acquisition Act (1950; 1953) – itself derived from the Crown Land Ordinance (1935), the Requisitioning of Land Act (1950; 1953) and the Lands Resumptions Ordinances (1887; 1955) were amended to reflect the conditions in which land could be expropriated 'free of encumbrance', including by the armed forces.[16] The Land Acquisition Act was considered to be the 'primary instrument for settling the dry zone by providing the government with the means of expropriating private land for public purposes'.[17] Crucially, the Act included provisions for rapid appropriation at the discretion of the Minister of Lands. For example, Article 38 allowed for the Minister to mandate district and divisional secretaries to appropriate land within forty-eight hours and was invoked on several occasions for 'political purposes and with a certain amount of force'.[18]

From the 1950s onwards, the government began supporting hundreds of new peasant settlements in north, central and eastern districts, areas comparatively densely populated with Sri Lankan Tamils and Muslims. They ranged from minor schemes with fewer than fifty households to larger units in Minneriya and Gal Oya that included over ten thousand 'settlers' (Figure 3.2). Settlements were usually formed in ribbon patterns alongside roads and irrigation canals. Village expansion schemes were more common in the dry zone than settlement schemes, leading in certain cases to the breakdown and liquidation of existing villages (Wickramasekera 1985; Weeramunde 1982). With few exceptions these settlement and resettlement schemes did not resolve alleged population pressures in the wet zone. Instead, they acquired a miserable reputation due to their lacklustre social amenities and line services, inefficient irrigation management and weak culture of community participation (Uphoff 1996). According to Attanayake et al. (1985: 31) 'not much attention has been paid to the physical planning of settlements and service centres'. Many settlements thus gradually become sites of discontent, vice and poverty, and fell far short of the expectations of their planners.

The introduction and enforcement of nation-building policies such as discriminatory language and land legislation in the 1950s and 1960s hastened the deterioration in Sinhalese–Tamil relations. Sri Lankan Tamil politicians condemned the Sinhala-Only language policies championed by Bandaranaike's SLFP government in the mid-1950s.[19] Also, for the first time, Tamil politicians openly accused the government of using colonisation schemes as a pretext to relocate Sinhalese peasants

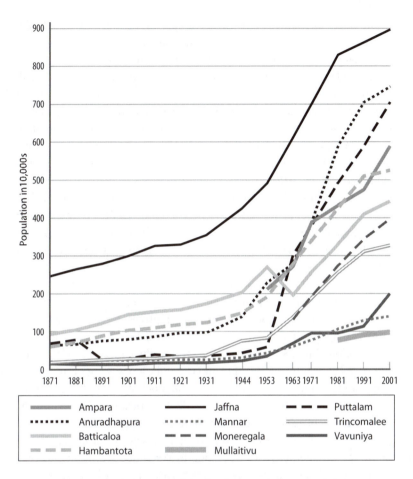

FIGURE 3.3 Population growth in the dry zone (1871–2001) *Source*:
Data drawn from Sri Lanka Department of census and statistics and
Annex 1a–1d. Note that Jaffna, Vavuniya, Mannar, Trincomalee, Batticaloa and Ampara have not had full censuses since 1981 and data are
collated from more specialised registration exercises in the 1990s.

into electoral districts in order to render Tamils 'minorities in their
own provinces' (Manogaran 1994). These fears were prescient. Between
1946 and 1971 the Sinhalese proportion of the total population in five
dry zone districts increased from 33 to 41 per cent, largely because of
government-supported settlement (Figures 3.2 and 3.3).[20] Owing to the
populist appeal of colonisation, Sinhalese MPs quietly ignored the marginal economic and social performance of the schemes: what mattered
was the distribution of countable units of land to countable numbers

of Sinhalese peasants. Pfaffenberger (1990: 392) observed how 'there are few political resources in Sri Lanka that can equal the vote-getting potential of handing out a clear title to a plot of land'.

In the decade following independence economic and ethnic national-ism was on the ascendant. In addition to nationalising key sectors of the economy, macro-economic debates were dominated by calls for an import-substitution industrialisation strategy to guide national develop-ment.[21] A major concern of the newly independent government was the reduction of the country's food dependency on India, an uneasiness that exhibited echoes with the recent and distant past.[22] Political independ-ence was considered a 'hollow shell' if not accompanied by meaningful economic independence, a feeling shared by the leaders of many other newly independent countries at the time (Chandraratne 2003: 141–3; de Silva, K. M. 1981). Ongoing transformations to Sri Lanka's economy opened the door for monumental development projects focused on en-hancing national agricultural productivity and self-sufficiency.

A growing number of politicians revisited national land legislation in order to prepare the ground for massive appropriation. In response to domestic opposition to excessively centralised land policies – a legacy of the colonial period – the government introduced a series of tentative reforms. For example, a second Land Commission was appointed by the Governor General in 1955 to review the policy of Crown Land distribution. Within a few years it issued a set of highly critical conclusions on the inadequacies of existing compensation arrangements for settlers and resettlers stipulated in the Land Development Ordinance (1935). It also identified the inefficiencies generated by systemic corruption and poor planning and implementation in land settlement programmes more generally. The findings of the Commission were quietly brushed aside by government authorities and only minor cosmetic changes were made to the Land Development Ordinance in the 1960s. There seemed to be little appetite among the growing Sinhalese upper and middle classes to alter the status quo which continued to favour presumption of title to the Crown.

The era of the grand development project: 1948–82

Independence marked the era of grand development schemes and a tendency towards more centralised settlement and resettlement policy. Sri Lanka earned the distinction of fielding two of the world's largest multi-purpose irrigation, electrification and settlement programmes in the second half of the twentieth century: the Gal Oya Irrigation Project (1948–52) and the Mahaweli Development and Irrigation Programme or

MIDP (1970–2000). These mega-projects were spawned by a modernisation ideology that fused capital-intensive interventions with centralised national planning. They signalled the arrival of newly independent and industrialising economies on the international stage (Scott 1998). In addition to guaranteeing national self-sufficiency in agriculture and the generation of electricity for industrial and domestic consumption, large development projects were expected to resolve persistent social and economic challenges.

Settlement and resettlement schemes following independence shared some continuity with previous interventions. They combined the civilising impulse and the colonial bureaucratic machinery with carefully regimented and clearly titled allocations of land. By distributing land in countable units, the state was able to easily count and publicise the number of households settled and resettled, plots allocated and acres given over for the preservation of the peasantry (Shanmugaratnam 1985). The paternalistic approach was encapsulated by the first elected Prime Minister of Sri Lanka (UNP), D. S. Senanayake, who noted that such settlement and resettlement should be devised so as to 'secure the welfare of [the peasant] classes even against themselves' (Senanayake 1935b: 4). By portraying themselves as the true champions of the peasant, the Sinhalese elite obscured their own strong and growing presence in the plantation sector and laid a convincing claim for increased political legitimacy.

Settlement and resettlement were thereafter centrally planned and managed by bureaucratic entities and entailed permanent changes to the spatial demography of the country. Moreover, the Gal Oya and the MDIP inevitably required 'sacrifices' at the altar of national progress with settlement actively promoted in order to restore the ancient Sinhalese civilisation to its previous glory. The Gal Oya Board (1949) was intended to oversee the settlement and resettlement of landless Sinhalese peasants, and the amended Land Acquisition Act (1950) reinforced the Board's powers of eminent domain. Advanced alienation necessitated the physical clearance of Sri Lankan Tamil and Muslim 'encroachers' from the marginal areas of planned project sites, including throughout the eastern districts. This was shortly followed by the 'voluntary' settlement of Kandyan Sinhalese 'peasants' – some of whom came from middle-class families – from the Central Province to districts in the north and east (Tambiah, S. J. 1986: 83–94).

These massive projects proved controversial. Though cloaked in the benign discourse of national development and cast as pro-peasant, minority MPs were alarmed.[23] As early as 1949, the founder of the Federal Party

Chelvanayakam warned in his inaugural address that the government's settlement and resettlement policies were more dangerous to Tamils than the proposed Sinhalese-Only Act. The post-independence period witnessed the emergence of a more assertive nationalism, with the Federal Party defining Sri Lankan Tamils as a distinct nation entitled to self-determination. The Federal Party presented its foundational manifesto in 1951, declaring that:

> [t]he Tamil-speaking people in Ceylon constitute a nation distinct from that of the Singhalese [sic] by every fundamental test of nationhood, firstly that of a separate historical past in the island at least as ancient and as glorious as that of the Singhalese, secondly by the fact of their being a linguistic entity entirely different from that of the Singhalese ... and finally, by reason of their territorial habitation of definite areas which constitute over one-third of this Island. (cf. Kearney 1967)

Significantly, Tamil nationalists equated the 'distinct nation' with the administrative boundaries of the northern and eastern districts.

The newly articulated demands advanced by Sri Lankan Tamil nationalists ensured that the settlement and resettlement enterprise was pursued with renewed vigour. In 1951, Prime Minister Senanayake was an avid supporter of the process.[24] Between 1950 and 1970, no fewer than thirty Acts clarified the conditions in which the state could undertake DIDR, providing only a limited set of rights and entitlements for those evacuated or whose land was appropriated.[25] Additional Acts, while also concerned with settlers involved in agricultural schemes, called for collective settlements and transferred the burden of planning, clearing, developing and managing these schemes to the settlers themselves.[26] The government was keen to relocate more people in less time than ever before.

Settling Gal Oya At the time, the Gal Oya project was the largest settlement and resettlement programme ever attempted in the country. Endorsed by foreign donors, including many who later assumed a key role in forging the DIDR regime, it was modelled on the TVA. Financed almost exclusively from domestic sources, the Gal Oya Board oversaw the construction of physical reservoirs, canals and irrigation ducts by US-based firms (MacFadden 1954). Straddling the districts of Batticaloa and (later) Ampara, the Gal Oya project was expected to provide irrigation for over 125,000 acres though the total surface area covered never surpassed 95,000 acres (FAO 1975). As part of its declared mandate to redress Sinhalese landlessness in the wet zone more than 10,000 Sinhalese *families* with an average size of approximately eight people – more than 80,000 in total – were 'settled' into forty numbered colony units between 1949 and 1952, though the process continued well into the 1960s (Peiris, G. H. 1996).[27]

Each Gal Oya colony unit benefited from the welfarist tradition accompanying colonisation schemes in Sri Lanka. Every unit was provided with an educational facility, village hall, recreation centre, cooperative market and related extension services. While there is virtually no published material on the social and economic profile of Sri Lankan Tamil, Muslim or Sinhalese households 'evacuated' as a result of headwork construction, flooding or village expansion, policy guidelines at the time stated that such populations should be 'first served'.[28] Each settler family was provided with four acres of irrigated land for paddy production and three acres of non-irrigated land for housing, though these allotments were later curtailed to three and two acres respectively (Uphoff 1996). The clearing of land, the laying of irrigation canals, the provision of water and sanitation infrastructure and the settlement and resettlement of colonies was completed by the mid-1960s. The Gal Oya Board was converted into a River Valley Development Board in 1965, though was mired in internal controversy following accusations of suspected overspending and corruption in 1969.[29]

Even its most ardent supporters concede that the outcomes of colonisation were highly uneven in relation to durable solutions. Administratively, the Gal Oya project was characterised by an inflated bureaucracy and a high degree of paternalism (Ellman 1975). Far from achieving permanent self-reliant communities, colony units were poorly planned and prepared and agricultural extension services failed to anticipate the requirements of second- and third-generation settler households (Uphoff 1996; Tambiah, R. 1958).[30] Due also to uneven land allocation, confusion generated by various types of deeds and unequal inheritance rules, new generations of settlers opted to vacate the schemes rather than become destitute. Despite efforts to redress these limitations, including experimenting with cooperative farming arrangements and alterations to leasehold arrangements, Weeramunde (1982: 16) described a 'mentality of dependence on the Government ... in the minds of settlers, which has been hard to eradicate to this day'. Instead, settlers were repeatedly described as uncooperative and prone to conflict, with 'very few of them having come voluntarily in the first place' (Uphoff 2001: 116). Much later it emerged that many of the original settlers had in fact been 'cleansed' from their home villages by the local *kachari* and coercively resettled into colony units, while others included convicts released from village jails.[31]

The colonisation strategy adopted by the Gal Oya Board subtly discriminated against Sri Lankan Tamils. Not only were they disproportionately excluded from the colony units, but the usual challenges of distributing irrigation water between head and tail-end areas were complicated by escalating ethnic rivalries in the areas where canals were built (Pfaffenberger 1990). Experts close to the process claim that the exclusion of Tamils was not universally supported by government agents and public authorities in the Gal Oya basin – many of whom routinely attempted to keep ethnic violence from 'boiling over'.[32] Indeed, certain episodes of violence can be attributed to the engineering bias of the builders of the Gal Oya reservoirs and their failure to grasp the social dynamics arising from external technological intervention. Another reason for lingering tensions related to the choice of crop cultivation, including (water-intensive) sugar plantations, which resulted in water shortages in primarily Sri Lankan Tamil and Muslim-populated areas (Thangarajah 2003: 25). An indicator of the ethnic polarisation accompanying Gal Oya included the deliberate targeting of settlers during outbursts of internecine violence (1956, 1958) in other parts of the country.[33]

The Gal Oya project constituted a visible expression of the ways in which the Sinhalese-dominated government pursued exclusionary policies. According to Spencer (1990b: 39): 'the Tamils of the North and East ... tended to lose out in terms of access to economic resources – particularly of access to the fruits of major development projects'. Iriyagolle (1978: 60), a local consultant associated with the International Bank for Reconstruction and Development (IBRD), observed how this was a continuation of a long-standing pattern of support for the peasantry: 'it would be correct to say that ... all public investment on irrigation in the dry zone has been exclusively for the [Sinhalese] peasant or small farmer class in the past 50 years'. In much the same way as early Israeli frontier settlements established in the Occupied Palestinian Territories created a legacy of grievances in the region, the Gal Oya settlements unintentionally laid the spatial and ethnic fault-lines of the armed conflict to follow.

Settling the Mahaweli International donors and government authorities were simultaneously preparing an even more ambitious project that would define the landscape – literally and figuratively – for the subsequent four decades. Between 1958 and 1969 multilateral and bilateral agencies associated with the nascent DIDR regime crafted a blueprint, or Master Plan, to divert the Mahaweli Oya (river) and expand agricultural production and electricity generation. The MDIP was expected to solve multiple developmental challenges once and for all, including the alleged crisis of landlessness and over-population (Barnabas 1967). The original blueprint divided the MDIP into three phases over a thirty-year period. Initiated in the late 1960s, the project included the construction of several interlocking reservoirs with hydro-electric plants and irrigation services spanning more than half a million acres. The Plan called for the development of thirteen separate 'Systems' spanning nine districts in the central, northern and eastern districts and required the settlement and resettlement of hundreds of thousands of (Sinhalese) peasants into the newly irrigated dry zone and areas of the north and east (Chapter 4).

The MDIP was conceived at time when the state was shifting away from a centrally planned economy to a more capitalist market-oriented development strategy. After almost two decades of aversion to the open economy, the election of then President Jayawardene's UNP government (1977) heralded a dramatic conversion to market-based orthodoxies, including structural adjustment and specific reforms to liberalise the economy, stimulate foreign investment, promote competition and privatise certain service delivery functions (Richardson 2005; Bastian 1995). Central planners were adamant that sizeable investment in capital-intensive projects could stimulate productivity and domestic consumption. A favourable domestic climate would in turn attract more foreign investment: they saw no contradiction in the principle of an open economy and an expanded role of government in capital formation. At the time considerable bilateral development assistance was already devoted to underwriting development projects. With Sri Lanka widely regarded as a 'success story' and having rejected socialist planning in favour of market-based reforms, President Jayawardene confidently announced that he would *accelerate* the MDIP from thirty to five years.

The preparation and physical construction of the Accelerated MDIP began in 1978. Presented to Parliament for a second reading by then Minister of Lands and Land Development Gamini Dissanayake, the Mahaweli Authority of Sri Lanka Bill created a centralised corporate body to implement a cabinet decision taken by the newly elected UNP government (Sri Lanka 1979a, 1979b). Like the Gal Oya Board before it, the Authority was granted wide discretionary powers and exemptions from many existing rules and regulations. A review of Hansard records from 1977 to 1980 reveals a string of objections raised by minority MPs over concessions granted by the government to the Mahaweli Authority.[34] For example, the Bill creating the Authority did not require the submission of accounts to the Parliament for approval, audits by the Auditor General or approval of the Parliament in allocating funds for development programmes (Sri Lanka 1979f). The settlement component in particular raised eyebrows:

according to planning documents, more than 140,000 families – including voluntary settlers and resettlers – were to be resettled into forty towns, 200 villages and hundreds of outlying hamlets (Sri Lanka 1979b).[35] In all, more than 700,000 people – more than 5 per cent of the country's population at the time – were expected to be relocated in less than six years.

Reviewed in more detail in Chapter 4, an international aid consortium was assembled to support the Accelerated MDIP including key proponents of the emerging DIDR regime (Sri Lanka 1979d). Consultancy contracts were issued to construction and engineering firms from participating countries. Though some doubted the feasibility of accelerating the programme in such a short time,[36] Sri Lanka was considered by bilateral donors to be a respectable creditor country and trusted to repay its loans. Moreover, there were considerable dividends to be reaped by donors, foreign contractors, the World Bank and the UNDP to the extent that a seasoned observer noted 'never would so much have been made so quickly by so few at the expense of so many' (Iriyagolle 1978: 47). Separate Systems were financed by different governments, and between 1970 and 1998 the World Bank extended six credits to the Authority, amounting to US$450 million (in 2001 dollars).[37]

The Accelerated MDIP registered two critical successes, one technical, the other demographic. First, in addition to generating sizeable economic returns for its donors,[38] it was widely lauded as an engineering marvel. Evaluations commissioned by the Mahaweli Authority regularly promised that within five years the dams, tanks and canals would contribute to major 'social improvements' (Attanayake et al. 1985). Second, by dramatically reconfiguring the ethnic ratios of northern and eastern districts, the government was able to justify a number of administrative adjustments to provincial and district boundaries to reflect changes in national population density and distribution. Five of the northern and eastern districts exhibited Sri Lankan Tamil majorities in the early twentieth century; by the end of the twentieth century these were much diluted in Mannar, Trincomalee, Batticaloa and Ampara, itself carved from south-eastern portions of Batticaloa in 1961.[39] These changes diluted the electoral potency of Sri Lankan Tamils and Muslims in these regions.[40] In addition to benefiting politicians in Colombo, the Accelerated MDIP successfully challenged the Tamil-speaking contiguity between the north and east, a stated goal of Sinhalese nationalists (Gunaratne, M. H. 1998; Manogaran 1994; Helmann-Rajanayagam 1986).

It is in examining the consequences of large-scale settlement and resettlement on *district-level* ethnic ratios that the logic of the MDIP becomes apparent. Demographic changes were especially pronounced

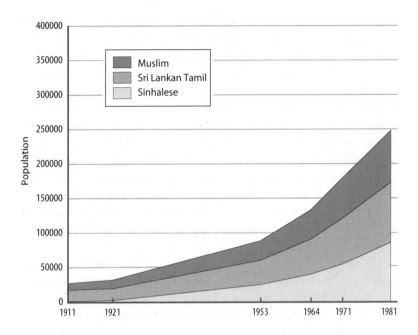

FIGURE 3.4 Population growth in Trincomalee (1911–81) *Source*: Reconstructed from census department figures (various years).

in Trincomalee, Batticaloa and Ampara. It is important to distinguish between natural population growth in these three districts and 'migrant' population growth: while Sri Lankan Tamil and Muslim population increases were 'internal', the Sinhala population increase was more colonisation-driven. Specifically, the ethnic distribution of Sri Lankan Tamils, Sinhalese and Muslims in Trincomalee in 1911 was roughly 65:4:26 respectively. After decades of colonisation and the launch of the Accelerated MDIP, the ratios in 1981 amounted to 33:33:29 (Figure 3.4).[41] Likewise, in Ampara district the Sinhalese proportion of the population, already comparatively large according to the 1963 census, expanded further still (Walkiewicz and Brockman 2004; Kearney 1987). By 1981, approximately 38 per cent of the population was Sinhalese as compared to 20 per cent Sri Lankan Tamil and 41 per cent Muslim (Figure 3.5). The Accelerated MDIP effectively fused the long-standing quest to populate the dry zone with the diversion of the Mahaweli *ganga*, hydro-power development and (Sinhalese) ethnic hegemony.

The colonisation experience in Trincomalee's China Bay provides an instructive illustration of how development-inspired resettlement can contribute to gradual changes in demographic profiles and related land disputes. In an area known as Kappalthurai, for example, a small group of Sinhalese 'settlers' inadvertently occupied 'waste land' in the 1970s and 1980s. Soon after, a Buddhist priest established a modest temple to cater to the growing population. Even as the settlement was disputed in the courts, a police post was erected to 'protect' the population. With increases in police presence, Sri Lankan Tamil locals were harassed and disputes began to emerge. Eventually, Tamils were driven out and new settlers arrived. After a decade or more, land tenure changed hands to the Sinhalese settlers, and land could be legally bought and sold. If Sri Lankan Tamils returned and contested ownership, multiple claims were likely to emerge and took years to work through the courts. But since the land registry in Trincomalee mysteriously burned down in the 1990s and the Colombo office resists locating copies of original titles, land claims were routinely dropped.[42]

The MDIP came under withering criticism in the 1990s. DIDR regime proponents and project planners were dismayed that an egalitarian society of smallholder farmers – or durable solutions – had failed to materialise. Benefits appeared to be accrued instead by the wealthy: typical of large-scale dam and irrigation projects in other developing countries, a disproportionate level of the output (e.g. electricity and paddy) was consumed in urban centres (Scudder 1991). Moreover, the strategy of introducing paddy monoculture failed to generate dynamic downstream linkages into the domestic economy.[43] As a result, employment opportunities generated by the MDIP were unable to expand sufficiently rapidly to absorb second- and third-generation settlers and resettlers (Scudder 1992). By the end of the 1990s expectations of achieving durable solutions in the wake of the MDIP faded entirely. A former director of the Mahaweli Authority described how '[we] moved many poorer people into slums [as a result of the Mahaweli] and the result is these areas became "criminal" fuelling drugs and crime'.[44] Following a series of damning reviews by the Operations Evaluation Department (OED) of the World Bank (2004b), the government sought to convert the Mahaweli Authority into a River Basin Authority, including reductions in personnel from approximately 11,000 to 5,000 in exchange for early retirement packages.

By far the most serious shortcoming of the MDIP was its impoverishment effects on settlers and resettlers. While the Mahaweli Authority reportedly 'lost' all longitudinal socio-economic baseline data on beneficiaries in the late 1990s,[45] virtually every published and internal assessment and impact evaluation between 1980 and 2001 revealed profound deteriorations in household livelihood indices among settlers and re-settlers. For example, Madeley (1983) reported that many families slated

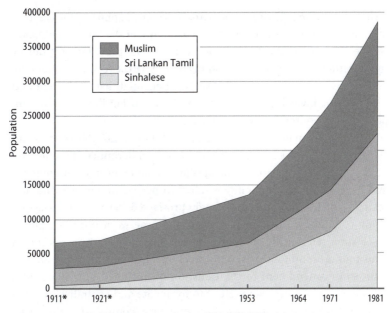

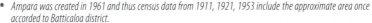

* Ampara was created in 1961 and thus census data from 1911, 1921, 1953 include the approximate area once accorded to Batticaloa district.

FIGURE 3.5 Population growth in Ampara* (1911–81) *Source*: Reconstructed from census department figures (various years).

for 'evacuation' and DIDR were not consulted prior to the launch of the MDIP. Goldsmith and Hildyard (1984) found that most settling and resettling families received far less land and compensation than was originally advertised. Although homeowners were supposed to be provided with market rate compensation, few could produce their title or deed and thus received no compensation following their eviction. Scudder's comprehensive panel survey of resettled farmers (1979–2001) detected serious problems shortly after the MDIP was accelerated:

> at a time when others were emphasising the project's ongoing success, we were the first to inform the Minister that the Accelerated Mahaweli Program risked replicating poverty with the Mahaweli systems ... the settlement component of the country's largest ever project was failing.[46]

As a result of the poor returns of the Gal Oya Project and the Accelerated MDIP, the state began to review its settlement and resettlement legislation in the late 1980s and early 1990s. Under pressure from DIDR regime proponents such as the World Bank and the ADB, the government revised its National Environmental Act (1988) and supported the creation of a Central Environmental Authority (CEA) under the Ministry of Land. Not coincidentally, the Act included many of the provisions set out by the Resettlement Guidelines promulgated by DIDR regime proponents and discussed in Chapter 2. The Act itself ensured that settlement and resettlement involving more than one hundred families were accompanied with 'comprehensive assistance'.[47]

The dispersion of institutional responsibilities among Ministries and Departments involved in land-related issues undermined the effectiveness of the new legislation. The absence of coherent lines of authority and lower-order accountability resulted in persistent gaps in land and related policies and correspondingly protracted delays in land acquisition (CPA 2005; RDC 2004). Indeed, the process of profiling, public disclosure, referencing to court, appeals, payment and possession of land took a minimum of seventy weeks and often much longer. The Thirteenth Amendment to the Constitution included provisions for a National Land Commission (NLC) to formulate and centralise national policy through representatives of the provincial councils; but this never got off the ground.

Proponents of the DIDR regime started vigorously supporting the codification of key norms and rules in national legislation from the 1990s onwards. Anticipating large-scale resettlement arising from road-building and infrastructure projects,[48] the government also began to acknowledge the need for a standardised approach.[49] After years of negotiation and building on World Bank- and ADB-supported guidelines established in the mid-1990s, a National Involuntary Resettlement Policy (NIRP) was approved by Cabinet in 2001. The Policy emerged against a backdrop of increasingly vocal opposition from human rights groups and resistance from those affected by DIDR.[50] The expression 'involuntary' was included in the bureaucratic lexicon of the Ministry of Land, revealing a discursive turn directly shaped by DIDR regime supporters. More fundamentally, the new NIRP promised fair, equitable and transparent resettlement.

Described as the first such policy in South Asia, the NIRP features an assortment of principles, norms and rules associated with protecting displaced populations and ensuring durable solutions. Overseen by the Ministry of Land, the Ministry of Housing and Planning Infrastructure and the Departments of Land Reform, Land Settlement and the Land Commission, the NIRP requires implementing agencies to submit detailed RAPs for all projects involving the 'evacuation' of twenty or more people and expects project authorities to pay compensation for land at replacement, rather than publicly valuated, cost. It includes provisions for participatory consultative mechanisms and provides special dispensation for indigenous populations. Crucially, it states that 'no impoverishment of people shall result as a consequence of compulsory land acquisitions for development purposes of the state'. In order to enhance the influence and effectiveness of the NIRP, a new Land Acquisition Law was drafted to replace the Land Acquisition Act with expectations of being presented to Parliament.[51] In the meantime, despite slower-than-anticipated enactment and implementation, the NIRP is equated by regime proponents with soft law and serves as a normative tool to address gaps in existing legislation. As with any policy, the success of the NIRP depends on its even application and enforcement.[52]

Resettlement during times of war: 1983–present

Conflict-induced displacement, return and resettlement occurred periodically during the twentieth century before its dramatic escalation in the wake of armed conflict in the early 1980s. Prior to the onset of war, the incidence of internal displacement was triggered by exclusionary policies designed to promote (majority) Sinhalese interests, including peasant colonisation, and periodic riots. In certain instances, settlers who themselves experienced DIDR were again resettled during the ensuing war. Well before the 1980s, state responses were typically reactive and confined to the provision of temporary rations and in some cases supplementary welfare assistance. More often, displaced populations were supported by existing social networks and left to their own devices. Where resettlement was pursued, interventions were hastily assembled and often amounted to physical relocation back to the district or division of origin. For example, in the wake of race riots between Sinhalese nationalists and Muslim traders in 1915, populations spontaneously relocated into emergency or 'temporary' shelters before being shunted home (Navaratnam 1995; Tambiah, S. J. 1986).

The first major incidence of CIDR occurred between 1956 and 1958 in the wake of discriminatory language legislation and the violence that ensued. Following Prime Minister Bandaranaike's election (1956) and the initiation of the Sinhala Only Act, Tamil Federal Party politicians launched a *satyagraha* campaign in protest. The Bandaranaike–Chelvanayakam Pact (1957) provided a compromise by proposing that Tamil would become the administrative language for 'regional councils' in the north and east. The Pact also promised to mitigate 'government-sponsored migration of persons, many of whom were Sinhalese, to sparsely populated areas of the north-central and north-eastern Dry Zone, which were regarded by Tamils as their ancestral homeland' (Kearney 1985: 904). The

Pact was abandoned due to mounting pressure from Sinhalese politicians and Buddhist clergy in Colombo. Riots soon broke out in Colombo and the eastern districts. According to Vittachi (1980):

> the area most seriously affected [by escalating violence] was the Gal Oya valley – the newly-opened colony for the reclaiming and settlement of the eastern side of Ceylon. Over 150 people were killed ... National unity has been shattered.

The May–June 1958 riots resulted in the displacement of more than 12,000 Sri Lankan Tamil *families* from the capital. Many estate and Sri Lankan Tamils were housed in temporary shelters close to their original homes before being permanently resettled to Jaffna (de Silva, K. M. and Wriggins 1994).

Another episode of internal displacement and resettlement was triggered by communal violence in southern Sri Lanka during the early 1970s. Between 1967 and 1970, a Marxist group of lower-caste Sinhalese (Karava and Durava) youth led by Rohana Wijeweera were fomenting an insurrection. Grievances ranged from systemic unemployment in the south and the reported shortcomings of the island's communist and socialist parties to paranoia of Indian hegemony. Following the release of their manifesto naming the group Janatha Vimukthi Peramuna (JVP) or the People's Liberation Front and the arrest of Wijeweera, armed violence engulfed the southern districts. The insurrection was met with aggressive counter-insurgency operations and the declaration of a state of emergency between March 1971 and February 1977.[53] Under the auspices of martial law, more than 10,000 Sinhalese youth were estimated killed or disappeared in 1971 and tens of thousands more were temporarily displaced (Abeyratne 2004; Tambiah, S. J. 1990). Many were cared for by neighbours and local faith-based groups, with limited welfare entitlements supplied by the state.

Another bout of internal displacement in Jaffna occurred in the wake of communal violence in 1977. Embryonic Tamil guerrilla groups began emerging in the early 1970s drawing inspiration from the JVP insurrection of 1971 and the creation of Bangladesh from Pakistan in the same year (Spencer 1990b; Helmann-Rajanayagam 1986). The 1976 Vadukkodai Resolution formed the TULF[54] and called for the creation of a separate Tamil state. With general elections approaching, Sinhalese–Tamil relations deteriorated precipitously. The UNP won the elections in July 1977 but the TULF secured the second largest number of seats in Parliament and formed the official opposition. Indeed, the bulk of electoral support for the TULF also roughly corresponded with Sri Lankan Tamil-dominated districts in the north and east.[55] Anti-Tamil riots broke out soon after in August 1977 in Colombo, Kandy, Panadura, Kalutara, Jaffna and other districts, leading to the killing of hundreds of Tamils and Sinhalese and resulting in the internal displacement of more than 10,000 Sri Lankan and estate Tamil *families* (Nissan 1996). With emergency legislation already firmly in place,[56] the government, with support from the armed forces, provided nominal rations in designated temporary shelters and encouraged the swift relocation of these families to various areas of the country.

There was a marked intensification of the Tamil insurgency between 1978 and 1982. This was met with an equally repressive state response, including counter-insurgency operations in Jaffna and other northern and eastern districts and the assassination of moderate Tamil and Sinhalese public authorities and politicians by Tamil militants (Seneratne 1997). Covert support was provided to Sri Lankan Tamil guerrilla organisations by India's Research and Analysis Wing (RAW), while Sinhalese extremist elements associated with the UNP promised a general crack-down (Swamy 2003). Even as the prospect of large-scale displacement became increasingly real, the state was caught unawares by the scale and dimensions of the crisis. Accountability for assisting displaced populations shifted between an array of ministries and departments in Colombo with modest interventions launched according to perceived domestic (predominantly Sinhalese) priorities. Discussed at length in Chapter 5, the provision of relief was devolved through government agents, district secretaries and ultimately *grama niladari*. In real terms, state-issued 'assistance' often amounted to little more than warm meals and dry rations for six months and (temporary) access to public buildings and warehouses (Lankaneson 2000).

The onset of armed conflict By far the most significant incidence of displacement occurred in the 1980s following the declaration and onset of war. Foreign and local academics conventionally portray the armed conflict as a violent contest between exponents of the majority Sinhalese community and the largest ethnic minority in the country, the Sri Lankan Tamils (Bush 2003; Venugopal 2003; Goodhand 2001). Explanations of the so-called root causes are roughly divided according to greed and grievance as proposed by Collier and Hoeffler (2000). One school interprets the conflict as a function of competition over scarce resources such as land, education and employment in an uncertain economic environment (Richardson 2005). Another frames the war as a struggle over identity and ethnic hegemony between a Sinhalese majority and a

Tamil minority, all set against a backdrop of dynamic socio-economic change (Peiris, G. H. 2001; Perera, J. 1992; Rogers 1987; de Silva, K. M. 1986). While Winslow and Woost (2004) contend that 'an explanation of origins no longer serves as an explanation of [conflict] persistence', they also concede that the control of resources in the north and east by the LTTE had more to do with social control and the pursuit of international legitimacy than greed per se.

With the origins of the conflict at best described as multi-causal and epiphenomenal, observers typically divide it into distinct chronological phases. The state was forced to contend with both refugees and internally displaced people for the first time during the first phase (1983–87) of the conflict. For example, more than 200,000 Sri Lankan Tamils reportedly fled to India as de facto refugees, with even more claiming asylum in western countries (UNHCR 1998b). Though statistically impossible to verify, at least another 400,000 Sri Lankan Tamils were also reportedly internally displaced during this period. The majority of the displaced settled with friends and relatives while others lived in deplorable conditions in so-called transit centres (UNHCR 1994a, 1998b).

A temporary peace agreement was engineered in the late 1980s and lasted until the withdrawal of Indian peace-keepers in 1990. The Indo-Sri Lanka Peace Accord was signed by Sri Lankan President Jayawardene and Indian Prime Minister Rajiv Gandhi in July 1987. The Accord set out a range of concessions to LTTE demands such as a modest devolution of authority to the provinces, the prospect of a merger of the northern and eastern provinces and official recognition of the Tamil language. An Indian peace-keeping force (IPKF) was installed to guarantee the provisions of the ceasefire and disarm the LTTE. The Constitution was amended in 1987 to establish provincial councils and district development councils and to limit further changes to ethnic ratios within provinces and districts (Sri Lanka 1978, 1987a, 1987b), though these amendments were largely cosmetic. Against a backdrop of escalating violence and ethnic tension,[57] Premadasa was elected president on a populist platform in 1989 and demanded that the IPKF withdraw within three months.

Tens of thousands more refugees and hundreds of thousands more Sri Lankan Tamils were internally displaced during the second wave of conflict (1990–94). Even as the majority of those internally displaced spontaneously settled on their own, the state began to broaden its approach from one focusing on temporary relief and internment in transit centres to temporary relocation in 'welfare centres' and resettlement as appropriate. Welfare centres were first established in Colombo, Kandy, Nuwara Eliya and Vavuniya and later spread to most districts in the north and east including Mannar, Kilinochchi, Vavuniya, Jaffna, Trincomalee, Batticaloa and Ampara. The centres were complemented with extensive restrictions on mobility between and within districts and a complex system of passes and identity cards to regulate population movement (Monitor 2002; Sri Lanka 1991).

The human and financial burden of prosecuting the conflict and responding to displacement escalated higher still during the third phase of the armed conflict (1995–2001). Complaints about the expanding network of welfare centres, the costs exacted on the public treasury and fears that such settlements served as havens for LTTE cadre and new recruits rose to fever pitch in Colombo. In addition to encountering difficulties in identifying suitable land for return and resettlement,[58] the government received alarming signals from the World Bank, ADB and UNHCR that subsidies for welfare centres and associated entitlements were unlikely to endure indefinitely. From the mid-1990s, senior state authorities began issuing directives, many of them orally transmitted, from Colombo to government agents so that they might begin adopting a new tack.

There were also signs that internal displacement arising from the conflict threatened to transform northern and eastern district ethnic ratios. Sri Lankan Tamils were pouring into Sinhalese-dominated districts and divisions while others were contained by the LTTE in areas where Sri Lankan Tamils sustained majorities. The twin policies of 'crash liquidation' of welfare centres and creation of relocation villages were pursued by the newly elected government of Chandrika Kumaratunga (1994) to counter these 'threats'. The Thirteenth Amendment of the Constitution technically restricted the 'relocation' of internally displaced persons to public land in any *district* other than that of their origin (Sri Lanka 1987a). Nevertheless, between 1995 and 2001, with the authorisation of Cabinet Ministers in Colombo and the support of the CGES, district-level authorities and the armed forces established more than seventy relocation villages. These villages were frequently conflated with welfare centres in the same way that return and resettlement were treated as synonymous.

The Sri Lankan armed forces were frequently deployed to support resettlement during the 1980s and 1990s. Despite evidence of the nascent CIDR regime's influence in enhancing the state's rhetorical commitment to protection promoting (voluntary) return and resettlement through existing bureaucratic structures, the army adopted a different tactic. For the armed forces, resettlement entailed the 'clearing' of land of both LTTE and 'terrorist sympathisers' and where possible the return of displaced people to their 'homes'.[59] While proponents of the CIDR regime issued guidelines advocating a 'voluntary' approach and the importance of establishing 'safe and secure' areas of reception, these were seldom adhered to in a context where martial law held sway (Seneviratne and Stavropoulou 1998). According to the CPA (1998), by the mid-1990s, more than half a million internally displaced individuals were forcibly returned or relocated to districts in the Vanni from Jaffna after being housed in welfare centres over the previous decade. There were several attempts to centralise the decision-making structure to enhance protection and durable solutions while retaining a decentralising delivery system. In order to hasten the process, a presidential task force issued an 'action plan' as the basis of a national programme to address the issue in 1999.

Under heavy pressure from donors and the domestic private sector, the government[60] agreed to a Norwegian-brokered ceasefire agreement (CFA) with the LTTE in February 2002.[61] The CFA included provisions for various joint state–LTTE interim arrangements and verification mechanisms (Sri Lanka 2002d).[62] Funded by the North East Reconstruction Fund (NERF),[63] a subcommittee on immediate humanitarian and rehabilitation needs (SIHRN) and a subcommittee on de-escalation and normalisation (SDN) were introduced as interim arrangements to build confidence. These sub-committees also advocated for protection and durable solutions for conflict-displaced peoples (Chapter 5). Meanwhile, the Sri Lanka Monitoring Mission (SLMM) was expected to oversee ceasefire violations by the armed forces and the LTTE and hasten relocation and the unimpeded return of affected populations to their homes. With these institutions in place, bilateral donors and multilateral aid agencies convened a series of conferences to define recovery and reconstruction needs.[64] The government and the UNHCR, anticipating a major repatriation of refugees from Tamil Nadu and possible return and resettlement programmes for internally displaced persons, expanded their interventions.

The internationally backed interim arrangements did not take account of existing pro-peasant legislation favouring the rights of existing tenants. The Prescriptive Ordinance (1871) included provisions entitling

> unauthorised secondary occupants who have ten years of undisturbed and uninterrupted possession of immovable property to claim legal ownership, adverse to or independent to the legal title of the real owner who was forced to leave the property.

Likewise, the Land Development Ordinance (1935), State Lands Ordinance (1947) and Land Grants (Special Provisions) Act (1931) all included provisions requiring regular occupation by the legal owners for land to be 'owned'. Indeed, a significant proportion of the internally displaced had occupied state land 'illegally' for generations with land conferred between relatives through a 'permit' of some type. For many others residing in 'welfare centres' or 'relocation villages', permits were often cancelled altogether (Pinto-Jayawardena 2006). The resettlement of internally displaced was intensely contentious since the rights of the conflict-displaced to their properties required balancing against the rights of encroachers and squatters, many of whom had themselves been repeatedly displaced. Prescriptive law favoured the rights of encroachers resulting in considerable difficulty to legally sanction return and resettlement.[65] The SIHRN and the SDN also avoided the inflammatory issue of the HSZs discussed in Chapter 5. Though hailed at the time as 'a testament to the commitment of both parties to work creatively', these interim arrangements were eventually abandoned in 2004 (Sriskandarajah 2003).

CIDR regime proponents expected that protection and durable solutions could be ensured through existing state structures. Despite efforts to coordinate state approaches to resettlement following the CFA, there were more than twenty ministries and departments with varying levels of engagement on the issue. By 2003 a newly created Ministry for Rehabilitation, Resettlement and Refugees sought to centralise approaches to CIDR and began a registration and census exercise with UNHCR. In addition, a variety of non-governmental bodies actively disseminated the Guiding Principles. Information-gathering and monitoring increased exponentially, and violations were more regularly reported to the national Human Rights Commission (HRC) of Sri Lanka.

Even so, cross-border and internal displacement intensified in the north and east following the election of the SLFP–JVP coalition government (2005). The newly created Ministry for Nation Building and Development (that replaced the Ministry for Rehabilitation, Resettlement and Refugees) and the Ministry of Resettlement were accorded responsibility for coordinating the protection and durable solutions agenda. Meanwhile, despite inroads suggested above, few policy analysts or practitioners outside of government – including those within the UNHCR and the World Bank – could explain the locus of accountability, the division of labour between particular public authorities, or the extent to which compliance to the norms and rules of the CIDR regime were monitored or enforced. According to the then senior adviser to the Ministry of National Building and Estate Development the logic was straightforward enough: 'our current priority is to resettle people as fast as possible ... though UNHCR objected to our crash programmes, we are moving ahead'.

Pressure by regime advocates to centralise bureaucratic responsibilities for CIDR generated modest results. In 2007, the Parliament passed legislation to create a 'Jathika Saviya' or Resettlement Authority (Sri Lanka

2006a, 2007). Vested with the 'power to formulate a national policy and plan, implement, monitor and coordinate the resettlement of internally displaced persons and refugees', it explicitly acknowledged the core principles, norms, rules and decision-making features of the CIDR regime. Though some regime advocates were understandably sceptical of its potential to ensure genuine protection and durable solutions, its creation suggests that the regime may finally yield concrete institutional gains after two decades in Sri Lanka.

Resettlement after the tsunami: 2004–present

Less than three years after the CFA, the island experienced the most dramatic natural disaster in its history. An earthquake off the coast of Sumatra, Indonesia, generated a series of massive waves that struck Sri Lanka's northern, eastern and south-western coastlines in December 2004. The effects of the waves on acutely vulnerable populations were devastating: at least 38,000 people were killed, 22,000 injured and hundreds of thousands were rendered homeless and dispossessed of their assets. The reconstruction needs were immense and, owing to the scale of the event, the international response was exceptionally generous (Chapter 6). The country was rapidly flooded with aid and relief agencies, thus offering a kind of natural experiment for testing the shape and impact of an emergent NIDR regime.

Despite the significant presence and authority of NIDR regime proponents, the government's response was shaped primarily by the political situation in the north and east and its own domestic lobby. A dispute ensued almost immediately after the natural disaster between the government and the LTTE over the *modus operandi* of the recovery process (Bastian 2006a; Uyangoda 2005). The combination of a potentially massive injection of foreign capital coupled with the possibilities of re-engineering the ethnic composition of the region raised the stakes on both sides.[66] After months of bargaining, the two parties compromised on a joint administrative mechanism for post-tsunami reconstruction (e.g. the Post Tsunami Operational Management Structure or PTOMS) in June 2005. But despite massive pledges of assistance[67] donors were manifestly reluctant to disburse without evidence of a more transparent decision-making mechanism and clarity in relation to land acquisition for return and resettlement (World Bank 2005).

The PTOMS was a national mechanism that included several interim arrangements expressly designed to enhance protection and durable solutions for all tsunami-affected populations. Financed by a World Bank-supported fund (NERF), the PTOMS was expected to be composed of a high-level committee, regional committees and district committees. The high-level committee included representatives from the government, the LTTE and Muslim 'stakeholders' and a rotating chair and was mandated to formulate policy and disburse funds.[68] With the headquarters based in the LTTE stronghold of Kilinochchi, regional committees were to be composed of a multi-party structure with a transparent system to verify proposals and operate in six tsunami-affected districts. Meanwhile, district committees were expected to identify and prioritise proposals and submit recommendations to the regional committee.

Expectations that the PTOMS would form an integral component of the peace process quickly evaporated. Indeed, the PTOMS collapsed because of extreme opposition from the JVP and Sinhalese nationalists. It was aggressively challenged in the Supreme Court on the grounds that the authority vested in the committees was 'governmental' in nature and thus unconstitutional. Moreover, it was argued that since the funds were established by a Parliamentary Act, they were not subject to scrutiny by the Auditor General – an intolerable concession to the LTTE. Finally, the petitioners contended that since the committees focused on only six districts in the north and east, they discriminated against those living outside these areas on the basis of birth and residence, thus violating Article 12 (2) of the Constitution (Satkunanathan and Rainford 2008). The Supreme Court ultimately restricted provisions for the regional committees and the funding mechanisms, thus compelling the LTTE to withdraw. The subsequent proposal of a National Disaster Management Council effectively made PTOMS redundant.

An unanticipated setback for the promotion of protection and durable solutions was the introduction of a coastal 'buffer zone' soon after the tsunami struck the island. The buffer extended to all coastal areas of the island and effectively limited the return of coastal populations to their homes or resettlement elsewhere, thus depriving them of their land and livelihoods. The government and the LTTE quickly agreed to establish a prohibition on the construction of new homes within its threshold (Chapter 6). Publicly described as a 'preventive' measure to prevent further risks from a natural disaster, it was privately considered a carefully crafted land grab owing to exemptions it provided to tourism and commercial entities (Leckie 2005). Although relaxed ten months later – 'depending on the vulnerability of the area to future threats' – and ultimately abandoned in 2006, the buffer vastly complicated the core objectives of NIDR regime supporters.[69]

As with regimes for development and conflict-induced internal displacement and resettlement, the NIDR regime actualises core norms and rules through a network of state structures and institutions. In the case of Sri Lanka, activities were contracted to and administered by multilateral and primarily foreign non-governmental agencies, local contractors and in 'uncleared areas', agencies affiliated with the LTTE such as the Tamil Rehabilitation Organisation (TRO).[70] Though a series of committees and task forces were established in Colombo and staffed by public servants, government agents, district secretaries and municipal authorities were expected to execute programmes associated with resettlement, employment, public service provision and upgrading of national infrastructure (OCHA 2005).

With support from NIDR regime proponents, the Sri Lankan government ultimately launched a multi-prong strategy of relief assistance aligned closely with 'transitional' and 'permanent' housing. Owing to the exigencies of the tsunami and the visibility offered by humanitarian assistance, permanent resettlement was awarded a comparatively low priority. Over a period of six months, UNHCR distributed more than half a million non-food relief items to more than 160,000 internally displaced people, the majority of them in southern districts, Ampara, Batticaloa and Trincomalee. The UNHCR also assumed responsibility for establishing 'transitional shelters' for over 50,000 temporarily relocated households[71] with UN-HABITAT and its partners focusing on building more 'permanent' housing in the south. Though promising to permanently resettle within a year the majority of those affected, by the end of 2006 approximately 250,000 displaced people still lived in transitional shelters in northern and eastern coastal districts.[72] As in the case of the CIDR, most of those displaced included Sri Lankan Tamils and Muslims though several thousand Sinhalese were also affected and ultimately resettled in southern districts.

The state's longer-term resettlement strategy, described as permanent housing, was purportedly slowed by an inability to secure land and concerns with disturbing ethnic ratios in strategic areas. Of the estimated 98,000 permanent dwellings destroyed in late 2004, less than half were built by December 2006.[73] Even so, the majority of completed donor- and owner-driven resettlement schemes were located in Sinhalese-dominated districts in the south, suggesting that principles of parity were not being realised. Many of those supplied with land and livelihood opportunities in the interior and away from the coastline refused to move from their 'traditional areas' citing loss of livelihood (Perera, A. 2005). In certain cases households began to fracture, with some seeking casual employment while others waited in 'transitional shelters' for their reconstruction grants to materialise.

The state's response to the tsunami was highly centralised in terms of decision-making (in the executive) but displayed a decentralised approach to delivery. A complex array of Ministries, Authorities and Departments were mobilised to coordinate the response. According to government and UN informants working in severely affected areas such as Trincomalee, Batticaloa and Ampara, however, it was government agents, working together with district committees and often with the LTTE-backed TRO, who were ultimately essential in promoting emergency relief and longer-term return and resettlement.[74] Contemporary incidences of NIDR provide an indicator as to whether lessons were learned by the state and the international community in the wake of the tsunami. For example, land-slides in 2007 in Nuwara Eliya district affected more than 160 villages and over 4,000 families. An estimated 18,000 individuals were resettled into sixty-four emergency shelters and thirty welfare centres, with consider-able numbers spontaneously settling on their own. Authorities in the Ministry of Land contend that unused plantation or 'estate' land would be located for them, though few had resettled more than six months after their displacement. While the rhetoric may have advanced, it has not necessarily yielded dramatically changed practice.

Conclusions

Sri Lanka is not a *tabula rasa* on which regime proponents 'construct' protection and durable solutions. This chapter has demonstrated that forced migration generated demographic transformation over the course of thousands of years. Planned population settlement and resettlement were pursued aggressively by colonial and post-colonial authorities for a combination of reasons, ranging from the stimulation of economic growth to nation-building and ethnic nationalism. A wide variety of civilians were purposefully resettled, ranging from Sinhalese peasants to war-affected Sri Lankan Tamils and Muslims. Over time, the distinc-tions between colonisation, settlement and resettlement were blurred by accident and design. It is in examining the process and outcomes of displacement and resettlement within a historical and unitary perspec-tive that a coherent narrative can be discerned. This chapter has traced out how settlement and resettlement of Sinhalese peasants to the north and east were pursued by ethnic nationalists as a strategic priority of the first order. Coupled with discriminatory policies introduced by a majoritarian state, colonisation schemes came to represent a real and perceived threat to the political and cultural integrity of Sri Lanka's largest minority community, among others. Though systematic evidence of the demographic outcomes of the process is obscured by the absence of reliable longitudinal data, the available information is damning: between 1946 and 1981 the dry zone districts in the north and east experienced a dramatic increase in population density and disproportionately rapid growth of Sinhalese settlements (Sri Lanka 1981, 1951). As a result of DIDR, the ethnic composition of key northern and eastern districts witnessed considerable changes in their ethnic ratios (Kearney 1987).

Different categories of internal displacement and resettlement came together in the early twenty-first century. In the case of DIDR, majority populations expanded and diffused into ostensibly minority-dominated areas. In the case of CIDR and NIDR, minority groups were constrained within existing areas, relocated away from strategically important sites and immobilised so as not to alter ethnic ratios. Population containment was entrenched following amendments to the Constitution in 1987. Proponents of the three regimes sought to graft certain universalising norms and rules on to state responses and supported the development of local decision-making structures, but were patently unable to contend with the political imperatives at play. The social and economic consequences of settlement and resettlement schemes were discouraging. Few schemes lived up to their potential to create egalitarian communities of 'peasant-owner proprietors' or durable solutions. In fact, resettlement schemes in the early twenty-first century reflected pathologies and levels of impoverishment common to those documented in the nineteenth.

4 | Resettlement for development: Systems L and B

'We have to go to the border, or the border will come to us.'
President Jayewardene 21 February 1985

Forced migration researchers in Sri Lanka focus predominantly on conflict-induced displacement, including refugees and internally displaced people. Yet a long-standing and tense debate persists over the consequences of development and social engineering projects on the country's demographic landscape. Despite the perverse political and social consequences of such interventions, comparatively little evidence has been mobilised to demonstrate the strategic rationale, modalities and outcomes of state-sanctioned resettlement schemes in the north and east. Over the past five decades attention has focused instead on specific categories of colonisation and technical aspects of assisted migration, including tenure arrangements and agricultural productivity. With the exception of certain studies undertaken in the 1980s and 1990s,[1] the political, ethnic and military dynamics of settlement and resettlement were only rarely broached. This, in spite of the fact that the 'ethnic dimension constitutes the most contentious issue concerning the subject of settlement development' in the country (Peiris, G. H. 1996: 205).

The conventional narrative put forward by certain politicians and policymakers is that population settlement since independence was voluntary and motivated by the macro-economic imperatives of nation-building. Colonisation was expected to expand agricultural productivity and reduce population pressures, including landlessness. Assisted migration was inextricably linked to national development planning, including the assertion of state control and authority over ostensibly 'backward' areas. In Sri Lanka, population settlement and resettlement were pursued as a strategic process of permanent demographic and political transformation. Given the highly antagonistic parliamentary debates over land legislation and appropriation between the 1940s and the 1970s and the strategic concerns over territory arising from the civil war since the early 1980s, it is perhaps not so surprising that so few empirical studies on the politics of resettlement were assembled, much less made public and disseminated.

This chapter contends that the settlement and resettlement of Sri

Lankan civilians were driven by more than developmental aspirations expounded by successive governments and exponents of the nascent DIDR regime. It is true that a series of massive state-led irrigation and power projects established in the Mahaweli basin promised to redress structural social and economic inequalities attributed to population pressure and landlessness in the south, the arid interior, dependency in the smallholder paddy (rice) sector and the cultural erosion of the country's majority population. DIDR was simultaneously embedded in a historical process associated with the purposive and irreversible realignment of district and divisional ethnic ratios, the consolidation of new administrative and electoral boundaries and ultimately the strategic and counterinsurgency imperatives of the security forces. Resettlement was intimately wedded to the politics of ethnic nationalism and militarism. Due to endogenous constraints within the nascent DIDR regime and specific exogenous factors, regime proponents[2] unintentionally contributed to a process that at best cemented Sinhalese hegemony and at worst led to ethnic cleansing. The real and perceived contradictions generated by the externally financed MDIP did not go unnoticed. Certain DIDR regime supporters and parliamentarians expressed reservations even before the concrete dams, reservoirs and irrigation canals were built but were no match for those responsible for shaping the intervention.

The outcomes of the MDIP reveal the limitations of the DIDR regime in relation to ensuring protection and promoting durable solutions. Notwithstanding the fact that the international regime was still in its early stages of formation, its proponents were unable to minimise displacement, protect minority populations or restore the livelihoods of resettlers. This chapter considers the experiences of two components of the MDIP: Systems L and B. These Systems were located in eastern and ethnically heterogeneous districts, which distinguished them from others executed in more stable and ethnically homogeneous (Sinhalese) districts to the west and south. Resettlement served to deepen ethnic fault-lines in specific districts and exacerbate armed violence in the early 1980s. Development and conflict-induced internal displacement and resettlement thus came together in insidious ways. The nascent DIDR regime was not only unable to minimise the onset of impoverishment of Sinhalese settlers and resettlers, but its proponents indirectly contributed to their prolonged dependency and militancy and ultimately the onset of CIDR (Chapter 5).[3]

Situating the Mahaweli programme

The post-independence literature on DIDR in Sri Lanka is dominated by the experience of Gal Oya and the MDIP. As noted in the previous chapter, the scale of their anticipated development dividends was exceeded only by their monumental size. Considered to be one of the largest development projects in the world at the time, the MDIP was expected to resolve the perceived population crisis in overcrowded southern districts; achieve domestic self-sufficiency and marketable surpluses in paddy production; resolve the country's power and electricity requirements; and instal a self-reliant peasant sector in allegedly sparsely populated areas of the country. From an engineering perspective, the simultaneous construction of four massive dams and reservoirs in under six years was an impressive accomplishment. Between 1978 and 1984, the reservoirs were impounded and dam headworks established with two large-voltage hydropower-generation facilities put into operation. By 1988, each of the four dams was considered operational, even if facing certain technical frailties related to their structural integrity. But the rapid construction of MDIP infrastructure generated a significant economic and social cost. Notwithstanding favourable reports issued by the Ministry of Irrigation, the Ministry of the Mahaweli Authority and the Mahaweli Authority, it is uncertain whether the MDIP achieved more than a few of its declared objectives.

By the early 1990s, the settlement and resettlement components of the MDIP were considered a failure. Rather than creating an egalitarian society of rural landholders or durable solutions for resettlers, the evidence generated by geographers, agronomists and sociologists revealed new patterns of impoverishment (Kumar 2003; Scudder 1980, 2001; Wanigaratne 1987). A baseline study commissioned by the Mahaweli Authority (1993) found that the economic gains in many of the systems were far below expectation. An interim assessment commissioned by the World Bank (2004d) described socio-economic conditions among second- and third-generation settlers as 'nightmarish'.[4] The study detected a sizeable decrease in the local labour pool among resettled households together with diminished prospects for employment:

> the demand for jobs too has increased but there were no employment opportunities in the Mahaweli zones, compelling a majority of job seekers to join the armed forces ... [l]and ownership of the second and third generations has declined to marginal levels and only four per cent owned high land, while only three per cent owned paddy land. (ibid.)

This chapter is not an indictment of the MDIP but rather explains the contradictions in rationale, approaches and outcomes of an externally financed development programme crafted to promote protection and durable solutions for landless peasants.[5] There are many attributed reasons for the failures of the MDIP. Despite the programme's avowed commitment to sustaining welfare systems and centralised planning mechanisms, studies highlighted the overly ambitious expectations of planners to establish self-administered and self-reliant 'settlement schemes' and 'colonies' in a short time (Pain 1986). Other critiques revealed the weak social infrastructure and limited agency – the attributes and endowment sets – of peasants 'selected' for (re)settlement (Gunaratne, M. H. 1980). Certain experienced technocrats affiliated with the MDIP observed that by far the majority of participants were not carefully selected settlers, but rather resettlers involuntarily evicted from their lands and original villages (Wanigaratne 1987). There is some evidence that thousands of settlers and resettlers included former convicts and 'undesirables' relocated from the south, a trend also detected in the Gal Oya project decades before (Peiris, G. H. 1996). As this chapter shows, many of these resettlers were later recruited as home-guards and local defence units in the frontier settlements separating Sinhalese and Sri Lankan Tamil areas in the north and east.

The preparation of the Mahaweli Master Plan

The MDIP was heavily influenced by foreign consultants and multilateral institutions associated with the nascent DIDR regime.[6] Aspirations of harnessing the 335-kilometre Mahaweli *ganga* (river) for industrial and agricultural development in the interior resonated with British colonial officials well before independence (Farmer 1957; Moore 1985). More determined plans to launch a large-scale project in the Mahaweli basin were promulgated by the first Prime Minister of Sri Lanka, D. S. Senanayake. In the wake of the Gal Oya Project (1948–52), a US-sponsored feasibility study was launched in 1958 to review the possibility of a trans-basin diversion of the Mahaweli *ganga*. The Sri Lankan government shelved the so-called United States Operation Mission Proposals soon after their completion and pushed the United Nations to elaborate a bolder vision. The UN Special Fund, with technical assistance from the UNDP, agreed to undertake a series of geological and hydrological surveys to examine soil, river flows and water requirements for a massive irrigation programme in the Mahaweli basin. Drafted by early supporters of the DIDR regime, including foreign consultants and applied researchers affiliated with the United States Agency for International Development (USAID), UNDP and the FAO over a ten-year period, these surveys formed the outline of a Master Plan (Map 4.1). The Master Plan was submitted to the Sri Lankan government in 1968 and publicly released in three volumes amid great fanfare in 1969.

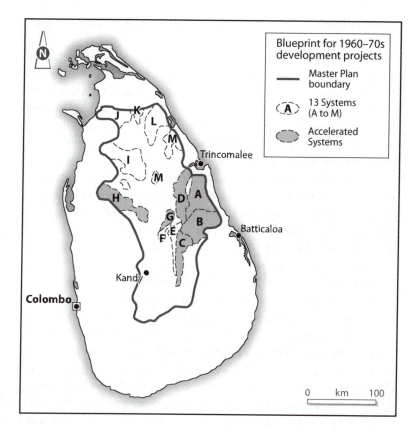

MAP 4.1 Mahaweli Master Plan (1969) *Source*: Reconstructed from archival records (PMU-Colombo).

The Master Plan embodied a development paradigm consistent with modernist ideologies of the 1950s and 1960s. Development planners – including Western-trained Sri Lankan policymakers – were convinced that smallholder agriculturists constituted the primary engine of national economic growth. In harnessing mechanised technology and know-how, overall peasant sector performance could be enhanced. There were widespread expectations that a 'uni-modal' agricultural strategy could strengthen urban–rural growth linkages (Mellor 1976). In keeping with these aspirations, the Master Plan proposed a comprehensive multi-phase (foreign) capital-intensive strategy to simultaneously stimulate growth in the peasant sector and resolve structural inequalities between densely and sparsely populated areas of the country. It also provided a useful entry-point for Western governments to tighten geo-political and economic relations with a country they felt was drifting worryingly towards socialism (Chapter 3).

In the 1960s the Master Plan was one of the most elaborate and complex rural integrated development proposals in the world. As with dam and irrigation interventions launched in Africa, Latin America and South-east Asia, it promised tremendous social and economic transformation that could comprehensively redirect the country's development trajectory. In adding a major power generation component, the Master Plan guaranteed that creditor countries would be ensured satisfactory returns on their investment. The technical ambition and audacity of the Master Plan caught the imagination of prospective DIDR regime proponents from the beginning.[7] It envisaged the construction of a series of interlocking concrete storage reservoirs and hydropower-generation plants in the Mahaweli basin over a thirty-year period. These reservoirs featured a series of irrigation diversions in order to deliver water to thirteen separate Systems (labelled A to M) covering almost 40 per cent of the country's land cover. The Master Plan also proposed a building-block approach to the construction of irrigation infrastructure, with internal checks and balances built into the process. The total estimated budget for the proposed irrigation, electrification and settlement components of the MDIP in 1968 was over US$1.28 billion. Approximately half (US$626 million) was allocated to settlement and *purana* (village) expansion and rehabilitation schemes. Typical of large-scale development projects, however, the budget profoundly underestimated absolute costs.[8] As a result of repeated delays, financial shortages and sporadic political unrest, a network of irrigation and canal systems, power-generating stations and settlement schemes was eventually established in only five of thirteen Systems by the mid-1980s.

Settlement under the MDIP

The Master Plan envisaged the settlement and resettlement of more than one million landless peasants from densely populated districts in the southern wet zone into the more arid central, northern and eastern districts. The *proposed* settlement components met many of the minimum pro-poor standards expected of bilateral donors such as USAID, the Canadian International Development Agency (CIDA), the then UK Ministry of Overseas Development,[9] the Japan International Cooperation Agency (JICA), the Central Committee for Swedish Cooperation (CCSC)[10] and others such as West Germany, the Netherlands and the European Economic Community (EEC). Though the Resettlement Guidelines reviewed in Chapter 2 had yet to be released, the importance attached to an equitable population settlement component that supported the basic needs of civilians and evacuees was also stressed by, among others, the World Bank, the ADB, UNICEF and the WFP. The anticipated scale of the settlement and resettlement featured in the Master Plan was unprecedented. The Master Plan provided a rough outline for the sequenced settlement and limited resettlement of a quarter of a million peasant *families* to so-called colony units and expanded villages. Evaluations undertaken by foreign consultancy firms in the 1970s lauded the technocratic innovations accorded by public officials to settlement and resettlement plans. Particular praise was directed at the use of central place theory as a means of spatially organising the colony units into interconnected and self-reliant settlement systems (TAMS 1980; NEDECO 1979). These consultancy firms were as heavily invested in the MDIP as their donor patrons.

The original Master Plan proposed by then Prime Minister Dudley Senanayake (1960, 1965–70) positioned the MDIP at the centre of the country's national development strategy. Conscious of the long-standing and tense parliamentary debates over the potentially destabilising effects of the project, he publicly advocated for an ethnically balanced approach. Though most of those targeted for voluntary settlement were expected to consist of landless peasants from the (supposedly over-populated) south, the Master Plan also included provisions for the incremental expansion of irrigation channels into western, northern and eastern areas that suffered from extreme water shortages and shorter growing seasons than the south (Scudder and Vimaladharma 1985, 1989; Vimaladharma 1982).

The physical construction of the MDIP reservoirs, dams and irrigation canals was expected to proceed in two phases and occurred during the tenures of SLFP Prime Minister S. Bandaranaike (1970–77) and UNP President J. R. Jayewardene (1977–89).[11] As anticipated in the Master Plan, construction was originally supposed to proceed over a period of two to three decades in order to stagger costs and allow for evaluation and adaptation over time.[12] The first phase included the construction of several System reservoirs in Sinhalese-dominated southern and central districts from 1970 to 1974. Specifically, the MDIP included the Polgolla diversion and the Bowatenna reservoir in 1970 which, combined with the trans-basin canals of Kalawewa, were designed to feed System H, a Sinhalese majority area. Approximately 500 'voluntary' settler families were reportedly evacuated from the reservoir catchments in Bowatenna and resettled elsewhere in System H, ostensibly to begin paddy production.[13] In 1973, MDIP planners began building the Victoria reservoir (System C), the largest of all the reservoirs. Both System C and System D

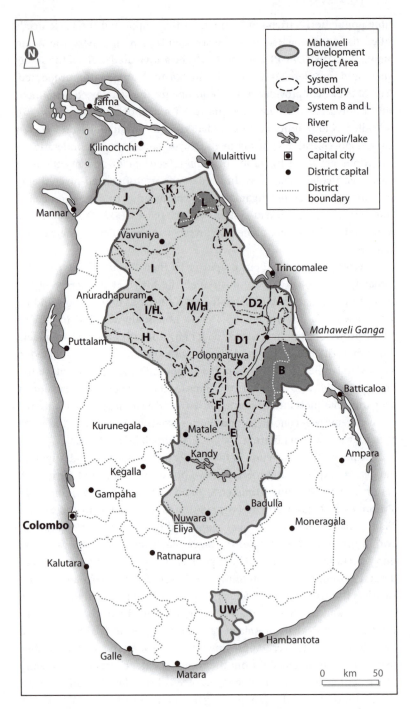

MAP 4.2 MDIP Systems (1975–2005) *Source*: Reconstructed from PMU Archives.

(Moragahakande reservoir) were expected to be completed in 1980. Two smaller canals in Thaldena (System A) and Pallewela (System B) adjoined the Uma Oya (river) and were subsequently connected to the Maduru Oya which acted as the central storage reservoir. The second phase of the Master Plan outlined the expansion of irrigation canals, reservoir systems and settlements in Sri Lankan Tamil and Muslim-dominated districts to the north, though few details were provided to guide the process. This second phase was never completed.[14]

The acceleration of the MDIP The exigencies of the ballot box led to profound changes to the original Master Plan. Following the successful election of the UNP in 1977, Prime Minister Jayewardene requested engineers and contractors to rapidly accelerate the MDIP from thirty to six years (de Silva, K. M. and Wriggins 1994). On the recommendation of twelve commissioned consultancy reports from a Dutch firm (NEDECO), the MDIP was streamlined from its anticipated thirteen Systems to just eight (Map 4.2). The newly elected government established a highly centralised bureaucratic mechanism modelled on the TVA to oversee and administer the accelerated programme (Chapter 3). The Mahaweli Authority, as it was called, was immediately granted unprecedented control over the design, planning, execution and monitoring of all facets of the MDIP, including land expropriation and acquisition (Sri Lanka 1979a, 1979b, 1979f). Under the Minister of Mahaweli Development, Dissanayake, and generous funding from multilateral and bilateral donors, a series of supplementary legal and bureaucratic institutions was created from late 1977 to 1980 to support the work of the Authority and expand eminent domain. State entities such as the Mahaweli Economic Agency (MEA), the Mahaweli Development Board (MDB), the Irrigation Department and the Central Engineering Consultancy Bureau assumed core decision-making functions of state-sanctioned population (re)settlement.

The decision to accelerate the MDIP by the UNP government in 1978 signalled the first tentative break with the nascent DIDR regime. While a combination of Western donors and international aid agencies financed and supported the MDIP, including its settlement and resettlement process, the resolve to redouble construction efforts was accepted as the prerogative of a sovereign state. Following renewed solicitations by Minister Dissanayake, financial support was secured from several bilateral donors and construction was brought forward. From 1979 onwards, the Mahaweli Authority worked to complete Victoria and Kotmale on schedule leading to the eviction and resettlement of more than 3,000 families in Kotmale by 1985 (Ministry of Mahaweli Development 1987). The Authority also initiated construction of Systems B and C with financing from the United Kingdom, Sweden, Germany and Canada (TAMS 1980).

In spite of a preoccupation with the construction of physical infrastructure, the Mahaweli Authority repeatedly advertised the pro-poor settlement components of the accelerated MDIP. Shortly after establishing credit agreements with the World Bank in 1980, a Mahaweli Settlement Division was established within the Mahaweli Authority to ensure that emerging DIDR regime rules were explicitly taken into account. Though construction agencies were criticised at the time for harbouring an engineering bias (Müller and Hettige 2004), Mahaweli Authority planners maintained that the positive execution of the settlement component was essential to the country's national development. As with the Gal Oya project, the Mahaweli Authority guaranteed compelling and sustained social returns from resettlers (Uphoff 1996). The Mahaweli Development Board (1979) expected that it would eventually 'create an integrated rural society with an acceptable standard of living, while simultaneously contributing to the economic wellbeing of the country as a whole'.

The importance attached to equitable and sustainable settlement – including for minorities and 'indigenous people' – was also emphasised by DIDR regime proponents. Foreign-commissioned surveys and assessments highlighted that '[c]onstruction is not an aim in itself; the aim is the creation of a reasonably satisfied rural society' (NEDECO 1979: 14). Studies commissioned by the Mahaweli Authority reported that 'the efficiency of the Accelerated Mahaweli Programme will one day be judged not by the colossal concrete structures and social infrastructure, but by the success of the settler in creating a physically healthy and economically viable society with a high sense of moral values' (Attayanake et al. 1985: 61). The Sri Lankan government repeatedly emphasised the critical role the MDIP would play in retaining and enhancing village structures and supporting Vedda populations in becoming 'productive paddy farmers'.[15] On the surface such declarations placated regime supporters, including international and bilateral donors while simultaneously advertising the dividends of the MDIP to the future electorate, including settlers and resettlers.

The decision to accelerate the MDIP came under criticism from without and within. Most of these early expressions of concern were tied to financial and technical aspects of the programme. Certain proponents of the nascent DIDR regime, including the World Bank, raised concerns over the potential inflationary consequences of a rapid injection of foreign investment over a comparatively short period of time, though these were brushed aside by the Sri Lankan government (de Silva, K. M. and Wriggins

1994). Other donors doubted that the new benchmarks set by President Jayewardene would be reached within six years. Meanwhile, opposition MPs complained of massive budgetary overruns – expenditures that later undermined other aspects of the programme (Hansard 1978–80). They argued that the acceleration of the MDIP resulted in much greater reliance on capital-intensive construction equipment, techniques and foreign labour, thus offsetting potential domestic employment gains. A former employee of the Mahaweli Authority warned that the massive influx of foreign currency combined with the absence of competitive tendering processes and poor accountability would exacerbate already high inflationary pressures and systemic corruption (Iriyagolle 1978). His concerns were prescient: by 1980 the projected costs of the acceleration rose three times above the 1978 estimate (Karunatillake 1983a). According to former consultants associated with the Mahaweli Authority and the World Bank in the 1980s, such cost overruns and adverse socio-economic outcomes were anticipated by certain regime supporters from the beginning.

The limitations of the programme's social infrastructure were increasingly difficult to conceal. The overt centralisation of administrative authority into a single entity with a clear bias towards infrastructure development resulted in comparatively weak coordination with extension workers recruited to support settlement, agricultural extension personnel and the new (primarily Sinhalese) settlers. The Mahaweli Authority proposed to build a vast network of grass-roots farmer associations and associated line services to promote self-sufficiency and reduce potential dependency, regarded as vital institutions on the basis of the Gal Oya experience and international practice. But any gains were overshadowed and marginalised in the rush to complete the headworks and canals (Tennekoon, M. T. 1982; Tennekoon, S. T. 1988). Immediately following the completion of most of the major reservoir works and canals in 1982, doubts began to surface as to whether the MDIP would achieve any of its settlement targets at all (Shanmugaratnam 1985).

Resettlement outcomes of the MDIP The MDIP was expected to resolve two interconnected demographic concerns. First, it was supposed to alleviate overcrowding of the (Sinhalese) coastal or wet zones. Second, it was expected to redress (Sinhalese) landlessness. These objectives were to be accomplished by voluntarily relocating enterprising settlers and landless peasants from the south to the newly established Systems in the Mahaweli basin. A review of publicly available census data reveals that these two fundamental objectives were not achieved (Chapter 3). According to the PMU director of the Mahaweli Authority and senior civil servants affiliated with the Ministry of Irrigation, approximately three-quarters of settlers and peasants who were ultimately granted land consisted of evacuees or resettlers from the same districts where Systems were built and not 'settlers' as intended in the Master Plan and promised by the Mahaweli Authority.

The majority of people ultimately relocated by the accelerated MDIP were internally displaced from upstream areas due to reservoir and related infrastructure construction within their districts or forcibly relocated across comparatively short distances as part of *purana* expansion schemes. Most 'settlement' was in fact intra-district and between heterogeneous divisions (Chapter 3). Less than one-quarter of the 'beneficiaries' of the MDIP actually consisted of voluntary 'settlers' from the south but rather instead included Sinhalese from adjoining districts. This fact is not clearly documented in a single Mahaweli Authority report or externally commissioned evaluation. The comparatively limited effects of the MDIP in relation to alleviating overall population pressure or resolving landlessness in the wet zone almost went virtually undiagnosed. The geographer G. H. Peiris (1996) described how in many settlements:

> a large proportion of the resident population had been drawn from the same districts in which the settlements were located ... it is unlikely that the Accelerated Mahaweli Development Programme as a whole will have a significant impact on prevailing pressure of population on agricultural land in the main rural population concentrations of the country such as those in the wet zone and Jaffna.

The acceleration of the MDIP coincided with general elections in the late 1970s, the intensification of martial law and marked deterioration in relations between the government and minority opposition groups. With the second largest elected party, the TULF effectively disbarred in 1983 after refusing to take an oath of loyalty to the government following their (unconstitutional) demand for secession, President Jayewardene easily won a second term virtually unopposed.[16] Despite the prospect of open war between the state and separatist Sri Lankan Tamil militants in the north and east, the acceleration process continued especially in divisive districts (Kearney 1985). Systems A, B, C, D, L and M in the northern and eastern districts (i.e. Vavuniya, Mullaitivu, Trincomalee, Batticaloa and Ampara) were considered to be especially volatile. Nevertheless, under the supervision of senior officials associated with the Mahaweli Authority and others,[17] the settlement of settlers into these areas in the 1980s followed on the heels of state-sanctioned eviction of Sri Lankan Tamil and Muslim residents.

After the 1982 elections settlement and resettlement in Systems B and L was pursued aggressively and at times covertly by the Mahaweli Authority. Evacuations of both Sri Lankan and estate Tamils and the relocation of Sinhalese into contested areas were undertaken by stealth. The former were in some cases declared 'absentee landowners' (including refugees then residing in southern India) and had their land annexed. Others were labelled 'encroachers' on designated MDIP land and, unless able to demonstrate formal ownership through presentation of deeds, were forcibly evicted. In Trincomalee, Batticaloa and Ampara the Mahaweli Authority annexed private, Crown and Buddhist clergy land and, with district-level approval, reallocated parcels to newly (re) settled populations. Once former residents were evicted, Sinhalese settlers and state-sponsored encroachers in turn were regularised by squatting[18] and through the legitimate designation and allocation of appropriate land by district and divisional authorities and private landholders. The Mahaweli Authority then immediately began supporting the installation of new settlement schemes (later described as 'frontier settlements' or 'border villages') (Jayasena and Senanayaka 1999). Crucially, drawing on the provisions of the Renaming of Towns and Villages Ordinance, previously Sri Lankan Tamil-dominated hamlets and villages were renamed in Sinhala, thus completing the transfer.

The exclusionary dimensions of the MDIP settlement programme were not immediately detected by DIDR regime proponents in the early 1980s. Because donors literally adopted separate Systems and owing to the complexity of the intervention, they failed to appreciate how the entire process was unfolding. Even so, a number of negative features were detected by international and local human rights activists[19] along with the Sri Lankan Tamil political and militant leadership and Indian politicians in Tamil Nadu (Nithiyanandam 2000; Manogaran 1994, 1996; *Frontline* 1985; Leary 1981). It was more than a decade later that the Jaffna-based University Teachers for Human Rights (UTHR) described how 'state-aided colonisation schemes' advanced by the Gal Oya Board and Mahaweli Authority contributed to the ethnic segmentation of districts and divisions through strategic alterations to their ethnic ratios (Satchithanandan 2000; UTHR 1993).[20] As noted above, the TULF repeatedly agitated against the MDIP. The LTTE, for its part, charged in a 1983 statement that:

[t]he most vicious form of oppression calculated to destroy the national identity of the Tamils was the state-aided aggressive colonisation which began soon after 'independence' and now swallowed nearly 3,000 square miles of *Tamil Eelam* (Tamil homeland). This planned occupation of

Tamil lands by hundreds of thousands of Sinhala [sic] people, aided and abetted by the state, was aimed to annihilate the geographical entity of the Tamil nation. (cf. Ponnambalam 1983: 260)

The government and Sinhalese nationalists, far from disagreeing, insisted that population settlement was essential to ensuring the integrity of the *national* ethnic ratio and combating 'terrorists'. Certain Cabinet Ministers and parliamentarians contended that 'strategic settlement' was the only way to dismantle the spatial contiguity of *Eelam* which stretched from the northern to the eastern districts and included two-thirds of the country's coastline (Sri Lanka 1985). According to former senior Mahaweli Authority bureaucrat M. H. Gunaratne (1998: 34): 'in regional development, particularly in selecting projects for development under the Mahaweli programme, it is possible to effect fundamental changes to destroy the *Eelam* aspiration and to restructure the country's geopolitics to strengthen its territorial integrity and internal stability'. These Systems, Gunaratne (ibid.: 35) continued:

> would become an intensive development area with a dense population, which is strategically located in relation to *Eelam* and it would destroy the land basis for the very existence of *Eelam* ... After completing development ... the other death stroke should be to develop the Mawatu Oya Basin in the West.

The Sri Lankan President Jayewardene confirmed the strategy following the outbreak of war in 1983. During an address at the ceremonial opening of Parliament in 1985 he announced that 'we have to combat "terrorism" and defeat it with all the resources at our command. We may have to equip ourselves to do so at the expense of development and social and economic welfare plans' (Sri Lanka 1985). Moderate observers also discerned the strategic logic of the MIDP settlement strategy. According to G. H. Peiris (1996: 207), an axiom of state policy from the mid-1980s onwards was the distribution of land 'after making allowance ... for evacuees and resettlers ... strictly on the basis of ethnic ratios, according to which the extents of land received by each ethnic group will be proportional to its percentage of the national population'. The fulfilment of national ratios thus required strategic population shifts to the north and east.[21] The remainder of this chapter considers two cases where the outcomes of state-administered population settlement diverged dramatically from the aspirations of DIDR regime proponents: System L and System B.[22]

System L: from Manal Aru to Weli Oya

Although it is included in the Master Plan, System L was not awarded an especially prominent position in the accelerated MIDP in the late 1970s. Straddling the districts of Mullaitivu, Vavuniya and Trincomalee, System L was initially expected to service a combination of Sinhalese, Sri Lankan Tamil and Muslim populations in an area later renamed Weli Oya in 1988 (Map 4.3). Against a backdrop of increasing political tensions in the early 1980s, the Mahaweli Authority publicly announced that land in Manal Aru would be alienated and voluntarily settled by peasants. Then Minister for Lands and Mahaweli Development, Dissanayake, designated large tracts of the Manal Aru area 'priority sites' for System L 'settlement schemes' (Mahaweli Development Board 1979). Regime proponents at the time expected that settlement and resettlement interventions in System L would subscribe to the minimum principles and rules articulated in state planning documents and government declarations. Having funded the Mahaweli Authority, DIDR regime supporters demonstrated confidence in the state's 'decision-making' capacities.

The Official Settling of System L Considerable land in Manal Aru was occupied and privately owned prior to its formal annexation by the Mahaweli Authority in 1984. Predominantly Sri Lankan Tamil agriculturists and Muslim traders reportedly held multiple plots under long-term leases (Perera, N. 1985). For example, a range of agricultural corporations such as Navalar Farm, the Ceylon Theatres Farm, Railway Group Farm, Postmaster and Group Farm were presiding over a wide variety of cash-crops and subsistence cultivation.[23] According to anonymous informants residing in 'relocation villages' in Trincomalee district who were themselves internally displaced from Manal Aru in 1985, at least sixteen such farms presided over more than ten thousand acres of paddy during the 1970s. Many of these farm owners were issued ninety-nine-year leases following their arrival in the mid-1960s.[24]

Even before the 'official' launch of System L, a modest-sized Sinhalese settlement scheme was quietly established in Padaviya, a frontier town in the southern area of the proposed System (Map 4.2). As early as 1983, Padaviya included a heterogeneous mixture of Sinhalese residents relocated from neighbouring districts and some Sri Lankan and estate Tamils. Some of these early settlers included convicts previously released under 'special terms' by local government authorities from jails in southern districts.[25] Padaviya was not immune to armed violence, having experienced periodic clashes between earlier Sinhalese settlers and Tamils in 1978 and 1982.[26] By 1984 Padaviya also included Sinhalese settlers originally 'settled'

119

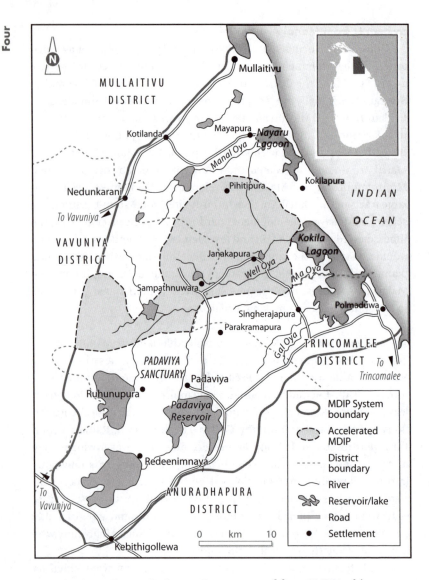

MAP 4.3 System L *Source*: Reconstructed from PMU Archives.

and subsequently 'resettled' from neighbouring Maduru Oya (System B), treated in more detail below. A review of Mahaweli Authority evaluations from the period suggests that the settler profile of the expanded Padaviya settlement scheme differed from analogous schemes elsewhere in the MDIP – with more designated 'non-farmer families' than 'farmer families', even as they failed to mention the presence of former convicts.

Procedurally, the acquisition and administration of land for System

L also differed from other MDIP Systems. In June 1984, a year after the outbreak of war, the Mahaweli Authority legally acquired land for System L under an extraordinary gazette notification. But the land was formally purchased and related activities 'officially' launched only four years later, in 1988.[27] To preempt international and domestic criticism, the Mahaweli Authority (1987) publicly stated that no official settlement or resettlement was taking place in System L from 1984 to 1987, though did not rule out the possibility that resources were channelled to the area in the interest of encouraging 'development'.

Immediately after the acquisition of land, administrative responsibilities were transferred to the government agent and district secretary in neighbouring Anuradhapura district (Map 4.3). The new Sinhalese settlers nevertheless remained on electoral lists in the Tamil-dominated Vavuniya district, rather than being transferred to (predominantly Sinhalese populated) Anuradhapura. Though retired civil servants from Mullaitivu conceded that large numbers of Sinhalese resettlers were displaced following attacks by the LTTE in late 1984, over 3,000 Sinhalese settler names remained on electoral lists – a significant number given the relative population sparseness in the area. Authorities in Colombo thereafter instructed the Assistant Commissioner of Elections in Mullaitivu and Vavuniya to regularly register the Sinhalese resettlers in L System.[28] The strategic imperatives were clear: to ensure a proportionately higher presence of Sinhalese in a potentially unstable part of the country.

The Mahaweli Authority suspended formal disbursement to System L but surreptitiously initiated settlement and resettlement between 1984 and 1987. Retired government agents interviewed in Trincomalee and Vavuniya districts[29] confirmed that the Mahaweli Authority and the Sri Lankan armed forces promoted the advanced alienation[30] during the intervening period (Mahaweli Authority 2006). Though the official population of settlers and resettlers appeared to remain comparatively stable, successive Mahaweli Authority monitoring missions revealed a tripling of the budget from R56 million in 1988 and over R150 million by 1993.[31] At a time when expenditures in all other MDIP Systems were falling, they rose dramatically between 1988 and 1993 in System L. Thus, by the end of 1988, over 3,200 new Sinhalese 'settler' families (estimated to include 14,890 individuals) were reportedly residing in System L, including the Padaviya scheme. From 1989 onwards, the MEA openly financed the 'development' of the area while the Mahaweli Engineering and Construction Agency (MECA) began building roads, electricity lines and homesteads and supporting 'self-reliant', 'productive' and 'viable' settler communities (Mahaweli Authority 1994).

System L exhibited a number of peculiar administrative anomalies that distinguished it from other Systems. For example, the number of registered clerical and agriculture extension-related personnel was proportionately lower than for other Systems. For a population of more than 3,000 households, System L featured no engineers or technical specialists, three engineering assistants and two typists, compared with proportionately higher numbers of such specialists in other schemes.[32] After the official (re)launch of the System in 1988, international regime proponents could not adequately explain how and to whom funds were being disbursed in System L; whether the 'settlement' achieved self-reliance; or why the Mahaweli Authority persisted with a development programme in areas of extremely high tension. In two cases, bilateral donors threatened to withdraw their funds entirely given the negative repercussions of 'failed settlement'.[33] By the late 1980s there were mounting concerns among domestic human rights activists that the Sri Lankan armed forces were de facto authorities of the 'settlement scheme', effectively curbing free movement of local populations.[34]

The 'unofficial' settling of System L The intensification of armed violence in mid-1983 required that the government adopt a cautious approach to settlement in the north and east. With mounting concerns in Colombo about an international and domestic backlash in response to strategic relocations to Manal Aru, among other places, 'official' development to the region was temporarily suspended. TULF-affiliated politicians and growing numbers of civil servants within the Mahaweli Authority were growing increasingly wary of the agency's impacts in System L. Moreover, unpublished assessments and interim reports prepared by the Mahaweli Authority (1984) in the aftermath of communal violence in Colombo in July warned of the likelihood of increased violence in Manal Aru (Karunatillake 1983b).

System L emerged as the site of unprecedented violence with far-reaching implications for the country as a whole. The warning signs were evident in parliamentary records and Mahaweli Authority assessments. For example, members of the National Christian Council raised their objections over resettlement in Parliament while the TULF, unable to officially express their views, strongly criticised the moves in other fora (Kearney 1987; 1985). A feasibility study commissioned by the Mahaweli Authority on land, irrigation facilities and settlement infrastructure in System L revealed a number of ominous trends: new Sri Lankan Tamil encroachers were reported and groups of young Sri Lankan Tamils 'from the north' were visiting the area to 'train' local youth.[35] There were also reports that Tamil encroachers were being paid substantial subsistence allowances by 'northern' Sri Lankan Tamils, while Sinhalese *chena* cultivators in Padaviya were alarmed over the appearance of *Eelam* flags in the area.

State-administered settlement in System L before, during and after 1983 deviated from the rule-based approach advocated by proponents of the nascent DIDR regime. The circumstances presented by the armed conflict undoubtedly accounted for some discrepancies. Beginning in late 1983 and under the aegis of emergency law, the Sri Lankan armed forces began to systematically clear Tamil populations from System L.[36] The Mahaweli Authority declared that the presence of Tamils in southern Mullaitivu was potentially 'illicit' and furthered 'anti-national' activities (Karunatillake 1983b). Despite the Mahaweli Authority's pledge to accord those evacuated first rights to new land, an estimated 13,000 Sri Lankan Tamil residents were displaced from forty-two villages and explicitly excluded from the settlement component of System L (Thangavelu 1998). According to a former government agent '64 traditional Tamil villages were displaced ... the occupants were given 24 or 48 hours [to leave]' (Government Agent 2005). Though overall numbers of internally displaced are impossible to verify, interviews with residents of Systems L in December 2003 confirm that (original) Tamil inhabitants were given between two and three days to 'vacate' their homes.

Awareness of developments in System L from late 1983 to 1988 was undoubtedly obscured by military escalations in other regions. Though media reports from Colombo and Tamil Nadu documented hundreds of extra-judicial killings and scenes of widespread conflict-induced internal displacement of both Sinhalese and Sri Lankan Tamils from the area, no official inquiry was ever conducted (*Frontline* 1985; *Saturday Review*, 2 December 1984). Nevertheless, as in other districts of the north and east, internal displacement was accompanied by severe restrictions on the mobility of the civilian population and a campaign of widespread harassment and executions of suspected LTTE cadres (Chapter 5). With the area declared an HSZ, official development of System L reportedly waned.[37] Few received compensation or new land in exchange for their properties, despite having lived in the area for at least a generation. The security situation in System L deteriorated precipitously in late 1984 as development-induced internal displacement gave way to conflict-induced internal displacement. In response to clearances initiated by the armed forces, between November and December 1984 the LTTE launched a series of counter-raids against the new Sinhalese settlers and resettlers occupying Kent and Dollar Farms. They also targeted Sinhalese settlers who had relocated to Kokila[38] and Nayarur, where the principal livelihood was fishing. Many of the newly displaced settlers from these two divisions were temporarily relocated to state-administered welfare centres in southern areas of Sri Lanka such as Negombo. Others were resettled to Pitipana division in Trincomalee, Gampaha division and the capital, Colombo.[39]

The reopening of System L System L was quietly reopened following the arrival of the IPKF in 1987. The Mahaweli Authority reported that the Manal Aru area (renamed Weli Oya in 1988) included 3,564 Sinhalese settler *families* presiding over 10,000 acres of coconut plantation. Despite considerable political unrest and violence, the population size reported in 1988 was virtually unchanged from the estimate rendered in 1983 (Mahaweli Authority 2004). Likewise, System L reportedly included a newly constructed North Central Province (NCP) canal and covered 100,000 acres, of which 6,200 were expected to be irrigable. While difficult to independently confirm, the actual amounts of land under cultivation, due to persistent security restrictions in the area, the estimates rendered by the Mahaweli Authority were considered by civil servant and armed forces personnel consulted to be gross exaggerations.

According to former government agents, public servants and even a Mahaweli Authority assessment of 1992, the reported agricultural activity and related infrastructure simply did not exist. In addition to official restrictions on direct funding from 1984 to 1987 which should have curbed agricultural productivity, the Mahaweli Authority had not actually commissioned the construction of new infrastructure or functioning irrigation canals in System L. Following short field visits, it appeared that the anticipated NCP Canal project was abandoned in the mid-1980s for technical and economic reasons, including limited water availability from the Polgolla Diversion.[40] Most water from Kokila Lagoon in fact came from Periya Aaru (renamed Ma Oya) and was impounded for the Padaviya scheme (Map 4.3).

The social infrastructure in System L during the 1980s and 1990s was similarly marginal. Mahaweli Authority monitoring reports revealed that public services and welfare benefits were 'virtually non-existent' contributing to lower-than-average health and educational conditions among settlers. The registered 3,564 settler *families* were apparently provided 'a couple of school buildings in a few settlements, one or two dispensaries, a few sub-post offices and a few co-operative retail shops' (ibid.). According to key informants in the area, settlers were forced to walk between 30 and 40 kilometres to access the nearest hospital or functioning clinic.[41]

Their long-term prospects were described by Mahaweli officials as 'dire': there were no facilities to promote transport, marketing, banking or credit boards in the project area (Ministry of Lands, Irrigation and Mahaweli Development 1991). The Mahaweli Authority (1994: 2) reported:

> The majority of the settler community are still without irrigable farms. Even those who have been provided with irrigable farms do not own alienated allotments for which ownership can be claimed ... it has to be mentioned that [civic amenities] are virtually non-existent.

The livelihood situation for the average settler deviated far from the 'integrated rural society with an acceptable standard of living' promised by the Mahaweli Authority and DIDR regime supporters.

Following its reopening in 1988, it was apparent that the reported numbers of settlers residing in System L was an exaggeration. Owing to the limited physical and social infrastructure and irrigation facilities in the area, retired government agents from the district commented that there were probably fewer 'settlers' than reported – including those included on Vavuniya electoral rolls.[42] Independent sources, including key informants formerly associated with the Mahaweli Authority, explained that the number of settler *families* likely could not have exceeded 400 in the mid-1980s.[43] Moreover, a Ministry of Lands, Irrigation and Mahaweli Development report (1991) reported a decline in settlers by 1990 such that 'the original number of settler *families* (3,564), which existed for a couple of years since the inception, has now been reduced to about 2,800 *individuals* [italics added]' – though it did not indicate how these numbers were determined or why the decline occurred. Indeed, a re-vised statistical assessment by the Mahaweli Authority (2004) reported that 2,035 settlers and resettlers in System L 'abandoned their land in 1999 due to insecurity' and indicated, confusingly, that fewer than 800 *families* remained.

The militarisation of System L Following the resumption of conflict in 1990, the Mahaweli Authority renewed investments in System L. In 1991, an Action Plan Committee composed of senior officials in the Mahaweli Authority and military authorities called for enhanced security of the settlers and resettlers through jungle clearances, strategic relocation of populations along key access roads and an expansion of overall 'development activities'. For its part, the Mahaweli Authority (Ministry of Lands, Irrigation and Mahaweli Development 1991: 10) recommended that settlers become more involved in their own security: '[t]he military personnel recommend that the area on either side of the road from

Padaviya to Kambiliyawewa be cleared of jungle with a view of settling people on the two sides'. These clearing operations were executed immediately so that 'security operations could be launched effectively' (ibid.: 11). The government justified these interventions as 'an interim measure to console the settlers, who are bravely holding a land of strategic importance' (Ministry of Lands, Irrigation and Mahaweli Development 1991: 18).[44]

By the early 1990s, it was clear that these new settlers were expected to shore up the military campaign against the LTTE. System L served to expand the aggregate and proportional Sinhalese presence in key northern and eastern districts. The settlement schemes themselves amounted to strategic buffers encircling army camps and demarcating 'cleared' territory from 'uncleared' areas controlled by the LTTE.[45] The spatial distribution and physical location of these resettlement schemes coincided with tactically vital areas. As M. H. Gunaratne (1998: 25–6) argued: '[e]stablishing Sinhala [sic] settlements, as it is being done in the Weli Oya basin ... is a desirable and strategic move'. Former (Sri Lankan Tamil) residents who periodically returned during lulls in the conflict to reclaim land were reportedly harassed and intimidated, in some cases killed and described posthumously in the press as 'terrorists'.[46]

The settlements increasingly appeared to form part of a deliberate state strategy of localised militarisation and counter-insurgency. Under the guidance of the newly constituted Joint Security Services Operation (JOSSOP), the Sri Lankan armed forces were effectively the sole administrative authority in System L throughout the mid-1980s and 1990s.[47] Sinhalese settlers by virtue of their geographic location were drawn into the armed conflict while the Mahaweli Authority sought to reduce (in theory) their dependency on the armed forces. Settler households were provided with extensive 'home-guard' training, assigned assault rifles and munitions and provided a daily stipend of R50–100. As early as 1985, paramilitary trainers and weapons were reportedly transported from Vavuniya to Padaviya.[48] The strategy of recruiting and arming civilians as territorial defence units was openly acknowledged and popularly advertised by Members of Parliament in the early 1980s (Thangarajah 2003; Seneratne 1997) and appeared to draw explicitly from the concept of people's war doctrine (Neff 2005).

Far from self-reliant, (re)settlers appeared more dependent on externally provided public services than ever. A Mahaweli Authority mission concluded in 1994 that: '[t]hese settlers in Weli Oya are badly in need of sources of revenue which could keep them on their lands ... Unless we create sources of revenue to meet their daily needs, it would be difficult to sustain ... where even basic facilities and needs are not available.' Rations and fresh produce were provided to settlers from outside the area, educational facilities remained under-serviced and only moderately functional and supplementary goods provided by Buddhist associations, such as Sarvodaya, on the condition that settlers and resettlers remained in the district. Organisations such as the All-Ceylon Buddhist Congress, Bhikku Peramuna and others also provided financial and material inputs.

By the mid-1990s, the Mahaweli Authority began to centralise services and facilities and moved to redouble population resettlement into System L. In addition to increased investment in building access roads, it resettled the Sinhalese fishing families relocated to the south seven years earlier back to Kokila Lagoon. Despite the deteriorating security environment and the failure to catalyse self-reliant resettlement schemes, the Mahaweli Authority recommended *expanding* the existing settlement (then alleged to number 2,800 settlers) almost fivefold to 12,650 settlers between 1995 to 2002 (Meemeduma 1994). The population reportedly grew to 19,000 individual settlers by 2001 before halving inexplicably in 2002 to approximately 10,750 and plummeting to less than 800 *families* as noted above (Mahaweli Authority 2006).

In the late 1990s there were some 25,000 infantry and home-guard militia occupying the border villages of System L. Field visits in 2003 and 2004 confirmed that the area remained intensely militarised and a major site of contestation between the army and the LTTE even before the resumption of outright hostilities in Trincomalee in 2005 (Introduction). By resuming official financial support in 1988, the Mahaweli Authority provided 'developmental cover' for advanced alienation and territorial consolidation by the military. A decade later, System L was described by representatives of the armed forces as 'very important militarily. Our presence will not allow the north-east merger. Terrorists cannot win *Eelam* as long as we stay here. If we go, there will be a threat to Padaviya, Kebigollewa and eventually Anuradhapura.'[49] Weli Oya therefore offered the paradigmatic model of settler militarism and paved the way for an approach replicated in Mannar, Wilpattu and Malwathu Oya in the western districts and Tantirimale, near Anuradhapura.

System B: resettling the right bank

System B was originally awarded a more prominent position than System L in both the Master Plan and the accelerated MDIP. Located in the fertile Maduru Oya (river) delta, System B spanned more than 125,000 acres and reached as far west as Polonnaruwa district and extended south and eastwards to Ampara and Batticaloa. In total it incorporated three districts and fifteen divisions (Map 4.4). According to the Master Plan, reservoir and canal developments in System B were intended to supplement the Maduru Oya and irrigate the equivalent of 115,000 acres of paddy land. They were also expected to provide the agricultural basis for a monumental transfer of settlers from the south.

Preparing for settlement The districts included in System B were characterised in early feasibility studies by a relatively high degree of ethnic heterogeneity but comparatively low population density. Prior to launch of the settlement component, foreign consultancy assessments described the area as 'sparsely populated' with just over 21,500 original residents – of which almost two-thirds (64.5 per cent) were Sinhalese, a quarter Tamil and less than 8 per cent Muslim (NEDECO 1979).[50] Fewer than 1,150 resident *families* were considered 'legitimate' or legally titled land-owners. Another 2,550 *families* were described as 'encroachers' and a further 210 as 'landless' *families*. All told, the existing population reportedly occupied less than 5,300 acres of land. While the authors of these feasibility studies anticipated that these people would be internally displaced by System B, they also expected, in line with the prescriptions of the emerging DIDR regime, that the oustees would be first in line for resettlement benefits regardless of their ethnicity or socio-economic status (Niyangoda 1979).[51]

The labels and categories introduced by the Mahaweli Authority ensured a skewed distribution of entitlements along ethnic lines. Ascribing spatial and demographic legibility to resettlement sites was an essential feature of resettlement planning for both MDIP planners and proponents of the DIDR regime. As noted in Chapter 1, the categories and labels introduced by Mahaweli Authority officials and regime supporters were inherently exclusionary. Specific 'beneficiary groups' (i.e. settlers) were defined according to pre-assigned categories of need: the label ascribed determined the relative benefit or entitlement. Many population groups potentially affected by the proposed creation of System B were excluded from initial feasibility studies and subsequent assistance packages. Estate Tamils, displaced from Nuwara Eliya by communal riots in the late 1970s and resettled in the Maduru Oya delta by divisional secretaries in Batticaloa, were not explicitly classified as beneficiaries in early preparatory assessments.[52] Rather than being identified as viable candidates for resettlement by the MDIP, they were described as *purana* village residents, colonialists, as residents of Vedda villages or more likely, new (illegal) encroachers to be evicted without compensation.

Before launching System B, the Mahaweli Authority identified at least

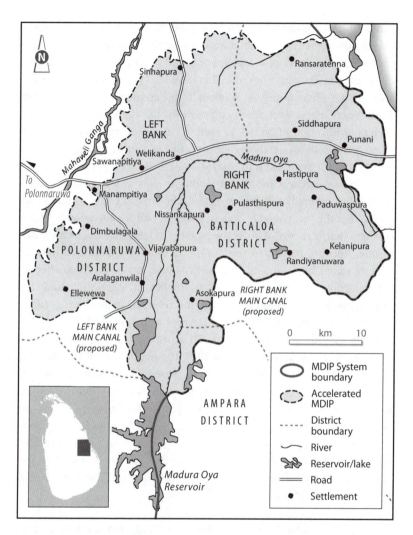

MAP 4.4 System B *Source*: Reconstructed from PMU Archives.

MAP 4.4 System B *Source*: Reconstructed from PMU Archives.

two pre-existing colonisation schemes in the Maduru Oya delta for 'special assistance'. These included 1,460 (Sinhalese) families settled in Pimburattewa (Polonnaruwa) from 1969 to 1976 and 126 (Sinhalese) families in Wadumunai (Batticaloa), initiated in 1952 (Chapter 3). The schemes included a total of 4,700 acres and were described in 1979 as suffering from deplorable conditions with fewer than half of all houses considered 'liveable' (NEDECO 1979). These and other pre-existing *purana* villages were confined largely to the Sinhalese-dominated Polonnaruwa district on the left bank of the Maduru Oya, though some also spanned the Sri

Lankan Tamil-dominated right bank.[53] Other smaller Sinhalese-populated colonisation schemes stretched from the south of Maduru Oya[54] into the predominantly Tamil and Muslim-dominated coastal areas of Ampara district.[55] A modest number of Vedda were also believed to have assimilated with Sinhalese and Sri Lankan Tamil communities, while estate Tamil encroachers were most common on the right bank. Areas with high concentration of Sinhalese received access to more benefits than those with proportionately higher densities of Tamils or Muslims.

MDIP settlement aspirations for System B were nothing short of breathtaking. Socio-economic feasibility studies and cadastral surveys undertaken immediately before the establishment of the System estimated that the 'net irrigable area suitable for paddy cultivation is 34,300 hectares [84,700 acres]. This is the amount of land that can be allocated in one [hectare] parcels to settlers ... the total of upland and lowland settlers would be 35,300 [87,300 acres]' (Acres 1980: 3). Thus, after accounting for certain geographical anomalies, it was anticipated that over 34,000 farmers could be settled and resettled in short order (ibid.: 4–5).[56] When dependants and non-farmers were added, the number of individuals rose dramatically. The CIDA-backed study confirmed that: 'as a result of the development [MDIP], the population of the area will increase tenfold, from about 25,000 to close to 250,000 in the next 10 years' (ibid.: 7). The consultancy firm speculated that this figure included all settler and resettler families, their dependants (estimated at four per family), the existing population and adjustments for population growth. The report also noted ominously that '[t]he influx of such a large number of people into relatively virgin territory over a brief period of time will require a planning effort commensurate with the size of this monumental migration' (ibid.).

Settling the left bank As in System L, the expected outcomes of an unprecedented increase resettlement in such a short period time were abundantly clear. Mahaweli Authority officials and nationalists in Colombo anticipated that the new 'settler' population would be predominantly Sinhalese.[57] The rapid population increase would dramatically alter the ethnic composition of districts in the Maduru Oya delta while leaving the ethnic configuration of Sinhalese-dominated districts inside and outside the System intact. The prospect of returning Sinhalese settlers to the area was in fact eagerly anticipated because of the symbolic resonance of 'returning' the region and its rightful people to their former glory (Chapter 3). Many ancient tanks, religious icons and ruins in Dimbulagala and Kandegama held tremendous historical and symbolic currency and figured prominently in the development and nation-building discourse of the era (Woost 1990, 1993; Tennekoon, S. 1988). That the settlement of System B would occur during a period of escalating tensions in the north and east only increased its appeal among certain parliamentarians and nationalists in Colombo.

A lingering concern related to whether the MDIP should begin on the right or the left bank (Acres 1979, 1980). Many within the Mahaweli Authority advocated the advanced alienation of the right bank owing to the apparent threat of Sri Lankan Tamil 'encroachers' who were also increasingly suspected of being aligned with northern Tamil militants. Nevertheless, the decision to ultimately begin construction and settlement on the left bank was supposedly rendered principally on technical grounds.[58] Those identified in earlier feasibility studies as prospective candidates for resettlement were accorded first priority for resettlement in line with stated DIDR regime and MDIP policy. For example, the Mahaweli Authority (1981: 8) reported that:

> [t]he available farms will be allocated to eligible farmer families who are already living in the project area under informal arrangements (this includes Youth settlement and Pol Colony schemes), persons who are displaced by the civil works under the construction of infrastructure programmes, or those who have been displaced by areas proclaimed wildlife reserves ... total capacity is 7,769 farmers.

As early as 1980, System B exhibited a real potential to incite ethnic violence by radically changing ethnic ratios at the district and divisional levels. MDIP plans were nevertheless readily endorsed and financed by stalwart DIDR regime proponents, particularly USAID and CIDA, but also Australia's Aid Department (AusAID) and other bilateral donors.[59] As sole executing agency, the Mahaweli Authority was responsible for developing both the left and right banks of System B. Dam-construction tenders for the left bank development were awarded between 1979 and 1980 and a number of key reservoirs and canals were completed by 1982 despite insufficient financing. While the actual building of infrastructure on the left bank began in 1980, downstream efforts were only partly completed by 1987 and then left idle.

Investment in System B proceeded despite reports of sectarian violence on both the left and right banks in the early 1980s. Construction on the left bank main and branch canal began in 1982. Some tentative building also began on the right bank, though as in System L, these were regarded as politically contentious by opposition parties. Facing budgetary shortfalls, in early 1983 the Sri Lankan government requested additional financial support from the World Bank. While certain DIDR regime proponents expressed reservations over the inflationary effects of rapid capital inflows, intensive lobbying by Dissanayake yielded a five-year loan from the World Bank.[60] What is more, a report of the subsequent World Bank mission (1984) proposed an implementation programme to enhance canal developing commencing in 1985, with CIDA and Saudi Arabia (Saudi Fund) also providing support. Other donors such as the EEC and Japan endorsed the World Bank strategy by providing supplementary funding later in the 1980s.[61] UNICEF (1984) and the WFP were also contracted to provide food assistance to (re)settlers.

The settlement strategy for the left bank entailed a rapid inflow of new settlers that voluntarily relocated to the area as well as intra-district resettlement. In contrast to MDIP Systems where three-quarters of the resettlement schemes were populated by resettlers from the affected area, System B experienced a sharp surge in 'assisted migration' facilitated by the Mahaweli Authority and others.[62] The large-scale relocation was publicly justified by certain parliamentarians on the basis of assessed population-to-land ratios in those districts that a 1981 national census revealed were sparsely populated. Any unease with evicting the estimated 3,900 Sri Lankan Tamil families[63] already living in Maduru Oya was offset by the promise of tremendous (Sinhalese) population expansion along both banks.

Settling the right bank The settlement aspirations for System B began to diverge fundamentally from those espoused by DIDR regime proponents from late 1983 onwards. According to retired civil servants from Batticaloa and Ampara districts, there was an almost manic compulsion among Colombo-based politicians to settle the right bank. The drive to rapidly relocate populations was motivated in large part by growing unease with Tamil encroachment and not a principled concern with protecting minorities or restoring the livelihoods of those forcibly evicted by the MDIP. Encroachments, which were observed from 1976–79, increased on both the left and right banks as news of the MDIP began to circulate. Such encroachments are a common feature of land-related investment and development projects. But elites in Colombo worried that such encroachment was motivated less by landlessness, opportunism or labour migration than with the strategic objectives of the LTTE to secure a homeland. Sinhalese politicians were convinced that such encroachments were goaded on by Tamil politicians affiliated with the TULF, militants and district-level bureaucrats. According to M. H. Gunaratne (1998: 60):

[o]rganised settlements around numerous small tanks were taking place in Maduru Oya. They were being made in a systematic and methodical manner. Food supplies were coming into the unauthorised settlers from an organised body ... Houses were coming up over night. Villages were being given Tamil names. District boundaries were being altered. The illegal Tamil settler was stabilising his holding on the Maduru Oya area with the active assistance of the administration from Batticaloa.[64]

While the Tamil encroachments were derided by Sinhalese nationalists and certain Buddhist clergy, the advanced alienation of the left and right banks by Sinhalese settlers was also considered a threat by Tamil interests.[65] Many of these so-called encroachers were estate Tamils who were previously internally displaced in the 1970s and not northern or eastern Sri Lankan Tamils. Their 'encroachment' was in fact resettlement that had been overseen by local authorities.[66] Despite protests lodged by sympathetic (Sinhalese) government agents and district secretaries against redisplacing estate Tamils through eviction, their discretionary powers were curtailed by the Mahaweli Authority. The Authority had already alienated land designated in the left and right banks of System B, thus stripping control over land issues from municipal authorities. As a result, most estate Tamils were ultimately evacuated from the area in 1982 and 1983.

Following their effective settlement on the left bank the advanced alienation of the right bank by Sinhalese settlers began in earnest. The process was symbolically led by a leading representative of the district's Buddhist clergy in August 1983 – a provocative gesture given the recent ethnic violence in Colombo a month earlier – and allegedly received covert financial and political backing from the Mahaweli Authority.[67] The violent encroachment by Sinhalese settlers in the Meerandavillu-Wadamunai, Mathanvansi-Mahaella and Punanai divisions led immediately to the widespread internal displacement of hundreds of remaining estate and Sri Lankan Tamils and Muslims and renewed concern about the potential for escalations of communal violence.[68] The Indian media, as well as local Sri Lankan Tamil officials and activists, described the settlement programme as an invasion or, more euphemistically, 'demographic aggression' (*Frontline* 1985).

The initial settlement of System B turned out to be more successful than even the most ardent (Sinhalese) nationalist planners could have anticipated. By the end of 1983, the number of Sinhalese settlers on the right bank swelled from several hundred to the tens of thousands. According to M. H. Gunaratne (1998: 49) a 'pioneer army was in the making'. Despite mounting international and domestic pressure to reduce the number of new settlers, the situation rapidly deteriorated. The Minister of Education and Youth Affairs, Ranil Wickremasinghe, was sent on a fact-finding mission by President Jayewardene to Maduru Oya in October 1983. His report indicated that some 40,000 Sinhalese settlers occupied the right bank.[69] As in System L, a combination of international and domestic pressure temporarily stalled the continuation of overall investment in System B.

Certain DIDR regime proponents acknowledged the way resettlement fuelled domestic tension. By the beginning of 1984 'official' construction and settlement on the right bank was described as 'delayed' in official government documents. As in the case of System L, however, it resumed following the arrival of the IPKF (Mahaweli Authority 1987). Construction and investment in the right bank was officially 'suspended' again in 1988 and 1989[70] as a result of pressure from the World Bank. By 1990, there were real concerns that the entire System might be forced to be prematurely terminated despite the importance attached to the programme by the Mahaweli Authority (1992: 2):

> System B right bank is the first area with significant settlement of ethnic minorities within the Accelerated Mahaweli Development Programme. The GOSL [Government of Sri Lanka] considers the speedy implementation of System B-RB [right bank] as a top priority.

As in System L, however, the development of viable and productive settlement schemes 'lagged behind considerably in System B' (Peiris, G. H. 1996: 185).

The militarisation of the new Sinhalese settlers in System B proceeded rapidly during the 1980s. Under the auspices of the Mahaweli Authority and the Sri Lankan armed forces, a thirty-member security unit was formed on the right bank. The security unit budget amounted to some R200,000 in 1983 and funds were released by the director general of the Mahaweli Authority.[71] As in System L, it was anticipated that selected settlers, including women and youth, would be made 'combat effective' and trained as home-guards. An elaborate communications and informant system was designed to ensure effective surveillance of insurgents (described as 'terrorists') and settlers were trained in the handling and use of assault rifles and basic strategic defence postures.

The advanced alienation of the right bank of System B and its subsequent militarisation eventually triggered an internal investigation. Parallel criminal investigations were also initiated as a result of accusations of illegal land acquisition in Maduru Oya and Yan Oya (System M). Following the appointment of a new District Minister for Polonnaruwa, considerable numbers of new settlement schemes were dismantled with the assistance of the Sri Lankan armed forces. Settlers were assembled in groups of between two and three hundred and resettled elsewhere, including System L. Though 'officially' exonerated by a presidential subcommittee on Maduru Oya, Director General Panditharatne of the Mahaweli Authority nevertheless resigned in late 1984. Although many Sinhalese settlers in Madura Oya were subsequently relocated from System B, the trend towards militarisation continued apace into the 1990s.

Conclusions

Settlement and resettlement constitute a process of spatial socialisation. In Sri Lanka, they contributed to what Yiftachel and Ghamem (2004: 652) describe as the 'Sinhalisation of contested space' and the reinforcement of state hegemony in non-state places. The creation of discrete Systems and the progressive addition of resettled populations into contested areas served to blur the boundaries between Sinhalese and Tamil settlements, bringing into sharp relief the competition for territory and strategic military advantage. Sri Lankan Tamil militants, including the LTTE, adopted equally conspicuous tactics to promote spatial reterritorialisation in areas under their control, but these were seldom described by outsiders as 'development programmes' or anything less than ethnic cleansing and terrorism.

Development-induced internal displacement and resettlement in System L and B constituted social engineering *par excellence*. It affected every dimension of the lives and livelihoods of those who were forcibly relocated. The MDIP as a whole was expected to enhance national agricultural productivity and increase hydro-electric power generation capacity. Widely lauded by donors, international agencies and the Sri Lankan government, it was shaped by the principles and norms of an emerging DIDR regime expressly to redress long-standing concerns associated with landlessness, over-population and the promotion of minority-sensitive development. Whether executed formally by the Mahaweli Authority or informally by the armed forces and the LTTE, relocation inevitably served purposes extending far beyond the durable solutions anticipated by DIDR regime supporters.

Some of the outcomes of the MDIP can be described in more positive terms. The engineering and physical infrastructural outcomes of the Accelerated MDIP are impressive, on a par with the hydrological initiatives launched 2,000 years earlier (Chapter 3). On paper, the settlement strategy also appeared to draw from progressive thinking in urban planning: it introduced an array of safety-nets and self-reliance strategies and seemed to resolve certain political concerns regarding the problem of the 'over-crowded' south (Peiris, G. H. 1996; Karunatillake 1983a). Moreover, the Mahaweli Authority adopted many of the core decision-making functions considered by donors and non-governmental agencies to be essential for the actualisation of the regime (Chapter 2).

But as the experiences of Systems L and B show, the planned settlement and resettlement strategy also serviced a set of instrumentalist ends. One explanation for the limited influence of the nascent DIDR regime is endogenous to the regime: its proponents were required to account for the sovereign interests of the Sri Lankan state. Agencies such as the UNDP, the World Bank, UNICEF and WFP were often reactive and lacked certain sensibilities with respect to the political dynamics of conflict that were then stirring in the country. The MDIP was underwritten and supported by international donors and development agencies – their mandates arguably circumscribed from interfering in what were ostensibly internal (political) affairs – at a time when Cold War tensions appeared to warrant Western support. But more than three decades after the first canal was constructed, the MDIP impoverished many whom it originally intended to assist.

It is inescapable that the principle of doing no (intentional) harm was side-stepped by proponents of the international DIDR regime in the case of Systems L and B. The MDIP served a set of geo-political interests, promised visibility and the enhancement of reputations, as well as considerable return on investment and a boon to foreign contractors – many of whom actively supported regime objectives. The programme fitted neatly into modernist ideology and mirrored analogous projects under way in other countries at the time. It is noteworthy that reports and evaluations commissioned by multilateral and bilateral donors and the Mahaweli Authority rarely alluded to the impoverishment effects, systemic violence, or CIDR that resulted until it was already clearly in place. While support was advanced on the principle of developing the country and stimulating agricultural productivity, the relative influence of the early DIDR regime should ultimately be measured as a function of words, deeds and outcomes.

5 | Resettlement during war: Trincomalee and Batticaloa

Internal displacement and resettlement of civilians in northern and eastern Sri Lanka is deeply interconnected to war and the consolidation of land. The short-term causes and consequences of displacement are actively documented by human rights activists and relief agencies, although comparatively less attention is devoted to the longer-term strategic imperatives of return or resettlement. Despite two decades of armed conflict and the government's creation of a Resettlement Authority to oversee protection and durable solutions, staple concepts such as 'return' and 'resettlement' are blurred and manipulated. Such confusion is especially problematic given the far-reaching implications of resettlement to all parties of the conflict, not least the internally displaced. This chapter finds that despite shifts in the rhetoric and bureaucratic approach to protection and durable solutions in Sri Lanka since the late 1980s, the shape and character of protection and durable solutions were heavily shaped by factors exogenous to the regime. Although international agencies such as UNHCR and the World Bank infused state policymaking and programming with core regime rules, they also indirectly bolstered containment and ethnic enclaves. Successive Sri Lankan governments, the armed forces, militia and non-state armed groups deliberately reordered the ethno-demographic landscape, thus revealing the limited purchase of the CIDR regime.

A host of spatial and social characteristics distinguish CIDR from other forms of forced migration in Sri Lanka. Armed conflict is geographically confined to specific northern and eastern districts such as Jaffna, Mannar, Kilinochchi, Vavuniya, Mullaitivu, Trincomalee, Batticaloa and Ampara.[1] As a result, Tamils and Muslims residing in rural and peri-urban areas of these districts are more likely to be affected by CIDR than the majority Sinhalese concentrated in the south and west. As noted in Chapter 3, the conflict is also frequently divided into discrete 'phases', from the 1970s until 1982; 1983 to 1987; 1990 to 1995; and 1996 to the signing of the CFA in late 2001. A comparatively virulent phase began in 2005 and has escalated dramatically since 2007. Temporal fluctuations in the severity of armed conflict influence the incidence and protractedness of cross-border and internal displacement.

Sri Lanka's conflict represents a kind of natural experiment for testing the influence of the CIDR regime in relation to state behaviour and resettlement outcomes. Since the mid-1980s, a combination of multilateral and bilateral donors and international non-governmental agencies played a central role in implanting the principles, norms and rules of the regime on state bureaucracy. Although Sri Lanka is not a signatory to the 1951 Refugee Convention or the 1967 Protocol, a number of agencies such as the UNHCR and the World Bank, together with public authorities, have promoted core tenets of the CIDR regime since the early 1990s. Regime proponents sought to provide 'flight alternatives' to would-be refugees to keep them from leaving the island. They also promoted rights to return and to remain. All the while, they encouraged state institutions to adopt the Guiding Principles which advocated protection and (voluntary) durable solutions and invested in 'welfare centres' and 'relocation villages'. In the wake of the CFA, CIDR regime proponents expected to further entrench regime aspirations through 'interim arrangements' in order to strengthen decision-making procedures and reduce collective action dilemmas.

The chapter finds that CIDR regime influence on state practice and resettlement outcomes were mixed. On the one hand, the regime appeared to partially contribute to a reduction in refugee outflows during the 1990s while simultaneously bolstering the government's rhetorical commitments to protect and pursue durable solutions for internally displaced people. Formal bureaucratic institutions including ministries, authorities and departments endorsed and operationalised a standardised approach to dealing with returning and resettling populations through the creation of guidelines and classifying groups into tidy categories of need. The formation of a national framework for return and resettlement backed by an agglomeration of (new) public entities since 2002 suggests that the CIDR regime achieved some of its stated ends.

Ultimately, the overall impacts of these interventions were muted by factors exogenous to the regime, notably ethnic nationalism and the strategic imperatives of the Sri Lankan state and the LTTE. While regime proponents advocated for more attention to protecting rights and needs, the latter conceived resettlement as a highly politicised form of spatial and ethnic segregation.[2] To paraphrase Clausewitz, resettlement was the continuation of war by other means. Despite their efforts to do no harm, the UNHCR and other international agencies unintentionally sanctioned forcible resettlement and return. This chapter reviews trends in CIDR from the late 1970s to the present. In examining discrepancies between the expectations and effects of internal displacement and resettlement *in situ*, it is possible to detect certain intrinsic limitations of the CIDR regime.

Contemporary CIDR trends

The incidence of conflict-induced internal displacement, return and resettlement predates the onset of armed conflict in Sri Lanka. Chapter 3 reviewed how earlier incidences of CIDR were linked to the radicalisation of nationalist Sinhalese and Sri Lankan Tamil factions in the wake of discriminatory language, education and land settlement policies of successive Sinhalese-dominated governments. Sri Lankan Tamil opposition groups became progressively radicalised in the face of settlement and resettlement schemes advanced by the Gal Oya Board and the Mahaweli Authority, the introduction of Sinhala as the official language of administration and the courts (1956), the special protections awarded to Buddhism[3] and the imposition of educational quotas on Tamils (Sri Lanka 1972, 1978). The LTTE emerged as the dominant extremist armed group supported as it was by RAW, the Tamil diaspora and an increasingly marginalised Tamil community in Sri Lanka. It is useful to recall that there were at least thirty separate guerrilla groups operating in northern Sri Lanka during the early 1980s of which the LTTE was the most brutal. The Sri Lankan government refers to all of them as 'terrorists'. From the 1980s to the present, the incidence of CIDR can be divided into three overlapping phases: a *refugee-producing* period (1983–present), an *internal displacement* period (1990–present) and a *return and resettlement period* (1995–present). Each of these phases is treated separately below.

The limitations of internal displacement data Before turning to the CIDR experience in Sri Lanka, it is important to review certain intrinsic methodological challenges when invoking longitudinal and spatial trends in forced migration. These can be attributed to the complex phenomenology of internal displacement and resettlement as well as institutional variation and even ambivalence in relation to labelling and data collection.[4] As noted in Chapter 1, displacement and resettlement are inherently fluid and dynamic concepts, and scholars and practitioners have long grappled with defining their beginning, middle and end. Conceptual dilemmas have in turn generated terminological confusion and problems with clarifying the referent. For example, the Sri Lankan media, public officials and non-governmental agencies describe the internally displaced alternately as 'refugees', 'internal refugees', 'IDPs', 'conflict migrants', 'returnees', 'settlers', 'inmates', 'relocatees' and 'others of concern'. These people live in 'refugee camps', 'relief centres', 'transit centres', 'welfare centres', 'relocation villages' and 'settlements'. As in the case of settlers and resettlers discussed in Chapter 4, conflict-affected populations are disaggregated alternately into 'individuals', 'families', 'households' and 'groups'. The registration of affected populations simultaneously as 'IDP families', 'returnee families' or 'individuals' by public and non-governmental authorities was common during the 1980s and 1990s. As a result, internally displaced people were alternately double- or under-counted and in some cases excluded from national and district-level registration exercises.

Owing to the intermittent physical access afforded to census enumerators in conflict-affected districts and the partial nature of national census surveys since 1981, it is difficult to verify or validate historical data on internal displacement, return or resettlement. There was no systematic state-led registration or reliable centralised census mechanism to monitor CIDR until the 2002 ceasefire. National censuses administered in 1971 and 1981 captured partial data on populations residing in violence-prone areas but subsequent surveys administered during the 1990s did not register even basic demographic information in the northern and eastern districts. Before and after the arrival of UNHCR in 1987, public entities such as the CGES and international agencies like WFP and UNICEF under-reported internal displacement by accounting only for those registering (self-selecting) for daily food rations.[5] Spontaneously settled displaced populations or those electing not to obtain state-issued benefits were excluded from registration exercises unless they reported to local land *kacheri* offices. Despite these gaps, CGES and related assessments periodically supplied aggregated data to the National Treasury and the General Auditor (Figure 5.1).

Throughout the 1980s and 1990s a variety of advocacy and non-governmental agencies issued annual reports on internal displacement trends in Sri Lanka. Data published by the USCR, Amnesty International and the IDP Database (renamed the Internal Displacement Monitoring Centre or IDMC) relied primarily on publicly supplied data, or on non-generalisable incident-reporting systems that collated information from community and faith-based organisations and media reports. By their very nature these approaches were biased, often under- and over-counting the incidence of displacement by an order of magnitude. Because they aggregated annual statistics they also tended to gloss over temporal fluctuations. Likewise, relief and development agencies such as Oxfam and Save the Children (SCF) administered cross-sectional surveys and focus groups in order to gather specific data on the socio-economic profile of displaced populations. These assessments are non-generalisable due to the lack of denominator data and also limited physical access, which distorted random sampling methods.[6] Although the UNHCR reported credible statistics on Sri Lankan refugees living in other countries, it was only in the late 1990s that public and non-governmental reporting

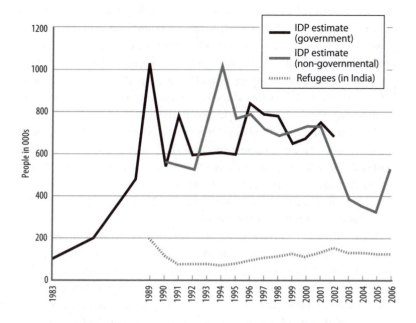

FIGURE 5.1   Estimating refugee and IDP trends (1983–2006)

Sources: Displacement statistics are drawn from a variety of public and non-governmental sources. Figure 5.1 above features published estimates of registered IDPs and refugees (in Tamil Nadu only) in December for each year available. Data sources include UNHCR (2000g, 2004d, 2005d, 2006a); USCR (1994-2004); and the Ministry of Development, Rehabilitation, Reconstruction of the East and Rural Housing Development (2001) and various confidential reports issued by the Ministry of Rehabilitation, Resettlement and Refugees and CGES since 1983.

and surveillance systems were capable of monitoring expulsions and returns within and between districts. Until UNHCR and the Ministry of Resettlement, Refugees and Rehabilitation launched a national IDP census (i.e. 'IDP profiling') in 2002, there was virtually no consensus on the numbers or profiles of people who had been displaced, returned, or resettled. Despite substantial improvements in national and district-level surveillance capacities since 2002, conceptual and semantic opacity continues to frustrate reliable accounting.

From refugee flows to internal displacement: 1983–87   A prolonged period of cross-border and internal displacement began in mid-1983. In late July that year, thirteen Sri Lankan soldiers were killed during an LTTE-led ambush in Jaffna. At their state funeral in Colombo, ethnic tensions exploded between Sinhalese and Sri Lankan Tamils and the government and armed forces showed little inclination to intervene. On the eve of district elections, internecine violence spread from Colombo to Ratnapura and Jaffna districts and throughout the rest of the country during what came to be known as 'black July'. In addition to the killing of several thousand Sri Lankan and estate Tamils another 15,000 were internally displaced from southern and central districts and spontaneously relocated to the central and northern areas such as Vavuniya and Mannar – though many would eventually return (Herring 2001). As the government prepared to counter a full-scale insurrection led by the LTTE, it also experienced the first glimmers of mass displacement.

International observers focused primarily on refugee movements during the initial stages of the armed conflict. Tens of thousands of primarily Sri Lankan Tamils initially fled across the Palk Straights separating north-western Sri Lanka from Tamil Nadu in India, though others sought asylum further afield. Between 1983 and 1985 an estimated 130,000 Sri Lankan Tamils sought de facto refugee status in India (UNHCR 1987a).[7] By 1987, despite acquiring only partial access to the camps, UNHCR (1987b) claimed that the total number of Sri Lankan refugees in Tamil Nadu state alone exceeded 210,000, reflecting the viscidities of the civil war. According to Kendle (1998), evidence also emerged at the time that India was forcibly repatriating Sri Lankan Tamil refugees to Sri Lanka despite repeated warnings from UNHCR that conditions were not conducive for (voluntary) return.

Though most civilians suffer during war, some suffer more than others. Sri Lankan Tamils with more extensive social networks and endowment sets sought asylum or resident visas in western Europe, North America and Australia. From 1983 onwards literally hundreds of thousands of Sri Lankan Tamils claimed *de jure* asylum in high-income countries. UNHCR (2000d, 2000e) reported at least 256,000 asylum claimants in western Europe alone by 1999.[8] Comparatively few ultimately returned home. While an estimated 75,000 refugees repatriated from India and other countries after the signing of the Indo-Sri Lankan Peace Accord and the arrival of the IPKF in 1987, most asylum claimants and refugees were reluctant to repatriate (Muggah 2007a; USCR 1991). Many Sri Lankan Tamil professionals and students living outside of the country simply elected to stay abroad whether as failed asylum claimants (illegal migrants) or residents of their adoptive state (McDowell 1996b).

Far from most international media headlines, internal displacement quietly expanded during the 1980s and early 1990s. Owing to considerable domestic interest in the Sri Lankan Tamil cause in Tamil Nadu, the Indian media scrutinised local developments. Early dispatches from the *Hindu* and other Indian media reported between 400,000 and 700,000 Sri Lankan Tamils and Muslims internally displaced by the end of the first Eelam war lasting from 1983 to 1987 (Gupte 1984; *Newsweek* 1983). Many of these people were reportedly living in what would later be described as 'protracted situations' – despite expectations that their circumstances were temporary (UNHCR 1994b, 1998a). Unlike in the case of refugees who were technically afforded international protection by the international refugee regime, the Sri Lankan state was expected to assume primary responsibility for caring for the victims of war, including internally displaced Sri Lankan Tamils and Muslims.

The provision of protection and durable solutions were not considered to be an overriding priority during the opening stages of the conflict. Indeed, the CIDR regime had still not emerged in any fundamental way in the 1980s. State-led responses to internal displacement focused instead on the provision of non-perishable food rations and temporary shelters, including hastily assembled 'transit centres'.[9] Restrictive policies introduced by the government such as pass systems sought to contain displaced Tamils as many were believed to harbour connections with the LTTE in their home villages. The government reinforced and expanded a series of national emergency measures that had been installed a decade earlier (Chapter 3).[10] Though the majority of internally displaced opted to spontaneously relocate and relied on existing social networks as a means of support, many of those registering for relief assistance were forcibly interned in 'welfare centres'.[11] These welfare centres were soon institutionalised by the state, with support from UNHCR and others. The centres served a dual function: providing temporary sanctuary to repatriating refugees while simultaneously offering safety for 'would be refugees' or internally displaced persons.

The government's policy of rapidly returning refugees together with internally displaced populations encountered obstacles from the beginning. The first challenge was how to encourage people to leave the welfare centres. By 1990, more than 700 such centres were operating in northern and eastern districts. Despite initially supporting their creation, proponents of the nascent CIDR regime were alarmed by their disconcerting proximity to garrison camps, army barracks and the LTTE's forward defence line (FDL).[12] As the centres became increasingly overcrowded and expensive to maintain, demand for return gave way to the pragmatic realities of resettlement. 'Relocation villages' were quietly launched as a durable solution from the early 1990s onwards.[13] Notwithstanding the escalating scale of internal displacement, Sri Lanka was still widely characterised as a refugee-producing country. Immediately before the signing of the CFA, Sri Lanka reported among the highest rates of cross-border and internal displacement in the world (UNHCR 2002a). In June 2001, UNHCR (2001c) registered approximately 817,000 'conflict-displaced' persons living abroad, most of who were considered *refugees* or *asylum seekers*.[14] Paradoxically, the overall numbers of refugees actively seeking asylum steadily declined during the latter 1990s while the number of people registering as internally displaced increased over the same period.

The IDP Crisis: 1990–present The dimensions of internal displacement intensified in the 1990s. The primary reason for the escalation can be traced to the collapse of the shaky Indo-Lankan Accord in 1989 and the resumption of armed conflict. Despite having technically 'invited' the Indian government to play a mediating role in brokering an end to the decade-old conflict, Sinhalese nationalists were intensely suspicious of their neighbour's hegemonic ambitions and the political formulation of the Accord. Certain politicians in Colombo were outraged by the role of Indian intelligence in providing training and tactical support to militant Sri Lankan Tamil organisations based in Indian refugee camps and the political autonomy granted by the Accord to Sri Lankan Tamils more generally.[15] In one of the supreme ironies of the decade-old conflict, elites within the Sri Lankan government together with the armed forces began covertly supplying the LTTE with arms to hasten the departure of some 100,000 Indian peace-keepers from Jaffna and the northern districts (Smith 2002; Seneratne 1997). Bolstered by an unprecedented victory over the better-equipped IPKF, the LTTE quickly resumed their insurgency.

The scale and distribution of internal displacement and resettlement in the 1990s expanded and contracted in direct proportion to the severity of the armed conflict. For example, following directives issued by the LTTE in October 1990, more than 100,000 Muslims were forcibly displaced from Jaffna and northern Mannar (Brun 2003; Refugee International 2000).[16] The LTTE claimed that Muslim communities were sympathetic to the armed forces and also saw in their expulsions a possibility to secure political and commercial advantages in their so-called homeland. Most displaced Muslims spontaneously relocated to the western districts of Puttalam, Anuradhapura and Kurunegala as well as Colombo (Hasbullah 1999).[17] Throughout this period the LTTE were increasingly preoccupied with 'clearing' the north and east of non-Tamils, including Muslims and Sinhalese who were suspected of being aligned

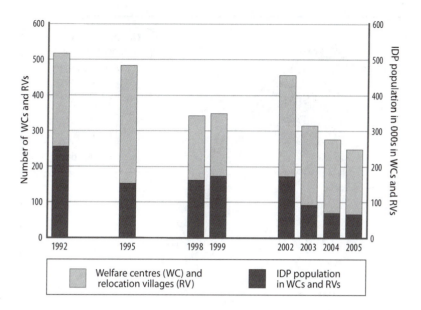

FIGURE 5.2 Welfare centres and relocation villages (1992–2005)
Sources: Return and resettlement statistics are drawn from a variety
of public and non-governmental sources. Figure 5.2 features published estimates of registered returnees and relocates in multiple
years. Owing to the difficulties among officials of distinguishing
between welfare centres and relocation villages, the data must be
treated as approximate. Data sources include UNHCR (2000g, 2004d,
2005d, 2006a); USCR (1994–2004); and the Ministry of Development, Rehabilitation, Reconstruction of the East and Rural Housing
Development (2001) and various unpublished reports issued by the
Ministry of Rehabilitation, Resettlement and Refugees and CGES
during the 1990s.

with the government or the armed forces. But while the LTTE pursued
these operations in so-called 'un-cleared' areas north of the declared
FDL, the armed forces also undertook strategic evacuations of Tamil
populations in areas under their control (Chapter 4).

The 1990s were notable for the quantitative and qualitative expansion of CIDR. Depending on the data source consulted, the number of
registered internally displaced people twice soared past the million mark
(Figure 5.1). CIDR was increasingly ethnically concentrated among Sri
Lankan Tamils and Muslims and geographically delimited to the north
and eastern districts to the extent that by 1996 over 50 per cent of the

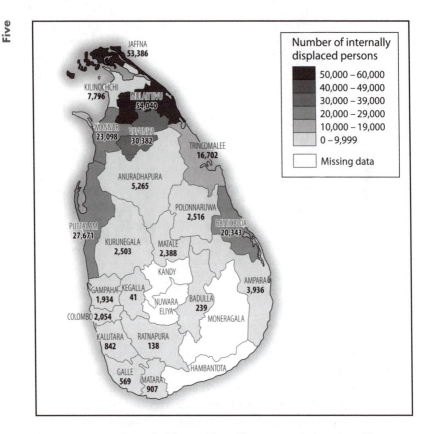

MAP 5.1 IDP households outside welfare centres/relocation villages (2005) *Source*: UNHCR database (Colombo).

total estimated population included in the North East Province were determined to have been displaced (UNHCR 2000g).[18] Owing to their geographic and strategic location, welfare centres and relocation villages also gradually came to occupy a new and purposive spatial boundary dividing the Sri Lankan Tamil-dominated north and east from the majority Sinhalese in the south and west.

The number and size of the welfare centres and relocation villages began to swell. Despite the issuance of guidelines from Colombo to liquidate welfare centres and reorient attention towards relocation and return, the incidence of displacement remained tenaciously stable. Faced with escalating recurrent costs and mounting social dysfunction within the welfare centres, UNHCR (1998b) eventually backed out from formally supporting them in 1998. Proponents of the CIDR regime continued to promote protection for the modest numbers of refugees trickling home even while quietly supporting relocation villages for internally displaced living in protracted situations. The situation did not improve. By 2000, there were between 600,000 and 800,000 internally displaced, including some 170,000 people who spontaneously fled or were forcibly evacuated before and after key battles in April 2000. Some populations spontaneously relocated only a short distance from their homes, while Muslims and Sinhalese living in the area moved further south in search of cooler ground (UNHCR 2001c).

Before the 2002 ceasefire, there were 'officially' 683,000 internally displaced persons, including more than 174,000 residing in 346 welfare centres and relocation villages (Figure 5.2). The persistently high incidence of internal displacement was attributed at the time to diminished support for new asylum claimants in third countries as well as improved registration procedures for accounting of new internally displaced populations.[19] Many representatives of donor and UN agencies and non-governmental organisations acknowledged at the time that official records probably omitted even more conflict-displaced persons including those not claiming rations, availing themselves of return or resettlement options, or living in the peri-urban and low-income areas surrounding Colombo (UNHCR 2002b).

Repatriation and resettlement: 2002–present CIDR regime supporters were optimistic that the peace afforded by the CFA would engender satisfactory conditions for durable solutions – particularly voluntary return (Chapter 3).[20] In particular, donors and UNHCR saw in the subsequent negotiations and interim arrangements an opportunity to leverage a decision-making mechanism to promote the protection and durable solutions for both repatriated refugees and internally displaced. Recognising that any sustained intervention would require acceptance or acquiescence on the part of the state, several subcommittees were created as part of the peace process in order to institutionalise a 'collaborative response'. These institutional mechanisms were supported by key proponents of the CIDR regime – including UNHCR, the World Bank, the ADB and the UNDP. But as predicted in Chapter 2, regime proponents considerably underestimated exogenous factors such as domestic political resistance on the ground and the military imperatives of the armed forces and LTTE. The splintering of the 'Karuna faction' from the LTTE in Trincomalee in 2004,[21] the assassination of the foreign minister in 2005 and increased violations of the ceasefire signalled a return to an undeclared conflict.

CIDR regime proponents recognised that their influence would be enhanced through the dissemination and codification of core principles

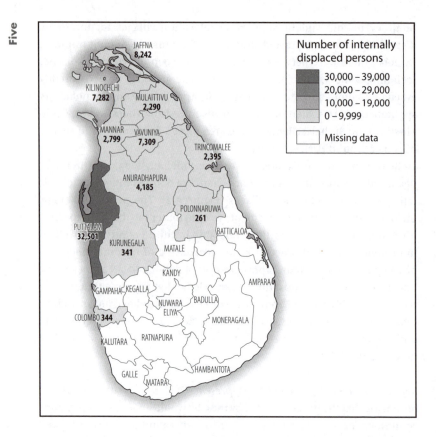

MAP 5.2 IDP households in welfare centres/relocation villages (2005)
Source: UNHCR database (Colombo).

and norms associated with preventive protection and durable solutions. A key focus, then, was on the establishment of effective decision-making structures and the generation and dissemination of information on prospects for return and resettlement (Chapter 2). Owing to the increased humanitarian space afforded by the ceasefire, they observed that it was possible to begin defining with precision the dimensions of the internal displacement and refugee caseloads. With support from the World Bank and the UNHCR, the newly established Ministry of Rehabilitation, Resettlement and Refugees launched an 'IDP survey' in mid-2002.

By the end of the year approximately 732,000 internally displaced persons were registered, of which an estimated 168,000 were residing in more than 300 welfare centres and relocation villages in the north and east. Shortly after, UNHCR alleged that the vast majority of the total IDP caseload rapidly (voluntarily) returned home or were living with 'friends and families' after spontaneously settling. Meanwhile, the Sri Lankan HRC observed that many properties were occupied by unauthorised secondary tenants and that (uncleared) minefields prevented durable settlement, raising a number of challenges for return (CPA 2003). A complementary census administered by WFP in 2002 focused exclusively on internally displaced receiving food rations and revealed that more than 250,000 individuals voluntarily 'returned' home immediately after the CFA, though it was unclear from either UNHCR or WFP demographers whether these respondents were also canvassed by the UNHCR-assisted survey.

While overall rates of refugee repatriation and return were lower than anticipated following the CFA, IDPs pursued their own durable solutions. UNHCR expected to facilitate the repatriation of more than 60,000 Sri Lankan refugees by the end of 2003 but fewer than 4,000 ultimately went home.[22] Meanwhile, the IDP census indicated that comparatively higher numbers of internally displaced populations were preparing to return home or settle elsewhere. Many had done precisely this without active support from CIDR regime proponents or the government. At the beginning of 2003, UNHCR registered a caseload of 447,000 'people of concern' – considerably lower than the estimates rendered in the 2002 census (UNHCR 2004b). By late 2003 a UN inter-agency working group on IDPs claimed that there were fewer than 332,000 'people of concern' remaining (UNHCR 2003c). Some observers close to the process disclosed privately that these estimates potentially reflected fewer than half of all internally displaced owing to the fact that many were in the process of returning or resettling when registration exercises were taking place. Nevertheless, by the end of 2003, 'rapid village assessments' undertaken by UNHCR and UNDP of more than 5,000 communities suggested that the caseload included 386,000 'people of concern' (including IDPs), observing at the time that many people still languished in welfare centres and relocation villages.

The tsunami in late 2004 vastly complicated the landscape in relation to conflict-induced internal displacement, return and resettlement (Chapter 6). According to Jayasinghe (2005: 9), there were approximately 496,000 conflict-displaced persons and 241 welfare centres in early 2005[23] and another 457,000 people displaced by the natural disaster. While it was never entirely clear how many previously conflict-affected populations were affected by the tsunami, concerns emerged early on about the importance of introducing a coherent strategy to avoid double-counting and ensure parity between both categories of displaced populations. There nevertheless manifested a 'clear disparity in the accommodation provided to conflict- and tsunami-displaced people, the package of relief they receive while displaced and the support they are given in order to return or resettle in another part of the country' (Amnesty International 2006).

Following the election of the SLFP–JVP coalition in 2005 and the increase in political violence, the incidence of both cross-border and internal displacement rose again. According to UNHCR protection officers in Colombo, approximately 350,000 individuals living in protracted situations in 2005 included as many as 19,000 *families* (between 76,000 and 152,000 individuals) confined to 256 welfare centres, though senior government and non-governmental officials could not validate these estimates.[24] Following severe clashes and reprisals between the armed forces and the LTTE in the interior of Trincomalee and Batticaloa districts in late 2005 and 2006, an additional 220,000 people were newly displaced, bringing the total to more than 570,000. Another 5,000 Sri Lankan Tamils simultaneously fled the north and east to India during 2006. In the absence of a national population census and in light of the continued disagreement over how internal displacement should be registered, the real incidence may never be known.

The policy and bureaucratic logic of CIDR

Over the past two decades an assortment of public, multilateral and non-governmental agencies has participated in promoting the principles, norms and rules and forging the basic decision-making architecture of a regime to protect and promote durable solutions for internally displaced populations. A burgeoning literature on the Sri Lankan forced migration experience emerged, much of it intensely critical of the cumbersome pace of international and domestic intervention. A notable exception is van Hear and Rajasigham-Senanayake (2006), who adopted a more favourable impression of the decision-making procedures promulgated by the nascent regime. The following section considers the bureaucratic logic of durable solutions as conceived by government entities, the armed forces and CIDR regime proponents such as donors, multilateral agencies and NGOs. It examines how the state's approach was informed as much by exogenous factors such as strategic advantage, political and electoral gains and ethnic ratios as by the rule-based approach espoused by regime supporters.

Public authorities The Sri Lankan government played a pivotal role in overseeing and managing durable solutions for the internally displaced during the two decades-long conflict. From the onset of mass displacement in the early 1980s, political actors and public authorities at the central and district level oversaw the direction, coordination, administration and monitoring of basic services, the distribution of rations and investment in return and more permanent resettlement options. Voluntary and dignified resettlement was actively promoted shortly after the arrival of UNHCR. This deliberate positioning of the (sovereign) state as a key decision-maker by regime proponents in regard to protection and durable solution was regarded as an essential means to overcome exogenous constraints to regime influence.

Approaches adopted by public entities in response to CIDR in the 1980s were qualitatively different from interventions launched in 1956, 1958, 1971 and 1977. This was partly due to the way internal displacement was conceptualised. It was previously characterised by state policymakers and planners as a *temporary* aberration amenable to short-term interventions. Bureaucratic responses were reactive, sporadic and decentralised. A rotating constellation of ministries, authorities and departments provided nominal non-perishable provisions or moderately expanded existing welfare services. The state relied heavily on faith-based associations, citizens' organisations and a small collection of non-governmental agencies to fill the gap (Vittachi 1980). A more proactive and forward-looking approach emerged in the wake of ethnic pogroms in mid-1983. The central government rapidly endowed the CGES with discretionary authority to operate autonomously from other line agencies. Large-scale relief operations were thereafter coordinated from the centre and partially decentralised through district, divisional and *grama niladari*-level authorities. These latter interventions drew consciously on principles of disaster relief, including established best practices in emergency assistance and shelter provision. For the first time, public authorities began consciously anticipating the consequence of large-scale return and resettlement on district and divisional ethnic ratios.

The first clear examples of CIDR regime influence in relation to state decision-making and bureaucratic orientation emerged shortly after the eruption of full-scale conflict. Between 1984 and 1986 a newly created Ministry of Rehabilitation established a rudimentary policy framework for responding to refugee repatriation and the return and resettlement of internally displaced people. This included the creation of a Rehabilitation of Persons and Property Authority (RPPA) to support the work of the Ministry.[25] With authorisation from the President's Office, the CGES oversaw relief logistics and certain durable solution functions in cooperation with district-level authorities. International donors such as USAID supplied consultants such as Fred Cuny[26] to work with Ministry and CGES officials in order to produce practical guidelines on protection and durable solutions in line with emerging international principles.[27] The

World Bank funded pilot projects to test the merits of low-cost housing and favourable loans for returning and resettling refugees and internally displaced households.[28]

The 'welfare centre' or IDP camp emerged during this period. Regarded at first as a second-generation 'transit centre', the welfare centre became an enduring legacy of the government's strategy to protect and promote durable solutions. Despite considerable effort on the part of district authorities and later UNHCR and NGOs, to stimulate self-reliance in welfare centres through the provision of grants and loans, dependency became entrenched during the 1980s. District-level officials claimed that restoring livelihoods and redressing impoverishment of affected populations 'would only succeed if people were made to stand on their own two feet' (Sri Lanka 1989). Unless they were made self-reliant, they argued, costs would rise indefinitely. Paradoxically, it was the military's policy of restricting movement – thereby constraining productive livelihoods – that contributed to prolonged dependency.[29] These early experiences with welfare centres instilled in local public officials a certain wariness of the ways in which protracted displacement could contribute to the degradation of cultural values and undermine durable solutions.

Successive government administrations introduced new initiatives to facilitate return and resettlement during the late 1980s and early 1990s. There were mounting concerns that if populations were not made to 'return', voluntarily, the government would be publicly discredited in the eyes of the world. In addition to demonstrating the peace dividend arising from the Indo-Lankan Accord, there were mounting concerns in Parliament that the central government could not fund welfare centres indefinitely. Led by the newly created Provincial Rehabilitation Ministry in 1987 an emergency reconciliation and rehabilitation programme (ERRP-1) was launched from 1988 to 1992 (Vamadevan 2007). With US$388 million provided by the World Bank and bilateral donors and support from the UNHCR, ERRP-1 introduced a unified assistance scheme (UAS) to supply dry rations and thus to encourage repatriated refugees and internally displaced households to locally integrate, return home or resettle elsewhere.[30] Despite the government's uneasiness with welfare centres, it nevertheless continued to support them together with area-based recovery programmes in the north and east.

Responsibilities for implementing return and resettlement were increasingly delegated to an expanding array of ministries and administrative and bureaucratic entities. By 1990, Lankaneson (2000: 3) counted 'more than ten institutions involved in human disaster management ... and most of them acted independently of each other resulting in fragmentation of the institutional framework and non-integration of projects'. Institutional fragmentation was aggravated by parallel decentralisation of governance functions to newly established (and deliberately underfunded) provincial councils and district and divisional level authorities following Constitutional amendments in 1987 (Aluwihare 2000).

Against a backdrop of renewed armed conflict and in order to consolidate the division of labour, a new Ministry of Rehabilitation and Social Welfare was created in 1991 followed by a Resettlement and Rehabilitation Authority and a Ministry for Resettlement, Rehabilitation and Refugees in 1996.[31] By the time a national policy framework for relief, rehabilitation and reconstruction (RRR) was created by the latter Ministry in 1999,[32] there were more than twenty-one different ministries, authorities and departments involved in promoting protection and durable solutions. Their impacts were comparatively meagre. UNHCR (2001c) concluded that after a decade, repatriations had not occurred in large number, return and resettlement was failing and that

> most welfare centres are overcrowded with little privacy, no appropriate cooking facilities for women, no traditional washing facilities, no available fuel for cooking, no choice in food purchases or supplies, no social activities for adults or children, nor any room to carry out activities, few religious outlets, education below standard and *poverty* is everywhere. (italics added)

CIDR regime partners such as multilateral and bilateral donors and UNHCR anticipated that a more robust framework for protection and durable solutions would emerge following the CFA. Indeed, peace negotiations sought to combine political representation between the state and the LTTE with enhanced district-level accountability. The ceasefire included provisions for the establishment of several interim arrangements to build mutual confidence. More important for the purposes of this chapter, these arrangements promoted incentives for return and resettlement. Specific arrangements included a subcommittee on immediate humanitarian and rehabilitation needs (SIHRN), a subcommittee on de-escalation and normalisation (SDN) and others focusing on political affairs and gender issues.[33] The SIHRN in particular prioritised 'activities aimed at [the] rehabilitation of internally displaced people ... and activities supporting the return of IDPs to their original homes and resettlement' thus providing a potential entry point in influencing approaches towards CIDR. The SDN also privileged resettlement as a core feature of the CFA, raising hopes that durable solutions for internally displaced were attainable.

SIHRN occupied a central position in the government's early post-ceasefire strategy. It was defined as 'a short-term mechanism for responding to the immediate needs of the population'. It was linked to the establishment of a broader and more contentious 'provisional administrative structure' demanded by the LTTE. SIHRN was to be funded by NERF, with membership from a combination of government and LTTE representatives as well as others from the Muslim community (Chapter 3). The Secretariat was physically based in the government agent office of Kilinochchi, a city that also served as the political and administrative capital of the LTTE. Because a provisional administrative structure was supposed to be established by separate agreement, the SIHRN lacked formal legal status. From the beginning, both NERF and the SIHRN came under pressure from extremist Sinhalese politicians including many in the JVP on account of its potential to politically legitimise the administrative and territorial authority of the LTTE.

The SDN was regarded by the armed forces as an intolerable concession to the LTTE, who they expected would use the arrangement as part of their campaign to win hearts and minds in the north and east. The SDN terms of reference also failed to explicitly account for HSZs in relation to return and resettlement, a major issue of contention between the LTTE and the armed forces. In order to mitigate these concerns, the government proposed that the armed forces craft an alternative strategy. The strategy, labeled the Fonseka Plan after the general of the armed forces, acknowledged that resettlement constituted 'the most important humanitarian need' but that it could yield a 'big political success to the LTTE' (Sri Lanka 2002b: Article 2). Moreover, the Fonseka Plan inextricably linked resettlement to a military strategy: 'resettling civilians in the HSZs would go hand in glove with a de-escalation process agreed by the GOSL and the LTTE' (ibid.: Article 3). Specifically, it required that resettlement be interwoven with the elimination of the long-range offensive capabilities and disarmament of the LTTE – understandably regarded as an unacceptable precondition by the latter (Satkunanathan and Rainford 2008: 39).[34] Predictably, neither the SDN nor the Fonseka Plan ever got off the ground.

The armed forces played a contradictory role in relation to the CIDR regime. On the one hand, the navy, air force and ground forces triggered considerable cross-border and internal displacement, return and resettlement before, during and after confrontations with the LTTE in the north and east. Welfare centres and relocation villages were frequently set up in close proximity to military bunkers and checkpoints. The armed forces thus came under international and domestic pressure from advocacy

coalitions, including proponents of the nascent regime, to protect populations in both cleared and uncleared areas during the 1980s and 1990s
(Gomez 2002; Cohen and Deng 1998b). At the same time, and partly in
response to such pressure but also in a bid to win hearts and minds, the
armed forces also occasionally provided a range of basic public services
such as water facilities, schooling and health clinics to support return
and resettlement in areas under its control. It supported comparable
services through the TRO – itself quite close to the LTTE – in so-called
un-cleared areas. Though the armed forces provided airlift and logistical
capacities for the CGES to promote assistance, its establishment of HSZs
undermined the CIDR regime in a number of specific ways.

The HSZs were spatial units set up by the armed forces in areas
they determined to represent a high risk of incursion or infiltration.
Initially designed to offer protection to soldiers from LTTE artillery in
Jaffna,[35] they were expanded to transport corridors, military encamp-
ments and entire villages throughout the north and east.[36] They also
frequently changed location and size owing to changing 'threat perceptions' (Pinto-Jayawardena 2006; Chandrasekharan 1993). In the process
of appropriating public land and tenements, the armed forces evicted
and evacuated residents, including recently relocated and returned households. Emergency legislation also facilitated the annexation of private
holdings in the interest of national security: permanent and temporary
land permits could be indefinitely suspended (Premaratne 2002). Thus
HSZs contributed directly to displacement and the dispossession of
property, contained populations through restrictions on mobility and
prevented individuals and households from returning or resettling.

The HSZs therefore created a visible and impermeable spatial boundary inhibiting durable solutions. Following the 2002 CFA, the armed forces
retained private land providing few clear options for original owners
to renew their permits or reclaim assets. Equitable compensation and
dispensation for appropriated assets and property was seldom issued
despite increased recourse to the courts.[37] In much the same way that
the presence of landmines and abandoned ordinance obstructed mobility, domestic investment or agricultural production, HSZs ensured that
population movement was kept to a minimum. The tensions between
HSZs and durable solutions were acknowledged at the time:

> [i]t is a fact that the return and resettlement of ... displaced people was
> invariably delayed by the existence of HSZs. Similarly, HSZ is a necessity
> if the [armed forces] were to perform their duty without hindrance.
> (Fernando 2006: 72)

But as signalled by Brun (2003: 386), 'the armed forces ... justified the need for HSZs ... on the basis of security until a permanent [political] settlement is reached' – a prospect as distant in 2008 as during the 1980s or 1990s.

There are signs that the CIDR regime may be exerting more influence in shaping national bureaucratic responses towards achieving meaningful protection and durable solutions. A Resettlement Authority was created to promote protection and durable solutions in early 2007. At the insistence of CIDR regime proponents and in the wake of several decades of experimentation, Parliament approved the creation of a centralised decision-making mechanism (Sri Lanka 2006a, 2007). The primary objectives of the new authority are to

> [e]nsure resettlement or relocation in a safe and dignified manner of internally displaced persons and refugees; facilitate the resettlement or relocation of the internally displaced persons and refugees in order to rehabilitate and assist them by facilitating their entry into the development process; facilitate the restoration of basic human rights including cultural rights to empower [them] ... to find solutions ... [and] to promote livelihood activities. (Sri Lanka 2007: 4–6)

The authority is mandated with the 'power to acquire and hold, take or lease and hire, mortgage, sell or otherwise dispose of immovable property', as well as to clear and redevelop land and enter into agreements with all government departments, local authorities and relevant public and private institutions to enable protection and durable solutions (ibid.: 7). The development of an authority tentatively satisfies the basic aspirations of CIDR regime proponents. Although some scepticism of the intent and capacity of the authority to discharge its functions persists, it represents a potential watershed.

UN agencies, non-governmental organisations and donors A constellation of UN agencies, multilateral and bilateral donors and NGOs encouraged the state to take on proactive activities on behalf of the internally displaced during the late 1980s and 1990s. Many of them launched parallel interventions to this end, recognising that Sri Lanka was not a signatory to key international legal instruments (Chapter 3). Depending on their size and the context in which they operated, these agencies exerted varying degrees of leverage on state policy and practice. Their capacity to influence change was not without precedent. Indeed, liberalisation processes under way in Sri Lanka throughout the 1970s fuelled a considerable expansion of aid in the country. According to Bastian (2006a), the World

Bank, the ADB and the International Monetary Fund (IMF) accounted for approximately three-quarters of total foreign aid by the mid-1980s, though dozens of NGOs were also present. During this period Sri Lanka received among the highest per capita levels of multilateral and bilateral aid in the world.

The normative and operational scope and influence of the emerging CIDR regime on Sri Lankan state institutions evolved in parallel with the growth of overseas assistance as well as other ongoing activities promoted by regime proponents. For example, during the 1990s the so-called Brookings Process played an important role in coalescing and normalising relevant principles, norms and rules among senior Sri Lankan authorities through repeated visits by the UN Special Representative Francis Deng (Chapter 2). Beginning in the mid-1990s, he called for domestic codification and diffusion of the Guiding Principles and encouraged UN agencies in Sri Lanka to examine ways of operationalising them (WFP 1999; Kunder and Nylund 1998). Outside of Sri Lanka, public policy networks supported various petitions at the UN Commission on Human Rights during the 1990s (Gomez 1996, 2002). Likewise, violations of CIDR regime principles and non-compliance with emerging rules were more regularly reported to the Sri Lankan HRC established in 1997.[38]

UNHCR UNHCR assumed a 'lead agency' role in promoting protection and durable solutions in Sri Lanka.[39] Following an exchange of letters, the Sri Lankan Ministry of Foreign Affairs and UNHCR established a memorandum of agreement in mid-1987 in order to provide 'assistance in the rehabilitation of returnees and displaced persons'. Though aspects of the agency's protection mandate were challenged at the time by Sinhalese nationalists, UNHCR nevertheless established small offices in Colombo and Mannar (UNHCR 1987a).[40] In keeping with the strictures of the refugee regime, UNHCR initially focused on crafting enabling legislation and incentives to facilitate refugee repatriation and return.[41] A special programme of limited assistance to returnees was rapidly implemented between 1987 and 1990 with the objective of speeding up their repatriation (UNHCR 2002b).[42]

A shift towards 'in-country' or 'preventive' protection was catalysed by the changing priorities of both India and the refugee regime (Kendle 1998; UNHCR 1998b). Anticipating a renewed surge in refugee movements out of Sri Lanka with the departure of the IPKF in 1990, certain countries encouraged UNHCR to adopt a more proactive role to prevent 'would-be refugees' from leaving the country. Following a series of oral requests from India in August of that year, UNHCR began actively exploring the possibility of channelling assistance to internally displaced Sri Lankan Tamils 'to which India could contribute, in order to provide them with an alternative to fleeing abroad' (UNHCR 1990b).[43] Likewise, with Sri Lankan refugees reluctant to return from India, subsequent amendments to the original memorandum of agreement in 1993 recognised that '*principles* established for assistance and protection of [refugee] returnees will apply to displaced persons wherever they live together with returnees'.

In the absence of a comparable precedent, UNHCR protection officers in Geneva were initially concerned that they lacked a clear normative basis for supporting the internally displaced in Sri Lanka. Specifically, UNHCR was unsure whether there was a legal basis to assist and protect them, the extent to which Sri Lankan returnees (both refugees and internally displaced) should be assisted once they returned or resettled and whether the agency should be undertaking activities in a country of origin aimed at reducing the flow of asylum-seekers at all.[44] Despite ultimately investing in protection and durable solutions for both refugees and internally displaced people, these concerns lingered in headquarters for the next two decades.

The resumption of armed conflict in the 1990s forced CIDR regime proponents, including UNHCR, to rethink durable solutions. During the early 1990s UNHCR found itself, for the first time in its history, with a physical presence in a country experiencing a mass exodus and a mass return of both refugees and the internally displaced. Coupled with increasing constraints to accessing refugee camps in Tamil Nadu and low levels of returnees, the agency resolved to orient its policies and programmes towards would-be refugees. This was not as radical as it may seem: advocacy coalitions and public policy networks were adamant that refugees and internally displaced people shared common vulnerabilities and required comparable forms of protection (Chapter 2).[45] At the urging of both Indian and Western diplomats, the Sri Lankan government formally requested UNHCR to provide 'assistance to displaced people on both sides of the FDL' (UNHCR 2002b).

With the blessing of the UN General Assembly and at the request of the Sri Lankan government, UNHCR's adoption of an IDP mandate generated several precedents that would shape international approaches to protection and durable solutions. For example, UNHCR's Sri Lanka operations were the first to receive formal designation from the Secretary General (in 1991) to undertake protection and durable solutions explicitly on behalf of internally displaced populations. As part of this mandate, UNHCR and its implementing partners actively promoted the Guiding Principles on Internal Displacement. Sri Lanka was thus the first country in which the Principles were consciously disseminated and applied (Geissler 1999). Although the Principles were not formally codified into national legislation, they featured prominently in soft law and related policy instruments.[46] But despite the active participation of the Sri Lankan government and the agency's expansion into districts with high concentrations of refugee returns and internal displacement, obstacles surfaced. Notably, the government requested that UNHCR not focus extensively on eastern districts and concentrate instead on ostensibly 'humanitarian' (as opposed to protection-oriented) activities in the north.[47] This push-back signalled the opposition of the government to certain key aspirations of the CIDR regime – notably impartial support for *all* internally displaced populations.

For the first time UNHCR assisted the state to implement programmes and projects purposefully designed to regulate the movement of internally displaced people and to facilitate durable solutions. Examples of specific innovations included 'open relief centres' (ORC) introduced to facilitate the return of refugees from Indian refugee camps to Sri Lanka and the movement of prospective asylum claimants out of Sri Lanka.[48] UNHCR supported two large ORCs in Madhu (Mannar district) and Pessalai (Mannar Island) with six more sub-ORCs eventually established in northern and eastern districts.[49] From 1987 to 1989 alone, ORCs reportedly processed the controlled departure and repatriation of 43,000 refugees and sheltered tens of thousands of internally displaced people (Clarence 2001; Seneviratne and Stavropoulou 1998). Though sharply criticised as a 'damage limitation' exercise and a surreptitious means of broadening its mandate, UNHCR, together with the armed forces and the LTTE, supported ORCs despite occasional breaches (Simmance 1991). A small number of former UNHCR officials nevertheless insisted that ORCs constituted an effort to contain refugee flows and protect the interests of India and the Sri Lankan government rather than those fleeing (Kendle 1998) and UNHCR ended its support in mid-1997.[50] Even so, ORCs were widely praised as an exercise in standard-setting (van Hear and Rajasingham-Senanayake 2006; Hyndman 2003).

UNHCR also moved towards enhancing durable solutions by reinforcing state institutions from the central to the local level. In order to bolster municipal planning capacities, the agency established 'district-level review boards' chaired by government agents. These boards were made responsible for identifying and implementing so-called quick impact projects (QIP) and a wide array of functions associated with promoting the fundamental rights of internally displaced populations. As noted in Chapter 1, these interventions were expected to enhance the capacity of areas of return and resettlement to absorb newcomers. UNHCR also established so-called return and resettlement committees in certain districts such as Jaffna and Vavuniya in order to promote relocation to the north and east (OCHA 2000). The UNHCR (1996b: 1) country plan for 1997–99 confirmed that the agency's 'main involvement in Sri Lanka is at present in the context of internally displaced persons'. By 1997, the UN Secretary General's office reaffirmed the UNHCR's mandate so that it could 'continue to coordinate the UN effort for humanitarian and relief assistance for internally displaced persons in Sri Lanka' (Schack 2000).

Multilateral agencies and bilateral donors actively supported core CIDR regime functions during the 1990s. UNDP, WFP, UNICEF and the ICRC in particular invested alternately in protection and durable solutions. The UNDP supported area-based programmes to enhance the absorptive capacity for return or resettlement through QIPs, 'micro-projects' and targeted assistance. The WFP continued its support (initiated in the 1980s) through supplementing CGES-led provision of food rations to welfare centres and significantly expanded its activities in the 1990s. Agencies within the non-governmental sector – including Oxfam, Care, SCF and Zoa Refugee Care[51] – all served at one time or another as implementing partners with UNHCR to promote return and resettlement. Other national NGOs and community-based groups acted independently of, or under contract with, the state, UN and bilateral donors, including national organisations such as Sarvodaya and Sewa Lanka Foundation. As highlighted in Chapter 2, however, the decentralised 'decision-making' apparatus of the CIDR regime is also its Achilles' heel.

A key objective of the CIDR regime is to influence the state to undertake protection and durable solutions in a predictable and effective fashion and in line with key norms and rules. An expectation is that states will adopt agreed 'decision-making procedures' in order to operationalise these norms and rules and ultimately to reduce informational asymmetries and transaction costs. The strategy pursued by UN agencies aimed to shore up state capacities while NGOs frequently adopted more adversarial positions. But not unlike the principle–agent problems arising from extreme decentralisation of responsibilities within government bureaucracy, UN agencies and NGOs frequently disagreed on how to enhance the state's capacity to fulfil its obligations.

To encourage a clear policy framework for protection and durable solutions, the UN helped instal a national framework for RRR in 1999 and a 'relief and rehabilitation thematic group' (RRTG) in 2000 chaired by the UN Resident Representative. The SIHRN and SDN installed in the wake of the ceasefire eventually supplemented these mechanisms even if elements of the RRTG remained. By way of contrast, NGOs rarely invested in supporting state capacity per se, but rather promoted inter-agency coherence through the creation of federated networks such as the Colombo-based Consortium of Humanitarian Agencies (CHA), an umbrella group set up in 1996 and devoted to information sharing and coordination.[52] Bilateral donors alternated between providing direct budgetary support to the state, supporting multilateral programmes and investing in NGOs. Countries such as Australia, Canada, Germany, Japan, the Netherlands, Norway, Switzerland, the United Kingdom and the United States expected that these approaches would allow for the monitoring of state compliance with the basic norms and rules set out in the regime.

The World Bank and the ADB The World Bank and the ADB were im-portant supporters of the CIDR regime and its aspirations from the beginning. Although commonly associated with the DIDR regime, inter-national financial institutions played an instrumental role in shaping the conceptual and programmatic foundation of durable solutions for conflict-affected populations in Sri Lanka. They exhibited potential to leverage basic norms and rules. Both agencies were engaged in pro-moting pro-market and liberalisation reforms in the 1970s and as the largest contributors of multilateral development assistance, they played an important role in orienting the recovery agenda throughout the war. In addition to supporting the CGES in the 1980s, the World Bank issued a US$100 million grant to the Sri Lankan government in 1999 for several inter-related projects designed to promote durable solutions (Vamadevan 2007).

Three of these projects formed a central plank of the implementation of the CIDR regime. The *first* was the North East Irrigated Agriculture Project (NEIP) launched in 1999. It consisted of a five-year US$32 million scheme designed to absorb conflict-displaced persons back to their origi-nal homes (UNHCR 2000f).[53] The *second* was a US$20 million North East Emergency Rehabilitation Project (NEERP) that focused on rebuilding critical infrastructure in areas affected by war.[54] A *third* was the creation of a North East Community Restoration and Development (NECORD) project to enhance the UAS (managed by the CGES).[55] All three projects were renewed on several occasions. The World Bank simultaneously established agreements with UNHCR to monitor its programmes in areas of return and resettlement so as to promote durable solutions in the north and east. Indeed, such collaboration was implicitly encouraged by public policy networks as anticipated in Chapter 2.[56]

CIDR regime proponents and state planners envisioned the UAS as a central pillar of achieving durable solutions, including resettlement. It included 'transitional livelihood assistance' designed to smooth incomes of returning and resettling populations. In theory, the UAS was seamlessly coordinated and implemented by the state and municipal authorities, financed by the World Bank and monitored by UNHCR. Funds were transferred directly to the Treasury by the World Bank and then on to the North East Provincial Council,[57] government agents and divisional secretaries and ultimately beneficiaries. A list of eligible returnees or resettlers was supposed to be provided to district authorities by so-called village rehabilitation committees (VRC), vetted by divisional secretaries and ultimately sent to district NECORD offices for payment directly into personal bank and post-office accounts.

A combination of food rations and housing grants was introduced amid great fanfare though funds were depleted relatively soon after the programme was launched. In practice, the administrative and eligibility requirements for the UAS grants were complex. The UAS consisted of a series of purpose-driven grants intended to support displaced populations to build *permanent* accommodation, establish productive enterprises, as well as compensate, in the case of (former) public servants and their dependants, for deaths, injuries and lost assets. The UAS was administered in combination with 'community-based assistance activities' (overseen by VRCs) (Jayasinghe 2005: 12).

From the beginning, the UAS engendered certain spatial and temporal biases. The UAS inevitably restricted mobility because it strongly encouraged permanent resettlement to original districts in government-controlled areas.[58] For example, access to UAS benefits required a bank account and a fixed address and many prospective beneficiaries could and would not open an account or had lost their property deeds. Only those who successfully registered with district-level authorities and were *returning* to their original homes or resettling *within* their original districts were entitled to benefits. Thus spontaneous settlers, welfare centre residents living outside of their original district and displaced populations with legitimate fears of reporting their status were excluded. What is more, upon fulfilling these minimum requirements, only those residing in state-controlled or 'cleared' areas were entitled to phased support. Disbursements ranged between US$250–1,500 depending on household size and social and economic status[59] and were capped at fifteen months of dry rations or an equivalent subsidy.[60]

The World Bank and UNHCR encouraged return and resettlement from the mid-1990s onwards, including support for relocation villages. Both agencies saw in the relocation village model an opportunity to liquidate welfare centres and advance real durable solutions. UNHCR (2002b: 10), in particular, was adamant that any durable solution be

> voluntary, dignified and carried out with the full knowledge and participation of IDPs, including in the design of their new homes. The process of resettlement (whereby IDPs return to their place of origin) and relocation (whereby they are moved from welfare centres to temporary or permanent sites where they can live safely and resume productive activities) is currently underway ... UNHCR's efforts to establish safe and well-provisioned relocation villages have made a significant positive impact, and meant that IDPs are consulted and involved in village planning.

The WFP (2001: 6), for its part, endorsed this view, acknowledging that:

> [w]ith recent government policies that promote resettlement/relocation, there are now further opportunities to establish more durable solutions that will enhance self-reliance ... [the WFP recommends] closer collaboration with partners to provide a more comprehensive package of assistance and encourage resettlement/relocation efforts.

UNHCR observed that together with the UAS, resettlement (or relocation) could be supported by 'reinforcing the protection available to the residents and affording privacy while simultaneously fostering a community feeling in the new villages' (UNHCR 2002b: 10). Moreover, UNHCR (ibid.: 11), together with the World Bank and ADB, played 'a valuable role in building local acceptance of the relocation villages through its efforts to ensure that these also bring tangible assets, such as access roads and wells, which the local population can share' arguing that the 'value of this goodwill should not be underestimated in a context where regular development activities have been severely curtailed'. A UNHCR (ibid.: 20) review concluded that:

> UNHCR should also continue and redouble its efforts to encourage the Ministry of the East to implement similar, voluntary relocation and resettlement initiatives in areas it administers. UNHCR should use its good relationships with local Government Agents as an opportunity to raise awareness and inform them of good practice in other areas.

CIDR regime proponents began to regard their approach to protection and durable solutions in Sri Lanka as an emerging gold standard (Muggah 2007a; UNHCR 2004c). UNHCR and other UN agencies reported that the material conditions and services of welfare centres and relocation villages in the 1990s while 'poor' were substantially improved before being 'handed-over' (Fardanesh and Walker 2002). The World Bank and the ADB continued to invest in the NECORD-sponsored UAS scheme well into the post-CFA period. UNHCR gradually transferred its programmes relating to durable solutions to line Ministries, municipal authorities and other UN agencies. The establishment of the Ministry of Rehabilitation, Resettlement and Refugees,[61] the Ministry of the North, the Urban Development Authority (UDA) and other public entities with UNHCR support appeared to signal the government's commitment to returning and the 'relocation of IDPs [from welfare centres] to relocation or resettlement villages'. By 2002, the Sri Lankan government claimed to have supported the development, diffusion and 'improvement' of welfare centres and relocation villages and contributed to durable solutions (Sri Lanka 2002a, 2003b).

On closer inspection these efforts to promote protection and durable solutions frequently deviated from the expectations of regime proponents. Contrary to the public pronunciations of UNHCR and the Sri Lankan government, conditions in welfare centres and relocation villages were widely regarded as deplorable. Fardanesh and Walker (2002), for example, described a host of social pathologies including 'dependence, learned helplessness, feelings of hopelessness, loss of self-esteem and breakdown of social norms'. Symptoms of this – alcoholism, drug abuse, depression, suicide and crime – were on the rise. Visitors to welfare centres and relocation villages found that reports of sexual exploitation, lower than average school attendance rates, reductions in income-earning activities and increases in feelings of worthlessness and lack of dignity were distressingly common.

In order to highlight the outcomes of CIDR regime efforts on resettled populations, we now turn to several 'relocation villages' established in Trincomalee and Batticaloa. As the proposed capital of an independent Eelam and the administrative nerve centre of the North and Eastern Province, Trincomalee was long a site of considerable instability. Batticaloa, a traditional base for eastern factions of the LTTE, also constitutes a site of bitter contestation. The lived experiences of households resettled into state-supported relocation villages are briefly considered in both districts.

The case of Cod Bay in Trincomalee

Trincomalee district is divided into eleven divisional secretary divisions and includes approximately 437 villages. Due to demographic changes discussed in Chapter 3, the district's estimated 340,000 residents exhibit an unusual ethnic distribution when compared to others.[62] A population census undertaken in 1871 ranked the Sri Lankan Tamil and Muslim populations as majority communities in Trincomalee. Less than 5 per cent of the overall population consisted of Sinhalese and Burghers. The next hundred years witnessed a dramatic transformation. By 1981, the ethnic ratios were divided equally into 36 per cent Tamil, 33 per cent Sinhalese and 29 per cent Muslim. The district-level population also increased at a faster pace than the national growth rate in the post-independence period. Since the 1981 census, Muslim and Sinhalese populations now reportedly outnumber all Tamils who are in any case unevenly represented in national population registration exercises.[63]

The early increase in Sinhalese population is commonly attributed to labour migration in the wake of the Second World War and colonisation and resettlement programmes initiated in the post-independence period (Chapter 4). A former government agent for Trincomalee observed that 'state-aided colonisation schemes were designed to shift the demography ... it was the principal aim of the government at the time to colonise [Sri Lankan] Tamil and Muslim areas'.[64] By contrast, contemporary demographic changes to the district are attributed to CIDR generated by the armed forces, their paramilitary factions and the LTTE. Though considerable numbers of residents fled the district as refugees, G. H. Peiris (2001) recorded an increase from 98 inhabitants per km² (1981) to 135 per km² (2001), mostly as a consequence of inter-district displacement of Sri Lankan Tamils from Mullaitivu, Batticaloa and Ampara to and from Trincomalee (Sri Lanka 2001b). Many of those resettled into welfare centres or relocation villages in Trincomalee were also original residents of the district rather than newcomers. Documents retrieved from the land *kacheri* and UNHCR sub-office reveals high rates of intra-district displacement of Sri Lankan Tamils and Muslims from divisions with 'delicate' ethnic ratios and spontaneous relocation to urban and peri-urban areas of the district capital during the 1990s.

Trincomalee district was long considered a strategic priority by the state and militant secessionist groups. Successive colonial and post-colonial administrations recognised the geo-strategic and commercial potential of the primary harbour, claimed to be one of the deepest and most well protected in the world. The district capital served as a major base for the British Royal Air Force and Navy: a series of military warehouses were then built in the China Bay area, many of which were later appropriated to serve as 'transit' and 'welfare' centres for internally displaced populations.[65] By the early 1980s Trincomalee was a major front of the armed conflict. From the perspective of the government,

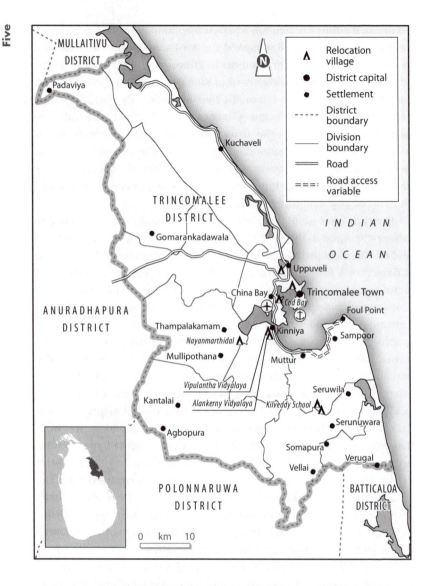

MAP 5.3 Relocation villages in Trincomalee *Source*: Reconstructed from site visits and consultations.

control over the district created a symbolic wedge dividing the spatial contiguity of the supposed *Eelam* homeland. It separated Mullaitivu district, a traditional stronghold of the LTTE, from Batticaloa district, where most guerrilla fighting cadres were traditionally drawn from (Narman and Vidanapathirana 2005).[66] Western districts such as Anuradhapura and

Polonnaruwa districts inhabited primarily by Sinhalese and areas from which the Sri Lankan armed forces traditionally drew elevated numbers of soldiers, formed yet another bulwark (Map 5.3).

Trincomalee district, given the political and military importance attached to it, became the site of considerable CIDR. Even before the outbreak of war, race riots flared up throughout the district in 1958 and again during the various JVP insurrections in 1971, 1977 and 1981 (Chapter 3). While characterised as 'calm' during the IPKF occupation in 1987 and 1989, parts of the district were engulfed in paroxysms of armed violence immediately prior to and following the withdrawal of peace-keepers in 1990. Throughout the 1990s, Sri Lankan Tamil and Muslim populations in Trincomalee were thus disproportionately affected by cross-border displacement with more than 25,000 former residents reportedly seeking refugee status in India by 1999.[67] An examination of *samurdhi* (welfare) benefits issued to displaced, returning and resettling populations reveals that the equivalent of between 50 and 90 per cent of the entire district population experienced some form of dislocation between 1983 and 2002 though more precise estimates were never issued (Sri Lanka 2002c).

The state introduced several measures to control and contain population mobility in Trincomalee. On the one hand, the district was spatially divided between the armed forces who occupied the capital, including the navy base and main arterial networks (e.g. roads and rail) and the LTTE who controlled large swathes of rural territory and extended sections of the coastline to the north and south of the district capital. Even while public administrative services nominally functioned in LTTE-controlled or 'uncleared' areas of the district, the LTTE successfully operated a parallel judiciary, police force and taxation system in areas under its control (Narman and Vidanapathirana 2005). The establishment of welfare centres and relocation villages, described colloquially in the district as 'refugee' or 'internment camps', were both a consequence of sustained military operations by the armed forces and non-state actors as well as specific government policies.

Evictions and displacement were pursued deliberately by the armed forces to secure the perimeter of transport infrastructure and related installations.[68] In order to clear particularly sensitive areas of scrubland and jungle, land was expropriated – through existing emergency provisions or the Tourism Act – and then quickly followed with strategic resettlement.[69] In practice, this implied the evacuation of ethnic groups, both Tamil and Muslim, who were perceived as a potential threat and the repopulation of these same areas with Sinhalese who were resettled and subsequently recruited and trained as home-guards (Chapter 4).[70]

The LTTE justified its attacks against (Sinhalese) settlers and resettlers in Trincomalee, claiming that they did not discriminate between home-guards and the security establishment.

During the early stages of the conflict, public authorities in Trin-comalee adopted analogous approaches to durable solutions as those described above. Though both Colombo and district-based authorities frequently advocated for displaced populations to return to their original homes, provisions were also made for resettlement. The state adapted its approach in line with CIDR regime expectations following a dramatic surge in displacement in the 1990s.[71] From 1990 to 1996, more than 56,000 people were reportedly internally displaced, of whom approxi-mately 46,000 were 'resettled to their original places'.[72] Thus, in addition to food rations, the district authorities sought to supply 'durable shelter ... and other necessary facilities depending on their need ... [including] grants and loan facilities to resettlers to take up their normal socio-economic life' in or outside of welfare centres (Sri Lanka 1997).[73] Despite such rhetorical commitments, in practice, compensation was seldom dispensed as planned.

Both the Sri Lankan government and exponents of the international CIDR regime required a legible population of countable units in order to supply protection and durable solutions. The welfare centre was an ideal interim solution. By the mid-1990s almost half of the district's known internally displaced population was clustered into more than a dozen welfare centres. A government agent memo reported at the time that: '1,785 *families* were living in 17 welfare centres and another 3,631 were living with friends and relations' (ibid., italics added). By 2001, the number of families registered in centres reportedly declined to 1,094 with another 2,576 families living outside welfare centres and relocation villages (UNHCR 2001c). Due to conflicting definitions (i.e. 'individuals' versus 'families'), self-selection and inconsistent monitoring, it is likely that overall rates of internal displacement were higher than officially rendered estimates.[74]

The number of registered internally displaced people declined after the 2002 CFA. Immediately following the ceasefire, UNHCR reported that fewer than 400 families remained in four welfare centres, though certain public authorities insisted that at least ten centres were still partially occupied. UNHCR memos at the time suggested that 'protracted displacement' and the persistence of welfare centres was a function of the unavailability of legitimate durable solutions, the diversification of landholdings such that former lands were already leased out and uncertainty over the 'political' environment. Two additional pull factors were cited that impeded the shutting down of welfare centres: the lack of birth certificates among residents (required for UAS benefits) and the presence of educational facilities in which children were enrolled.[75] With the resumption of armed conflict in the interior of the district near existing irrigation canals in late 2005, however, the numbers of displaced in the district swelled again.

Even before the 2002 CFA, UNHCR began to detect a host of social pathologies among resettlers in the welfare centres. Along with human rights groups, they noted the 'extensive' forcible recruitment of soldiers, including children, by the armed forces and the LTTE (UN 2006, UTHR 1995). Public health monitors and UNHCR programme officers also observed excessively high rates of substance abuse, teenage pregnancy and mental illness contributing to above-average rates of suicide.[76] Owing to their persistent stigmatisation by state institutions and host communities, many displaced populations displayed acute anxiety and psychosocial distress, under- and unemployment and a steady deterioration of 'cultural' values and technical skills.[77] As in other parts of the country, UNHCR began withdrawing direct financial and logistical support for welfare centres in the mid-1990s, opting instead for monitoring, advocacy and investment in protection and, to a lesser extent, resettlement in Trincomalee.

The gradual withdrawal of UNHCR support from welfare centres in Trincomalee coincided with the state's issuance of formal guidelines on return and relocation. There was considerable optimism in the new strategy promoting (voluntary) durable solutions. The government agent (1996) in Trincomalee at the time noted that:

> the majority of the displaced families are anxious to return to their original place of residence or relocate. These families are resettled according to carefully worked-out resettlement plans, with financial commitments, commitments of the administration, clergy, NGOs, and the resettlers themselves. They are convinced that the area is safe for resettlement and happy to return to their villages.[78]

In order to speed up the return and resettlement process, incentives such as dry rations and cash stipends in welfare centres were gradually phased out.[79] Both daytime and nocturnal mobility in and around centres was restricted and even the nominal informal wage labour that was earlier tolerated was curbed. Overall changes in the population of welfare centres were closely monitored and UNHCR supported the establishment of committees and services in the centres to stimulate return and resettlement in conditions of safety and dignity.

The resettlement of Cod Bay Several resettlement initiatives were quietly launched in Trincomalee during the mid- and late 1990s (Map 5.3). Resettlement was increasingly regarded as unavoidable due in part to the spiralling costs of the welfare centres and the inability of displaced people to return home given the occupation of their land by the armed forces or the LTTE. The initial relocation villages entailed the resettlement of a small number of displaced Sinhalese families living in 'transit centres' in north-eastern Trincomalee to areas near the district capital. They also involved the resettlement of modest numbers of both Sinhalese and Sri Lankan Tamil families to other districts such as Vavuniya, Kilinochchi, Batticaloa, Ampara, Mannar and Colombo. These resettlements were pursued without fanfare for fear of appearing to 'negatively' affect national and district ethnic ratios and in order to avert political repercussions should they be widely advertised.

The establishment of relocation villages was undertaken at the discretion of specific Ministers and MPs. As such, relocation invariably favoured displaced Sinhalese and to a lesser extent Muslims, rather than Sri Lankan Tamils who constituted by far the largest caseload but exhibited the least leverage in Colombo.[80] Because significant numbers of Sri Lankan Tamils were displaced from their lands in Trincomalee, nationalist politicians and army officers had little incentive to launch state-sponsored plans to return or resettle them. For all of their limitations, welfare centres were considered an adequate interim solution until the economic costs of their maintenance rose too high. For many politicians there were few obvious dividends to be gained from championing the return and resettlement of displaced Tamils, particularly if their original land was occupied by the armed forces and Sinhalese resettlers or was located in divisions where the ethnic ratios were considered 'sensitive'. The prolonged residency of Sri Lankan Tamils in welfare centres was in some ways the most logical decision for central authorities harbouring hegemonic ambitions or simply seeking to retain their office.

The Cod Bay relocation village was constructed in 2000 and located approximately twenty minutes' drive from the district capital (Map 5.3). The new village was expected to serve as a durable solution for 138 resettled fishing households of Sinhalese origin. According to leaders of the 'village', the majority of the families were originally displaced by the LTTE from Kuchaveli division (in north-eastern Trincomalee district) during clashes between the armed forces and the LTTE in June 1986. Many of them had in fact settled or were resettled to Kuchaveli during the 1950s as part of state-sponsored development-induced resettlement schemes (Chapter 3). According to key informants,[81] households were repeatedly displaced during the late 1980s and early 1990s, some as many as ten times. These displacements were violent and abrupt: most were given by either the armed forces or the LTTE less than two days to vacate. They described how they were first transported by the armed forces from Kuchaveli to Trincomalee town in 1986 while the navy reportedly annexed and subsequently occupied their privately titled lands.

Though overseen and managed by district-level authorities, the relocation village benefited from political patronage in Colombo. The Minister of Fisheries stood to benefit from the resettlement of Sinhalese into his electoral zone which included Cod Bay division. Before the launch of the initiative, households were registered as 'conflict IDPs' by the (Sinhalese) government agent in 1998 and relocated into a variety of welfare centres until 2000. The physical transportation of the families to the new sites in Cod Bay occurred relatively swiftly over a six-month period. Public land was annexed and assigned by the government agent and approval granted by the Minister of the Ministry for Rehabilitation, Refugees and Resettlement.

Both the Ministry of Fisheries and the Ministry for Rehabilitation, Refugees and Resettlement issued assistance packages for housing construction based on existing directives and the existing UAS scheme.[82] Several local public and non-governmental agencies were contracted to prepare the resettlement scheme and to lay submerged water pipelines, connections to the central electrical grid, sanitation and latrine services and gravel roads. Several civil society entities also supported the establishment of education, health and recreational services, including the district chapter of the Young Men's Buddhist Association, the Trincomalee District Development Association and the (Sinhalese) Rotary Club in Colombo.[83]

The physical resettlement of Cod Bay relocation village proceeded in two phases. The first phase was administered in the southern area of Cod Bay closest to the railway tracks and primary access road between 2001 and early 2002. Several dozen families were moved in advance in order to test the suitability of the site. A second phase was overseen by the Colombo-based Rotary Club in 2002, during which time the remainder of the displaced Sinhalese were relocated. While the process was described by public authorities as voluntary, resettlers were not directly consulted on either the design or layout of their homes or village as anticipated by regime proponents. Moreover, relocated populations were expected to contribute their own labour to the enterprise in what amounted to advanced alienation – a procedure long since discredited (Schickle 1969). According to local residents in Cod Bay, the Ministry of Fisheries provided them with approximately six months of dry rations, together with the above-mentioned grants and then left them to fend for themselves.

The spatial layout adopted in the Cod Bay relocation village was analogous to other model resettlement schemes visited by the author in Mannar, Vavuniya, Batticaloa and Ampara. A 'geometric approach to site planning' was pursued in much the same way as other relocation villages in Jaffna and Vavuniya (Fardanesh and Walker 2002). Homesteads were built in regimented columns within a grid-pattern, with each household allocated an equivalent-sized plot of land for subsistence food production ('home-gardens'). The symmetrical approach to housing potentially reduced the cost of construction, but it also resulted in settlement that differed markedly from the villages and towns left behind. Participatory mapping exercises undertaken with twelve families in Cod Bay revealed that while many of the homes were originally provided with water and electricity connections (subject to user-fees), less than one-fifth reported functional service two years later. Moreover, only two families claimed they earned sufficient income to pay for the newly introduced services. While this comparatively better-off minority adopted metered service and paid user-fees, the majority of families pirated electricity with the use of makeshift leads, relied on kerosene for lighting and cooking, or pooled resources and shared (either leased or cooperatively purchased) power generators.

The Cod Bay relocation village was in fact comparatively better-off than neighbouring resettlement schemes. Its relative 'success' is in stark contrast with other relocation villages and welfare centres in predominantly Sri Lankan Tamil and Muslim areas of Trincomalee district. In comparison to six other Sri Lankan Tamil 'relocation villages' visited by the author between July 2003 and August 2006, including Nayanmarthidal, Vipulantha Vidyalaya, Sampaltiru, Vilankulam, Kanniya and Vilgram Vihara, Cod Bay was visibly better serviced and resourced. In contrast to other schemes, public and private utilities and administrative support were originally provided to Cod Bay as a result of the personal intervention of the Minister of Fisheries. No other relocation villages or welfare centres were situated as close to an urban centre or the coastline, much less with access to markets, wharves or local transport services.

The distinctions between the Cod Bay relocation village and other resettlement schemes inhabited by minority populations were stark. In all cases, relocation villages established for Sri Lankan Tamils between 2003 and 2004 were at least double the size of the Cod Bay scheme, with as many as 500 families per village. While a small minority of residents in other resettlement schemes claimed to receive partial assistance through the NEERP and the UAS, they did not benefit from a clear patron. Respondents also complained of diminishing supplies of dry rations from the divisional secretary.[84] Where constructed at all, permanent houses were built almost exclusively by the TRO and other, primarily local Tamil-funded NGOs.[85] Moreover, households in each of the Sri Lankan Tamil resettlement schemes complained of the prospect of LTTE incursions, a concern made real since 2005 in the wake of heightened levels of violence in the district.

Though comparatively recently established, the Sri Lankan Tamil relocation villages cannot be considered 'durable solutions'. More than two years after their official relocation, resettlers complained that in only a few cases were the concrete foundations of their houses completed. Most of the tenements appeared extensively overgrown and under-utilised, suggesting that residents had settled elsewhere soon after their construction or were living there on a seasonal basis. During focus group sessions with both resettlers and (host) residents, it emerged that not one of the six Sri Lankan Tamil resettlement schemes had generated meaningful social or economic linkages with surrounding settlements. Indeed their relative distance from peri-urban areas – they were each more than an hour's drive from the district capital – precluded sustainable trade networks other than the occasional exchange of wood.

Meanwhile, the Cod Bay relocation village appeared to have contributed to the enhanced protection of the area, including of locals. Long-term (host) residents observed certain benefits that accrued from the relocation village. For one, relatively significant investment in the area provided new public infrastructure and potential markets. Moreover, it was widely conceded that their arrival led to enhancements in overall security. According to interviewed public authorities and a sample of local residents, during the late 1990s Cod Bay was regularly patrolled by LTTE cadres. Residents complained to the armed forces about the threats this presented and the importance of clearing out forest cover in nearby areas. Following the 'clearance' of land and the resettlement of the Sinhalese from Kuchaveli, residents observed a qualitative improvement in their own personal security. The extent to which this is correlated with the 2002 ceasefire or the specific interventions of the armed forces is more difficult to discern.

The Cod Bay relocation village achieved a partial durable solution. Despite the relative advantages of the Sinhalese relocation village when compared to the above-mentioned schemes, residents of Cod Bay commonly perceived their condition as the same or worse as compared to before their displacement. A range of grievances was signalled during participatory focus groups and non-representative surveys with a small sample of families. Instead of appealing to changes in fixed measures of well-being such as net income or asset ownership, they alluded to more customary indicators. For example, many argued that their fishing vessels were no longer personally owned but rather leased from wealthier host community residents in the area. These new arrangements reduced their marginal profit and lowered their social status in relation to neighbours. A livelihood ranking exercise focusing on expenditure and consumption patterns determined that monthly household income in Cod Bay ranged from R2,000 [US$20 in 2004 dollars] to R18,000 [US$172 in 2004 dollars], depending on fishing yields. But female respondents observed that the overwhelming proportion of their household income was devoted to food consumption – one of several benchmarks of socio-economic well-being.[86]

Despite their proximity to some of the largest markets in the district, Cod Bay residents noted that the informal wage-labour opportunities were considerably more limited than had been the case in Kuchaveli where existing social networks had facilitated such arrangements. An important concern registered by adult men was that land in the scheme was not legally or even customarily owned but rather subject to an annual renewable permit. Resettlers were uneasy about security of their tenure despite assurances from public authorities that land would be officially transferred after ten years of demonstrated residence, a requirement of prescriptive law (Chapter 3). As in the welfare centres, certain residents also reported an intensification in social and psychological pathologies ranging from domestic and substance abuse to adultery and petty crime.

Notwithstanding the important security dividends, the resettlement scheme did not appear fully integrated with host communities in the surrounding area. At the time of the visits, there were several distinguishable social spatial boundaries that separated the relocation village from other local residents. For example, host communities accorded subtle but lingering stigmas to resettlers four years after their resettlement. Many local Sinhalese residents described them as of an inferior 'social level' or caste, lacking in etiquette and generally 'unclean'.[87] According to some host community residents, 'while some people are clean, most of them [the resettlers] let themselves and their houses go ... most of them are from the same family [caste] ... we'll not go there unless we're asked to'. Sinhalese residents who claimed to meet regularly with resettlers at the local *stupa* (temple) differentiated themselves on the basis of the quality and colour of their clothes and religious 'purity'.

Resettlement experiments in Batticaloa

Batticaloa district experienced among the country's highest proportional rates of internal displacement, return and resettlement during the armed conflict, particularly near its volatile district borders with neighbouring Polonnaruwa and Ampara. Unlike Trincomalee, however, UNHCR and other agencies were only formally granted access to the district from 2002 onwards. The district exhibits a number of additional demographic and administrative differences with neighbouring Trincomalee. Divided into twelve divisions, its roughly 486,000 residents[88] are divided into Sri Lankan Tamils (72 per cent), Sinhalese (16 per cent) and Muslims (12 per cent). Indeed, Batticaloa is a new administrative creation, having been carved from the northernmost section of Ampara in 1961. Peebles (1990) controversially reported how changes to administrative boundaries between Trincomalee, Polonnuwara, Batticaloa and Ampara often facilitated Sinhalese access to canals and irrigation benefits at the expense of Sri Lankan Tamils and Muslims.

During the late 1980s and 1990s, Batticaloa district was considered a stronghold of the LTTE. Indeed, as Chapter 4 observed, the area was considered to be 'infiltrated' with Sri Lankan Tamil 'encroachers' and LTTE sympathisers as early as 1980. In 2002, the Sri Lankan armed forces reportedly controlled roughly 20 per cent of the territorial area of the district with the remainder described as 'un-cleared'. UNHCR (2001e, 2001f) noted that the 231st, 232nd and 233rd army divisions were based in the district before the CFA: the continued military presence in its aftermath was warranted due to the growing influence of the LTTE over the district capital and outlying areas.[89] Even while visible checkpoints and road-blocks eased after 2002,[90] considerable security precautions were in place during repeated field visits between 2003 and 2005. By mid-2006, access to the district was highly controlled and public train services postponed indefinitely.

The strategic concerns of the armed forces were not without precedent. Throughout the 1980s and 1990s a number of major confrontations ensued in the district (Seneratne 1997). Many of the later confrontations were not direct confrontation so much as war by proxy: the armed forces regularly cleared areas not directly under their control through tacit arrangements with local militia and paramilitary groups such as TELO, PLOTE, the so-called Razeek Group and later, the breakaway Karuna faction. As in Trincomalee, the armed forces also widely deployed locally recruited home-guards to protect frontier resettlement schemes and settlements, major transport corridors and key military and utility installations.[91]

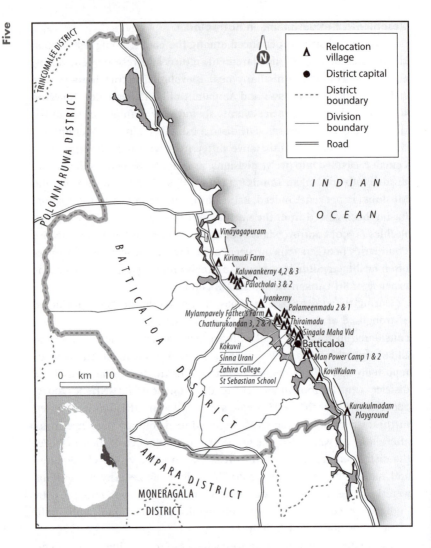

MAP 5.4 Relocation villages in Batticaloa *Source*: Reconstructed from site visits and consultations.

In fact, Batticaloa was long considered a site of strategic and highly contested settlement and resettlement. On the heels of Gal Oya, ambitious state-planned colonisation schemes between 1954 and 1962 resulted in the relocation of 'landless' Sinhalese peasants into areas traditionally dominated by Sri Lankan Tamil and Muslim paddy growers and pasture lands. Following the redrawing of Batticaloa and Ampara, a national census in 1963 registered a *tenfold real and proportional increase* in Sinhalese in both districts when compared to census undertaken ten years previously. As noted in Chapter 4, the Mahaweli resettlement schemes in System B were also singled out by Tamil MPs and the TULF owing to the diversion of water from their constituents and the progressive erosion of their district-level electoral base.[92] Periodic outbursts of internecine violence in other parts of the country spread to Porateenu, Pattu and Villavely divisions. At the time, CIDR was concentrated primarily among Sri Lankan Tamils, though a small minority of Muslims and state-sponsored Sinhalese settlers were also eventually affected (Peebles 1990).

Interventions launched by district authorities and proponents of the CIDR regime to promote protection and durable solutions transformed over time. In the 1970s, approaches were generally 'humanitarian' in character. In some cases ad hoc transit centres were established and dry rations provided over a period of up to three months and channelled through the Social Service Ministry (later the CGES) and divisional authorities. Even after more extensive and protracted internal displacement in the mid-1980s, the state response was described by the serving district secretary as 'half-hearted'. Modest aid resettlement packages were provided by the UNDP and the European Community Humanitarian Office (ECHO) to hastily assembled welfare centres with the aim of encouraging self-reliance and reducing the economic burden exacted on the state.[93] By the end of the 1980s, the state introduced a strict registration system for internally displaced people to maximise control and minimise abuse. Registration cards were issued only to those qualifying as 'IDPs', thus ensuring that assistance was exclusionary. Potential registrants were disqualified if they were not registered within a month of the displacement 'event', if they had been displaced more than once, or if they were married after their displacement.

A more coherent approach to protection and durable solutions emerged following the resurgence of conflict in 1990. The state began to officially promote and sanction welfare centres and relocation villages in Batticaloa in the early 1990s, though few details appear to have been made publicly available to the diplomatic and aid community based in Colombo. UNHCR made comparatively few inroads into Batticaloa until after the ceasefire.[94] The district was considered off-limits to the agency owing to reservations expressed by highly placed government officials during initial negotiations in 1987. As a result of national security concerns, the agency and its implementing partners were unable to fully monitor either protection or durable solutions in Batticaloa until 2002.[95] Return and resettlement were already highly politicised issues in the district – influenced as they were by ranking politicians in Colombo, but also vested interests at the provincial, district and divisional levels. But by the mid-1990s reports emerged that welfare centres established in Batticaloa were being gradually liquidated and either renamed, or replaced in some cases with relocation villages (UNHCR 1996b). As with resettlement schemes discussed in the case of MDIP System B, centres were later strongly discouraged for fear they might become infiltrated or serve as bases for recruitment and training of LTTE cadres.

Between 1994 and 1995 relocation guidelines were issued (in Sinhalese) from Colombo and distributed to government agents, including in Batticaloa. According to long-serving public servants in the district, two-week training initiatives were launched in 1995 and 1996 to inculcate district-level authorities in the mechanics of return and resettlement programmes. Government agents and district secretaries were also summoned to Colombo to review policy imperatives and guidelines associated with durable solutions. The relocation efforts were considered to be generally effective. By the end of 1997, the District Planning Secretariat and District Statistical Office of Batticaloa revealed that less than 350 families (1,539 individuals) remained in three welfare centres in two divisions. More than 5,300 families (21,949 individuals), over 90 per cent of the total estimated caseload in the district, were believed to be living outside of centres or in relocation villages.[96]

Despite launching a major drive to resettle populations, welfare centres continued to exert a strong pull on residents who had few alternative options to return or relocate. Unpublished non-representative surveys conducted by UNHCR in the 1990s (in districts other than Batticaloa) revealed that the majority of Sri Lankan Tamil respondents preferred to stay in welfare centres or relocate to alternative areas because of prevailing insecurity and the presence of HSZs. The LTTE, too, appeared unwilling to support strategic relocation of populations in cleared areas to areas under their control. According to a UNHCR (2004b: 4) memo summarising the findings of these early surveys:

> although most IDPs prefer to be relocated, and the government may be showing some interest, the LTTE has taken a stance by not accepting relocation as a solution on the basis that people have the right to return. Relocation is seen as a move to evict Tamils from their lands.

Many IDPs also rejected return or resettlement options owing to the pull-factors such as the availability of basic services in welfare centres, particularly education facilities and the availability of basic amenities relative to proposed areas of return or relocation.

In addition to the persistent matter of ethnic ratios, a key exogenous factor shaping the prospect for durable solutions related to the quality and availability of land. The question of where to resettle populations – whether on public or privately owned land – was a persistent dilemma for district and divisional-level authorities throughout Sri Lanka, including in Batticaloa. Municipal civil servants repeatedly lamented the scarcity of public land and the fact that, even where available, it was of marginal quality. Private landowners were not inclined to grant even temporary access to their lands because, as with encroachers or squatters, land legislation favoured the rights of the tenant and outright ownership after ten years (Chapter 3). They risked forfeiting their land with little compensation and few options other than to forcibly remove the displaced from their property. Examples of this were common prior to the ceasefire period. For example, approximately 287 families 'liquidated' from Pethalai welfare centre in 2000 resettled on private land near Valaichennai and Koralaipattu in 2002 after making petitions to the courts. In another case, private land provided for the Punanai welfare centre was sold in small parcels to between forty and sixty displaced households at well below market rate by the owner, himself resolved to eventually losing it to encroachers.[97]

Relocation village experiments A series of 'model' relocation villages were soon launched by district authorities to serve as demonstration projects in the late 1990s (Map 5.4). It was expected that these might encourage more welfare residents to leave welfare centres. They included Savukkady relocation village (42 Sri Lankan Tamil families), Thiraimadu (72 Sri Lankan Tamil families), Villopulanadaradudam (275 Sri Lankan Tamil families, Navatkudah East (120 Sri Lankan Tamil families) and Thirupperumthurai (37 Sri Lankan Tamil families). Other spontaneous relocations were also relabelled 'relocation villages', though only limited records of their whereabouts were maintained by the land *kacheri* office in Batticaloa. According to the then government agent of Batticaloa, these early relocation villages necessitated Cabinet-level approval and were carefully monitored from Colombo. The drive to promote resettlement was temporarily suspended in 2000 owing to increasingly vocal charges levied by the TULF that the relocation villages had the potential to make profound changes to the ethnic ratio of the district.

The UNP government elected in 2001 restarted the liquidation of welfare centres in Batticaloa while allegedly discouraging the establishment of new relocation schemes. The UNP appeared to broadly support certain Sri Lankan Tamil grievances and slowed down the construction of relocation villages. Newly posted civil servants in 2003 openly criticised the 'flawed logic of resettling specific displaced populations of one cultural [ethnic] background to a new cultural environment'.[98] They were also more conscious of the political hurdles associated with securing Cabinet-level approval to alter ethnic ratios given the new political configuration of the elected government. A former senior civil servant from Batticaloa explained that 'this [the ethnic ratio] was an important consideration ... if Muslims were settled in Tamil areas and vice versa ... they [their political representatives] would have been up in arms'.

The new relocation villages were expected to reduce the pressures generated by welfare centres while simultaneously regularising specific categories of displaced. In certain instances, they did precisely this. The Savukkady relocation village, for example, consisted of forty-two Sri Lankan Tamil families and was located less than twenty minutes' drive from Batticaloa town.[99] The residents were displaced from a neighbouring division in the early 1990s and sought temporary shelter in transit centres on the grounds of the Eastern University located in the outskirts of the district capital. In 1995, after years of inaction by district-level authorities, a number of families, some of them having relocated to welfare centres, spontaneously settled to (private) land identified by the Catholic Bishop of Batticaloa. The total resettlement scheme covered approximately five km^2 and each family was provided with between one and two acres depending on their demonstrated needs (e.g. size of household and occupation). With support from the Church, some basic provisions were supplied to resettling families including a modest shelter with cement foundations and tin sheets for roofing. As in the case of Cod Bay, the involvement of an external patron facilitated the overall resettlement process.

Residents of Savukkady claimed that their resettlement constituted a durable solution. Though the relocation village was visibly less well serviced and supported than Cod Bay, interviewed residents were generally satisfied with the resettlement scheme. The social conditions of the relocation village were described during participatory focus groups as comparatively positive in comparison with nearby welfare centres and even with their previous communities prior to displacement. The relative improvement in their socio-economic livelihoods following resettlement could be attributed, they contended, to the fact they considered themselves to have been comparatively poor before their displacement. Livelihood mapping exercises revealed average monthly incomes of approximately R4,000 [US$40 in 2004 dollars], considerably below the national poverty line.

While a number of residents expressed concerns with public amenities – including the poor state of access roads (which were prone to floods) and intermittent electricity supply – they claimed that these were highly seasonal in nature. As a measure of their uncertainty over property rights, a considerable number of residents claimed to have stowed away the deeds to their original land even though this limited their access to UAS benefits and additional state support. A number of enterprising residents already purchased land and were preparing to sell or release their original properties. Moreover, because Savukkady was located in primarily Sri Lankan Tamil-dominated areas, the level of local integration was comparatively robust as evidenced by the extensive market exchanges reported by residents.

The Villopulanadaradudam model relocation village was widely considered by district authorities and residents to be another success story. The relocation village was composed of approximately 275 Sri Lankan Tamil families from Batticaloa district who had arrived from neighbouring divisional welfare centres in three successive phases in 1990, 1994 and again in 2002. Villopulanadaradudam was established as a result of direct intervention by the government agent's office and like Savukkady, with support from the bilateral Danish development agency (DANIDA). Though the conditions of individual houses and land allotments were highly variable, each family was provided with the equivalent of a one-off payment equivalent to US$2,500 and some building materials to construct their own residence.

As in Savukkady, at first appearances the Villopulanadaradudam relocation village seemed to be failing to provide a durable solution. The level of infrastructure was meagre and public utilities and services had not been installed despite repeated promises by local authorities and NGOs. Unusually, the spatial layout of the relocation village did not mirror the typical grid-pattern as in Cod Bay or other conventional resettlement schemes. Rather, it displayed a more organic morphology in keeping with local custom. Crucially, residents perceived their situation to have improved in relation to their circumstances in the welfare centre. Likewise, because the relocation village was approximately thirty minutes from Batticaloa town, land plots were comparatively large (ranging from 2–5 acres each). Owing to the relative abundance of low-cost land in the area, resettled households reported that they immediately began diversifying their income streams by leasing and purchasing new and more desirable arable lands in the vicinity while (illegally) using their own non-titled land as collateral. Focus groups indicated that the level of local integration was positive signalled by increasing rates of intermarriage and commerce between resettled and host communities.

Though registering more positive assessments of their resettlement experience than Cod Bay resettlers, real livelihood and income-earning potential was comparatively more limited in both Savukkady and Villopulanadaradudam. As with many Sri Lankan Tamils living in relocation villages in Trincomalee, men and youth frequently migrated for seasonal and informal labour opportunities in neighbouring paddy fields or to collect fuel-wood. Others worked in rice mills as far away as Polonnaruwa district. Some respondents observed that they were competing with host communities for formal labour opportunities in nearby textile and apparel factories or other forms of unskilled labour. They noted that their willingness to work for lower wages engendered resentment from host communities.

Likewise, the resettlement process appeared to generate certain stresses on women and youth. Many resettled female respondents claimed that their spouses stayed away from welfare centres and relocation villages for months on end, indirectly contributing to the emergence of what were described euphemistically as 'social ills'. They also highlighted their intensifying exposure to physical insecurity, including detention, arrest and harassment by the armed forces and the LTTE. According to UNHCR (2001d; 2001e) reports written during sporadic site visits, women were less involved in direct household income-generation owing to traditionally ascribed gender roles but also the absence of adequate social mobilisation programmes. Because the provision of dry rations and UAS benefits was intermittent and unreliable, residents felt that a major failing of the resettlement schemes was the widening income gaps in relation to host communities.

Although drawn from a modest-sized sample, a range of general observations can be made about the Cod Bay, Savukkady and Villopulanadaradudam relocation village experience. The role of ethnicity, external patrons and proximity to 'stable' markets in particular were alleged to contribute to 'successful' protection and durable solutions.[100] The ascribed 'ethnicity' of displaced populations was considered to be a significant intervening factor affecting relative perceptions of resettlement outcomes. For example, Sinhalese resettlers registered comparatively more positive experiences in 'real' material well-being when compared with Sri Lankan Tamil resettlers, even if the former determined that their 'social' or 'economic' status diminished in relative terms. As such, comparative household surveys assessing varied relocation experiences may register substantial real differences in income or assets, but often fail to capture relative changes between different categories of resettled populations. In all three cases, direct support from an external patron prepared to lobby on their behalf proved to be essential in mobilising the necessary political and material resources for a durable solution. At the same time, the spatial proximity of relocation villages to urban centres and the possibility of resuming livelihoods also appeared to enhance physical protection and prospects for market and social integration.

Conclusion

This chapter traced out a number of ways that armed conflict directly shaped the spatial, ethnic and temporal dynamics of displacement, return and resettlement in Sri Lanka. Though disagreements on the scale and distribution of internal displacement since 1983 persist, there is little doubt that it ranks among the highest in the world in real and proportional terms. In addition to the estimated violent deaths of at least 70,000 civilians from 1983 to the present, millions of Sri Lankan men, women and children experienced some form of internal displacement since the late 1970s.[101] Since the resumption of an undeclared dirty war in 2005, at least 5,000 civilians were killed in the north and east and more than 300,000 forced to seek refuge. Two decades after the arrival of UNHCR, the case of Sri Lanka beckons humility as to what kind of protection and durable solutions can realistically be achieved in the context of war.

A great many misconceptions remain concerning what exactly is meant by resettlement in Sri Lanka. Part of the confusion can be attributed to the distortion and manipulation of core concepts. Both semantics and eclectic data collection systems limit robust comparative analysis. Clarity in nomenclature and the referent are essential preconditions for improved understanding. Notwithstanding the creation of a Resettlement Authority to centralise protection and durable solutions, after more than four years of intermittent field research in Sri Lanka it appears that few government or non-governmental officials could distinguish between basic concepts essential to the functioning of the CIDR regime. These misunderstandings have consequences. Despite policy prescriptions mandated from above, district and divisional-level officials were often confounded by the differences between transit centres, welfare schemes and relocation villages. Even as welfare centres were controversially 'liquidated' – including as many as 150,000 people between 2001 and 2002 alone[102] and another 35,000 in mid-2007 – the motives, character and outcomes of resettlement went largely unrecorded. A review of government directives and internal memos generated by UNHCR and WFP suggests that resettlement was often justified provided it reduced overall costs, amplified protection and promoted (voluntary) durable solutions.

We have here considered the relative influence of the incipient CIDR regime in relation to shaping state behaviour to promote protection and durable solutions. Findings suggest that at one level, the regime effectively contributed to the formation of progressive policies and practices directed towards internally displaced people, particularly after the arrival of UNHCR in 1987. The adoption of certain regime prescriptions was motivated partly by humanitarian impulse. The Sri Lankan government also saw in the promotion of protection and durable solutions a strategy to prevent refugee outflows and providing 'in-country solutions'. State institutions progressively adopted core tenets of the principles, norms and rules prescribed by the CIDR regime, including the Guiding Principles. Certain endogenous constraints on regime influence – including those relating to state sovereignty and collective action dilemmas – were anticipated by regime proponents and accounted for through the establishment of 'interim' and coordination arrangements. Even so, exogenous factors were not fully anticipated by regime exponents.

Return and resettlement policies came under scrutiny following the CFA and the election of the UNP government. For one, there was sufficient evidence for UNHCR, World Bank and non-government organisations to determine that the majority of welfare centre residents, while living in deplorable conditions, did not necessarily want to return home, much less their original district. State policy on resettlement militated against the provision of public land to internally displaced populations in districts other than that of origin. Durable solutions and related entitlements were provided only on the condition that the displaced returned to their original districts. Even at this basic level, there was evidence that 'government relocation policy ... threaten[ed] the right to freedom of movement of landless IDPs' (CPA 2003).

The CIDR regime offered a prescription for equitable protection and durable solutions in circumstances characterised by political turmoil. While international CIDR regime proponents advanced basic norms and rules, these aspirations were unevenly applied by the Sri Lankan government, armed forces, a politicised district-level bureaucracy and the LTTE. As options for return became more limited, regime proponents endorsed resettlement as the path of least resistance. Because the domestic discourse and interests conditioning CIDR were only partly grasped by donors and international agencies, the regime potentially did more harm than it intended. As with the experience of DIDR described in Chapter 4, the displacement and resettlement of conflict-affected populations constitutes in many cases a purposive and ongoing strategy to secure land, enforce legibility in 'border areas' – particularly those that remain 'uncleared' – and a means of reshaping ethnic ratios in potentially contested districts and divisions. The case of relocation villages in Trincomalee and Batticaloa highlight the limits of CIDR regime. Although the state and its bureaucratic machinery adopted certain rhetorical and institutional provisions of the regime, the government and the LTTE simultaneously pursued their own politico-strategic objectives such as consolidating land and ethnic ratios.[103] In some case, their approaches were inimical to those prescribed by the regime – alternately containing, restricting and controlling population movement.

6 | Resettlement after the wave: reflections on the north and east

In late December 2004 an earthquake off the coast of Sumatra (Indonesia)[1] generated a series of massive waves that contributed to the deaths of more than 187,000 people and the disappearance of another 42,000 in more than nine countries. The consequences of the tsunami for already densely populated communities in northern, eastern and southern Sri Lanka were considerable. More than 35,000 people were killed and another 22,000 seriously injured. The tsunami devastated a vast social and physical network of settlements and resulted in the internal displacement of almost half a million people. The disaster created a triple burden: many Sri Lankans previously internally displaced and resettled by development and war subsequently relocated once again. Since the tsunami, a burgeoning literature on the various linkages between vulnerability, natural disaster and population relocation emerged in and outside the country, some of which is reminiscent of DIDR and CIDR scholarship described in previous chapters.[2]

External evaluations of the quantity and quality of international, national and civil society responses to the tsunami are mixed.[3] On the one hand, there is near universal praise for the early initiative of a diverse array of civil society organisations composed almost entirely of individuals with existing religious, kinship and familial ties to the areas in which they intervened. Many faced enormous pressures and in some cases struggled to scale up their activities, and were routinely lauded for having provided culturally and locally sensitive approaches to meeting basic needs of affected populations in the aftermath of the tsunami (TEC 2006: ii). These local associations worked to reinforce the social resilience of displaced households even as they offered modest and short-term material assistance. The effectiveness of the larger organisations – including international and national donors, state entities and non-governmental agencies – is often characterised in less favourable terms. It is the character and structure of the response by these latter institutions that constitute the focus of this chapter.

A combination of multilateral donors and international financial agencies attempted to centralise their relief and reconstruction through state mechanisms. This chapter contends that, taken together, the efforts of these specific international and national actors were a tangible expression of the international NIDR regime. While at times uncoordinated and unfocused, their objectives were to achieve an equitable, voluntary and needs-based approach to the provision of protection and durable solutions. To this end, regime proponents advanced 'transitional' shelters and 'permanent' housing as key vehicles to achieve meaningful resettlement. Owing in large part to the unprecedented generosity of the international community immediately after the tsunami, regime proponents and the government publicly announced 'permanent housing for all' in less than a year and promised to 'build back better'. The proposed construction of almost 100,000 houses in a country that built between 5,000[4] and 15,000[5] per annum was unrealistic to the extreme.

The outcomes of the resettlement interventions endorsed by NIDR regime supporters were less successful than anticipated. Though approximately 55,000 'transitional shelters' were constructed with support from regime proponents in the first year, fewer than 2,500 of the anticipated 98,000 'permanent houses' were built by early 2007.[6] Indeed, approximately 130,000 tsunami-displaced were residing in 'temporary' and transitional shelters – referred to as 'refugee camps' by some public officials and the international and domestic media – at least three years after the disaster.[7] The vast majority of these shelters were located in the Sri Lankan Tamil-dominated coastal areas of the north and east.[8] Of the small number of permanent shelters constructed, the overwhelming majority were located in the Sinhalese-dominated districts in the south and south-west.[9]

We shall consider here the normative and bureaucratic architecture of the NIDR regime and its manifestations in Sri Lanka. The drafting of this chapter was undertaken while these processes were practically occurring – field research coinciding as it did with the tsunami. The natural disaster and the international and national response offered a natural experiment in which to examine the structure and influence of the nascent NIDR regime and the extent to which it overlapped with other parallel regimes. Interventions to promote protection and durable solutions for internally displaced people conformed in some respects to explicit prescriptions of the NIDR regime (Chapter 2). They focused sequentially on the equitable and voluntary provision of temporary and transitional shelter followed by more permanent housing.

The influence of the NIDR regime in Sri Lanka was shaped by both endogenous and exogenous constraints. Specifically, NIDR was taking place in a context of corrosive relations between the state and the LTTE and in an environment characterised by complex reconstruction operations involving massive inflows of resources and literally hundreds of NGOs and state entities. The creation of a highly centralised decision-making mechanism to undertake resettlement was one important reaction to these challenges, though it practically succumbed to collective action dilemmas. Exogenous limitations included, among other things, the introduction (and subsequent withdrawal) of a 'buffer zone' and the state's reluctance (or inability) to appropriate or grant adequate land for resettlement. In briefly tracing out the experience of 'donor-driven' and 'owner-diver' permanent housing schemes in specific districts such as Trincomalee, Batticaloa and Ampara, this chapter highlights the disjunction between the expectations of NIDR regime supporters and de facto outcomes. So-called transitional shelters and permanent housing schemes came to resemble in many ways the welfare centres and relocation villages reviewed in Chapter 5.

Enter the NIDR regime

The tsunami inspired one of the largest international emergency relief and recovery operations ever undertaken (TEC 2006). It also led to the most rapid and spontaneous outpouring of aid on record, stimulated in part, according to Hyndman (2007) by Western media reports of 'white suffering' in coastal resorts and game parks. An unprecedented US$7 billion was collectively raised for all tsunami-affected countries in less than two months. Approximately two-thirds of this was contributed by individuals and private sources and routed through international agencies such as the International Federation of the Red Cross/Crescent/Crystal (IFRC) and Red Cross societies[10] together with established international agencies such as Oxfam, Care and World Vision. It is hardly surprising that the tsunami overwhelmed the disaster response capacities of most affected countries. No coherent disaster prevention mechanisms were in place in Sri Lanka at the time.

The absence of a comprehensive national disaster prevention framework is surprising given the country's long experience with internal displacement, return and resettlement arising in the context of cyclones, landslides and droughts. Just eighteen months before the tsunami Sri Lanka appealed for US$30 million from donors to rebuild in the wake of the worst monsoon-induced floods in the nation's history: more than 235 people were killed with 108,000 families displaced (Twigg 2004). At the time of the tsunami, functional agencies charged with disaster response were highly dispersed and responsibilities were located alternately in the National Disaster Management Centre (Ministry of Women Empowerment and Social Welfare), the Human Disaster Management Council (Presidential Secretariat) and with the erstwhile Ministry of

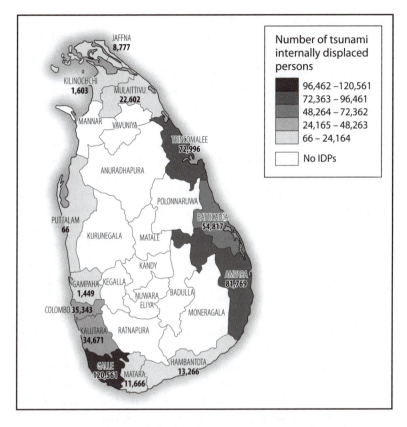

MAP 6.1 Tsunami-displaced (2006) *Source*: RADA (2006a).

Relief, Rehabilitation and Reconciliation (renamed the Ministry of Nation Building and Development), the Ministry of Health, the CGES and the Planning Unit of the Ministry of Finance. Despite their integral role in overseeing relief assistance, return and resettlement, none of these agencies had adopted cogent disaster management plans or displayed adequate competencies to deal with significant hazards in vulnerable areas (Parakrama 2006: 29).

While the state retained overall planning authority for NIDR, a host of international and national NGOs assumed a central role during the post-tsunami period. The state centralised coordination functions and contracted out responsibilities for transitional and permanent housing. In practical terms, the government established a Centre for National Operations (CNO) in the aftermath of the tsunami to identify priorities, centralise resources and implement discrete relief projects. Three separate interim arrangements were subsequently constituted: the Task

Force for Rescue and Relief (TAFRER), the Task Force to Rebuild the Nation (TAFREN) and the Task Force for Logistics and Law and Order (TAFLOL). Under the authority of the President's Office, these task forces were empowered to delegate responsibilities vertically and horizontally between state and non-state institutions. The appropriation of land, physical construction of shelters and houses and the rebuilding of social and economic infrastructure were activities effectively managed by government agents and district secretaries with programming interventions overseen by divisional secretariats (assistant government agents at the sub-district level) and *land kacheris* at the lowest administrative level.

The anticipated funding requirements to guide the transition from relief to development were formidable. Fearing major macro-economic set-backs due to the destruction wreaked by the tsunami, the government requested that a preliminary needs assessment be launched in January by the World Bank (2005), together with the ADB, the UN and the Japan Bank for International Cooperation (JBIC). The assessment determined that the country's recovery and reconstruction requirements exceeded US$2 billion, though this would later rise to US$3.3 billion. Aggregate damages accrued by the tsunami were forecast at the time to exceed 5 per cent of 2006 GDP (ibid.; OCHA 2005). Unusually, the amount pledged by the international community *exceeded* the requested appeal – with approximately US$661 million contributed by bilateral donors, US$1.29 billion from multilateral agencies and over US$853 million from newly flush international NGOs.[11] Fearing that a massive infusion of aid might contribute to exacerbating the conflict, funds were only gradually disbursed. Donors were also reluctant to provide sizeable financial transfers to either government- or the LTTE-administered areas without a transparent joint-institutional mechanism in place (World Bank 2005).[12]

The country's geography and a legacy of mutual mistrust between the government and the LTTE were decisive in shaping the parameters and influence of the NIDR regime. Political volatility in the north and east and corresponding difficulties accessing 'non-cleared' areas had long hampered reconstruction efforts, including prospects for locating durable solutions. Areas especially ravaged by the tsunami included LTTE-controlled coastal belts to which the government and the armed forces had comparatively limited access (Map 6.1).[13] Immediately following the tsunami, a dispute erupted between the government and the LTTE over the mechanics of administering aid to cleared and uncleared areas. The prospects of a massive injection of foreign and domestic investment coupled with the possibilities of consolidating political legitimacy, authority and strategic control over territory and affected populations raised the stakes. The LTTE considered itself an equal partner to the state in the recovery and reconstruction process, forming a Planning and Development Secretariat to coordinate activities and facilitating the work of the TRO to operate in uncleared areas (Uyangoda 2005: 30). Representatives of the government and armed forces in Colombo vehemently disagreed and doubted the sincerity of the LTTE at all stages. After a period of tense bargaining, the two sides eventually reached a compromise to establish a joint administrative mechanism, the PTOMS.[14] The Sri Lankan government agreed to the arrangement because it assumed that the LTTE was in a quantitatively weaker position after the tsunami – with rumours that its 'Sea Tiger' naval wing had been partially destroyed, thereby shifting the strategic equilibrium in favour of the state (ibid.: 30). Though widely hailed as an important step for reconciliation, the PTOMS proved enormously controversial and ultimately collapsed by the end of 2005 (Sambandan 2005).[15]

Proponents of the NIDR regime played an important role in shaping initial institutional responses to return and resettlement. From the beginning, promised durable solutions were conceived as a physical and linear shift from homelessness to transitional shelters, permanent housing and ultimately longer-term development activities. Following consultations with regime proponents such as the World Bank, the ADB and UNHCR, TAFRER and TAFLOL were merged into a single Task Force for Relief (TAFOR) in early 2005. TAFOR was expected to coordinate a transitional shelter strategy in cooperation with donors and non-governmental agencies.[16] Meanwhile, TAFREN was installed to ensure that land for resettlement would be readily identified and was charged with overseeing the eventual relocation of households residing in transitional shelters to permanent houses. Owing to the scale of NIDR, the government began to draft legislation to establish an Authority for Rebuilding the Nation (ARN) as a successor to TAFREN. Much like the Mahaweli Authority, it was expected that ARN would eventually be provided with broad discretionary authority to push NIDR forward. Predictably, given the considerable pressures to achieve meaningful transition and competition for land, tensions between TAFOR and TAFREN rapidly emerged.

While TAFOR and TAFREN coordinated the overall process and chaired committees responsible for tendering contracts, regime proponents asserted themselves at various stages. At the urging of certain donors such as the United States, Japan and the United Kingdom, the UNHCR and its implementing partners adopted a central role in the early transitional period. Meanwhile, the World Bank took on the mandate for permanent housing and infrastructure development as 'reconstruction was [their] forte'.[17] A multi-donor trust fund (MDTF)[18] was established to undertake, among other tasks, permanent housing, though it faced a US$75 million budgetary shortfall from the beginning that would affect NIDR over the coming years. Given the sheer diversity of actors involved and the aforementioned political constraints, the institutional and programmatic approach to establishing temporary shelters and permanent housing was bound to be complex, not least because TAFOR and TAFREN were expected to coordinate as many as twenty-three ministries to implement coherent emergency and development operations in eight affected districts (CPP 2006). At least ten ministries, departments and authorities were involved in specific aspects of NIDR.[19] The UDA, in particular, expanded and reasserted its authority over land appropriation and allocation immediately after the tsunami, requiring, for example, approval of 'development activities undertaken within the ... special control zone [the buffer]'.[20]

Meanwhile, de facto programming and implementation, including the preparation of transitional shelters and permanent housing, were devolved to government agents, district secretaries, divisional secretaries, *land kacheris* and *grama niladharis*.[21] This decentralisation process was described as 'a huge workload that was not only entrusted but also thrust upon the district administration without prior notice' (UNDP 2005: 313). For example, TAFREN was staffed by some sixty public servants in the capital, but was responsible for managing return, resettlement, employment generation, public service delivery and the restoration of national infrastructure in every single affected district (OCHA 2005). In theory, TAFREN was supposed to be decentralised at the level of implementation and to work with the government agent and district committees (or the TRO in 'uncleared' areas).[22] This state of affairs was symptomatic of the centralising impulses of the country's political-bureaucratic elite. Meanwhile, district and provincial structures were sidelined and their capacities largely underutilised.

Transitional shelters Owing to its experience and demonstrated capabilities, UNHCR was requested to directly support state planners in establishing an initial emergency strategy for undertaking protection and durable solutions for the disaster-displaced. The UNHCR and other agencies such as the Sri Lankan Red Cross sought to ensure that assistance and resettlement activities conformed to the basic rules set out by the NIDR regime. Key standards at the time included SPHERE and related UNHCR (2000c) guidelines (Chapter 2). The strategy promoted durable solutions by providing prospective recipients with the option to (voluntarily) return to their (original) land or to resettle elsewhere. From the beginning, UNHCR actively disseminated guidelines to infuse state policies (rules) with principles of equity and parity. Specifically, they were adamant that:

> forcible relocations should not be undertaken, whether from schools or to transitional settlements, or camps. Relocation will be voluntary at all times and affected people will be provided with full, free and impartial information on the Government plans and options available. The authorities will ensure the full participation of displaced persons in the planning and management of the return, resettlement and relocation process.[23]

Formal guidelines were issued to guide the construction of these shelters later than anticipated by UNHCR and RADA (2006b). Thus, transitional shelters were supposed to be designed in such a way that they offered 'safe, dignified and durable' housing, even if they were expected to endure for less than a year. UNHCR assumed this role because of its acknowledged 'comparative advantage'.[24]

It is worth recalling that the *emergency* phase of NIDR began immediately following the tsunami (or hazard). In Sri Lanka, temporary shelters[25] were supplemented with food rations. Though the emergency phase was expected to last between one and two months, for some tsunami-affected populations it persisted several years after the fact.[26] UNHCR, WFP and a variety of international agencies helped shape and direct the overall response during the period, particularly in regard to the distribution of rations and supporting the logistics and outreach capacities of district and divisional state structures. The government encouraged the liquidation of the remaining temporary shelters, in part because they signalled a visible failure of the NIDR regime to promote equitable and durable solutions.

The *transitional shelter* phase was originally intended to serve as an interim measure before permanent housing was established. During this stage, households were provided with temporary accommodation often consisting of a temporary shelter composed of two rooms and a tin roof, open dirt or mud floors, communal toilets and access to communal water points (TAFREN 2005a). The transitional phase was not expected to endure more than eighteen months. Nevertheless, NIDR regime proponents and state planners accepted the inevitable: that the period might be protracted because transitional shelters, as with welfare centres in the case of CIDR, were the only available option in the absence

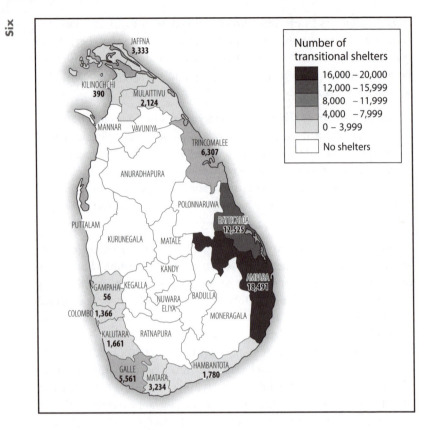

MAP 6.2 Number and location of transitional shelters (2006)
Source: RADA (2006a).

of possibilities for return or resettlement. As observed by experienced UN-HABITAT representatives, 'transitional housing is seldom transitional'.[27] Indeed, between 20 and 30 per cent of all tsunami-displaced were residing in these temporary shelters, especially in the north and east, three years after the tsunami (Map 6.2).

The outcomes of the UNHCR transitional shelter strategy were lauded by NIDR regime proponents. Between January and June 2005 the UNHCR, together with WFP, reportedly distributed over 500,000 'non-food' items working directly through government agents and local partners to more than 160,000 tsunami-displaced living in ad hoc temporary emergency shelters. These shelters, understood as an unavoidable component of the 'transition', were common and widespread. Superficially under the authority of TAFOR, the UNHCR later assumed responsibility for establishing 'transitional shelters' for some 55,000 resettled households.

RADA (2006c) announced that an additional 1,000 transitional shelters were completed by the end of 2005 though more than 6,000 of these were subsequently decommissioned by early 2006 owing to surplus production.

The lived experiences of those who relocated from emergency to transitional shelters were highly uneven. Following the often premature and forcible movement of tsunami-displaced from temporary to transitional shelters, many later reported that their situation was worse than before. Throughout the country, most transitional shelters were of variable quality, severely degraded and showing deterioration within six months of being constructed. Due to the pressures to respond quickly and the enormous variation in contracting and construction capacities in affected districts, transitional shelters were frequently poorly designed and constructed. Despite government pledges of a 'house for all' within the year, the planning and practicalities of both transitional shelters and permanent housing were not adequately thought through.[28] Even while a host of non-governmental, philanthropic and community-based groups emerged to assist with the transition strategy, local initiatives were largely supplanted by better-funded foreign NGOs that began to arrive in their hundreds in the first six months of 2005.

Permanent housing The requirements of executing the permanent housing strategy were far more complex than for transitional shelters. In order to enhance the coherence and focus of NIDR, TAFREN established a Tsunami Housing and Reconstruction Unit (THRU). This was mandated to plan, facilitate and monitor the reconstruction of an estimated 98,000 houses, including 45,000 within the buffer zone and approximately 53,000 outside (see Map 6.3).[29] The strategy was further complicated by a national election. Following the election of President Mahinda Rajapakse in November 2005, TAFREN and THRU were combined into RADA. In order to enhance the 'efficiency' of the state's response to NIDR, RADA was deliberately staffed with private sector employees new to government. The deleterious effects of their inexperience in terms of lost institutional memory and related transaction costs were immediately felt by governmental and non-governmental partners alike. As noted above, RADA (2006a) was designated as the key state institution to address tsunami recovery in all its aspects with several priority areas: 'transitional shelter, permanent houses, restoring livelihoods, health and education'.[30] Central to RADA's mandate was NIDR.

As in the case of the transitional strategy, proponents of the NIDR regime played a central role in shaping the mandate and design of

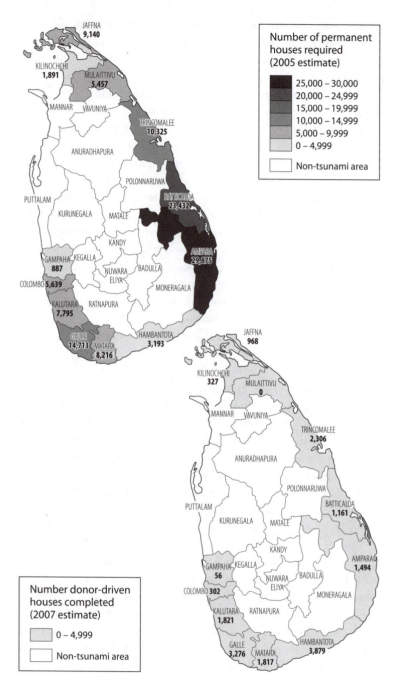

MAP 6.3 Total number of permanent houses required vs donor-driven houses completed (2007) *Source*: Reconstructed from UN-HABITAT documents and database (Colombo).

TAFREN (later RADA) and related rules associated with *permanent housing*. This was facilitated by regular donor coordination meetings organised by the UN, IFRC, the World Bank and others in Colombo and the district capitals as a means of enhancing transparency, predictability and reducing transaction costs. There, contracts were tendered and issued and memoranda of agreement hammered out on specific resettlement-related interventions between donors, NGOs and local community-based agencies. Donors outlined the number of permanent houses they expected to be built for specific beneficiaries and these commitments were aligned, in theory, with land identified by RADA together with district-level municipal authorities. Government agents essentially sub-contracted out resettlement schemes to a variety of non-governmental agencies and construction firms (who in turn sub-contracted out to smaller enterprises) on the basis of existing beneficiary lists supplied by the *grama sevekas* to divisional secretaries.[31]

Sri Lankan ministries and related line agencies were encouraged to establish guidelines and principles on resettlement in line with World Bank and ADB standards and on the basis of consultations with an array of donors and non-governmental agencies. These standards were not uncontroversial. For example, together with bilateral donors and the ADB, the World Bank initially determined that the mean value of a conventional permanent housing unit[32] was US$5,000. Certain representatives affiliated with UN agencies and NGOs felt this severely undervalued the real cost of permanent houses, arguing that the true estimate was probably two to three times higher. The escalating costs were attributed to runaway inflation in tsunami-affected areas. But owing to overall shortfalls in funding for permanent housing, the World Bank and its partners ultimately *reduced* the estimated value of housing to US$2,500 per unit.[33] Thus, the standard compensation for permanent housing was set far below the estimated mean value of a conventional home. The World Bank and its partners expected that resettling populations would cover the balance from their labour, savings and additional inputs from hundreds of non-governmental agencies.

Permanent housing was divided into two categories, and entitlements were issued on the basis of the geographic location of the beneficiary before the tsunami. Permanent housing was provided to those originally residing outside the buffer zone who could prove both title and that their home had been damaged (owner-driven) and those initially located inside the buffer zone and who were required to resettle elsewhere (donor-driven). 'Owner-driven' housing was based on the principle of providing a house for a house, encouraging owner participation in

197

housing development, the provision of phased grants for reconstruction and mobilising the existing banking system to distribute cash grants. Contributions to the owner-driven schemes included the World Bank, ADB, Swiss Development Cooperation, GTZ and the Dutch government. By way of contrast, 'donor-driven' housing was intended to relocate affected families from the buffer zone to a 'safer' location, provide a house for a house, ensure land was provided by the government and mobilise donor assistance at the local level to ensure construction of homes and related infrastructure.[34]

Permanent housing grants differed fundamentally from transitional support. The distinguishing feature of permanent houses was the granting of titled and non-transferable land to the owner after ten years. Owner-driven grants varied from US$1,000 to US$2,500 depending on whether houses were considered 'fully' or 'partially' damaged.[35] The World Bank, a core proponent of the NIDR regime, prepared a trust fund to support owner-driven housing schemes through commercial banks. Meanwhile, a host of donors, including the World Bank, supported the process on a district-by-district basis. By the beginning of 2007 more than 55,000 (owner-driven) permanent houses were built – slightly more than 50 per cent of the original target of 98,000. According to RADA (2006c), very few donor-driven homes had been constructed (Map 6.3). According to key informants, however, most permanent houses that were constructed remained unoccupied owing to the poor land quality, their isolation, lack of infrastructural connectivity and persistent levels of insecurity.

The donor-driven permanent housing schemes were perhaps the clearest expressions of the nascent NIDR regime. The planning and construction of these schemes tended to be organised by external actors – including donors, architects, engineers and development specialists – and presented as 'a menu of options' to prospective beneficiaries. The conception, design and execution of these schemes were typically top-down and highly standardised. For example, blueprints of community-based schemes presented to the UDA varied from 100 to 1,000 households and were frequently characterised by grid-patterned roads, stylised houses aligned in rigid linear patterns with homesteads of the same size and configuration. Resettlement schemes often featured communal facilities – such as water points, toilets and schools – located in the centre of the 'community'. Resettlers interviewed in Ampara complained that the outlay and location of public services and utilities in donor-driven schemes seldom accounted for their heterogeneous religious, cultural, ethnic and gendered needs. Moreover, blueprints seldom included green or recreational spaces. According to one urban planner:

the cultural aspects of purchasing and building on land was not taken into account ... astrology and the identification of auspicious times, as well as consultations on the size, layout, and ordering of homes is important, irrespective of the socio-economic status or literacy of the displaced.[36]

Efforts to promote permanent housing faced a number of major challenges early on. Despite the introduction of donor meetings, these included poor coordination among state and non-governmental actors and the application of varied standards, as well as a persistent emergency relief bias in aid. As signalled above, the state's response while institutionally centralised in a specialised unit in Colombo was operationally decentralised among an array of competing entities.

Owing to the unprecedented scale of the natural disaster and international response, a vast number of new international NGOs began operations in Sri Lanka. Many had no experience working in the country and expected to rapidly acquire a sophisticated appreciation of the state's political, administrative and legal structure and culture (Rajasingham-Senanayake 2006). Their capacity to develop a nuanced approach was aggravated by the absence of institutional memory or inter-sector cooperation between the state and non-governmental sectors.[37] Many of these new NGOs and other more established NGOs such as Oxfam and Care had comparatively limited experience in moving beyond emergency and transitional approaches. There were in fact few agencies with adequate development expertise, and approaches tended instead to reflect short-term relief priorities.

Endogenous limitations of the NIDR regime

A number of Sri Lankan scholars contributed to a lively theoretical critique of the NIDR regime and the international aid architecture through which it is enacted. Most criticism is levied at endogenous factors – the interests, actors and actions of those involved in administering assistance. Commenting on the contradictions of the international response to the tsunami, scholars such as Rajasingham-Senanayake (ibid.) presage Naomi Klein's (2007) critique of 'disaster capitalism' and the intentional and unintentional distortions of overseas assistance. UN agencies are singled out for singularly failing to meet project deadlines, unnecessarily extending timelines and putting disproportionate emphasis on 'building back better' (Bastian 2006a). Others criticised the uniform or blueprint approach to resettlement that insufficiently accounted for the socio-economic and cultural heterogeneity of those living in affected areas. The

Sri Lankan government is also chastised for essentially sub-contracting out its response to (foreign) NGOs instead of harnessing local talent and for favouring large-scale capital-intensive development projects rather than smaller-scale bottom-up initiatives (Fraser 2005a).

Despite the deteriorating political climate from 2005 onwards, it is important to recall that NIDR regime proponents and planners were initially optimistic about prospects for achieving successful durable solutions. Many donors openly wondered whether the international response to the tsunami might also foster conditions for conflict prevention and reconciliation (Fraser 2005b). Nevertheless, their approaches to NIDR reflected several basic assumptions, including the application of standardised labels and categories and the adoption of a linear sequenced approach to population return and resettlement. In the rush to promote durable solutions, however, considerably less attention was devoted to adequately promoting horizontal and vertical linkages between resettlement schemes and host communities, ensuring genuinely participatory consultations relating to the design of permanent housing settlements or meeting adequate standards during their construction.

The NIDR regime promoted standardised and instrumental *categories* of presumed need. As predicted in Chapter 1, complexity was glossed over and differences denied. Labels emerged such as 'tsunami-displaced', as well as temporary 'emergency shelters', semi-permanent 'transitional shelters' and 'permanent housing'. These labels presupposed tidy categories of need and a corresponding range of entitlements managed by NIDR regime proponents and state bureaucracies. Access to these benefits required the acquisition of an appropriate label, irrespective of stratifications according to class, caste, religion, language and socio-economic status. Because they did not always fit predetermined categories, certain groups of landless and squatter communities were explicitly excluded from the policy of replacing a 'house for a house'. According to Uyangoda (2005: 31) beneficiaries were viewed not as active participants but rather 'passive recipients of humanitarian assistance'. For example, fishing families and carpenters from coastal areas in Batticaloa or Ampara were resettled inland and therefore suffered corresponding losses in livelihoods. Newly arrived NGOs were ill-prepared to accommodate the complex social and cultural realities of relocation, including the implications of moving fishing castes into communities from agricultural castes. As a result, large schemes of permanent homes, including apartment buildings, remain unoccupied.[38]

NIDR regime supporters adopted a *linear and sequenced approach* to relocation. The approach mirrored the trajectory anticipated in Chapter 1.

There were essentially three stages to NIDR beginning with (i) an emergency or temporary shelter phase; (ii) a transitional shelter phase; and (iii) a permanent housing phase. Resettlement schemes were often constructed in such a way that resettlers were treated as homogeneous entities. An underlying assumption was that all resettlers were to be provided with support on an 'equitable' basis and according to pre-established metrics of need. As in the case of the CIDR, NIDR regime proponents presumed that the displaced anticipated a swift return to 'home' even if many of the supposed beneficiaries were vocally opposed to returning. In Sri Lanka, NIDR regime proponents anticipated a permanent resettlement process. Indeed, such was the optimism among regime proponents that they anticipated 'building back better' and reordering the social and economic networks of otherwise vulnerable coastal communities. According to an early pronouncement by the director of THRU:

> We do not want to create slum cities. Instead, one must plan for the
> future and take account of all environmental, social and livelihood issues
> in resettling these people. The new settlements will be based on a new
> concept of village equipped with all infrastructure, educational, and
> health facilities. We are confident of completing all reconstruction and
> settlement work by April 2006.[39]

A major shortcoming of owner- and donor-driven permanent housing schemes was the limited attention to *vertical and horizontal linkages* between sectors, markets and geographic spaces. Because of the central government's understandable preoccupation with achieving visible and tangible impacts, resettlement schemes were often hastily assembled. Immediately following the acquisition of land by government agents and *land kacheris*, resettlement scheme plans seldom included strategies to ensure adequate connectivity to public utilities, roads and markets or recurrent expenditures. Such experiences stood in stark contrast to the DIDR regime, which applied central place theory to ensure that social and economic networks were central to resettlement scheme design. Early blueprints for new 'permanent housing' schemes often omitted downstream linkages in order to make their bids more attractive to donors. As result, many new permanent housing schemes in Sri Lanka lack long-term growth or market strategies and are likely to be emptied of second- and third-generation resettlers and reduced to orphans or satellite communities. What is more, many of those resettled lack the lobbying capacity to promote 'sustainable' integration of resettlement schemes with neighbouring communities.

Despite considerable rhetoric to 'voluntarily' resettle the tsunami-displaced, both owner- and donor-driven permanent housing schemes seldom adopted *participatory approaches* in practice. According to local authorities consulted in Trincomalee, Batticaloa and Ampara, the impetus was on 'building back faster rather than better'. One of the attributed reasons for this related to the engineering bias that pervaded the design of resettlement schemes. Another relates to the incentives for local contractors to build rapidly in the rush to secure ever more contracts. By 2006, however, UN-HABITAT introduced a more consultative approach to permanent housing. The agency launched a permanent housing programme for more than 3,000 donor-driven and owner-driven houses in fourteen districts. In order to promote sustainable social infrastructure, the agency supported the creation of 'community development councils' and discrete action plans to enhance their lobbying potential with district-level authorities.[40] Their multi-sector approach differed markedly from that of the World Bank's owner-driven schemes which were limited to (cash) grants issued to individuals through commercial banks.

Owing to the *absence of national standards* for NIDR and the sheer diversity of actors on the ground, there was considerable variance in both the quantity and quality of resettlement schemes. For example, there were considerably more permanent housing schemes established in south and south-western areas than in the north or east. Moreover, there was extensive variation in the types of schemes being established. As a result, in both Sri Lankan Tamil and Sinhalese areas, there were impressive multi-storey and well-constructed homes amid shoddy and poor-quality sheds.[41] Many schemes rapidly fell into disrepair owing to the failure to monitor and enforce quality. At times, this variance led to contradictions in the support provided by the NIDR regime. For example, in a number of schemes, FAO provided more fishing vessels than could be absorbed by the new residents, while in others, there were insufficient inputs. FAO was likewise forced to repurchase excess boats it had provided in Jaffna on account of military concerns with the surfeit of cheap vessels. Predictably, the disparity in resettlement packages and the rapid influx of assistance led to considerable tensions and competition (Kumar and Vasanthan 2006).

Exogenous limitations of the NIDR regime

A number of critical exogenous factors undermined the character and influence of the NIDR regime in Sri Lanka. As in the case of DIDR and CIDR, these factors are tied to the country's pre-existing ethnic conflict and political economy and were not anticipated by regime proponents. The first was the aforementioned *buffer zone* introduced by the government in the immediate aftermath of the tsunami. The buffer constituted a new spatial area that immediately required all within it to either settle or be resettled to new locations. To remain would be considered a criminal offence even if tolerated in certain cases. As noted above, the buffer created two separate categories of resettlement: donor-driven permanent housing for those within the buffer area and owner-driven permanent housing for those living outside the buffer. The second exogenous factor relates to *land availability and management*. Without sustained access to appropriate land, the potential of the NIDR regime proponents to promote durable solutions is limited. For one, the differentiated access to land – and the relationship between human vulnerability and settlement patterns – is a significant predicator of the incidence of NIDR. On the other hand, the availability – or in this case, non-availability – of land played a major role in shaping the outcomes of resettlement.

The buffer zone Though certain restrictions associated with coastal property existed since the 1980s, a forcefully enacted buffer zone was introduced retroactively by presidential decree shortly after the tsunami. The buffer effectively divided the fourteen affected districts into two discrete zones: the south and west (i.e. Kilinochchi, Mannar, Puttalam, Gampaha, Colombo, Kalutara, Galle, Matara and Hambantota) and the north and east (i.e. Jaffna, Mullaitivu, Trincomalee, Batticaloa and Ampara). The first zone included a new 'no-go' area extending from the mean highwater line to 100 metres inland, though this was relaxed to 50 metres following an outcry from the tourism lobby. The second zone included restrictions more than 200 metres inland (TAFREN 2005b). In uncleared areas in the second zone, the LTTE extended its own perimeter to 300 metres.

The buffer introduced prohibitions on the construction and reconstruction of buildings within the proscribed limit. It effectively criminalised the repairing of so-called partially damaged buildings and thus denied several hundred thousand displaced people the right to return or rebuild their own homes. The buffer effectively amounted to constructive forced eviction (COHRE 2006b). It also included important exemptions. While no 'residential' tenements were permitted, the tourism sector was permitted to continue operations in order to 'jump-start the local economy'.[42] Certain fishing industries, religious buildings, historic monuments and archaeological sites were also allowed to remain, on a case-by-case basis. These restrictions were not without precedent. Earlier Coastline Conservation Department (CCD) laws (1997, 1981) had effectively banned construction in certain coastal areas. Although introduced well before the buffer regulations, they were summarily ignored.

The buffer was first described by government officials as a 'preventive' measure to prevent communities from further exposure to subsequent tsunamis and related natural disasters. Its introduction appeared at first to be reasonable and superficially consistent with human rights standards (Leckie 2005) and initially supported by tsunami survivors (TEC 2006: iii). Notably, the buffer effectively disconnected the tsunami event from pre-existing social and economic 'vulnerabilities' as noted in Chapter 1. Moreover, the buffer was introduced without consulting affected populations and despite the express desire of many to return to their coastal homesteads. Thus, the buffer not only undermined NIDR regime principles of *voluntariness* and non-coercion,[43] by exempting the tourism industry and property developments, it undermined the regime's emphasis on equity and parity. Predictably, the buffer came to be viewed by local residents and critics as a commercially motivated land grab at best, and a strategic effort to confine the activities of the LTTE at worst (Uyangoda 2005).[44] Leckie (2005: 15) felt that it 'provided a pretext for evictions ... unjustifiable land acquisition plans and other measures designed to prevent homeless residents from returning to their original homes and lands'.

Those previously living within the 'buffer zone' were expected for the most part to be resettled into donor-driven permanent housing schemes. Described above, these schemes were located on newly annexed land – often far from the original homesteads of the new residents – and included purpose-built houses and access to certain services depending on their geographic location. Incentive packages to stimulate rebuilding were occasionally provided, depending on the service provider, the socio-economic profile of the recipient households and patronage networks among the settlers. Ultimately a small number of cash grants were provided and a meagre assortment of permanent houses established. The participation rates in donor-driven resettlement schemes were much lower than expected owing to the slow pace of their preparation, but also clear biases in the selection of candidates.[45]

By way of contrast, 'owner-driven' permanent housing schemes were eligible only to those living outside the various buffer limits. Individuals who could demonstrate proof of land and house ownership (by presenting titles and deeds) and corresponding damage were entitled to special grants. Grants were provided only to 'named' individuals who were included on 'beneficiary lists' prepared by the *grama sevekas* and administered by the divisional secretary and the *land kacheri*. Unlike the case of donor-driven approaches above, cash packages were provided to individual claimants through existing banks for repairing and rebuilding homes *in situ* rather than resettlement to a new area. Assistance was also provided for those affected or living in or near 'railway zones', 'wildlife conservation areas' and zones determined by the CCD regulations. According to practitioners working with Practical Action, Care and Oxfam, despite facing similar challenges (e.g. increased salinisation of paddy land, reduced fish harvests and reductions in tourism), 'owner-driven' permanent housing schemes were more rapidly and efficiently established than 'donor-driven' schemes.

Amid mounting international and domestic criticism, the entire buffer zone was abandoned in early 2006. It was first relaxed to 80 metres in the north and east 'depending on the vulnerability of the area to future threats' in late 2005. Faced with growing scientific and domestic opposition, some of which was driven by advocacy coalitions, the government rejected the buffer entirely in January 2006 and renewed prior CCD laws. These existing laws included guidelines that demarcated the coast according to differentiated 'zonal' restrictions aligned to topographical contours and elevation rather than arbitrarily defined spatial areas (de Silva, R. 2005). The buffer thus varied from 1 to 60 meters according to the spatial layout of the land surface. The altered legal context introduced yet another layer of complexity to the owner- and donor-driven resettlement enterprise and undermined the credibility of the entire NIDR regime.

Land distribution and availability NIDR regime supporters failed to adequately anticipate the highly uneven patterns of land distribution and the structural challenges associated with land acquisition. As previously noted, the scale and spatial effects of natural disasters are shaped not just by the hazard itself, but more fundamentally by pre-existing human or societal vulnerability and endowments among residents. Thus, existing societal capacities and resources, public infrastructure and social capital condition the outcomes of a particular disaster. Moreover, these same pre-existing vulnerabilities also shape the relative access to land. Pre-existing land-use and ownership patterns and land scarcity are briefly considered below.

Many natural disasters in Sri Lanka, including the tsunami, are inextricably linked to existing land-use and landownership patterns (Bastian 2006b). Households living in low-lying areas, non-irrigated lands, or steep and hilly terrain are especially susceptible to natural disasters, whether droughts, floods or landslides. Though many of these areas are arguably unsuitable for human habitation, they were often selected by certain households precisely because of latent ownership patterns and socio-economic stratification. As Bastian (ibid.) observes, market forces literally push the poor and marginalised to the periphery, in some cases closer to low-lying marginal coastal areas in the north and east where the tsunami's impact was most severe. Institutional responses to natural disasters, however, often fail to acknowledge pre-existing and heterogeneous forms of vulnerability (Chapter 2). Bureaucratic mechanisms developed by NIDR regime participants, for example, are frequently unable to account for the variation in landownership.

An oft-cited challenge to resettlement in Sri Lanka – including donor-driven permanent housing schemes – is land scarcity. According to the Sri Lankan government and most international NGOs, land scarcity is the critical exogenous constraint to the realisation of the NIDR regime. NIDR regime proponents, including donors and certain NGOs, threatened to relocate and prematurely terminate their operations unless land was made available by government agents, district and divisional secretaries and *land kacheri* offices. In their view, land was not only limited in quantity, but also in *quality*. Land provided by the state for donor-driven and owner-driven housing is often of exceedingly poor (agricultural) quality, located in politically unstable or marginal areas and in some cases so far from the original homes of displaced populations as to require profound changes in livelihood strategies and potentially resulting in the deepening of impoverishment.

NIDR regime proponents are increasingly unwilling to encourage resettlement on to poor-quality land. This is not only because of its re-moteness and limited social and economic connectivity, but also because of the limited visibility and profile prospective projects in remote areas would garner. For example, in Batticaloa, most arable and available land is located in the existing flood plains and exposes households to further vulnerability. When land is made available, it tends to be remote from con-ventional markets and public services. At the same time, comparatively little effort was devoted to defining alternative power and water facilities and more appropriate technologies including rain harvesting, alternative cooking techniques and even solar or wind power technologies.

Higher-quality land is difficult to acquire in the north and east due to legal constraints, population density in arable areas, persistent insecurity and inflationary effects associated with the conflict and the tsunami itself. The cost of goods and services escalated dramatically following the tsunami and subsequent inflow of aid. Key informants, including 'barefoot contractors' in Batticaloa, observed that the costs of cement rose from R490 a kilo to R690 in less than twelve months, while labour costs tripled from R400 to R1,500 a day for carpenters and masons. Similar shifts were reported by key informants in Trincomalee, Ampara and Hambantota in the south. NIDR regime supporters misjudged the attendant costs of resettling populations from marginal and flood-prone land or of integrating new resettlement schemes to electricity and water grids. Cost-overruns were more often the rule than the exception. These challenges were aggravated by the limited pool of skilled labourers and the absence of quality assurance guarantees, much less enforcement of contracts, all of which led to poorer-than-anticipated permanent housing schemes.

On closer inspection, it appears that land availability was also reserved for particular ethnic groups. The UDA and other designated state entities experienced considerable difficulties alienating and preparing state land for hundreds of thousands of displaced Sri Lankan Tamil and Muslim populations owing to familiar complaints that this might disturb ethnic ratios and the intensity of land speculation. Indeed, government agents in the north and east repeatedly emphasised the issue of 'ethnic ratios' when asked why southern resettlement schemes were progressing at a faster rate than those in the north and east. There is anecdotal evidence that pressure was applied from central authorities on government agents and the district bureaucracies not to upset the ethnic ratios – particularly by TULF, SLMC and other MPs with vested interests.

Meanwhile, the majority of land parcels ultimately identified by state authorities in Trincomalee, Batticaloa and Ampara for NIDR were often described as 'inadequate' by prospective resettlers. Many of those provided with land in the interior and away from the coastline refused to move from their 'traditional areas', citing loss of income and social capital (Perera, A. 2005). Other households adopted more innovative coping strategies by dividing their members, with some seeking employment in neighbouring centres and others waiting in emergency and transitional shelters for their owner-driven reconstruction grants to materialise. These individuals were often derided as 'cheats' or 'opportunists' by public and private officials alike.

Case studies of NIDR

Though the macro-economic consequences of the tsunami were surprisingly limited, the human costs were significant. The total area affected included fourteen districts and over 1,142 villages (Map 6.1).[46] The majority of disaster-related fatalities occurred in Jaffna, Batticaloa, Ampara, Mullaitivu, Galle and Hambantota, while the least affected areas included Colombo and Puttalum. The most significant displacement took place in Galle (128,000) due to the proximity of the densely populated old city to the coast, followed by Trincomalee (82,000) and Ampara

(85,000) with similarly dense coastal settlements (TAFREN 2005b). While the NIDR regime played a pivotal role in framing the discourse and bureaucratic approach to resettlement, its proponents did not achieve their central objective: permanent housing based on equity and need. Indeed, hundreds of thousands of tsunami-displaced continued to live in emergency and transitional shelters almost four years after the tsunami. Where built at all, most permanent houses were relocated tens of kilometres from the original homes of displaced populations with severe consequences for achieving sustainable livelihoods and resuming productive lives.

Trincomalee Due to its strategic and historical importance to the LTTE and the Sri Lankan armed forces, Trincomalee is one of the more politically unstable districts in the country. Trincomalee district was also severely unsettled by the tsunami. Certain divisions such as Muttur, Kinniya, Etchalampattu, Kuchaveli and Seruwila were particularly badly affected, including fifty-two *grama seveka* divisions. According to RADA and UN-HABITAT some 3,893 houses were 'fully damaged' and another 3,638 'partially damaged' in and around the erstwhile buffer zone. Additional social infrastructure including almost 330 communal market places, as well as educational and hospital facilities, were reportedly destroyed. Despite the considerable impacts on the area, comparatively few permanent homes were built by 2006 and in 2007 the majority of the tsunami-displaced remained in temporary and transitional shelters, or settled spontaneously.

The district is also anomalous in Sri Lanka because all three major ethnic groups are more or less equally represented (Chapter 5). Moreover, tens of thousands of Sri Lankan Tamils and Muslims from Trincomalee and surrounding districts were affected by CIDR throughout the 1980s and 1990s and now reside in welfare centres and relocation villages. Both Sri Lankan Tamils and Muslims living in Muttur and Kinniya were doubly discriminated against owing to their persistent inaccessibility and the continued armed conflict. In many cases, those provided with relief *before* the tsunami found these provisions annulled *after* NIDR-related relief programmes were introduced.

According to the government agent of Trincomalee, a major challenge to NIDR relates to the overall scarcity of land, the marginal quality of land that is available for resettlement and the exceptional low quality (but high cost) of construction materials.[47] While transitional shelters expanded throughout the district, permanent housing construction was delayed on account of persistent confusion with the buffer zone policy and

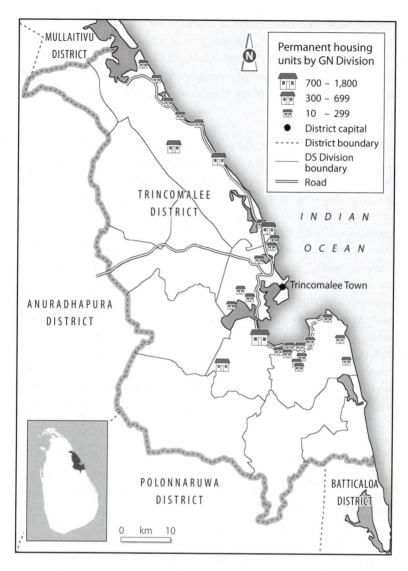

MAP 6.4 Permanent housing in Trincomalee (2006) *Source*: Reconstructed from UN-HABITAT records/database.

concerns with preserving the ethnic ratio (Map 6.4). Such unpredictability generated certain real and opportunity costs. Few donors or locals were prepared to invest in 'permanent housing' without guarantees that land tenure would be secure. Repeated field visits also revealed overt and subtle forms of resistance to resettlement from among the tsunami-displaced. Many preferred to remain in emergency and transitional shelters rather than relocate. Key informants complained that not just their assets and socio-cultural investments, but also their livelihoods would be displaced should they move further inland. Among those who availed themselves of donor-driven resettlement, many retained their (original) land in the buffer zone while simultaneously securing new land offered in the schemes.

Ampara Like Trincomalee, Ampara also exhibited an unusual population distribution in relation to other Sri Lankan districts. Of the estimated 604,000 residents in 2003, approximately 41 per cent are Muslim, 39 per cent Sinhalese and 19 per cent Tamil.[48] What is most important to recall is that well over 90 per cent of all Muslims and Tamils in the district were living in exposed coastal areas in twelve of the twenty divisions at the time the wave struck the island. Their location in extremely dense clusters – among the most densely populated human habitats in the world – in marginal coastal land is testament to their pre-existing vulnerability (Map 6.5). This stands in start contrast to the majority of Sinhalese 'settlers' and residents who live predominantly in the fertile interior.[49] Immediately following the tsunami, there were an estimated 10,436 people killed and more than 193,000 internally displaced scattered in some sixty-seven clusters of emergency shelters or transitional shelters (TAFREN 2005b). By mid-2005, TAFREN reported that at least 17,117 homes were 'fully damaged' and needed to be rebuilt and that an additional 10,000 were 'partly damaged'. The resettlement requirements were tremendous.

NIDR regime proponents encountered significant challenges in building either transitional shelters and permanent housing in Ampara. A number of obstacles were logistical in nature: the sheer costs of ensuring that goods and services were provided to isolated areas, in addition to the many accompanying security risks, reduced the overall volume of aid. In addition to the remoteness of Ampara district from the political and commercial centre of the country, a key factor shaping NIDR in the region related to ethnicity. Both Muslims and Sri Lankan Tamils lacked adequate bargaining clout to (re)negotiate their entitlements with state structures. Not just the quantity, but the quality of transitional and permanent housing appeared to be lower in Ampara than in other southern districts. During field visits, transitional houses were repeatedly described as being in poor condition and, indeed, many showed evidence of rapid erosion and decline.[50] A focus group with recent resettlers in Kalmunai complained that their (and their neighbours) houses were frequently 'too small, with poor ventilation, no electricity, made from shoddy materials,

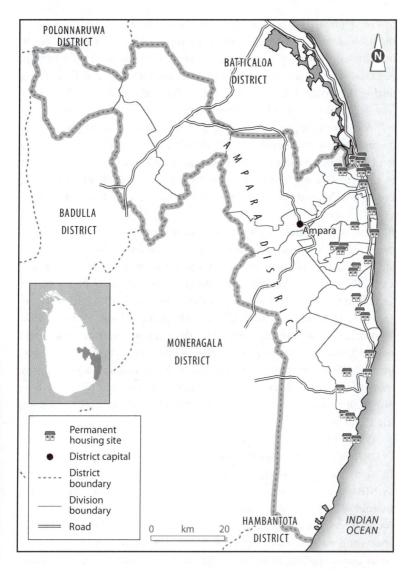

MAP 6.5 Permanent housing in Ampara (2006) Source: Reconstructed from UN-HABITAT records/database.

with virtually no access to health clinics or services' and that transport in and out was impossible after the rains.[51]

The acquisition and securing of title of reasonable-quality land for permanent housing was considered to be among the most significant challenges for NIDR in Ampara. Those living in 'emergency' and 'transitional' shelters and located on private land were often required to evacuate by existing owners and moneylenders – many of whom were positioning themselves to sell at higher prices. In some cases, residents living in transitional shelters on public lands were requested by local authorities to pay *solai vari* – or land tax – despite having lost virtually all of their assets during the disaster. Focus group respondents claimed that where land was declared unavailable by government agents or district secretaries, full compensation (as opposed to the equivalent of US$2,500) should be provided to those forced to leave 'buffer areas' in order to purchase land and build new homes. Moreover, those living with extended families in their homes before the tsunami felt that 'compensation' should be broadened beyond the 'roof for roof' and 'house for a house' policy.

Batticaloa According to 2001 census records there were at least 486,000 people living in Batticaloa at the time of the tsunami. Unlike Trincomalee or Ampara, the majority of the district's residents are Sri Lankan Tamil (Chapter 5). The principal source of livelihoods is paddy or rice agriculture, though those living in the nine coastal divisions were engaged, as in Ampara, in fishing. It was these coastal divisions that were among the most severely affected by the tsunami. Batticaloa was also considered to be one of the worst affected districts in Sri Lanka. According to TAFREN (2005b), there were some 29,000 'fully damaged' houses, more than one-third (37 per cent) of the total in the country. There were also approximately 11,486 'partially damaged' homes, or 28 per cent of the country's total.

As in other districts, the quality of the 'transitional shelters' erected by UNHCR and others was severely criticised by focus group respondents. In many cases, the standards set in Colombo and in district capitals by NIDR regime proponents were not followed through on the ground. Instead of free-standing edifices with steel reinforcements and concrete foundations, transitional shelters more often consisted of polyethylene sheets and wooden boards retrieved from nearby buildings. In other cases, transitional shelters built by donors and NGOs were used as 'storage spaces' or left empty because they were developed in inappropriate or marginal areas. Respondents repeatedly complained that their location and design was incommensurate with their needs and that they had not been consulted in their design or implementation.

The development of permanent housing proceeded more slowly in Batticaloa than in most other districts. Indeed, the policies introduced to administer the process were described as 'highly selective' and 'discriminatory' by focus group respondents.[52] According to some, they failed to take into account the multiple tenants and extended families in existing

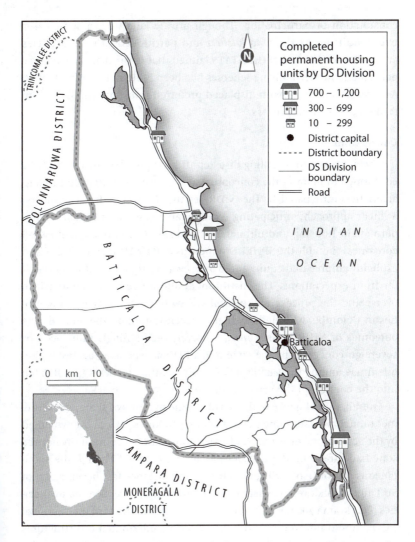

MAP 6.6 Permanent housing in Batticaloa (2006) *Source*: Reconstructed from UN-HABITAT records/database.

households. Families living in parental homes were ineligible for assistance under the NIDR regime. Permanent housing grants and schemes assumed a relatively smaller number of potential residents. Even for those entitled to owner-driven permanent homes, those households that deviated from the criteria (e.g. those with extended families or those without clear title), experienced extensive and protracted delays in supplying the US$2,500 grant. By way of comparison, donor-driven assistance was piecemeal and ad hoc with few clear provisions for community consultation or participation. Though private land was in some cases made available by the *land kacheri* and partitioned to state agencies and NGOs for NIDR, UN-HABITAT claimed that fewer than two or three permanent 'model' housing schemes had been built in the entire district. As a result, many tsunami-displaced preferred monetary compensation to the donor-driven process.

Conclusions

The approach to resettling disaster-affected populations in Sri Lanka conformed to many of the conceptual, normative and bureaucratic characteristics anticipated by the NIDR regime. Conceptually, it advanced a linear approach, anticipating a predictable shift from transitional to permanent housing and ultimately, handover. Normatively, it drew on core rules – notably the SPHERE Standards and UNHCR guidelines – and explicitly emphasised equity and parity, even if implementation deviated far from expectations. The institutional and bureaucratic approach to overseeing the process was centralised within a number of core entities in Colombo, with delivery highly decentralised on the ground. The outcomes of NIDR in Sri Lanka, however, were strongly influenced by sovereign concerns (by the state and LTTE) as well as collective action dilemmas among the vast array of implementing agencies that flooded into the country in the wake of the wave.

Overall, the influence of the NIDR regime in terms of shaping resettlement outcomes was superficial. Regime proponents were overwhelmed by the scale of the disaster. Neither the international community nor the state had experienced a disaster of such magnitude. Though the spontaneous response of civil society in the first instance fast became part of Sri Lankan folklore, the sheer level of devastation exceeded their capacities (Parakrama 2006; Fraser 2005a). As literally hundreds of international NGOs moved into the country, they rapidly undermined the structures of community and local organisational structures through aggressive recruitment, inflationary impacts and the rapid and misdirected distribution of assistance (Fraser 2005a: 40). Crucially, however, exogenous factors, including the introduction of the buffer and tensions over land availability, played a critical role in minimising regime influence.

Acknowledging and adequately preparing for exogenous factors, including pre-existing patterns of land availability and access, is essential to undertaking sustainable resettlement in the aftermath of natural disasters. By considering structural conditions of Sri Lankan society, including access and ownership of land, caste, class and ethnicity, it is possible to begin anticipating the potential risks and outcomes of

NIDR. Indeed, progressive interventions might even anticipate these constraints and include preventive relocation and the strengthening of 'disaster-preparedness' mechanisms for those compelled to reside in vulnerable disaster-prone areas. Owing to their inability to explicitly account for ethnic politics and pre-existing vulnerability NIDR regime proponents failed to anticipate these exogenous factors. The combined effects of these exogenous factors were to spatially segment resettlement assistance. According to R. Senanayake (2006: 61):

> districts with deeper poverty and higher concentrations of vulnerable communities affected by the tsunami and conflict (Jaffna and Vanni) have far fewer projects and organisations on the ground than some other tsunami-affected districts in the south where reconstruction is slightly more advanced.

In this chapter we have considered the parameters and outcomes of a declarative NIDR regime in Sri Lanka. As predicted by constructivists, the discursive expressions of principles, rules and decision-making procedures occur in 'official' fora such as the UN General Assembly or donor conferences in Tokyo or Colombo, but also in daily landscapes and interactions that characterise lived experience. We have also reviewed the diversity of displacement and resettlement experiences and entitlements arising out of the tsunami. In some cases, the tsunami-displaced availed themselves of owner-driven permanent houses and relocated from the eastern to the southern coast. In other cases, the displaced were provided with donor-driven assistance and resettled in land away from their coastal villages. In still other scenarios, displaced households received nominal grants to repair their partially destroyed home. Instead of including resettlers as active participants in a durable solution, the diverse needs of the tsunami-displaced were streamlined by the NIDR regime in such a way as to make them legible to outsiders.

Conclusions

This volume has found that a comparative analysis of different categories of internal displacement and resettlement can usefully reveal their common causes, conceptualisations and consequences. A unified perspective can therefore enhance theory-building and policy. In reviewing the origins and evolution of distinct advocacy coalitions and public policy networks, the foregoing has highlighted the emergence of distinct regimes with common clusters of principles, norms, rules and decision-making mechanisms. Although oriented towards promoting protection and durable solutions and drawing on familiar conceptual axioms in forced migration research, regime supporters have remained stubbornly isolated from one another. Despite much promise, the three regimes are less influential in inducing changes in state behaviour or fomenting protection and durable outcomes than expected.

In Sri Lanka, as elsewhere, regime influence is diluted by endogenous factors such as a narrow reading of sovereignty and collective action dilemmas. Regimes are born weak because of the widespread interpretation of sovereignty as non-intervention in national affairs.[1] Despite evidence of an ominous return to (military) unilateralism in the Middle East and Central Asia, the non-interference principle remains a cornerstone of the present international order (Evans, G. 2007). In deference to these legitimate concerns, regimes are frequently declaratory and decentralised. Related to this, regimes are manifest in the codification and dissemination of basic norms, the creation of decision-making mechanisms to implement rules and censure where core tenets of the regime are ignored or violated. In Sri Lanka, despite the absorption of certain regime norms and rules in national legislation, policy and programming, the decision-making apparatus for the three regimes translated into either highly centralised public entities in the case of DIDR or dispersed confederations of multilateral, bilateral and national non-governmental agencies in relation to CIDR and NIDR. The lack of accountability and unpredictability generated by these latter institutional mechanisms exacerbated collective action dilemmas among regime proponents, particularly those practically involved in undertaking resettlement.

Exogenous factors also shape regime influence and effectiveness, as the case of Sri Lanka amply shows. Despite the professed aim of contributing to enhanced protection and durable solutions, international regimes and their proponents are still relatively ill-equipped to contend with the diverse constellation of interests and factors shaping DIDR, CIDR and NIDR. In Sri Lanka, legislation associated with land acquisition, owner-ship, tenure and expropriation extends back to the nineteenth century and grew progressively politicised following independence. A combi-nation of economic and nationalist interests profoundly conditioned the character of DIDR. Likewise, the imperatives of war and strategic advantage influenced the state's approach to CIDR, while land availability and the political imperatives of elites shaped the direction and tenor of NIDR. Chapters 4, 5 and 6 highlighted the disjuncture between regime objectives and outcomes in Sri Lanka and the ways in which exogenous factors to regimes – including nation-building and ethnic nationalism – can undermine them.

This Conclusion compares the connections and relationships between DIDR, CIDR and NIDR, processes often conceived by policymakers and practitioners as autonomous and mutually exclusive. Specifically, it focuses on their multi-causality, bureaucratic logic and impoverishment effects. We then review prospects for regime convergence and examine the likely direction of international responses to internal displacement and resettlement in the twenty-first century. Notwithstanding the uni-lateral tendencies described above, an emerging rights-based discourse is encouraging an 'equitable' treatment of different categories of displaced people. However, unless basic assumptions concerning the function of state sovereignty are consciously broadened and collective action di-lemmas are reduced through the articulation of effective decision-making institutions, regimes are unlikely to achieve their professed aims.

Comparing internal displacement and resettlement

Over the course of the past five decades, since the 1960s, the forced migration field has undergone a process of theoretical and bureaucratic differentiation. As with the tendency towards theoretical and technocratic specialisation in the natural and social sciences more generally, the densification of parallel streams of forced migration studies made it increasingly difficult to bridge disciplinary divides and instead encour-aged the formation and consolidation of epistemic and bureaucratic silos. Nevertheless, the period witnessed a considerable horizontal transfer of ideas and knowledge between scholars and practitioners within specific specialist communities. This is because forced migration scholars – both action and applied researchers – are closely connected with policymakers and donors involved in promoting protection and durable solutions. As a result, there is significant cognitive exchange between the academic and policy realms. An unintended consequence of this is the unnecessary sheltering of communities from one another and continued standardisation and labelling in forced migration discourse.

Advancing a unitary approach A unitary approach to researching displacement and resettlement can potentially bridge latent segmentation in forced migration studies. In revealing the common approaches to modelling the causes of, and responses to, forced migration, it is possible to see how different categories of displaced and resettled populations share more commonalities than frequently assumed. Comparative analysis also highlights the similar political and economic agendas that underlie the process while revealing opportunities for learning and sharing between potentially disconnected epistemological communities. Likewise, a comparative assessment reveals the common effects and pathologies associated with resettlement and ways of potentially minimising them. Sutton (1977: 298) observed how 'comparability can stem from the traumatic effects produced by resettlement ... [and how] the stress of forced removal is so great that societies respond similarly' in his reflections on the commonalities between *regroupment* and dam-related resettlement in Africa. As noted by Cernea (2005: 26) almost three decades later, investment in inter-disciplinary and comparative research can potentially 'influence the public arena by mutually reinforcing their policy advocacy and operational recommendations'.

The dividends arising from enhanced exchange between certain forced migration streams – particularly scholars of DIDR and refugees – was observed almost two decades ago by Harrell-Bond at Oxford's Refugee Studies Centre (RSC) and Cernea (1990). Cernea in particular was concerned with the persistent 'unjustified dichotomies' in the forced migration literature and an absence of meta-theory building. Though separate 'streams' of enquiry coexisted, he detected little meaningful collaboration between experts focused on oustees and specialists concerned with refugees.[2] Another initiative led by Cohen at the Brookings Institution stimulated learning and exchange between action researchers focusing on conflict-induced and development-induced internal displacement in 2002, though these findings were not published (Kälin 2005b). Both initiatives signalled a renewed commitment to comparative analysis of displacement, but few follow-on studies were undertaken.[3]

The application of a unified approach requires basic consensus on fundamental concepts such as internal displacement and resettlement. Though the perspectives of different forced migration experts may diverge at various levels, Chapter 1 of this study highlighted some conceptual convergence on the basic parameters of both phenomena, and reviewed several core attributes assigned by forced migration experts to displacement: volition, temporality and spatiality. It noted how such concepts need to be critically examined in practice. By way of comparison, resettlement was described as being conditional on displacement and a function of clear planning and control and permanent reterritorialisation of populations to an area other than their place of origin. Although the terminologies and labels ascribed to the internally displaced and resettled are varied – whether 'settlers', 'oustees', 'refugees', 'IDPs' and 'tsunami-displaced' in 'colonisation units', 'welfare centres', 'relocation villages' or 'permanent houses' – a unified appraisal signals their many shared characteristics.

Across disciplines, understandings and approaches to conceptualising displacement and resettlement generally flow from attributed causes and presumptions of linearity. Policymakers and practitioners often attribute displacement to specific triggers such as the implementation of a development project, the outbreak of collective violence and the onset of natural or environmental disasters. In their haste to respond to and mitigate the effects of such events they often presume unidirectional causation: multi-causality may be unintentionally glossed over. Displacement and resettlement are cast as if on a continuum. Although structural and proximate factors associated with DIDR, CIDR or NIDR are noted, attention focuses instead on the incident catalysing displacement, associated strategies to enhance resilience or minimise risks and, ultimately, return, local integration or resettlement. As such, interventions are oriented around minimising triggers, protecting the displaced and supporting durable solutions rather than attending to the broader political or economic processes at work. Displacement and resettlement are thus compartmentalised – isolated from the constellation of intervening factors that gave rise to it or that directly inform its shape and character.

There are clear distinctions between development-, conflict- and natural disaster-induced internal displacement and resettlement. In Sri Lanka as elsewhere, DIDR regime proponents portray displacement as being an unintentional by-product of development interventions. Resettlement is frequently planned with detailed procedures laid out in hard or soft law as to how and when assets can be expropriated, the obligations of the acquiring agency and clearly defined valuations for compensation. In the case of conflict, internal displacement is cast by CIDR regime advocates as a purposive strategy or as 'collateral damage'. Resettlement is expected to adhere to norms laid out in human rights law, including the Guiding Principles. Depending on the intensity of the natural hazard and the relative vulnerability of affected populations, approaches to NIDR vary significantly, with resettlement outcomes contingent on international and domestic interests and capacities. Despite these perceived variations, the rationale for developing a unified approach to researching internal displacement and resettlement across contexts is compelling. All three processes entail the planned relocation of civilians *within* the boundaries of their original state. Most if not all resettlers *should* receive equal treatment as citizens within a shared jurisdiction.

Reflections on multi-causality Different categories of internal displacement and resettlement are seldom compared because development, conflict and natural disasters are often treated as exclusive processes. Though a simplification, development is cast by DIDR regime supporters, especially applied scholars, as a progressive process associated with expanding human capabilities and economic growth (Sachs 2005; Sen 1999; UNDP 1994). Whether defined in relation to macro-economic growth, sustainability, or human security, development as a process is supposed to expand opportunities and improve social and economic welfare. By way of contrast, armed conflict is commonly interpreted by CIDR regime proponents as a breakdown in development and a violent reordering of economic and social relations (Wallensteen 2005; Keen 1998). Whether measured as a function of 'battle deaths' or war, it is generally associated with diminished opportunities and various forms of exclusion and horizontal inequalities (Stewart et al. 1997; Stewart and Fitzgerald 2001). Natural disasters are frequently described simplistically as interconnected environmental hazards by NIDR regime advocates, invariably contributing to sudden social and economic decline even if the complex associations between human vulnerability, resilience and environmental stress are gradually being recognised (Oliver-Smith 2005; Twigg 2004). International responses to development, conflict and natural disasters were traditionally designed and executed by distinct public entities and multilateral agencies with specialised competencies in each sector.

There is a growing recognition that development, conflict and natural disasters are in fact multi-causal phenomena with multiple risk factors and outcomes. A political economy lens reveals a much more complicated and interconnected cluster of (independent) variables precipitating and prolonging all three processes. Monolithic paradigms alternately linking development with economic growth and well-being, conflict with socio-economic deterioration or natural disasters with social collapse are at odds with an emerging critical literature on the (anti)politics of development, new wars and environmental hazards (Duffield, M. 2001; Duffield, J. 2007; Kaldor 1999; Sachs 1992; Ferguson 1990). Indeed, all three processes overlap, and awareness of these synergies has potentially far-reaching implications for forced migration theory and practice. Acknowledging the web of factors contributing to internal displacement and resettlement could lead to rethinking the very nature of separate international regimes designed to address the problem to begin with.

Chapter 4 reviewed the way in which a well-resourced development intervention in Sri Lanka generated unintentional, unequal and ultimately violent outcomes in a context where political and ethnic dynamics were insufficiently taken into account. The uneven impacts of a host of other development-induced resettlement schemes since the 1970s are disconcerting reminders of how this was not an isolated event (World Bank 2004d; Dunham and Kelegama 1995). These findings coincide with emerging cognisance of the relationships between development, underdevelopment and armed conflict.[4] Demonstrated factors contributing to the onset of acute armed violence, for example, include sharp macroeconomic shocks, youth bulges, systemic under- and unemployment and rising horizontal inequality (Pugh et al. 2004; Collier and Hoeffler 2000; Berdal and Malone 2000; Keegan 1993). At the meso- and microlevels, Anderson (1999) describes how development and humanitarian assistance can also intensify and prolong violent conflict where it is inappropriately planned, managed and monitored.[5] The reverse is also true: armed conflict can undermine and even terminate prospects for equitable pro-growth and pro-poor development and can diminish opportunities for relief assistance.

As noted in Chapters 5 and 6, there is growing consciousness of the many ways that societies affected by underdevelopment and conflict are also connected with increased vulnerability to natural and environmental disasters. Though certain hazards remain difficult to predict, there is a marked increase in international capacities to estimate, anticipate and respond to such calamities – whether earthquakes, cyclones, hurricanes or encroaching deserts as well as measure pre-existing patterns of vulnerability (Homer-Dixon 2000, 2006; Black 2001a). In societies facing acute stresses such as unevenly distributed development or acute levels of violence, many households invariably face heightened susceptibility to even relatively minor hazards including floods and hurricanes (Gleditsch 1997). Likewise, contrary to expectations in post-tsunami Sri Lanka, dramatic natural hazards can also potentially aggravate political tension and exacerbate underdevelopment by creating the conditions for the onset of war.[6] Despite growing awareness of the robust connections between

221

development, conflict and natural disasters, the compartmentalisation by policymakers of various forms of internal displacement and resettlement into reified categories persists.

A growing number of forced migration scholars are acknowledging the many ways in which causal factors contributing to development, conflict and natural disasters are interlinked. As noted in Chapters 1 and 2, development interventions with resettlement components – large-scale land reform, resource-extraction schemes and power or irrigation projects – are regularly accompanied by violence and coercion before, during and after population movement takes place. Described by Oliver-Smith (1996) as 'economic violence', ethnic and religious minorities, low-caste groups and the (income) poor are often forcibly resettled without compensation or provision of land at replacement cost and usually as part of a broader process of strategic and commercial appropriation. At its most extreme, 'development-induced displacement is the ultimate expression of a state with its monopoly on the management of violence ... to be resettled is one of the most acute expressions of powerlessness because it constitutes a loss of control over one's physical space' (ibid.: 79). That the state is in most cases both a protagonist and arbitrator of displacement and resettlement – and the source of laws and regulations – raises a number of clear and difficult tensions. But systematic research on the ways in which settlement and resettlement feature coercion is still limited. Specialists tend to focus on violent resistance.

It is worth revisiting the interconnectedness of DIDR, CIDR and NIDR in the Sri Lankan case. Chapter 4 described how several hundred thousand Sinhalese peasants were alternately settled and resettled (often within their original districts) into state-assisted colonisation schemes and *purana* village expansion projects. These interventions displaced Sinhalese peasants as well tens of thousands of Tamil and Muslim 'encroachers' in the central, northern and eastern districts during the 1970s, 1980s and 1990s. Chapter 5 documented how many of the same populations displaced and resettled into colonisation units were (re)displaced as both refugees and IDPs and subsequently resettled into welfare centres and relocation villages where they were effectively contained. Chapter 6 recounted how almost half a million acutely vulnerable – Sri Lankan Tamils, Muslims and Sinhalese – many of whom were previously displaced and resettled by a combination of colonisation and development projects and protracted war, were again relocated into temporary, transitional and permanent shelters following a massive tsunami. Over a period of several decades, these successive episodes of displacement and resettlement contributed to the consolidation of ethnically homogeneous enclaves

(Annex 1a–1d). It is in assessing linkages between causal factors and effects that a fully unified narrative is rendered.

Bureaucratic logic Public and non-governmental entities supporting DIDR, CIDR and NIDR tend to apply a uniform bureaucratic logic and set of practices to achieving protection and durable solutions. Bureaucratic logic refers to the normative and operational assumptions adopted by states and non-governmental agencies to planning and implementing interventions on behalf of displaced and resettled populations. The expression is borrowed from Voutira (1997: 2) who notes how 'affected groups' are disaggregated and assigned specific attributes that reflect the interests and aims of 'the existing bureaucratic structures entailing a specific division of labour and responsibility among UN and non-governmental agencies'. Their common approaches are born in part from epistemic and causal assumptions reviewed in Chapters 1 and 2. The convergent bureaucratic logic is ultimately a function of sustained collaboration between multilateral and bilateral donors, international financial institutions and humanitarian agencies – the World Bank, UNHCR and IFRC prominent among them[7] – often on thematic issues that are relatively new to their institutional mandates (UNHCR 2004a, 2006c). The fact that many regime proponents collaborate on a regular basis on a vast array of activities potentially explains why certain bureaucratic responses share many common features.[8]

On the ground, the way in which regime proponents promote protection and durable solutions is often top-down and paternalistic despite a growing insistence among advocacy coalitions for participatory approaches. Chapter 3 described how, in Sri Lanka, legislation and interventions on behalf of the internally displaced frequently assumed that the latter were passive, risk-averse and dependency-prone. Authorities frequently attributed the slow pace and poor outcomes of resettlement to resettlers rather than to the original conceptualisation, the associated practices or the political environment and historical context in which it transpires. Sutton (1977: 283) described how in the case of DIDR, in many cases 'those who have been resettled now experience the additional insult of being dependent for food aid on the same central government agency that they blamed for uprooting them in the first place'.[9] The introduction of grassroots agricultural committees to identify and respond to local needs (Chapter 4), voluntary committees within welfare centres (Chapter 5) or individuated cash grants for owner-driven housing (Chapter 6) were all comparatively novel innovations designed to stimulate more consultation, 'self-reliance' and ultimately to avoid dependency.

Dependency – the reliance on state or non-governmental hand-outs and the manipulation of entitlements – is seldom interpreted by regime proponents as a kind of coping strategy. Since the nineteenth century, public authorities have reacted with dismay when resettled populations exhibited certain forms of opportunism – whether by taking advantage of the incentives on offer, exploiting loopholes in entitlements or resisting relocation efforts. Rather than harnessing and reinforcing their latent entrepreneurship, resettlers were instead derided for their delinquency and lack of creativity (Jamal 2003; Cutts 2000). Relatively few regime supporters questioned the ways in which their own policies and programmes reinforced apathy and fixed identities. It seems instead that the persistence of centralised top-down approaches to resettlement in Sri Lanka was motivated as much by a desire to control and (re)order communities as a genuine concern for the welfare of affected groups. During the 1960s and 1970s there was a general tendency towards experimenting with collective and cooperative tenure systems and interventions to avoid dependency, although a penchant for rational and individual-based incentives soon returned.

Resettlement is social and demographic engineering by another name. Whether shaped by the imperatives of national progress or ethnic hegemony, resettlement comprises spatial and social reconfiguration. It aspires to 'the administrative ordering of nature and society' (Scott 1998). Resettlement is expected to allow complex social realities to be read by outsiders (elites and planners) and frequently privileges technical knowledge over indigenous understandings. The sheer remit of resettlement is breathtaking. It anticipates the restoration and re-creation of coherent, functional and dynamic household and community structures, often in contexts where the socio-economic and cultural order is fragmented, rights and entitlements marginalised and familiar geographies replaced by foreign and potentially marginal spaces. As noted in Chapter 4, the MDIP was a 'modernization programme envisaging the improvement of living standards of all settlers in schemes concerned by intensifying land use' (Mahakanadaawa 1979).

Across time and space, resettlement targets poor and frequently rural populations and adopts a phased approach. Drawing from modernisation theory, large-scale agricultural resettlement schemes were often favoured in order to promote sedentarism and curb rural–urban migration. Durable solutions ranged from the creation of productive households across multiple generations to self-reliant communities in a relatively short period of time. Resettlement planners conventionally divided the process into discrete stages with a 'beginning' shortly before the displacement event, a 'middle' characterised by heightened risks and vulnerability and a 'handover' for which an exit strategy was ideally prepared in advance. Thus neatly packaged, interventions on behalf of internally displaced and resettled people follow a typical sequence. In Sri Lanka, they included sensitisation and early warning during the early onset of the 'incident', the provision of food and non-food rations following the event, physical relocation to transit centres, temporary shelters, transitional shelters or welfare centres and ultimately investment to promote self-reliant colonisation units, relocation villages or permanent housing schemes. Rations and development inputs were gradually reduced to deter dependency. Assistance was eventually terminated altogether when the new resettlement schemes were considered by outsiders to be self-sufficient and 'integrated'. Despite the repeated failure of such approaches, they are nevertheless reproduced again and again.

Impoverishment effects Forced migration scholars and practitioners scrupulously documented the social, cultural and economic pathologies accompanying displacement and resettlement. While their research straddles multiple contexts and disciplines, they register consistent and recurrent patterns and trends. In describing the costs and risks of DIDR, CIDR or NIDR, they observe that such populations universally face privation, loss of adequate shelter and assets, cultural dissonance, above-average unemployment, morbidity and mortality and real and relative poverty arising from the dislocation of both households and societal networks. In describing how populations under stress cope with their new environments, they also emphasise the many ways in which displaced and resettled people mobilise social and economic resources on their own in order to re-establish viable relationships and restore their material and social status, sometimes by resort to force. Oliver-Smith and Button (2005: 11) note that there are 'important similarities that we must recognize and understand both to minimize displacement and to assist in the material reconstruction and the social reconstitution of communities'.

Forced migration scholars thus focus overwhelmingly on the *risks, vulnerabilities* and *impoverishment effects* associated with internal displacement and resettlement. Through extensive ethnographic and anthropological research, many found that resettlement yielded the reverse of what was anticipated in theory: it exacerbated rather than deterred impoverishment. Though there is limited comparative evidence statistically measuring the strength of correlations between resettlement (independent variable) and impoverishment (dependent variable), there is a litany of anecdotal examples where resettlement administered as part of a development intervention, in the aftermath of an armed conflict, or following a major natural disaster, intensified a range of impoverishment risks (Cernea 2006; Garikipati 2005; McDowell 1996a).

There is in fact very limited research on the counterfactual – that 'spontaneous settlers' are better off than those who are physically relocated into planned schemes. A proxy counterfactual might include individuals and households affected by DIDR, CIDR or NIDR and spontaneously settling *outside* colony units, relocation villages and permanent housing schemes. Another approach might include comparing and contrasting the socio-economic profiles of resettling populations with control populations that were neither displaced nor resettled (Ellis and Barakat 1996; Chambers 1986). In the select cases where empirical studies compared resettlers with spontaneous settlers and host communities, they demonstrated that the latter generally reported higher indices of well-being and resilience, including more rapid rates of livelihood restoration, than those involved in resettlement (Boano et al. 2003). Intervening variables such as the *capacity* of public authorities to undertake resettlement and the *endowment sets* of populations selected for resettlement or who elected for spontaneous settlement are of critical importance. But even when accounting for diverse factors relating to the state capacities or the social capital, income, assets and agency of resettlers, the fact of being resettled remains a significant contributor to impoverishment.

Although internally displaced and resettling populations universally experience suffering, they do not suffer equally. Action and applied researchers observed certain differences in the impoverishment risks facing different categories of internally displaced and resettled populations. They recognise the heterogeneity of resettlement experiences even though the majority of those affected are represented in lower income strata, castes or minority populations. Moreover, they found that differences among specific categories inspired varying institutional responses that in turn shaped differential vulnerabilities. For example, in Sri Lanka, there were comparatively fewer services and inputs provided to households internally displaced and resettled by conflict than for those evicted as a result of irrigation projects, village expansion schemes or natural disasters, irrespective of the demonstrated need of the resettlers. The comparatively higher levels of visibility and interest accorded to specific categories of displaced and resettled populations clearly influenced the quality and quantity of inputs (entitlements) supplied on their behalf.

Regime convergence in the twenty-first century

Regime theory provides a conceptual framework through which to assess the vast assortment of principles, norms, rules and decision-making procedures established by states, international agencies and non-governmental organisations for different categories of internal displacement and resettlement. It potentially explains how and why states and other non-state actors cooperate and promote protection and durable solutions where no clear motive appears to exist. It reveals regularities and patterns and the ways in which international and national responses to internal displacement – far from directionless or inchoate – are often infused with the strategic calculi of their proponents.

It is useful to recall the distinction between regimes and their proponents. International regimes are created by states and for states, even if non-state actors influence their form and content. As noted in Chapter 2, advocacy coalitions and public policy networks were instrumental in fomenting shared expectations, understandings and, ultimately, cooperation. Regimes themselves do not possess agency, but are instead embodied in the shared principles and interests of a highly differentiated array of state and non-state entities. Moreover, while the interests and values of regime proponents may converge around areas associated with protection and durable solutions, they are not limited to these issues. For example, although the World Bank, UNHCR and the IFRC actively promote values, concepts and language that shape regimes for protection and durable solutions in the case of DIDR, CIDR and NIDR, as institutions they also have mandates that extend beyond those reflected in the content of the associated regimes.[10]

Regimes do not arise in a historical or political vacuum. Nor are regimes reservedly a function of humanitarian or altruistic impulse. Each of the regimes discussed in this volume reflects to varying degrees a combination of geo-political economic and ideological interests. According to Keohane (1984) regimes are (deliberately) created against a backdrop of inter-state competition and power that are reflected in the content of their principles, norms, rules and decision-making processes. Goodwin-Gill (2006: 4) referred to the refugee regime as being established to ensure a 'common public order' that did not necessarily conform at all times with common patterns of interest. More controversially, Dubernet (2001) contends that the containment and control of population movement is a central pillar of a competitive international system including in-country mechanisms designed to regulate groups that could potentially destabilise the system. In her view, the introduction of principles associated with preventive protection and the right to remain neatly fit a strategic agenda that is intensely hostile to most, if not all forms of 'irregular migration', whether pastoralism, human trafficking or displacement.

The desire to stabilise and sedentarise those 'out of place' figures into cognitive and ideational framings of displacement, return and resettlement. The idea that people are firmly *rooted* or *fixed* to specific territorially defined nation-states is an enduring feature of international relations and systems theory and strongly embedded in the evolution of the refugee regime. Across the social sciences, there is a persistent sense that people have a place where they ultimately *belong* and that they should stay *rooted* and socially connected to this space. The discourse on refugees and internal displacement to some extent transcends international practices and statutory processes. According to Zetter (2007: 185–6) it

> relays anxieties about the fear of the 'other' and social relations between newcomers and settled communities ... it somehow challenges notions of a cohesive 'national identity' ... [and] jeopardises commonly held norms and values by which a nation state ... identifies itself.

Viewed in this way, cross-border and internal displacement represents a kind of disorder or 'de-territorialisation' to be prevented and redressed. Malkki (1995) observed how the fluid or liquid metaphors so common in forced migration studies (e.g. flows, waves or trickles) reinforce essentialist presumptions of fixed, immutable and immobile populations, identities and relationships. The concept of in-country protection, as with the right to remain, return and resettlement, is conceived by refugee-sending and refugee-receiving states as a means of preventing and reducing cross-border disorder.

Chapter 2 revealed how certain regime supporters do not necessarily envision a contradiction between the containment of would-be refugees and the protection and preservation of the rights and needs of internally displaced people. Regimes combining advocacy for more robust adherence to human rights with protection and durable solutions for the internally displaced purportedly coincide with state interests in preventing and deflecting would-be refugees and keeping people in their place. Certain forced migration specialists vehemently disagree. Hyndman (2000), for example, issued a critique of the race and gender-blindness of the humanitarian, human rights and development community which she describes as the 'colonialism of compassion'. Building on Harrell-Bond's (1986) concern with the imposition of aid, she contends that while the humanitarian community aspires to universal humanism and ordering the 'disorder' of displacement, the project is untenable. She attributes this to the clear power asymmetries demarcating the aid community from their 'beneficiaries' and the former's unconscious denial of local complexity.

Principles such as preventive protection and the right to remain as well as respect for minorities, non-discrimination and voluntariness are comparatively non-threatening and uncontroversial to states. The prevention of displaced populations from *crossing* borders and restricting rights to asylum becomes politically and ethically tantamount to promoting return and resettlement to guarantee their safety and security *in situ*.[11] In Bosnia and Herzegovina, Colombia, Iraq, Uganda and Sri Lanka, in-country preventive protection mechanisms and internal flight alternatives were initiated with precisely these goals in mind. The domestic interests motivating containment, protection and durable solutions varied across time and space in Sri Lanka. In contrast to the case of DIDR, where relocation was planned by state (Sinhalese) authorities in such a way as to encourage ethnic hegemony, approaches to CIDR promoted international and domestic containment. In the latter case, regime proponents advocated for the return and resettlement of specific groups back to their original districts and divisions or to new relocation villages in such a way that reinforced outcomes antithetical to regime objectives. Despite the demonstrated success of DIDR, CIDR and NIDR regimes in shaping the national discourse and to some extent practice of resettlement to make it more participatory, voluntary and attentive to protection concerns, exogenous factors often undermined durable solutions.

In spite of their adoption by a large number of states and non-governmental agencies, the Principles, the Guidelines and even the Standards gave rise to controversy, especially among countries wary of any formulation that potentially opened the door for interference in their domestic affairs. Heavily proscribed relief and development assistance (conditional aid, in the vernacular) has been widely considered an unacceptable infringement on borrower sovereignty for decades. Owing to the fact that the principles, rules and decision-making procedures of the DIDR, CIDR and NIDR regimes are still in evolution, it is not surprising that tensions persist in certain contexts in which they are enforced. But refusal or denial of regime prescriptions by certain states does not necessarily lead to their collapse or even premature fragmentation. Indeed, regime theory predicts that they can continue to exist even if the interests of certain parties shift or if certain principles, norms and rules are contravened.

Certain enforcement mechanisms were introduced to the DIDR regime in order to encourage national compliance. As discussed in Chapter 2, in addition to the Guidelines, the World Bank sanctioned the Morse

Commission to investigate alleged violations of resettler rights in response to India's Narmada Sarda Sarovar project. The Commission determined that World Bank policies and loan agreements, particularly those pertaining to mitigating negative resettlement and environmental impacts, were systematically neglected and abused. The findings of the Commission led to the establishment of a permanent Inspections Panel to enforce strictures of the DIDR regime. The Panel detected no fewer than seventeen claims where the agency was accused of failing to enforce its own policies, procedures and loan agreements (Cernea 2005; Udall 1999: 1–3). The development of a mechanism to measure performance of specific interventions in relation to durable solutions but also to monitor non-compliance represented a significant contribution to DIDR regime coherence. The Panel also provided for an unprecedented legal entry point for citizens to directly contest the activities of an international agency.

By way of comparison, CIDR regime proponents encouraged norm and rule compliance by advocating for human rights-based criteria in relation to protection and durable solutions at the international, regional and national levels. The Guiding Principles were designed at the outset to accommodate multiple forms of internal displacement within a rights-based framework even if the operational focus remains on the war-displaced. The same is true of the Pinheiro Principles adopted in 2006, which rearticulate standards and practices associated with housing, land and property restitution for the war- and disaster-displaced.[12] The Guiding Principles include thirty provisions listing the international principles and norms relevant to protecting the internally displaced against arbitrary displacement and 'safe and dignified return or resettlement and reintegration'. In addition, they advocate for the principle of necessity and proportionality in resettlement. They were also rapidly endorsed by states and non-governmental agencies since their formal adoption in 1998.[13] In 2004 the UN Commission on Human Rights called on the Secretary General to give greater focus to the human rights dimensions. The Principles were again affirmed at the 2005 World Summit 'as an important international framework for the protection of internally displaced persons' (UN 2005b: para. 132). Moreover, a manual emphasising key human rights provisions was developed to support legislators and executive policymakers at the national level (Mooney 2005).

NIDR regime proponents exhibit the least capacity to leverage compliance with core principles, norms and rules. While the Standards offer a needs-based framework for ensuring that protection and durable solutions are addressed, they are entirely voluntary and at the discretion of intervening state and non-governmental agencies. The development of Guidelines on Human Rights and Natural Disasters offers a series of general and operational principles. Core protection functions are linked to 'civil and political, as well as economic, social and cultural rights' (IASC 2006b: 5). In addition to highlighting core humanitarian entitlements for internally displaced people, the Guidelines (ibid.: 14–15) privilege their rights to 'speedy transition from temporary or intermediate shelter to temporary or permanent housing ... security of tenure ... [and] sustainable and long-term planning of resettlement and reconstruction'. But these rules are only in the earliest stages of dissemination and robust enforcement seems unlikely.

Sovereignty as responsibility There are tentative indications that the three regimes are converging in the twenty-first century. The prospects for regime convergence are growing precisely because a key endogenous constraint – sovereignty – is being consciously reappraised in multilateral forums. Since the 1990s, the narrow parameters of national sovereignty conceived from a Westphalian perspective were consciously re-evaluated by moral entrepreneurs (Deng 2007; Hathaway 2006; Cohen 2001; Annan 1999). The concept of sovereignty in the highly positivist ideal as an absolute assertion of power and authority over a territory amid competing nation states has long been challenged (Evans, G. 2007; Philpott 2001; Kelsen 1960). The corollary right to non-intervention, long enshrined in international law, was also fundamentally unsettled with the emergence of human rights discourse since the 1950s but most forcefully in the late 1990s.[14] Certain countries, such as Canada, Norway, Austria and Japan, began aggressively advocating a paradigm of sovereignty that assigned human rights as the organising normative principle and held states and non-state actors to account to international and national statutory obligations (Muggah and Krause 2007). In the meantime, concepts such as human security, civilian protection, the responsibility to protect (R2P), individual responsibility for international crimes, and human- or rights-based development[15] began to acquire legitimacy in multilateral fora such as the UN Security Council and the General Assembly – testament to their combined efforts to operationalise this reformulation of sovereignty.

The referent for sovereignty is not so much shifting, as expanding. There is a conscious effort on the part of the norm entrepreneurs identified above to shift the focus from an exclusive concern with national territorial jurisdiction and security to one that simultaneously advances domestic priorities, including the responsibility to protect the human rights of all citizens.[16] An early proponent of the CIDR regime, former UNHCR High Commissioner Sadako Ogata argued that the re-orientation of sovereignty as civilian protection is 'the most powerful idea that has emerged in the international arena in the last decade' (cf. Deng 2007). A particularly assertive articulation of 'sovereignty as responsibility' emerges from the Canadian-supported International Commission on Intervention and State Sovereignty (ICISS 2001):

> sovereignty implies a dual responsibility: externally – to respect the sovereignty of other states – and internally, to respect the dignity and basic rights of all the people within the state. In international human rights covenants, in UN practice, and in state practice itself, sovereignty is now understood as embracing this dual responsibility. Sovereignty as responsibility has become the minimum content of good international citizenship.

The repositioning of sovereignty as a renewal of the social contract in a Lockean sense, while not necessarily new, has immediate implications for regime coherence and convergence. With the establishment of the International Criminal Court (ICC),[17] the threat of international sanctions and forceful intervention in the event of clear violations of responsibility, including genocide, offers a possible deterrent to alter state and non-state behaviour. Despite optimism in the possibilities of a paradigm shift, prospects for forceful intervention in defence of gross violations receded in the opening decade of the twenty-first century.[18] Renewed US unilateral military action in Iraq and potentially in Iran and Syria, together with the return of power-politics among emergent super-powers such as India and China, redirected the debate away from humanitarian intervention and negotiated settlement to one emphasising traditional neo-realist security doctrine. An especially poignant test of the limits of sovereignty as responsibility is protracted defiance of successive UN Security Council resolutions by the Sudanese government in the context of alleged genocide in Darfur since 2004. Notwithstanding the ICC's charge of war crimes against Sudan's President in 2008, the inability of the international community to agree on decisive action and to fully deploy Chapter VII UN missions in Darfur, Chad and Central African Republic suggests the practical limits of a genuine paradigm shift.[19]

Nevertheless, the reframing of sovereignty as responsibility reinforces the declaratory potential of regimes to promote protection and durable solutions for internally displaced and resettled people. Owing to the inherent weaknesses of their decision-making mechanisms – weaknesses that are likely to endure – the potency of the three regimes is less in their regulative power than their constitutive potential. Their capacity to influence resides in large part on the discursive capacities of regime proponents to convince, cajole, sanction, rebuke and even potentially indict actors that systematically violate core norms and rules in international and national tribunals or panels. As observed by Cohen (2001), the 'creation of an effective international system for the internally displaced will be the true test of an expanded and more responsible notion of sovereignty and will give greater meaning to existing concepts of human rights and protection'.

Overcoming collective action dilemmas Notwithstanding the discursive shift towards sovereignty as responsibility and the countervailing resistance in the form of renewed unilateralism, the rules and decision-making procedures guiding regimes reiterate the basic principles of non-intervention. While the World Bank, UNHCR and IFRC play a central role in facilitating resettlement, states occupy a central role in all aspects of the regimes. They are awkwardly positioned as the perpetrators of development, conflict and to a lesser extent natural disaster-induced internal displacement and resettlement but also as arbitrators of protection and durable solutions. With the exception of extreme cases where expelling and hosting states are either unable or unwilling to intervene to protect displaced populations, interventions on behalf of the internally displaced are virtually always mediated by and through states in collaboration with a wide array of international and national non-governmental organisations.

Theoretically subservient to states, multilateral and non-governmental agencies regularly pressure them into adopting international standards and changes in behaviour. Dependent on state consent in the absence of aggressive international mandates, international financial institutions, the UNHCR and its implementing partners and the IFRC are all active proponents of the three regimes. But because they are generally deferential to states and predominantly 'reactive' entities, their power to enforce regime rules is limited. In the case of DIDR, certain developing states can renegotiate or shirk relevant conditions attached to specific loan agreements, opting instead for private capital if they disapprove of the terms issued by the World Bank. As noted in Chapter 2, weaker and more fragile states with fewer opportunities to access private capital may therefore be more susceptible to regime influence. In the case of CIDR and NIDR, states can selectively engage specific (more compliant) donors and agencies. In some countries, states are expert at manipulating interventions and contesting or blocking initiatives that do not suit their sovereign interests. As a result, regime influence is comparatively limited except in instances where financing strictures are imposed from without. Regime proponents therefore emphasise the importance of adapting domestic legislative and regulatory frameworks, improving governance and enhancing (domestic) state enforcement capacities in order to expand regime influence.[20]

It has been observed in this book that the decision-making functions of regimes for internal displacement and resettlement are frequently diluted by loose and highly decentralised state and inter-agency structures. The absence of clear centralised mechanisms constituted a kind of 'grand bargain' between those advancing a set of enlightened international principles and those calling for guarantees of non-interference in domestic affairs. In each regime, some discretionary decision-making authority is vested in existing multilateral institutions in collaboration with international and national agencies but all under the aegis of the hosting government. Despite the important role played by moral entrepreneurs within advocacy coalitions and public policy networks, regime proponents also face important mandate constraints that restrict their capacity to engage with exogenous factors.

In Sri Lanka, as elsewhere, regime proponents recognise that internal displacement and resettlement are politicised. But due to the absence of a centralised decision-making mechanism, bureaucratic interventions are shaped by institutional mandates that may not be geared ostensibly towards protection and durable solutions. Thus, the World Bank, UNHCR, the IFRC and other non-governmental agencies are 'invited' by the hosting state and potentially walk a thin line: criticism or antagonism can undermine their work. In becoming actively involved in sensitive (domestic) matters such as internal displacement, return or resettlement, donors and non-governmental agencies potentially compromise mandated priorities and the investments of their shareholders. The World Bank, for instance, attaches considerable weight to preserving and safeguarding its institutional reputation and its executive board is especially sensitive to investing in activities that could affect mandated priorities such as the issuance of loans and debt repayment. The extent to which agencies are therefore prepared (or not) to adopt an assertive role in enforcing regime compliance raises still more fundamental questions ranging from the limits of their mandates and capacities for intervention to the safety of their personnel (Verdirame and Harrell-Bond 2005).

The influencing potential of international non-governmental agencies should not be underestimated. For example, in addition to the subtle political and moral leverage applied by agencies such as the World Bank, the UNHCR or the IFRC, these organisations also wield considerable discretion over access, allocation and disbursement of funds. In many cases, financial agreements or memoranda of understanding signed between governments and multilateral agencies exhibit legal authority. For example, funding agreements with the World Bank and the ADB or formalised cooperation agreements between host states and UNHCR can have comparable standing to international treaties.[21] Likewise, the DIDR Guidelines and to a lesser extent the CIDR Principles are imbued with (soft) legal status. Cernea (2005: 21) observed how in the case of the DIDR regime:

> resettlement action plans resulting from the Bank's policy are included not only in the content of the projects that entail resettlement, but are explicitly recorded and their content is reflected, in the project's legal agreements. Thus, they are binding as international treaties on borrowing countries despite absence of domestic legislation.

Put another way, the World Bank finds that such contracts are 'valid and enforceable in accordance with their terms, notwithstanding the law of any State or political subdivision to the contrary' (IBRD 1988: 10.01).

Closing reflections

This volume has considered the evolution of distinct regimes that alternately contain, protect and promote durable solutions for the internally displaced. Regimes were from the beginning state-centric even while non-governmental actors played a central role in their formation and implementation. The principles, norms, rules and decision-making procedures of these regimes were moderately influential. They suffered from endogenous constraints owing to a narrow interpretation of sovereignty and collective action dilemmas. We have challenged the extent to which these international regimes achieved their intended goals in Sri Lanka, a country affected by multiple forms of internal displacement and resettlement. Their outcomes were mitigated by exogenous factors – namely ethnic nationalism and the military imperatives of an insurgency. In contexts of development, war and natural disaster, the regimes seldom achieved what their proponents most valued: they were manipulated by states and non-state actors.

While the three regimes share many commonalities and a tendency towards convergence, they are unlikely to realise more substantive gains without a fundamental renegotiation of sovereignty. Moreover, a more conscious engagement with where power lies in countries affected by displacement and the silences of the regimes is critically important. Internal displacement and resettlement signal a qualitative deterioration in claims to citizenship and governance. In the case of cross-border displacement, signatories to international legal instruments are compelled to protect designated refugees and ensure a range of lasting solutions on their behalf. Analogous types of commitments are increasingly demanded by proponents of three nascent regimes for development, conflict and natural disaster-induced internal displacement and resettlement. Where states are unable or reluctant to secure the basic rights of their own civilians, regime proponents contend that their sovereignty is circumspect. As such, there is an international responsibility to fulfil these rights (either through direct intervention or, more likely, through supporting a state's capacities).

A comparative assessment of regimes suggests they are normatively merging but remain bureaucratically segmented. The Guiding Principles in particular are assuming more prominence largely through the efforts of the Secretary General's Special Representative for Internal Displacement and a growing constituency of advocacy coalitions and public policy networks. As the case of Sri Lanka reveals, activities on behalf of internally displaced and resettled populations remain disparate with separate 'framings' of the issue and distinct ministries, departments and agencies involved. It is possible to detect a subtle shift favouring a more coherent and unified approach to protection and durable solutions. The newly created Resettlement Authority, Ministry of Resettlement and Disasters Relief Management and Ministry of Nation Building and Estate Infrastructure Development announced a rash of new policies and activities to 'resettle' both CIDR and NIDR affected populations (Vamadevan 2007). Despite persistent lobbying by regime proponents, conscious efforts of certain states to reposition sovereignty as responsibility and ongoing attempts to promote inter-agency coordination (in the absence of a centralised agency), it is likely that regimes will continue to be weakened by their extreme decentralisation.

Growing numbers of DIDR, CIDR and NIDR regime proponents believe that the best way to ensure a more coherent response is through the purposive application of a rights-based approach (Grabska and Mehta 2008). Such an approach probably resonates more for specialists focusing CIDR or NIDR than those working on DIDR. A rights discourse was traditionally avoided in the latter case for fear of being construed by recipient governments as interventionist. As signalled above, however, the changing discourse on sovereignty as responsibility is reshaping the possibility for rights-based interventions more generally. An increasingly urgent objective of advocacy coalitions and public policy networks is to reinforce and operationalise the principle of sovereignty as responsibility: 'to stipulate that sovereignty entails responsibility is to imply accountability for failure to conform' (Deng 2005: 1). Traditional avenues to exhort states to adopt more responsibility include the UN Security Council, the newly created UN Human Rights Council[22] and the UN General Assembly, but the true measure of effectiveness will be demonstrated protection and durable solutions on the ground.

Endogenous constraints to regime expansion such as collective action dilemmas are being addressed through investment and promotion in decision-mechanism arrangements intended to enhance collaboration and norm and rule promotion. Owing in part to ongoing UN reforms initiated in the late 1990s[23] to strengthen coordination, promote integration and reduce uncertainty, there are increasingly attractive incentives for key regime proponents to work together. This has facilitated the brokering of inter-agency alliances – for example between the World Bank, UNHCR and UNDP, among others. These agencies worked together to promote protection and durable solutions for tsunami-affected populations in several countries, including Sri Lanka. While the regimes will probably never exert much punitive potential, increased attention to shared understandings, habituation and ultimately internalisation of core principles, norms and rules, the development of inspection panels, the coupling of internal displacement and resettlement to human rights sanctions and 'naming and shaming' are nevertheless crucial steps towards fundamentally changing state and non-state behaviour.

Appendix: mapping ethnic distributions, 1911 to 2001

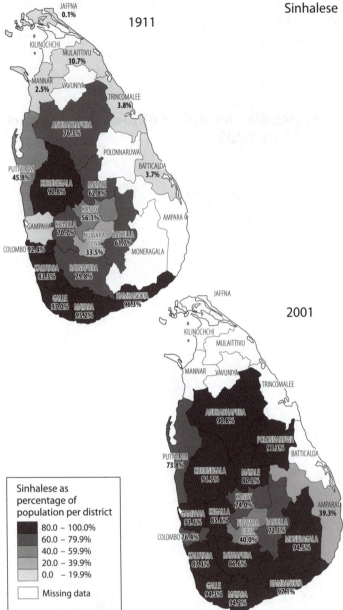

MAP 1A Demographic changes: 1911–2001 *Source*: Reconstructed from Sri Lankan census data and regional demographic surveys. Note that the districts of Jaffna, Kilinochchi, Mannar, Vavuniya, Trincomalee and Batticaloa do not register data owing to the lack of reliable census registration since 1981.

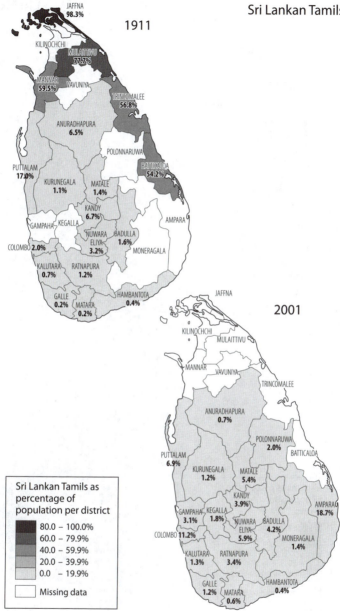

MAP 1B Demographic changes: 1911–2001 *Source*: Reconstructed from Sri Lankan census data and regional demographic surveys. Note that the districts of Jaffna, Kilinochchi, Mannar, Vavuniya, Trincomalee and Batticaloa register data from specific census registration exercises undertaken in 1991 by provincial councils.

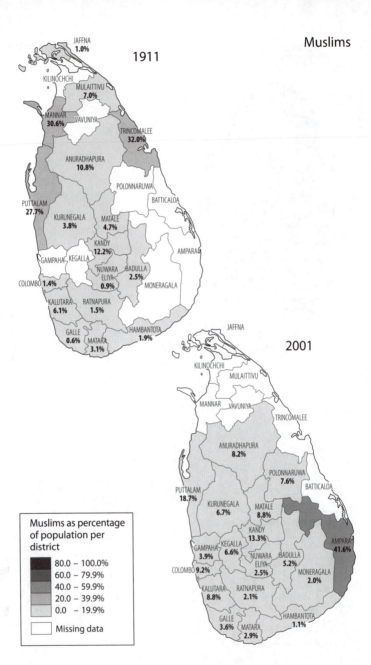

MAP 1C Demographic changes: 1911–2001 *Source*: Reconstructed from Sri Lankan census data and regional demographic surveys. Note that the districts of Jaffna, Kilinochchi, Mannar, Vavuniya, Trincomalee and Batticaloa do not register data owing to the lack of reliable census registration since 1981.

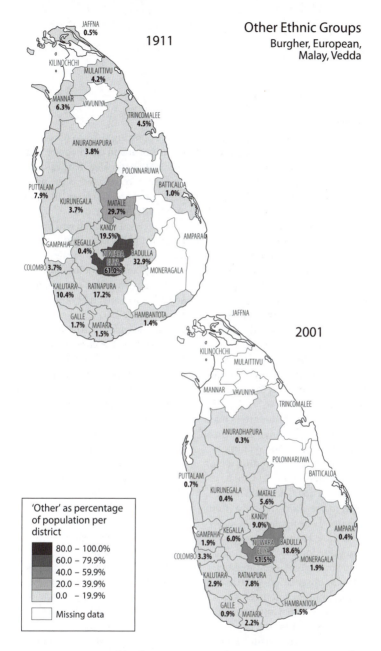

MAP 1D Demographic changes: 1911–2001 *Source*: Reconstructed from Sri Lankan census data and regional demographic surveys. Note that data quality and reliability may vary in Jaffna, Kilinochchi, Mannar, Vavuniya, Trincomalee and Batticaloa.

Notes

Introduction

1 Sending and Neumaan (2006), borrowing from Foucault, describe this process as a form of 'governability' – a process involving the extension of state control in a rational process defined according to certain practices and actions.

2 It is useful to note that sovereignty is seldom equated with 'absolute power' over a population or territory and is based in large part on internationally mediated legitimacy.

3 Observations of the author based on country visits and field research on forced migration and disarmament, demobilisation and reintegration (DDR) in ten countries from 2001 to 2007. See, for example, Muggah (2008a).

4 The Geneva headquarters maintains a twenty-year moratorium on all internal documentation relating to country operations, including reports and communiqués on Sri Lanka. Beginning in 2007, unpublished UNHCR material on Sri Lanka (from before 1987) was made available for the first time, though this was not of special value for this volume.

5 In some cases, I resorted to participant observation – particularly as an intermittent volunteer with various international and national agencies in Sri Lanka and other countries between 2003 and 2006. My provision of occasional services on a voluntary basis facilitated access to relevant evaluation reports, archival material and personnel on the ground without compromising the integrity of independent research.

6 Following visits to nine districts in the north and east in 2003, Mullaitivu, Trincomalee, Batticaloa and Ampara were selected as the primary sites of field research on DIDR, CIDR and NIDR for 2003–07.

7 Archival research was undertaken primarily at the national archives and the J. R. Jayawardena Cultural Centre in Colombo.

8 These included more than 35 separate Sri Lankan key informants in the case of DIDR, 50 key informants in the case of CIDR and 40 key informants in the case of NIDR. Other face-to-face, phone and Skype interviews were administered with European and North America-based scholars and practitioners between 2002 and 2007.

9 This is not the preferred approach to participatory research. In order to enhance the ownership and exchange of ideas and findings, the author has typically encouraged participants to keep outputs *in situ*, and often to publish or disseminate them locally if appropriate.

10 See, for example Muggah (2005a), Muggah and Samanayeke (2004) and Banerjee and Muggah (2002) for a review of participatory methods tested in Sri Lanka and other 'conflict' contexts.

11 Specific participatory tools piloted and used in the course of the thesis field-work included livelihood and wealth mapping to discern patterns of well-being before and after resettlement, timelines to highlight key events during the resettlement

experience and pair-wise ranking of locally determined risks and challenges encountered as a result of relocation.

12 In other cases, however, certain focus group respondents asked that their views be directly communicated to federal and district-level political authorities, a request that was acted upon by the author in various circumstances.

13 For example, the use of survey questionnaire instruments without a clearly identifiable 'partner' or 'patron' became less feasible owing to perceptions by local actors about how collected data would be stored and used.

14 In mid-August 2006, seventeen Action against Hunger employees were murdered in Muttur, a town immediately south of the district capital, Trincomalee. No arrests or prosecutions were made and the investigation was widely considered to be flawed, including by an executively appointed eminent group of international experts.

1 A unified approach

1 In Sri Lanka alone, social scientist-cum-resettlement specialists such as Robert Chambers, Fred Cuny, Tad Scudder, Norman Uphoff, Antonio Barnabas, Mark Vincent, Bill Frelick, Erin Mooney, Francis Deng and others published in peer-reviewed journals while simultaneously consulting with agencies such as the US Agency for International Development (USAID), UNHCR, UNDP, FAO and the World Bank.

2 A refugee, for example, acquires an international legal status with a set of recognised rights. These rights are guaranteed by the 143 countries that acceded to the 1951 United Nations Convention relating to the Status of Refugees and its 1967 Protocol.

3 Recognising the many ways that the two concepts can merge, certain scholars such as Cernea (2005) and Castles (2003) cautioned *against* applying too rigid a distinction between migration and displacement.

4 Vernant (1953) introduced a political–economic dichotomy to distinguish between displacement and migration, though this was eventually abandoned due to the practical difficulties of distinguishing between overlapping and competing motivations.

5 Other approaches emphasised the attainment of specific geographic or livelihood-based criteria, such as the de facto return to their place of origin, the relocation of a population to a camp or settlement scheme, or the attainment of socio-economic parity with host populations (Muggah 2007b).

6 The idea that displacement ends on the basis of fundamentally 'changed' or 'safe' circumstances is linked to the concept of 'cessation' as articulated in the Refugee Convention. The 'cessation clause', while seldom invoked by UNHCR, requires a 'complete political transformation of the refugee's country of origin'. In practice, this is exceedingly difficult to measure (UNHCR 2003c).

7 Other pathologies include increased exposure to illness and related morbidity, social marginalisation, loss of access to common property, the erosion of social and customary ties and behavioural changes such as risk adversity and increased propensity towards dependency (Cernea and McDowell 2000; Cernea 1997).

8 Similarly, Cernea (1997, 2006) described how the designation of

areas as parklands and reservoirs can result in restrictions on hunting and grazing rates, thereby contributing to various forms of risks that can lead to distortions in established migratory patterns.

9 Naomi Klein (2007) described resettlement in the context of post-Katrina floods in US coastal cities as a kind of 'shock therapy'. She claims that a Milton Friedman-inspired response to disasters includes aggressive urban planning and wholesale privatisation of the relief and reconstruction process.

10 White (1994) describes civil society as 'an intermediate associational realm between state and family populated by organisations which are separate from the state, enjoy autonomy in relation to the state and are formed voluntarily by members of society to protect or extend their interests or values'. There is nothing inherently positive in civil society per se.

11 See, for example, Principles 29 and 30 of the UN (1998) Guiding Principles on Internal Displacement that outline the rights and entitlements for those people who choose to 'voluntarily' pursue resettlement.

12 Translation by David Gellner, Oxford University, January 2008.

13 The TVA was comprised of a series of controversial hydroelectric dams and over 1,000 kilometres of canals stretching from Tennessee to Kentucky. See, for example, Hargrove (1994); Kollgaard et al. (1988); and Selznick (1964).

14 See, for example, the work of Picciotto et al. (2001); Mathur (2000); de Wet (2000b); McDowell (1996a); Guggenheim (1994); Rew (1996); Cernea (1991); Appell and Appell-Warren (1985); Collier (1984); Scudder (1980); and Barnabas (1967).

15 Third-country resettlement included the transfer of refugees from the state in which they initially sought asylum in another state that agreed to provide permanent residency. This strategy was adopted for most European refugees following the Second World War as well as for many Latin American and South-east Asian refugees throughout the Cold War and African refugees following the independence struggles of the 1960s and 1970s.

16 It should be noted that 'refugee camps' predate the Second World War. They first appeared in the 1920s following the First World War, the break-up of the Austro-Hungarian Empire and during the Russian Revolution, when a major preoccupation of the time was resolving the 'refugee' issue in the absence of agreed homelands. The use of such camps was the exception rather than the rule until the reported success of camps following the dissolution of East Pakistan and the establishment of Bangladesh in the early 1970s (UNHCR 2000b, 2002a).

17 Refugees and IDPs who are more skilled and socially connected tend to stay out of camps or adopt seasonal migration strategies. See, for example, Harvey and Lind (2005); Cutts (2003); and Kibreab (1989).

18 The idea that underdevelopment played a role in exacerbating the severity of disasters became increasingly entrenched by the 1990s. Between 1992 and 2001, over 95 per cent of all deaths from natural disasters were estimated to occur in countries classified by the UNDP (2005) as of medium and low development.

19 The US-based Committee on International Disaster Assistance counts as many as ten major and

fifty-one minor causal agents leading to natural disasters (Davis and Seitz 1982).

20 Davis and Seitz (1982: 548) observe how these 'phases' were divided into pre-disaster conditions, warning, threat, impact, inventory, rescue, remedy and recovery.

21 Wisner et al. (2004: 11) describe vulnerability as 'the characteristics of a person or a group in terms of their capacity to anticipate, cope with, resist and recover from the impact of a natural hazard (an extreme natural event or process). It involves a combination of factors that determine the degree to which someone's life and livelihood is put at risk by a discrete identifiable event ... in nature or in society.'

22 Twigg (2004: 16) described how a 'natural disaster' is a misnomer and that there are only 'natural hazards'. In his view, 'a disaster takes place when a society or community is affected by a hazard ... the impact of the disaster is heavily influenced by the degree of the community's *vulnerability* to the hazard'.

2 Protection and durable solutions

1 Ruggie, cited in Duffield (2007) observes that the concepts 'norms' and 'rules' are assigned numerous meanings in the international relations literature: 'typically ... these meanings are quite similar, and the words are often used interchangeably'.

2 That said, according to Young (1980: 332–3), regimes may be 'more or less formally articulated and they may not be accompanied by explicit organizational arrangements'.

3 The Refugee Convention and its 1967 Protocol were ratified by 134 states. There are forty-five state parties

to the 1969 OAU Refugee Convention and eighteen states party to the 1984 Cartagena Declaration on Refugees.

4 The refugee regime is moderately coherent on account of the number of states that ratified significant conventions and covenants. The Refugee Convention and its 1967 Protocol have been ratified by 134 states. There are forty-five state parties to the 1969 OAU Refugee Convention and eighteen states party to the 1984 Cartagena Declaration on Refugees.

5 In the case of the Refugee Convention and Protocol, the number of state parties exceeds the one-third proportion that regime proponents claim indicates 'norm cascades' which ultimately result in 'internalisation' (Finnemore and Sikkink 1998).

6 Along with UNHCR, certain UN treaty and non-treaty bodies such as the UNCHR (established in 1993 and relaunched as the UN Human Rights Council following recommendations issued by the UN *High Level Panel on Threats and Change* in 2004), also play a role in monitoring compliance.

7 In certain contexts, however, UNHCR has taken on more robust bureaucratic functions on behalf of governments – including assuming responsibilities for processing asylum claims and durable solutions.

8 In 1979, for example, a paper synthesising the social costs of resettlement was circulated in the World Bank. It would later prove crucial to the formulation of Guidelines ultimately approved by then President McNamara in 1980. Communication with Michael Cernea, September 2005.

9 See, for example, Resolution 1990/17 and 1993/77 of the UN Sub-Commission on the Prevention

of Discrimination and Protection of Minorities.

10 An internal task force was created in 1996 to review DIDR from 1986 to 1993. The published findings recommended a host of strategic and operational changes. Importantly, it also called for 'policy replication' in developing countries as a major objective (Cernea 2005: 15).

11 The IADB and ADB followed shortly after, in 1994 and 1995 respectively, with inspection panels of their own.

12 There was a decrease in large-scale publicly driven capital invest-ments in infrastructure projects in the 1990s. Instead, emphasis was on privatisation – the deregulation of the power sector, the reduction of subsidies, a concerted focus on macro-economic probity and reduc-tion of budget deficits and a renewed focus on renewable and smaller-scale energy production.

13 The IFC issued its own social and environmental safeguard policies on resettlement. These have drawn mixed reviews from civil society organ-isations but represent the standards now applied by the Equator Principles affiliated banks. Interview with Picci-otto, November 2006.

14 For example, Shell Inter-national (2004) initiated a DIDR programme in West Papua, Indo-nesia that ascribes to the principles, rules and practices advocated by the DIDR regime. Communication with Cernea, November 2006.

15 Certain refugee scholars, however, were strongly opposed to 'confusing' the refugee regime with formal responses to internal displacement (Hathaway 2006: 6–12; Barutciski 1998, 1999, 2000).

16 For example, in 1988 and 1989, the UN hosted the International

Conference on the Plight of Refugees, Returnees and Displaced Persons in Southern Africa (SARRED) and the International Conference on Central American Refugees respectively, to raise the questions of 'institutional-ised assistance to internally displaced people' (OCHA 2003: 21).

17 The Guiding Principles define internally displaced people as 'persons or groups of persons who have been forced or obliged to flee or to leave their homes or places of habitual residence, in particular as a result of or in order to avoid the effects of armed conflict, situations of generalized violence, violations of human rights or natural or human-made disasters, and who have not crossed an internationally recognized State border'.

18 This stands in contrast to the observed global decrease in the number of armed conflicts over the same period. See Liu Centre (2005).

19 It is important to stress the clear cleavages between supporters of the CIDR regime (Mooney 2005; Mar-tin, S. 2004; Cohen and Deng 1998a) and its critics (Hathaway 2006; Dubernet 2001; Barutciski 1999) with regard to the 'containment' of IDPs. While critics claim that containment was designed to mask the withdrawal of European states from their refugee protection responsibilities, Mooney describes this as 'containment con-spiracy theory'.

20 See UNGA (1993b). This would later be reinforced by UNGA (1995) and UNHCR (1994b, 1999b).

21 Austria was a major supporter of moving the issue into UNCHR with Norway as a co-sponsor. Norway also aggressively pushed the IDP issue in the UN General Assembly. Norway and other Scandinavian countries actively supported increasing trans-

parency on the issue through the Norwegian Refugee Council (renamed the IDP Monitoring Centre).

22 UNHCR issued policy guidelines in 1993, updated in 1997 and ultimately leading to a comprehensive policy paper in 2000. This latter report is the 'main policy document on UNHCR's role with internally displaced persons' (UNHCR 2001g).

23 By 2005 the Principles were available in more than forty languages.

24 Crisp claims that UNHCR envisions the cluster approach as a way of addressing 'conflict IDPs', though notes that 'other agencies see it as broader than this'. Correspondence, January 2008.

25 The IASC established an operational framework with the UN at its centre and required all relevant agencies in situations of 'mass displacement' to work together under the coordination of the UN Resident Representative and/or the Humanitarian Coordinator.

26 The IDD monitored eight countries where there are conflict-affected displaced populations to ensure that the 'collaborative response' was followed and adhered to. It had no formal enforcement capabilities but could apply pressure through advocacy and high level consultations (IASC 2005).

27 See UNGA (2004) which requests the strengthening of 'inter-agency arrangements and the capacities of the United Nations agencies and other relevant actors .... [for] an effective, accountable and predictable collaborative approach'.

28 In mid-December 1987 during its 42nd session, the UN General Assembly designated the 1990s as the International Decade for Natural Disaster Reduction.

29 There is no universally agreed definition of what constitutes a 'rights-based approach' to humanitarian action or development. It is generally defined as a conceptual framework for assigning priorities that is normatively based on international human rights standards and the obligations of states to meet them. It has a legal basis, a normative framework and a process of realising the overall goal. See, for example, Ljungman (2004).

30 As with rights-based approaches described above, there is no agreed definition of what exactly comprises 'needs-based approaches'. There is some consensus that it shifts the focus from state obligations to the bio-physical needs of the beneficiary and is therefore inherently more objective and demand-driven than the former (Grabska and Mehta 2008).

31 According to SPHERE representatives, thousands of individuals from over 400 organisations representing eighty countries participated in various aspects of its development.

32 Brookings Institute (2008) followed up these Guidelines with operational standards and a field manual on protection in situations of natural disaster.

3 A short history of settlement

1 This stands in contrast to other South Asian countries that are only rarely situated in the colonial and post-colonial experience of land colonisation and agricultural expansion during the nineteenth and early twentieth centuries.

2 Sri Lanka was known as Ceylon until it changed its name in 1972. For the purposes of this chapter, the term Sri Lanka will be used throughout.

3 For the purpose of this chapter, the expressions Sinhalese, Sri Lankan Tamil, estate Tamil and Muslim will be used throughout.

4 The *Mahavamsa* includes the *Dipavamsa* and the *Culavamasa* which together trace out a contiguous (and contested) record of settlements, tanks, temples and Sri Lankan and Indian dynasties from 550 BC to 1815. All references in this chapter to the *Mahavamsa* are taken from Geiger (1964).

5 Full population censuses were administered in 1871, 1881, 1891, 1901, 1911, 1921 and 1931 and partial censuses were carried out in 1946, 1953, 1963, 1971, 1981 and 2001. The 2001 census excluded key northern and eastern districts entirely. Batticaloa was split into two districts in 1961, Batticaloa and Ampara. Likewise, Mullaitivu district was created in the late 1970s from the northern part of Vavuniya and a small portion of eastern Mannar.

6 Each district was subsequently divided into several 'divisions' and, ultimately, cities, towns and villages.

7 By 1870, more than 300,000 acres were given over to European-owned plantations (Moore 1985; Farmer 1957).

8 As many as 500,000 Indian Tamils were supposed to be repatriated under the Sirima-Shastri Pact of 1964.

9 In fact, overall population growth steadily declined from the 1940s onwards – from a crude birth rate of 36.1 per 1,000 (1941–45) to some 28.1 per 1,000 (1976–80). Similar declines were observed with respect to fertility rates – from 5.3 (1953) to 3.3 (1981) (Sri Lanka 1981).

10 Rogers (1987: 592) observes a number of incidents of collective violence between 1886 and 1903 and again in 1915 that were tied to the growth of Buddhist revivalism.

11 Roberts (2004), by contrast, believes that conspiratorial theories that associated colonisation policy with land-grabbing between 1920 and 1950 remain unsubstantiated.

12 Though it 'protected' the tenant from (foreign) predation, it was also criticised for preventing the sale, lease or mortgaging of holdings and limiting domestic investment (de Silva, K. M. 1981).

13 In a bid to heighten the appeal of colonisation, Dudley Senanayake claimed direct genealogical descent from ancient Buddhist kings of the dry zone civilisation when he was made Prime Minister in 1952 after his father's sudden death (cf. Jiggens 1979).

14 See K. M. de Silva (1986).

15 The new electoral presence in the east was expected to be pro-Sinhalese. By the late 1950s and 1960s 'control of the east' came to form a major political and military strategic objective of successive administrations.

16 These Acts provided for nominal compensation. See, for example, the Requisitioning of Land Act (1950: No 33, Section 2/1).

17 Interview with Weerawardna (Ministry of Lands), June 2007.

18 Ibid.

19 The government's policy of supporting both Sinhala and Tamil as official languages changed following the passage of the Official Language Act No. 33 of 1956. The Act led to a sharp decline in employment prospects for Tamils in the public service to some 10 per cent by the late 1990s.

20 Peebles (1990) describes how the population of Tamankaduwa division (Polonnaruwa) increased

from 20,900 to 263,000 between 1946 and 1981. More than 70 per cent of the growth was attributed to settlers and resettlers and 91 per cent of the entire population was Sinhalese in 1981 as compared to 56 per cent less than four decades earlier.

21 Import substitution entailed increased tariffs, rigid export and import controls and price control legislation (Richardson 2005).

22 Sri Lanka was dependent on India for rice several hundred years before. The *Mahavamsa* recorded that erstwhile kingdoms had become disorganised by the fourteenth century. See Geiger (1964).

23 Moreover, while the system of centralised and imposed management was not immediately resented by managers and resettlers themselves, it came under increasingly vocal criticism in subsequent years (Ellman 1975).

24 In an infamous speech to newly arrived colonists in Padaviya that year, Senanayake is alleged to have said: '[t]oday you are brought here and given a plot of land. You have been uprooted from your village ... The final battle of the Sinhala [*sic*] people will be fought on the plains of Padaviya. You are the men and women who will carry this island's destiny on your shoulders ... The country may forget you for a few years, but one day very soon they will look up to you as the last bastion of the Sinhala.' This extract is drawn from M. H. Gunaratne (1998) and was discussed during an interview at the author's residence in August 2006.

25 These acts focused on housing development (National Housing Act 1954; 1955), urban planning (Town and Country Planning Acts 1946; 1950; 1953; 1955), plantation and mining (Ceylon State Plantations Corporation Act 1961; Mines and Mineral Law 1983), as well as Crown land (Sale of State Lands Law 1973; and Land Reform Law 1972), among others. See, for example, Ellman and Ranaweera (1974).

26 See the Paddy Lands Act (1958) and the Agricultural Land Law (1983), see also Ellman (1975) and Ellman and Ranaweera (1974).

27 Between 1951 and 1953, for example, some 25,740 people were settled into Gal Oya. Families grew from four members in 1951 to over nine members in 1953 (MacFadden 1954: 12).

28 Interview with Norman Uphoff (Professor, Cornell University), August 2004.

29 Ibid.

30 Ibid.

31 Interview with Bradman Weerakoon (former government agent in Batticaloa and Ampara), August 2006.

32 Uphoff describes how certain MPs from Ampara and the Government Agent, D. A. Ariyaratne, sought limit ethnic divisions among farmers – distinct from the 'thugs that many MPs kept at their disposal'. Interview with Uphoff, August 2004.

33 Uphoff notes that while certain sections of the Gal Oya comprised 'zones of peace', there were regular threats to settlers and resettlers levied by both Tamil militants and the JVP. He claims that ethnic killing genuinely emerged in the Gal Oya basin only after 1990 when the LTTE kidnapped and murdered several hundred police and army forces in one evening in a town at the headworks of the scheme. Ibid.

34 A parallel, but related, debate on families displaced by the widening of the Colombo–Katunayake

road during the late 1970s was also ongoing. Hansard records were reviewed at the J. R. Jayawardena Cultural Centre in September 2004.

35 By 2004, a review of Mahaweli Authority statistics reveals that in fact more than 148,633 families (estimated to include 743,165 individuals) were eventually relocated by the MDIP – an astonishing 75 per cent of whom consisted of 'resettlers' or 'evacuees'. Based on correspondence with Wanigaratne, September 2000.

36 NEDECO, a Dutch consultancy firm undertaking a feasibility study in just one of the Systems in 1979 highlighted these risks: 'on the basis of the scenario adopted by the consultants, about 50,000 families or 250,000 people have to be settled between 1980 and 1985. It is hard to find examples elsewhere in the world of successful settlement of such a large number of people in such a short time.'

37 Dams in Kotmale were supported by Sweden, Victoria reservoir by the United Kingdom, Maduru Oya by Canada, Randenigala by West Germany and Moragahakande by Japan. Moreover, Saudi Arabia, Kuwait, the OPEC Special Fund and others also invested in the MDIP.

38 According to the director of the Mahaweli Authority PMU, the project yielded a benefit–cost ratio of 1.57 and led to the repayment of debts to the aid consortium. Interview with Director of the PMU, August 2005.

39 It should be noted that there have been several changes to administrative district boundaries since independence. For example, in 1955 Chilaw district disappeared and Anuradhapura and Polonnaruwa districts were created. In 1979, the districts of Gampaha and Mullaitivu

were created, followed by Kilinochichi in 1984 (Sri Lanka 1979c).

40 These arguments were made repeatedly during parliamentary debates on the acceleration of the MDIP in the late 1970s. Mr A. Amirthalingam described certain administrative changes resulting from the MDIP as a calculated act to reduce Tamil-speakers to minority status. Written communication, July 2004.

41 Likewise, the ethnic profile of Batticaloa remained comparatively stable over the same period, with Sinhalese constituting a negligible proportion.

42 Communication with COHRE officials and Jay Maheswaran, May 2008.

43 Based on site visits to resettlement schemes in Trincomalee, Batticaloa and Ampara and interviews with Scudder and Ranjit Wanigaratne (former agriculture adviser to the Mahaweli PMU), August 2004 and May 2006.

44 Interview with Weerawardna, June 2007.

45 After repeated requests for access to disaggregated data on resettler profiles between July 2003 and July 2005, this 'fact' was revealed to the author in August 2005 by the chief of the PMU of the Mahaweli Authority.

46 Scudder (2001) reported more than fifteen years later that 'since our negative assessment ... Vimaladharma and Wanigratne's recent survey has further documented settler poverty and lack of multiplier effects'.

47 The CEA received support from the ADB (2003b) to promote capacity-building so that it could play a more prominent role in promoting 'progressive' resettlement.

48 Plans for a large Southern

Transport corridor were being prepared in the 1990s with financial backing from the ADB and the JBIC. It had not begun as of 2007. Interview with Mr Karunatillake (former Secretary, Ministry of Lands), June 2007.

49 The World Bank-supported Land Titling and Related Services project documents no fewer than seventy-one separate laws, acts and ordinances associated with land appropriation. Interview with Weerawardna, June 2007.

50 Approximately 5,000 families – some 21,000 individuals – were resettled from Mahawa, Wariyapola and Maspotha as a result of the Deduru Oya Irrigation project between 2001 and 2005. During a visit by the Irrigation Minister in June 2007 residents turned violent owing to failed promises. Interview with then Irrigation Minister, June 2007.

51 The Land Acquisition Law was not presented as of July 2008, with no clear sense of when it would be approved by Parliament. There is also speculation about the creation of a new resettlement law being drafted by the Ministry of Planning (at the request of the Ministry of Resettlement and Disaster Relief), but these plans appear to be in their infancy. Interviews with senior officials at the ADB (Manila) and World Bank (Colombo and Washington DC) in June 2007 and Tod Wassle June 2008.

52 Moreover, because the NIRP is a 'policy', abuses are more difficult to present in court as the provisions are not legally actionable (unlike the Tsunami Housing Policy, for example).

53 Though proscribed between 1971 and 1977 and again in 1983, the JVP would later contribute to massive levels of violence between 1987 and 1989 (Gunaratne, R. 1990). Following a wave of Sinhalese nationalism in the wake of the Indo-Sri Lankan Accord, an offshoot of the JVP, Deshapreni Janatha Viyaparaya or the Patriotic Liberation Organisation, began a campaign against the state and pro-Tamil sympathisers. After attempting to assassinate the President and Prime Minister in 1987, the group launched a campaign of intimidation against the ruling party, killing more than seventy MPs between July and November (Chandraprema 1991).

54 The TULF was an amalgamation of the 1972 Federal Party, the All Ceylon Tamil Congress and other organisations that banded together in 1972 to form the Tamil United Front (Kearney 1985).

55 Kearney (1987: 570) writes that it is 'possible to point to a rough correspondence between the TULF's proportion of the vote by district and the Sri Lankan Tamil proportion of district population at the preceding 1971 census'. Indeed, Sri Lankan Tamil proportions of the district populations were virtually identical to subsequent 1981 census, with the exception of the newly created Mullaitivu district created just before the latter census.

56 States of emergency were also declared from 29 November 1978–28 May 1979. The country experienced successive states of emergency since 1979 with the exception of brief reprieves in 1980, 1981, 1982 and 1989.

57 Over 1,000 Indian peacekeepers and more than 5,000 Sri Lankan civilians were estimated to have been killed during the mission (Seneratne 1997).

58 The CPA, for example, estimates that over 80 per cent of all

land in Sri Lanka is 'owned' by the state, though they offer no systematic evidence. Interviews conducted with Anita Amuthini, Samita Ananthan, Neranjana Gunetilleke and Fiona Remnant between November 2003 and August 2006 and June 2007.

59 The army did not necessarily interpret 'home' to imply the original properties or structures of the displaced but, rather, the home 'division' or 'district'.

60 President Kumaratunga (SLFP) and Prime Minister Wickremasinghe (UNP) occupied an uneasy coalition government at the time.

61 An LTTE attack on Katurayake international airport and a subsequent report by the Central Bank (2001) announcing the first ever contraction of the economy (–1.4 per cent of GDP) since independence concentrated minds. The LTTE too faced an international climate less tolerant to armed groups following the 'terrorist' attacks in the United States in September 2001.

62 Articles within the CFA agreed on the structure and membership of the SLMM which included sixty monitors in headquarters and six district offices. Members were drawn from Norway, Sweden, Finland, Denmark and Iceland. Following the EU proscription of the LTTE in May 2006, the SLMM was limited to Norway and Iceland.

63 The NERF was advanced by the World Bank, the ADB and the UNDP. According to Jay Maheswaran, despite Norwegian commitments, NERF was never actually activated. Both parties agreed on the formation of the fund, but the Attorney General allegedly procrastinated, and eventually the LTTE pulled out of SIHRN.

64 Between November 2002 and July 2003 donors pledged more than US$4.5 billion on the condition that certain preconditions were met. The four co-Chairs of the Tokyo conference, including the EU, Japan, Norway and the United States, together with the World Bank and the ADB, promised sizeable financial packages with favourable repayment rates.

65 Protections against encroachers and prescriptive law are also extended to tsunami-affected populations by the Tsunami (Special Provisions) Act no. 16 (2005).

66 The government calculated that the LTTE sustained considerable losses, including the destruction of part of its naval wing, thus shifting the strategic equilibrium in its favour. Meanwhile, the JVP objected to providing political concessions or resources to the LTTE.

67 The World Bank (2005: 7) estimated in its needs assessment that bilateral donors pledged US$661 million, multilateral agencies US$1.29 billion and NGOs US$853 million.

68 Interview with negotiator, Jay Maheswaran, May 2008.

69 The relaxation was alleged to have been precipitated by a visit of former US President Bill Clinton, appointed the UN special tsunami envoy. A Special Committee was established by President Kumaratunga to review the situation, which issued a recommendation in October 2005. The CGES, however, contended that the non-availability of land was a major obstacle and the reason for rescinding the zoning rule. See, for example, A. Perera (2005).

70 The TRO is publicly registered with the government of Sri Lanka and has offices in eight districts. Its mandate and statutes are accessible at www.trousa.org.

71 According to Jeffels (2005: 36) these include some 3,000 temporary shelters in Jaffna and Ampara by mid-2005.

72 Ibid.

73 Reports suggest that considerably more are in the process of being finished – even if the majority remain unoccupied (Chapter 6). Interview with Evans, June 2007.

74 While the LTTE was lauded for mobilising an emergency response with 'military precision' through the TRO, the government's emergency response was ponderous and almost dysfunctional.

4 Resettlement for development

1 See, for example, Sørensen (1997), Bastian (1995b), Peebles (1990), Kearney (1985, 1987), Moore (1985) and Dunham (1982, 1983) who focused on the political dynamics of 'colonisation'.

2 Regime proponents include bilateral aid donors from at least seven Western countries, international financial institutions such as the World Bank and the ADB and multilateral agencies such as the UNDP and FAO.

3 In mid-July 2006 armed violence erupted between Sri Lankan armed forces and the LTTE over the shutting off of water supplies from the Mavil Aru anicut and sluice gates in the Kellar area of Trincomalee district (System B right bank). The dam allegedly services as many as 30,000 first-, second- and third-generation Mahaweli (re)settlers in government-controlled areas of Batticaloa. Subsequent violence in the area triggered the resumption of the armed conflict and the *formal* termination of the 2002 CFA by early 2008.

4 The study focused on System H and was undertaken in 2003 by Dr Henegedera, W. Shantha and D. W. Senevirathne from the Hector Kobbekaduwa Agrarian Research and Training Institute.

5 While protection and durable solutions were implicit objectives of the MDIP, they were not classified as such in foundational documents and proposals.

6 As noted in Chapters 1 and 2, international consultants such as Scudder and Uphoff undertook extensive studies on behalf of the Sri Lankan government and international financial institutions, while also publishing extensively on resettlement.

7 Indeed, the 'blueprints for the Master Plan were heavily influenced by donors in the 1960s' according to Weerawardna. Interview, June 2007.

8 By the late 1980s and early 1990s, against a backdrop of waning international interest, approximately 50 per cent of all public sector 'capital expenditure' was devoted to servicing the MDIP (World Bank 2004a; Peiris, G. H. 1996).

9 In 1970 the UK Ministry of Overseas Development was converted into the Overseas Development Administration (ODA). In 1997 it was converted to the Department for International Development (DfID).

10 The CCSC was later renamed the Swedish International Development Agency (SIDA) in the 1970s.

11 J. R. Jayewardene was elected Prime Minister in 1977 but oversaw changes to the 1972 Constitution shortly after attaining office. The new 1978 Constitution shifted the state from a Westminster-based political system to a republic with a directly elected president who selected the prime minister and could dissolve Parliament.

12 Based on a review of Hansard

records in Colombo (1970–80) at the national archives.

13 This evacuation was documented in Hansard records in 1971. There is no further documentation available from the Mahaweli Authority on the outcome of the initial resettlement process. Land *kacheri* officials interviewed in Anuradhapura and Polonnaruwa in August 2003 did not know of the whereabouts of the resettlers.

14 Intriguingly, in late 2006 the newly elected SLFP coalition government announced that they would be resuming elements of the MDIP, in both contentious northern areas and southern districts (Colombo Page 2007).

15 Interview with Weerawardna, June 2007.

16 After being elected in 1977, Jayewardene had SLFP presidential nominee S. Bandaranaike stripped of power (Samarasinghe 1982).

17 There was in fact considerable support among national elite and others in the private sector for the 'settlement' of volatile communities in Colombo. According to Gunaratne, in one instance approximately R3.5 million was privately raised to fund settlement programmes between September and October 1983, particularly in Systems M and B (Gunaratne 1998: 101–2). Interview with Gunaratne, August 2006.

18 UTHR (1993) observed that 'there is a seeming connivance by the authorities in encouraging Sinhalese encroachments under protection of the [Sri Lankan armed] forces and consequent moves to regularise them'.

19 A UK Parliamentary human rights investigation reported that '[w]e can say, without doubt, that the Government is driving Tamils from their homes and does intend to settle

Sinhalese people in these areas. This, at least, lends support to the more extreme version believed by most Tamils' (Kilroy-Silk and Roger 1985).

20 The reports of the UTHR are of course also subjected to intense criticism from certain quarters for being biased and non-verified. Nevertheless, the organisation has been awarded several honours, including the Hellman/Hammett award for human rights reporting.

21 Yiftachel and Ghanem (2005) claim that the number of Sinhalese living in the north and east increased by more than 650 per cent between 1946 and 2001, though these figures are not backed up with reliable census data.

22 Note that 'Manal Aru', 'Weli Oya' and 'System L' are used interchangeably. Similarly, the terms 'Maduru Oya' and 'System B' are also synonymous.

23 Key informant interview with government agent (Vavuniya), July 2004.

24 Two landholdings in particular, Kent Farm and Dollar Farm, were managed by comparatively recently arrived estate Tamils who themselves were displaced by communal violence in Nuwara Eliya district during the race riots of 1977 (Chapter 3). Their farms were subsequently appropriated by the Land Commission and the Mahaweli Authority for the development of the System L settlement schemes.

25 Interview with former government agent and two divisional secretaries of Mullaitivu, September 2004. All three officials requested anonymity.

26 Ibid.

27 Drawing on section 3(1) of the Mahaweli Authority Act of 1979, the Minister for Lands and

Mahaweli Development issued a gazette notification in April 1988 declaring the region a 'special area'. Divisions annexed included Kokilai, Kokkuthoduvai, Karnaddukerni, Kumulamunai East, Kumulamunai West, Maruthodai, Oottukulam, Kayadikulam and Koddaikerni.

28 Interviews with retired and sitting government agents in Anarundhapura, Vavuniya and Batticaloa between September and October 2004.

29 Interviews with former government agents and retired civil servants working with a local World Bank-funded project in Vavuniya, Trincomalee and Colombo, July 2004. All requested anonymity.

30 It should be emphasised that this type of settlement was tested in the 1960s and abandoned due to its inefficacy (Schickle 1969, 1970).

31 When adjusted for 1988 and 1993 dollar values, this represents an increase from approximately US$2.4 million to US$7.5 million.

32 Interviews with district-level officials in December 2003 and Mahaweli Authority officials in September 2005. All interviewees requested anonymity.

33 Certain aid officers associated with the UK and Canada expressed concern with the rising levels of violence before and after the arrival of the IPKF in 1987. Interviews with Weerakoon, November 2006. Officials with DfID recalled certain 'anomolies' but claimed that all documentation before 1990 had been destroyed.

34 According to UTHR (1993) 'even administrative officials of the three Tamil districts of which it was a part could not enter the area without military clearance'.

35 The Mahaweli Authority undertook the study in order to assess possibilities for resettling populations from System B to Pada-viya (Karunatillake 1983b).

36 These areas included Kokila, Kokkuthoduvai, Karnaddu, Kerni, Kayadikulam and Koddai Kerni divisions.

37 There are also reports that in the months preceding the massacres, Israeli advisers were hired to assist in the development of security-based settlement policies in System L. See, for example, Otrovsky (1990) and *Saturday Review*, 8 September 1984). An official inquiry launched by the Sri Lankan government soon after the publication of Otrovsky's volume revealed no criminal malfeasance on the part of Sri Lankan citizens.

38 'Kokila' is also written Kok-kilai in Tamil.

39 Schickle 1970.

40 See also G. H. Peiris (1996: 184) for a brief treatment of canal development in System L.

41 Interview with former government agent and two divisional secretaries of Mullaitivu, September 2004. All three officials requested anonymity.

42 Population census data in System L/Weli Oya were not provided by district or divisional authorities because the district itself was subject to emergency legislation and such data were declared 'unavailable' by ranking Sri Lankan military personnel.

43 These include UTHR (1993); *Sunday Times* (1993); *Sunday Island* (1993); and key informants in Trincomalee. Independent confirmation is impossible due to the military presence and the classified status of the relevant documents since 2005.

44 Total estimated costs for the capital works for the entire MDIP were estimated at R117 million

in 1991 and R314 million in 1992
(Ministry of Lands, Irrigation and
Mahaweli Development 1991: 24).
According to Meemeduma (1994: 5),
annual budgets for System L alone
were R45 million in 1988, R45 million in 1990, R57 million in 1991,
R75 million in 1992, R50 million in
1993, R150 million in 1994, R200
million in 1995, R666 million in
1995, R479 million in 1999 and R344
million in 1998.

45 As noted in Chapter 3, cleared
land refers to those areas controlled
by the armed forces while 'uncleared'
land includes territory otherwise
controlled by the LTTE. Author's
observation from short field visits to
Weli Oya in 2003 and 2004.

46 As of 2005, there were approximately fifteen registered 'villages'
in Weli Oya that remain apparently
vacant.

47 Headed by former navy
general Askoka de Silva, JOSSOP
was based in Vavuniya and designed
to oversee security and allied civil
affairs, including land settlement in
Mullaitivu, Trincomalee, Vavuniya
and Mannar, while Jaffna was under
separate command.

48 The operation was allegedly
coordinated by the son of President
Jayewardene, Ravi according to
M. H. Gunaratne (1998: 219–23) and
Otrovsky (1990).

49 Quoted by Brigadier Hiran
Halangoda, cited in the *Sunday
Observer* (1998).

50 The number of estimated
residents was expanded to 25,000
in subsequent Mahaweli Authority
Reports on Left and Right Bank Development in System B. See Mahaweli
Authority (1984, 1987).

51 In addition, some 2,285
individuals were identified outside of
System B who owned allotments of

more than five acres. Later estimates
put the total number of families
likely affected at 4,000 though
this estimate did not include the
residents of Pimburettewa, Vakaneri
and Punanai schemes. These latter
families would 'likely qualify for
settlement under the Mahaweli
Programme, being near landless
and earning below-average incomes'
(Acres 1980: 5).

52 Estate Tamils were from
Kegalle, Matale and Ratnapura in
the south and were alleged to have
encroached on broad tracts of state
land. Many were assisted by Sarvodaya, the WFP and a local Gandhian
Movement. Bradman Weerakoon was
government agent of Batticaloa at
the time and involved in relocating
encroachers to Vadumanai.

53 Most of the *purana* schemes
identified were located in Karapola,
Mutugala, Katuwanwila, Alinchipa-
tana, Soruwila, Alavakumbura, Man-
ampitiya, Damminna and Vilaya in
Polonnaruwa, as well as Akkuranai,
Pettanai Kallichchai and Maduran-
gani in Batticaloa.

54 These include divisions such
as Kathiriveli, Vakarai-Mankerni and
Panichankerni.

55 See, for example, a representative household survey (n=4,094)
undertaken by Niyangoda (1979) in
System B.

56 Acres (1980: 4) later cautioned
that: '[t]he estimate of the number
of one hectare parcels may, however, overstate what can actually be
achieved with existing small tanks
in terms of reallocation, though it
would not overstate production'.
By 1984, P. de Silva (1984: iii) of the
Mahaweli Authority contended that
some 114,300 acres was available
within the irrigated and command
non-irrigated areas, though no

estimates on settlement were provided.

57 Against this backdrop, the recommendations regarding the involvement of Tamil encroachers and drawing on neighbouring supplies of Tamil labour by Acres (1980: 11) seem especially naive: '[a]reas adjacent to System B should receive preferences for settler selection. The coastal area between Trincomalee and Batticaloa, the area south of System B and the area north of Polonnaruwa should all be able to supply settlers familiar with the living conditions in the dry zone.'

58 This argument is made by G. H. Peiris (1996), who examines the hydrology and topography of the area and rendered judgements on the cost benefits.

59 USAID provided US$95 million for main and branch canal construction while CIDA provided US$76 million for headworks production (Acres 1982: iv).

60 See, for example, Acres 1982.

61 CIDA provided a further US$40 million, the World Bank some US$42 million and the balance of US$28 million came from the Sri Lankan government. By 1986, the EEC expressed its willingness to fund part of the project while Japan supported the outstanding construction needs in 1987.

62 System H had only one-quarter of farm families from the area (18,000) as compared to farm families from 'outside'. System B had 4,000 families from the area and some 31,000 families from 'outside'. See Acres (1980: 7).

63 This estimate was established in the 1981 census.

64 According to M. H. Gunaratne, this was not a recent process: the renaming and settling of these areas by Tamils had been going on for fifteen to twenty years.

65 These interests included the Ceylon Workers' Congress – a party traditionally representing the rights of Tamil plantation workers – as well as the TULF and the LTTE.

66 These Indian Tamils included some forty-eight families sent to Batticaloa from Hambantota after the 1977 disturbances and settled on approximately fifty acres of land. Their presence there was communicated to the Ministry of Lands and Land Developments. In 1974 an additional ten households were allocated land in the Wadamunai Colonisation Scheme.

67 Reports published in various local papers (*Riviresa* 1983) noted that 'land from the Dimbulagala [is] to be distributed free for cultivation', particularly for youth with no land and the 'poorest of the poor peasant families'. By September 1983, it is alleged that between 700 and 5,000 Sinhalese volunteer settlers from Polonnaruwa, Gallewela, Mahiyangana, Matara, Kantale, Kurunegala and Kandy were occupying land. Led by the Dimbulagala monk, the settlers entered the area in a convoy with Buddhist flags. Mahaweli Authority vehicles were observed in the procession.

68 These concerns were relayed by the government agent for Batticaloa to the Mahaweli Authority and various ministries throughout September and October 1983. See Government Agent (1983).

69 This was strongly contested by Dissanayake, who insisted the number was closer to 5,000 'squatters' (Gunaratne, M. H. 1998: 108).

70 Further confusion emerged following the Sri Lankan government's announcement that it would

'postpone the commencement of System B-RB (right bank)' in 1989. See Mahaweli Authority (1992: 2).

71 The unit was headed by Abeygunasekera, an officer with the Sri Lankan navy appointed 'chief security officer' of the Maduru Oya settlements. Interview with M. H. Gunaratne, August 2006.

5 Resettlement during war

1 An exception includes the Muslim population in the western district of Puttalum, discussed at length by Brun (2003) and Hasbullah (1999).

2 The literature on the heterogeneity of internally displaced people and their coping strategies is vast and includes Brun (2003); Sørensen (2001); Seneviratne and Stavropoulou (1998); and O'Sullivan (1997).

3 The special rights attached to Buddhism are noted in the 1972 Constitutional Preamble, the contents table and Articles 1 to 65, 134 and schedules A and B.

4 Crisp (1999: 4–5) considers the challenges of enumerating refugees and IDPs due to the lack of clearly defined units of measurement. He notes that established categories and definitions are often undermined by operational realities.

5 The Sri Lankan government and WFP, among others, recorded IDP status on the basis of whether or not populations registered for dry rations and cash assistance.

6 Two qualitative studies in particular – the UNHCR 'RRR framework' and the 'listening to the displaced' project introduced by Oxfam-GB and SCF-UK – undertook census studies (Van Hear and Rajasingham-Senanayake 2006: 56–8).

7 Because neither India nor Sri Lanka has ratified the 1951 Convention or the 1967 Protocol, Sri Lankan asylum seekers are not classified as *de jure* refugees (Muggah 2007a).

8 Approximately 20 per cent of the asylum applicants arrived by 1985, another 31 per cent between 1989 and 1992 and the rest between 1993 and 1998 (UNHCR 2001c).

9 Retired public servants interviewed in Colombo, Trincomalee and Batticaloa between 2003 and 2006 referred to these as 'refugee camps'. All officials requested anonymity.

10 Such measures had been introduced in 1970 by Prime Minister Bandaranaike following the JVP insurrection. Her SLFP government suppressed the revolt and declared a state of emergency that lasted six years (Seneratne 1997).

11 Interview with Weerakoon, November 2006.

12 Interview with Neill Wright (former UNHCR Representative), December 2006 and Roland Schilling (former senior UNHCR programme officer), September 2004.

13 The other so-called durable solutions include 'return' and 'local integration'.

14 This included over 400,000 Sri Lankan Tamils in Canada, 200,000 in Europe, some 68,000 in southern India, 40,000 in the US, 30,000 in Australia and another 80,000 living in a dozen other countries (UNHCR 2002a).

15 The Indo-Lankan Accord sought to change existing administrative structures in Sri Lanka, many of which were expected to enhance the 'federated' autonomy of Sri Lankan Tamils. The prospect of 'merging' the North East Province and renewed support for the District Development Councils are two examples. See, for example, Bastian (1995).

16 According to Brun (2003: 9)

the 'LTTE directed all of the Muslims living in LTTE-controlled areas of the Northern Province to leave all their belongings behind and leave the Tamil homeland within 48 hours ... Since 1990, about 60,000 Northern Muslims have lived as IDPs in Puttalam together with about 90,000 local people, with very weak prospects of return.' Thousands more would arrive in 1991 and 1992.

17 More than fifteen years later at least 75,000 remained in resettlement schemes on private land in Puttalam. Based on interview with Brun and author's visit to Puttalum in September 2004.

18 CPA (2003) would later estimate that over four-fifths of the entire population of the LTTE-controlled areas in the north and east were displaced though failed to explain their methodology for attaining the estimate. CPA representatives were unable to explain their methods in subsequent interviews in July 2004, August 2006 and June 2007.

19 Interview with Wright, July 2003.

20 Interviews with EU, Japanese, US, Norwegian and Canadian embassy representatives and Harrold in Colombo, July 2003.

21 In 2004 Vinayagamoorthi Muralitharan (alias Colonel Karuna) announced that he was splitting from the LTTE. Karuna claimed that the northern-led LTTE exploited the eastern Tamil forces and was aggrieved over the lack of consultation prior to the assassination of non-Tamil politicians by the LTTE. Approximately 6,000 armed cadres out of a total LTTE force of 15,000 joined Karuna. Interview with Fernando, August 2006.

22 By 2004, UNHCR recognised that the much anticipated 'mass

repatriation' was not going to take place.

23 This figure was reportedly determined from an assessment of government agent reports.

24 Multipliers of between four and eight were used interchangeably from 1983.

25 Retired Admiral Alfred Perera was the executive secretary of an affiliated agency.

26 The late Fred Cuny, an internationally recognised humanitarian and development specialist, was assigned to the post and worked in Sri Lanka from 1986 to 1987.

27 Austin Fernando, then Secretary for the Ministry of Rehabilitation and later chairman of CGES (1986–88), recalls how the volume *Disasters and Development* by Cuny was especially important to early planners.

28 From 1987 to 1990 loans were commercialised through state banks and the ADB provided a credit to support agricultural development in areas of return and resettlement.

29 SAHR (2007: 24) notes, however, how 'border villages' and recruitment of home-guards created 'a strong inter-dependency between Sinhala villages and the military'.

30 The UAS provided certain 'entitlements' for returning refugees and internally displaced populations. These grants were rarely effectively allocated and not adjusted for inflation until 2003.

31 By 2005, these Authorities and Ministries were replaced again with a Ministry of Nation Building and Development (2005), a Ministry of Resettlement (2005), a Ministry of Disaster Services (2006), a Ministry of Disaster Management and Human Rights (2006), a Ministry of Resettlement, Disaster Relief and

Relief Services (2007) and a Ministry of Nation Building and Estate Infrastructure Development (2007).

32 The RRR framework was in fact connected to the government's national poverty reduction strategy issued in November 2000. It was expanded and updated to national coordinating committee status in 2002.

33 The subcommittee on political affairs never met and the subcommittee on gender met only once and was later disbanded (Satkunanathan and Rainford 2008).

34 A senior LTTE-affiliated strategist, the late Balasingham, declared that the group would 'fiercely oppose and reject any proposal that makes resettlement of refugees conditional upon de-commissioning of LTTE weapons' (Tamilnet 2003a).

35 The first HSZ was established in Palaly camp in Jaffna. By 1990, the armed forces expanded them to protect the area from LTTE *pasilan* mortars. These were expanded again with the purchase of shoulder-fired missiles by the LTTE and the acquisition of 130mm artillery with a range of more than 25 kilometres (US State Department 2005).

36 For example, there is one large HSZ in the western coast of the Jaffna peninsula, but there are also some 152 army camps that are essentially HSZs and many others in 'cleared' areas.

37 Though in some cases ad hoc leasing arrangements were established with (primarily Sinhalese) landowners, such agreements were more the exception than the rule (Leckie 2005).

38 The Human Rights Commission (HRC) of Sri Lanka Act of August 1996 gave the institution a mandate that combined the functions of two other institutions which preceded it: the Commission for the Elimination of Discrimination and Monitoring of Human Rights (CEDMHR) and the Human Rights Task Force (HRTF).

39 According to UNHCR (2002b: 9): 'UNHCR's programme in Sri Lanka is rigorously based upon UNHCR's statutory tasks of protection and the pursuit of durable solutions'.

40 Fernando (then Secretary for the Ministry of Rehabilitation) and Sampath Kumar (UNHCR Representative in India) were responsible for negotiating UNHCR's entry to the country. See also Ministry of Reconstruction, Rehabilitation and Social Welfare (1987) for a review of the initial agreement.

41 Protection functions focused initially on advocacy for 'others of concern', including internally displaced populations.

42 UNHCR claimed to have a legal basis for assisting asylum-seekers in the form of EXCOM Conclusions (UNHCR 1980, 1985). Protection officers at the time argued that internally displaced persons should be considered a priority only in so far as their inclusion might encourage voluntary repatriations from India (UNHCR 1990b).

43 India broached the issue with the ICRC a year earlier, but the agency declined to support the request (UNHCR 1990a).

44 These concerns were raised in a note for the file recording the conclusions of a series of meetings held in November 1990 to discuss the programme, signed by C. J. Carpenter and dated 21 November 1990. It was ultimately agreed that the legal basis did exist and that legal authorisation was required from the UN Secretary General.

45 Interview with Crisp, March 2003.

46 For example, the 'guidelines on confidence building and stabilisation measures' refer explicitly to the Principles (UNHCR 2007b). Moreover, the Human Rights Commission launched a project to draft a national 'IDP Bill' and 'resettlement policy' though work remains in the formative stages.

47 The Ministry of Foreign Affairs of Sri Lanka frequently urged UNHCR to adopt a more 'humanitarian' rather than 'protective' approach (UNHCR 1998a).

48 ORCs were introduced in the wake of the Indo-Lanka Accord and UNHCR involvement was agreed by both headquarters and the Sri Lankan government.

49 As the closest land mass to India, Mannar was a site of considerable inflow and outflow of refugees as well as internally displaced populations. The ORC was initially established in a famous church shrine where some 13,000 internally displaced people had sought sanctuary.

50 Kendle (1998) also criticised the repatriation of Sri Lankan Tamils from Switzerland in 1994 from where, he argues, they were effectively *refouled*.

51 The author considered a short-term consultancy with Zoa Care (Trincomalee) in August 2006 to support an agency-wide review of durable solution activities.

52 By 2006, CHA included 153 professional staff in field offices in twelve districts in the north, east and south.

53 The NEIP was extended by the World Bank (2005–10) for a total of R8 million or US$800,000 (2004 dollars) (Vamadevan 2007).

54 In 2002, the World Bank restructured the NEERP, contributing a further US$42 million. The NEERP was extended again until 2008.

55 Funding for NECORD was renewed by the ADB and Sweden (2005–08) for US$43 million (2004 dollars) (NECORD 2005a).

56 A rapprochement simultaneously took place between the World Bank President James Wolfenson and the High Commissioner for UNHCR, Sadaka Ogata, with a view of enhancing coherence. Interview with Sadaka Ogata, November 2007.

57 The north-eastern province includes Jaffna, Kilinochchi, Mannar, Mullaitivu and Vavuniya and the Council was forged by the Indo-Lankan Accord signed by Rajiv Gandhi and J. R. Jayawardene and a constitutional amendment in 1987. Amid growing pressure from Sinhalese politicians, the merger was declared unconstitutional by the Supreme Court. In January 2001, the government appointed a governor for the Eastern Province though no governor has yet been appointed to the Northern Province.

58 Interview with Mr Bugendram (NECORD Project Director of Planning in Trincomalee), July 2005.

59 Government documents reported that UAS grants were issued for resettlement (R2,500), economic support (R4,000), shelter repair (R15,000), assistance for deceased (R50,000), housing loans (up to R250,000) and economic enterprise support (up to R500,000). But some confusion emerged over the dimensions of the entitlements. According to the Inter-Agency IDP Working Group (2002), the UAS was limited to: 'R 15,000 start-up grant for returning IDPs and refugees to acquire basic tools, inputs and temporary shelter

to restart productive livelihood. It also includes an additional R50,000 grant for permanent housing allowance. However, due to fiscal constraints only a very limited number of returning IDPs or refugees has received the full amount.'

60 The dry ration stipend amounted to approximately R1,260 or approximately US$20 a month in 1995. All currency conversions are set in the year mentioned unless otherwise stated.

61 The UNHCR provided budgetary support to the Ministry of Rehabilitation, Resettlement and Refugees between 2003 and 2004.

62 The 1981 census listed a population of 255,948 inhabitants while the 2001 census included 340,158, though this is considered incomplete. See, for example, Sri Lanka (2001b).

63 According to the Department of Statistics, only eighteen of twenty-five districts were surveyed in the 2001 census. Importantly, Trincomalee was only partially covered. As a result there are no official statistics on the total population or ethnic distribution of Jaffna, Trincomalee, Mannar, Vavuniya, Mullaitivu, Kilinochchi and Batticaloa.

64 Written statement by a former government agent and divisional secretary, Trincomalee, September 2003.

65 In mid-1991, the temporary relocation of displaced populations there led to the expression 'warehousing', though they were eventually vacated in 1994.

66 There is a widely perceived distinction between Jaffna Tamils and so-called eastern Tamils. Related, there are differences according to rank and status accorded LTTE factions from Jaffna and Trincomalee, some of which are believed to have

contributed to resentment among eastern recruits.

67 Interviews with UNHCR sub-office director and personnel in Trincomalee and on-site review of archival records, September 2003 and August 2005.

68 The role of the military in setting up resettlement schemes for displaced populations in Trincomalee district was confirmed by several Sri Lankan armed forces personnel in Trincomalee and Colombo between 2003 and 2006. All informants requested anonymity.

69 See, for example, Sri Lanka (1989, 1991 and 1994) for consideration of emergency regulations.

70 There are apparently no Sri Lankan Tamil or Muslim homeguards in Sri Lanka and despite discussion of a 'Muslim battalion', comparatively little is known about how they are appointed (Tamilnet 1998). The University Teachers for Human Rights and Dr S. H. Hasbullah, however, are currently investigating the role of home-guards.

71 Directives issued by Colombo in 1996 instructed district authorities in Trincomalee and Batticaloa to provide eligible candidates with 'a grant of R2000 [US$37 in 1995] for the purchase of kitchen utensils and other basic requirements ... productive enterprise grants ... of R4000 [US$74 in 1995] ... to revive economic activities ... and housing assistance of R25,000 [US$467 in 1995] to repair and reconstruct their damaged/ destroyed housing'.

72 Documents retrieved from Trincomalee government agent offices (circa 1996).

73 Additional compensation mechanisms were also introduced to account for 'destroyed permanent homes (R7000) [US$130 in 1995],

dry rations for six months from the payment of the productive enterprise grant, or for dependents injured or killed in "terrorist actions" (from R25–30,000) [US$467–560 in 1995]' (documents retrieved from Trincomalee government agent offices, circa 1996).

74 See, for example, Ministry of Development, Rehabilitation, Reconstruction of the East and Rural Housing Development (2001).

75 Moreover, they found that the reasons for staying or relocating varied according to security, on the one hand, and property rights, illegal occupation of homes, the absence of government assistance and the quality of the terrain in original homes. See, for example, UNHCR (2000g).

76 Records located at the Trincomalee sub-office archives.

77 Key interviews with IDP leaders in four welfare centres (all located in Alice Gardens) in Trincomalee, July 2003–September 2005. All respondents requested anonymity. Analogous pathologies were observed by the author in UNHCR-administered camps in Nepal where some 101,000 Bhutanese refugees resided for over ten years (Muggah 2005b).

78 Letter from the Trincomalee government agent to Trincomalee UNHCR sub-office, November 1996.

79 In 1990, these rations were allotted on a monthly basis and according to family size. These allotments remained the same for more than fifteen years, despite changes in inflation and rising real prices.

80 Sri Lankan Tamils had no 'official' representation in Parliament owing to the proscription of the TULF in 1982 (Chapter 3).

81 Cod Bay, as with other 'relocation villages' visited in Trincomalee

and Batticaloa, was described as a 'success' during preliminary meetings with senior government officials in Colombo and the district capitals. Field research was carried out in Cod Bay between June and July 2004 and again in August amd September 2005.

82 The Ministry of Rehabilitation, Refugees and Resettlement provided R32,000 (US$450 in 2000 dollars) and the Ministry of Fisheries R50,000 (US$700 in 2000 dollars) for permanent shelter construction to each resettling household.

83 Interview with Mr Arumaniyegam (land *kacheri* officer, Trincomalee), June 2004.

84 The divisional secretary, Mr Arumainayaham, as well as local officials Mr Kumar, Mr Ariyannyagan and Mr Sarath, were interviewed in August 2005.

85 According to local informants, the LTTE prohibited direct state involvement in these areas.

86 According to respondents in various participatory focus groups undertaken in Cod Bay, between 85 and 90 per cent of all income is consumed by food, schooling and health-related functions.

87 Interview with four host community resident key informants in Cod Bay in August 2005.

88 The 1981 population census registered 330,333 residents in Batticaloa. As in Trincomalee, estimates for 2001 are based on partial censuses conducted in the area.

89 According to SLMM officials based in Batticaloa, the LTTE carried out thirty-six extra-judicial killings in 2003 and these rose again in 2005 and 2006. Moreover, key informant interviews in Batticaloa town revealed that the LTTE controls liquor, tobacco, cement and public

transport concessions. Also, there were rumours that many of the 4,000 internally displaced people receiving UAS support in Batticaloa and Ampara were being extorted by LTTE representatives, though these were difficult to confirm after 2005. Interviews, August 2006.

90 Vehicles are regularly required to turn off their headlights when approaching checkpoints, front fences of homes are required to have holes/slots enabling patrols to look in and arrests and detentions under the Emergency Regulations and Prevention of Terrorism Act were common.

91 Sri Lankan defence expenditures reported an increase of 30 per cent on previous years in 2006. While the recurrent expenditures for Sri Lanka Army (SLA) and Sri Lanka Navy (SLN) account for the biggest increases, the capital expenditure for the SLN decreased in 2006. See, for example, Tamilnet (2005).

92 Many of these colonies would fall into disrepair. For example, the Punanai colonisation scheme launched in the early 1980s was later abandoned owing to increased insecurity. Visit by the author in July 2005.

93 Certain donors and non-governmental agencies also supplemented state-provided rations with the temporary shelters, primary health-care services and support for dispensaries and educational facilities.

94 By early 2003 the office was modestly staffed in comparison with other UNHCR sub-offices in the north and east. Though the office acquired two expatriate programme officers in 2004, at the time of the field research it only included one local protection officer and two support staff.

95 In fact, the author's repeated visits in 2003, 2004 and 2005 stimulated the first official meeting of UNHCR's Batticaloa sub-office with residents of a 'relocated village'.

96 Oddly, by 2002, the government agent of Batticaloa reported that the number of welfare centres had swollen to five. There were four welfare centres at the time of visits between 2003 and 2005, most of which were reportedly in the process of closing.

97 According to the divisional secretary, more than three-quarters of the households in Punanai were eventually able to purchase land by resorting to private sources (such as family networks and moneylenders). Because they originally inhabited areas close to the site they were considered 'resettled' and thus entitled to resettlement allowance and housing funds issued by the UAS. Interview, August 2004.

98 Informants requested anonymity.

99 Field visits were carried out in Savukkady and Villopulanadaradudam between July and August 2004 and again in August and September 2005. A small-scale survey and two participatory focus groups were administered in both relocation villages. All participants requested anonymity.

100 These findings coincide with household surveys carried out among internally displaced populations in Batticaloa, as reported by Kamirthalingam and Lakshman (forthcoming).

101 A significant proportion of the internally displaced remain in temporary and permanent resettlement schemes in the north and east. Another 68,000 Sri Lankan Tamil 'refugees' languish in unofficial 'camps' in Tamil Nadu state (UNHCR 2006a).

102 This estimate was floated by a number of senior politicians in 2001. The state ultimately targeted some 8,000 'families' in 2001 and was expected to resettle more than 27,110 families in 2002 with the support of UN agencies (Sri Lanka 2002b; UNHCR 2003c).

103 A UNHCR (2002b: 8) evaluation noted belatedly that both 'parties to the conflict have tried to manipulate the UNHCR programme and the IDPs, including by the movement or location of people to suit political and military strategic aims' and that UNHCR had taken steps to avoid being implicated in this.

6 Resettlement after the wave

1 The earthquake registered 9.2 on the Richter scale (de Silva, R. 2005).

2 See, for example, Bastian (2006b); Rajasingham-Senanayake (2006); and Uyangoda (2005).

3 See, for example, DEC (2006); Parakrama (2006); RADA (2006b); TEC (2006); TAFREN (2005a, 2005b); and UNDP (2005).

4 'For a country like ours which was building an average of 4–5,000 houses a year this is a gigantic challenge', Interview with Gamini Alawattegama (THRU Chief Executive Officer), November 2005.

5 Evans contends that the number of buildings constructed annually is probably closer to 15,000 a year. Interview, June 2006.

6 Ibid.

7 See, for example, Kumar and Vasanthan (2006); Jagtiani (2006); and Gill (2005).

8 According to UNHCR, there were an additional 40,000 conflict-displaced families (200,000 people) already resettled in 'welfare centres' and 'relocation villages' on marginal land near the coast in late 2004.

Interview with Patel, July 2006.

9 For example, the southern Hambantota district exhibits 'a 91 per cent oversupply of [permanent] housing whereas the East has a [permanent] housing completion rate of less than 21 per cent'. Interview with Evans, June 2007.

10 The IFRC allegedly received more than US$500 million in voluntary contributions to respond to the tsunami internationally. Interview with Lackenbauer, June 2007.

11 Interview with Evans, June 2007.

12 Likewise, the Sri Lankan government – as well as minority parties such as the JVP – were concerned with monitoring international and national NGOs, many of which were long considered to be sympathetic with Tamils and the LTTE.

13 As noted in previous chapters, the Sri Lankan state retained a nominal capacity in certain LTTE-controlled areas, unusual for countries facing similar conflict-like circumstances. District secretaries and government agents, divisional secretaries and *land kacheris* still function in the four districts under LTTE control. Following the escalation of armed conflict in 2005, however, the state with support from a breakaway faction of the LTTE managed to secure territorial control of many areas of the east and hold elections in early 2008.

14 Communication with Jay Maheswaran, a former lead negotiator of the PTOMS, May 2008.

15 According to Sambandan (2005), LTTE leader Prabhakaran reportedly claimed that 'with the demise of the tsunami mechanism, the Sinhala-Buddhist chauvinism killed the last hope of the Tamil people'.

16 The Transitional Accommoda-

tion Project was the focal point for coordinating emergency shelter – or tents and 'transitional shelters' with the UNHCR, the IOM and other NGOs. See circular issued by the CGES (2005).

17 Interview with World Bank focus group, August 2006.

18 The World Bank expected that of the US$3.5 billon pledged by donors, some US$150 million would be allocated to the housing reconstruction sector. The World Bank was also expecting to pocket the 5 per cent interest on the MDTF as overhead costs. Interview with Gamaathage, June 2007.

19 These included the UDA, the Ministry of Housing, the Ministry of Finance, the Ministry of Highways, the Ministry of Social Services, the Ministry of Health, the Ministry of Education, the Ministry of Telecommunications, Power and Energy, the NHDA, the Environment Authority and later, RADA.

20 The Memorandum further observes that 'the powers delegated to local authorities by the UDA in approving development activities within those areas have been temporarily suspended until further notice'.

21 In fact, the decentralisation of both emergency and developmental interventions to the district, divisional and GN levels is the conventional response adopted by the Sri Lankan state, described as a 'good structure for community development' by most observers. In the case of food ration distributions, the National Cooperative societies were used, with WFP supporting distribution through district and divisional chapters.

22 But while the TRO intervention was lauded for mobilising an emergency response with 'military-like precision', the government's

initial response was described as dysfunctional (Uyangoda 2005).

23 These guidelines also emphasised the retention of family units in resettlement, special protections for women, children and groups with special needs, rights to documentation, protection of the civilian character, avoidance of multiple relocations, respect for cultural and conflict sensitivities and access to education and participation. See, for example, UNHCR (2005c: section 1).

24 Moreover, UNHCR had recently accepted 'temporary housing' as one of its core responsibilities under the UN-mandated 'cluster approach' agreed by the IASC and discussed in Chapter 2.

25 This distinguished them from transitional shelters which were reinforced with steel poles and brick foundations; emergency shelters usually consisted of a cadjew hut, tent or tarpaulin and were frequently situated on public property (e.g. school, community centre, road, etc.) or by private agreement.

26 According to personnel affiliated with RADA, approximately 1,500–2,000 (Sri Lankan Tamil and Muslim) families were still living in emergency shelters in Colombo alone in mid-2006.

27 Interview with de Tissera and Weerapana, August 2006.

28 The role of the World Bank and UN-HABITAT, as well as the UDA and National Housing Development Authority (NHDA) in setting up permanent housing is treated in more detail below.

29 Interview with Alawattegama, November 2005.

30 Interview with RADA officials, July 2006.

31 Importantly, the government agent and divisional secretaries were

selected by the central government as the primary mechanism for administering DIDR rather than the provincial councils. It is important to note that government agents are appointed and representatives of the provincial councils are elected. At the time of the tsunami, the SLFP did not have significant representation in provincial councils: they were largely UNP candidates. In order to minimise the legitimacy of these structures – to ensure that they did not reap the potential dividends of providing assistance – the government opted instead to channel relief and development support through the government agent structures.

32 Permanent houses were described as having 'deeper cement foundations, a house with roof tiles, full floors and plastered walls, some connectivity to electricity and water services' according to a small sample of tsunami resettlers in Batticaloa.

33 The World Bank also encouraged the government to provide land grants valued at a flat rate of US$2,500.

34 Minimum dimensions for housing were set (500 ft^2), off-site infrastructure was supposed to be provided by governments and on-site by local investors.

35 So-called 'fully damaged' houses included those with repair costs exceeding 40 per cent of the replacement cost. Likewise, 'partially damaged' homes included those with repairs requiring less than 40 per cent of the replacement cost and included grants up to US$1,000 over two stages.

36 Interview with urban planner with RADA, August 2006.

37 A notable exception is the NHDA, which drew lessons from the 'village awakening programme' of the early 1980s launched by Prime Minister Premadasa wherein some one million houses were reportedly built over a short period of time.

38 Author visits to Batticaloa and Ampara in June 2006.

39 Interview with Alawattegama, November 2005 and Prashan Malalasekera (UNDP), April 2007.

40 The budget for the UN-HABITAT programme reflected this shift, in that 70 per cent was devoted to housing, 20 per cent for community services, 2 per cent for 'livelihood' support and the rest for overheads and staffing costs.

41 In some cases, names of resettlement schemes reflected attendant stigmas, such as *dumpwata* (dump flower) scheme, located near Colombo.

42 Interview with RADA officials, August 2006.

43 CPA (2005: 30) observes that the 'coastal zone policy may violate the principle of voluntary return contained in the Guiding Principles and the right to freedom of movement and the freedom to choose one's residence contained in the International Covenant on Civil and Political Rights (ICCPR)'.

44 The buffer was widely criticised. Not only did it introduce an arbitrary distance – which would later be replaced with existing contour buffers established by the CCD – but planned housing interventions were neither reflexive nor innovative. There was an emphasis on physical relocation rather than rebuilding of disaster-resistant homes, including buildings on stilts. Owing to the considerable number of ministries, departments and non-governmental agencies it involved – and the intense politicisation of the process – it lead to 'chaos' in the words of planners,

public health officials and civil servants interviewed in 2005 and 2006.

45 Interview with tsunami resettler focus group in Ampara district, May 2006. All participants requested anonymity.

46 The ADB (2006: 184–9) reports that economic impacts were 'not strong enough for economic growth to deviate significantly from its recent trend. Gross domestic product (GDP) grew at an estimated 5.7 per cent in 2005. The sectors most badly hit, fisheries and tourism, continue to struggle. However, tourism accounts for only 1 per cent of GDP and fisheries about 2 per cent and the industrial belt in the western part of the country was largely unhurt.'

47 One divisional secretary bemoaned the shortage of appropriate surveyors and contractors who might speed up alienation and building of new sites. Interview, May 2006.

48 See, for example, the 2003 Department of Health Survey.

49 Ampara accounts for one-quarter of all rice production in the country, with massive irrigation schemes set up as part of the Gal Oya scheme reviewed in Chapter 3 servicing the entire district.

50 Interview with tsunami resettler focus group in Ampara district, May 2006. All participants requested anonymity.

51 Ibid.

52 Participatory focus group in Koralai and Mamunai North, in August 2006.

Conclusions

1 Intervention in this sense can be forceful (i.e. military), but more likely includes other forms of political and social interference. Based on the principle of territorial integrity discussed above, the UN Security Council can sanction collective action through a Chapter VII mandate for collective interventions to be taken to prevent and remove international threats to peace and security.

2 In an effort to bridge the divide, Harrell-Bond and Cernea organised two conferences at RSC (1995 and 1997). One outcome of these sessions was a volume by Cernea and McDowell (2000) that sought to stimulate further dialogue between the refugee and DIDR communities.

3 Cernea (2006) published an overview of various types of resettlement in the context of development projects, mining and resource extraction schemes, war and violence and certain natural disasters in Africa.

4 See, for example, www. genevadeclaration.org for a review of these relationships and their empirical basis.

5 Interview with Mary Anderson (DSA), November 2006 and February 2007.

6 See Hyndman (2007) and Le Billion and Waizenegger (2007) for a comparative review of the experiences of Sri Lanka and Aceh following the tsunami.

7 UNHCR collaborates with the Organisation for Economic Co-operation and Development (OECD), especially with regard to post-conflict development cooperation and with the World Bank. In the latter case, it advocates more systematic inclusion of population displacement in the Bank's poverty-reduction strategies and development-oriented approaches to 'durable solutions' (UNHCR 2006c).

8 Interview with Sadaka Ogata (JICA) in November 2007.

9 Harrell-Bond (1986: 20) de-

tected similar experiences in other local resettlement processes, targeting Sudanese refugees in Uganda: 'the failures of [local] settlement policy, while evident and largely known, are [erroneously] considered to lie with the displaced and symptomatic of a dependency syndrome'.

10 For realists, the influence of regimes does not extend further than the direct policies and programmes associated with internal displacement and resettlement. As the experience of the World Bank Inspection Panel Shows, they have comparatively less capacity to exert changes in state behaviour in parallel interventions and projects. Interview, Picciotto, December 2006.

11 The ICIHI (1986: 119) argued that 'it would be wrong to suggest that the organised removal of displaced people inevitably involves the violation of humanitarian principles. Indeed, in situations of intense communal conflict, voluntary relocation might be the only certain form of protection available to the minority community'.

12 See COHRE (2007: 6).

13 Along with the UN Inter-Agency Standing Committee (IASC) and the World Bank, the OAS, OSCE, Council of Europe, AU, ECOWAS, IGAD and SADC all formally endorsed the Principles.

14 The supposedly 'humanitarian' intervention in Kosovo is widely regarded as the principal precedent in this regard. See, for example, G. Evans (2007).

15 There is an expansive literature on 'human security' and 'human development', both concepts that have been advanced by the UN throughout the 1990s. See, for example the *Human Security Report* (Liu Centre 2005); King and Murray (2002); and UNDP (1994).

16 Interview with Lloyd Axeworthy (Former Foreign Minister of Canada), July 2003 and Andy Mack (Director, Liu Centre for Human Security), November 2005.

17 See Rome Statute of the International Criminal Court, Rome 17 July 1998 (2187 UNTS 90).

18 It could equally be argued that UN Security Council-sanctioned interventions in Somalia and Haiti in the 1990s were triggered not so much by 'international threats to peace and security' but to ostensibly domestic crises relating to democracy and extreme humanitarian disasters with limited international destabilising consequences.

19 By mid-2007 the UN Security Council sanctioned a 26,000-member peace-keeping mission in Darfur ('heavy support package') with support from China (Muggah 2007c).

20 For example, there is growing interest on the part of the World Bank, UNDP and UNHCR, among others, to ensure that core provisions of the regime – protection and durable solutions – are enshrined in Poverty Reduction Strategy Papers (PRSPs), United Nations Development Assistance Frameworks (UNDAF) and other national development planning instruments.

21 Interview with MacNamara, June 2006, Cernea, November 2006 and Chiara-Gillard, December 2006.

22 See, for example, www.ohchr.org/english/bodies/hrcouncil/.

23 See, for example, UN (1997b) and www.un.org/reform/.

Bibliography

Abeyratne, S. (2004) 'Economic Roots of Political Conflict: the Case of Sri Lanka', *World Economy*, 27(10): 1295–314.

Abeysekera, C. (ed.) (1985) *Capital and Peasant Production: Studies in the Continuity and Discontinuity of Agrarian Structures in Sri Lanka* (Colombo: ARTI).

Acres (1979) *Maduru Oya Project Feasibility Report: Main Report* (Colombo and Niagara Falls: Acres International Limited).

— (1980) *Maduru Oya Project Feasibility Report. Settlement Planning* (Annex 1) (Colombo and Niagara Falls: Acres International Limited).

— (1982) *Maduru Oya: Right Bank Development Project* (Colombo and Niagara Falls: Acres International Limited and the Canadian International Development Agency).

ADB (Asia Development Bank) (1995) *Policy on Involuntary Resettlement* (Manila: ADB, draft).

— (1998) *Handbook on Resettlement: A Guide to Good Practice* (Manila: ADB).

— (2001) *Guidelines on Involuntary Resettlement in ADB Projects* (Manila: ADB).

— (2003a) *Addressing Immediate Rehabilitation Needs in Conflict-Affected Northern and Eastern Sri Lanka* (Manila: ADB).

— (2003b) *Report and Recommendation of the President to the Board of Directors on Proposed Loans to the Democratic Socialist Republic of Sri Lanka for the Conflict-Affected Areas Rehabilitation Project* (Manila: ADB).

— (2006) *Asian Development Outlook: 2006* (Manila: ADB).

— (2008) 'Asian Development Bank Will Not Weaken or Dilute Existing Social and Environmental Policies, Panel Told', Bank Information Center; www.bicusa. org/en/Article.3356.aspx (accessed June 2008).

AfDB (African Development Bank) (1995) *Guidelines on Involuntary Displacement and Resettlement in Development Projects* (Addis Ababa: Sustainable Development and Poverty Reduction Unit).

— (2003) *African Development Bank and African Development Fund: Involuntary Resettlement Policy* (Addis Ababa: PDSU).

Alexander, D. (1993) *Natural Disasters* (London: UCL Press).

Aluwihare, A. (2000) 'Patterns of Displacement: Responsibilities and Consequences', *Refugee Survey Quarterly*, 19(2): 64–9.

Amnesty International (2006) 'Sri Lankans Waiting to Ho Home – The Plight of the Internally Displaced', web.amnesty.org/ library/Index/ENGASA370042006 (accessed December 2006).

Anderson, M. (1999) *Do No Harm: How Aid Can Support Peace – or War* (Boulder, CO: Lynne Rienner).

Annan, K. (1999) 'The Legitimacy to Intervene: International Action to Uphold Human Rights Requires a New Understanding of State and Individual Sovereignty', *Financial Times*, 31 December.

Appell, G. and L. Appell-Warren (1985) 'Resettlement of Peoples in Indonesian Borneo: The Social Anthropology of Administered Peoples', *Borneo Research Bulletin*, 17(1).

Apthorpe, R. (ed.) (1968) *Land Settlement and Rural Development in East Africa* (Kampala: Transition Books).

Ariyaratne, R. (2003) 'Sri Lanka: On the Edge of Ending Internal Displacement?', *Forced Migration Review*, 17: 33–4.

Arulanantham, A. (2000) 'Restructured Safe Havens: A Proposal for Reform of the Refugee Protection System', *Human Rights Quarterly*, 22(1): 1–56.

Associated Press (AP) (2006) 'Mahaweli Dream Turns Nightmarish', *Lankanews*; www.lankanewspapers.com/news/2006/10/8877.html, October (accessed November 2006).

Attanayake, A., C. Bandara, J. Dissanayake and B. Hemapriya (1985) *Mahaweli Saga: Challenge and Response* (Colombo: Mahaweli Authority of Sri Lanka and Aitken Spence and Co.).

Axelrod, R. and R. Keohane (1985) 'Achieving Cooperation under Anarchy: Strategies and Institutions', *World Politics*, 38(1): 226–54.

Bagshaw, S. (1998) 'Internally Displaced Persons at the Fifty-Fourth Session of the United Nations Commission on Human Rights, 16 March–24 April 1998', *International Journal of Refuge Law*, 10(3): 548–56.

— (2000) 'Developing the Guiding Principles on Internal Displacement: The Role of Global Public Policy Network', UN Vision Project on Global Public Policy Networks; www.globalpublicpolicy.net/fileadmin/gppi(accessed October 2005).

— and D. Paul (2004) 'Protect or Neglect? Toward a More Effective United Nations Approach to the Protection of Internally Displaced Persons', Paper for Brookings-SAIS Project (Geneva: Inter-Agency Internal Displacement Division).

Baker, G. and D. Chapman (eds) (1962) *Man and Society in Disaster* (New York: Basic Books).

Bakhet, O. (1987) 'UNHCR Experiences in Implementing Rural Settlements', Conference Box, mimeo (Oxford: RSC).

Balaam, D. and M. Veseth (2001) *Introduction to International Political Economy* (New Jersey: Prentice Hall).

Banerjee, D. and R. Muggah (2002) *Small Arms and Human Insecurity: Reviewing Participatory Research in South Asia* (Colombo: Regional Centre for Strategic Studies).

Barnabas, A. (1967) 'The Sociological Aspects of Resettling People in Ceylon', Paper for Seminar on Mahaweli Scheme with FAO (Rome: FAO).

Barrows, H. (1923) 'Geography as Human Ecology', *Annals of the Association of American Geographers*, 13(1): 1–14.

Bartelson, J. (1995) *A Genealogy of Sovereignty* (Cambridge: Cambridge University Press).

Barutciski, M. (1996) 'The Reinforcement of Non-Admissions Policies and the Subversion of UNHCR: Displacement and Internal Assistance in Bosnia-Herzegovina (1992–1994)', *International Journal of Refuge Law*, 8(1-2): 49–110.

— (1998) 'Tensions Between the Refugee Concept and the IDP

Debate', *Forced Migration Review*, 3: 1–14.

— (1999) 'Questioning the Tensions Between the Refugee and IDP Concepts: A Rebuttal', *Forced Migration Review*, 4: 35.

— (2000) *Addressing Legal Constraints and Improving Outcomes in Development-Induced Resettlement Projects* (Oxford: RSC and DfID).

Basnayake, S. (1975) 'Possession in a Mixed Legal System: The Sri Lanka Experience', *International and Comparative Law Quarterly*, 24(1): 61–81.

Bastian, S. (1995a) *Land and Ethnic Politics* (Colombo: International Centre for Ethnic Studies).

— (1995b) *Control of State Land: The Devolution Debate* (Colombo: International Centre for Ethnic Studies).

— (2006a) 'Sri Lanka's International Straightjacket', *Himal Magazine*, December.

— (2006b) 'Tsunami Rehabilitation – Reflections', *Polity: Special Issue on the Tsunami*, 3(2) (Colombo: Social Scientists' Association).

Batiampillai, B. (1998) 'Displaced Persons and Their Plight in Sri Lanka', Conference of Scholars and Professionals Working on Refugees and Displaced Persons in Asia (Bangladesh, February).

Bechert, H. (1978) 'The Beginnings of Buddhist Historiography: Mahavamsa and Political Thinking', in B. Smith (ed.), *Religion and Legitimating of Power in Sri Lanka* (Chambersburg, PA: Anima Books), pp. 19–27.

Bennett, J. (1998) 'Forced Migration within National Borders: The IDP Agenda', *Forced Migration Review*, 1: 4–7.

Benthal, J. (1993) *Disasters, Relief and the Media* (London: Taurus).

Berdal, M. and D. Malone (eds) (2000) *Greed and Grievance: Economic Agendas in Civil Wars* (London: Lynne Rienner).

Betts, A. (2005) 'International Cooperation Between North and South to Enhance Refugee Protection in Regions of Origins', Working Paper Series 25 (Oxford: Queen Elizabeth House, RSC).

Betts, R. (1984) 'Evolution of the Promotion of Rural Integrated Development Approach to Refugee Policy in Africa', *Africa Today*, 31(1).

Beyani, C. (2006), 'Recent Developments in the Treatment and Protection of Internally Displaced Persons', unpublished paper.

Biggs, S. and F. Ellis (2001) 'Issues in Rural Development: Evolving Themes in Rural Development 1950–2000', *Development Policy Review*, 19(4): 437–48.

Birch, J. (1857) 'Report on the Patipola-aar', CO 54/328 enclosure.

Black, R. (1988) *Refugees, Environment and Development* (London: Longman Development Studies).

— (1994) 'Forced Migration and Environmental Change: The Impact of Refugees on Host Environments', *Journal of Environmental Management*, 42: 261–77.

— (1998) 'Putting Refugees in Camps', *Forced Migration Review*, 2: 2–7.

— (2001a) 'Fifty Years of Refugee Studies: From Theory to Practice', *International Migration Review*, 35(1): 57–78.

— (2001b) 'Environmental Refugees: Myth or Reality?', UNHCR Working Paper 34, pp. 1–19.

Blaikie, P., T. Cannon, I. Davis and B. Wisner (1994) *At Risk: Natural Hazards, People's Vulner-*

ability and Disasters (London: Routledge).

Boano, C., A. Rottlaender, A. Sanchez-Bayo and F. Viliani (2003) *Bridging the Gap: Involuntary Population Movement and Reconstruction Strategy* (Oxford: Oxford Brookes University).

Boekle, H., V. Rittberger and W. Wanger (1999) *Norms and Foreign Policy: Constructivist Foreign Policy Theory* (Tubingen: University of Tubingen).

Bond, G. (1988) *The Buddhist Revival in Sri Lanka* (Columbia: University of South Carolina Press).

Boserup, E. (1965) *The Conditions of Agricultural Growth: The Economics of Agrarian Change Under Population Pressure* (Chicago, IL: Aldine).

Brayne, C. (1928) 'The Problem of Peasant Agriculture in Ceylon', *Ceylon Economic Journal*, 6: 35.

Britton, N. (1986) 'Developing an Understanding of Disaster', *Journal of Sociology*, 22(2): 254–71.

Brohier, D. (1934) *Ancient Irrigation Works in Ceylon*, Part 2 (Ceylon: Government Press).

Brokensha, D. and T. Scudder (1968) 'Resettlement', in N. Rubin and W. Warren (eds), *Dams in Africa: An Inter-Disciplinary Study of Man-Made Lakes in Africa* (London: Frank Cass), pp. 20–62.

Brookings Institution (1999) *Handbook for Applying the Guiding Principles on Internal Displacement* (Washington, DC: Brookings Institution Project on Internal Displacement).

— (2005) *Addressing Internal Displacement: A Framework for National Responsibility* (Washington, DC and Berne: Brookings Institution and University of Berne).

— (2007) *When Displacement Ends: A Framework for Durable Solutions* (Washington, DC and Berne: Brookings Institution and University of Berne).

— (2008) *Human Rights and Natural Disasters: Operational Guidelines and Field Manual on Human Rights Protection in Situations of Natural Disaster* (Washington, DC and Berne: Brookings Institution and University of Berne).

Brun, C. (2003) 'Local Citizens or Internally Displaced Persons? Dilemmas of Long-Term Displacement in Sri Lanka', *Journal of Refugee Studies*, 16(4): 376–97.

Bush, K. (2003) *The Intra-Group Dimensions of Ethnic Conflict in Sri Lanka: Learning to Read Between the Lines* (Basingstoke/New York: Palgrave Macmillan).

Butcher, D. (1971) *An Organisation Manual for Resettlement: A Systematic Approach to the Resettlement Problem Created by Man-Made Lakes, with Special Reference for West Africa* (Rome: FAO).

Castles, S. (2002) 'Environmental Change and Forced Migration: Making Sense of the Debate', UNHCR Working Paper 70.

— (2003) 'Towards a Sociology of Forced Migration and Social Transformation', *Sociology*, 77(1): 13–34.

— and M. Miller (3rd edn, 2003) *The Age of Migration* (New York: Palgrave Macmillan).

Central Bank (2001) *Central Bank Statistics: 2001* www.centralbanklank.org (accessed November 2005).

Cernea, M. (1990) 'Internal Refugee Flows and Development-Induced Population Displacement', *Journal of Refugee Studies*, 2(2): 320–39.

— (1991) 'Involuntary Resettlement:

Social Research, Policy and Planning', in *Putting People First: Sociological Variables in Rural Development* (New York: Oxford University Press), pp. 188–216.

— (1993a) 'Social Science Research and the Crafting of Policy on Population Resettlement', *Knowledge and Policy*, 6(3–4).

— (1993b) 'Anthropological and Sociological Research for Policy Development on Population Resettlement', in M. Cernea and S. Guggenheim, *Anthropological Approaches to Resettlement*.

— (1994) *Resettlement and Development: The Bank-wide Review of Projects Involving Involuntary Resettlement: 1986–93* (Washington, DC: World Bank Environment Department).

— (1995) 'Understanding and Preventing Impoverishment from Displacement: Reflections on the State of Knowledge', *Journal of Refugee Studies*, 8(3): 245–64.

— (1996) 'Bridging the Research Divide: Studying Refugees and Development Oustees', in T. Allen (ed.), *In Search of Cool Ground: War, Flight and Homecoming in Northeast Africa* (Oxford: James Currey).

— (1997) 'Reconstruction and Risk', *World Development*, 25(1): 1569–87.

— (ed.) (1999) *The Economics of Involuntary Resettlement: Questions and Challenges* (Washington, DC: World Bank).

— (2003) 'The Question Not Asked: When Does Displacement End?', *Forced Migration Review*, 17.

— (2004) 'The Typology of Development-Induced Displacements: Field of Research, Concepts, Gaps and Bridges', Paper presented at the workshop on Typologies of

Relevance in Forced Migration, US National Academy of Sciences, Washington, September.

— (2005) 'The Ripple Effect in Social Policy and Its Political Content', in M. Likosky (ed.), *Privatising Development: Transnational Law, Infrastructure and Human Rights* (Leiden: Martinus Nijhoff), pp. 65–101.

— (2006) 'Concept and Method: Applying the IRR Model in Africa to Resettlement and Poverty', in I. Ohta and Y. Gebre (eds), *Displacement Risks in Africa: Refugees, Resettlers and their Host Population* (Kyoto: Kyoto University Press), pp. 195–258.

— (2007) 'Financing for Development: Benefit Sharing Mechanisms in Population Resettlement', *Economic and Political Weekly* (India), 42(12): 1033–44.

— and S. Guggenheim (eds) (1993) *Anthropological Approaches to Resettlement: Policy, Practice, and Theory* (Boulder, CO: Westview Press).

— and C. McDowell (eds) (2000) *Risks and Reconstruction: Experiences of Resettlers and Refugees* (Washington, DC: World Bank).

— and H. Mathur (eds) (2008) *Can Compensation Prevent Impoverishment? Reforming Resettlement Through Investments in Benefit-Sharing* (New Delhi: Oxford University Press).

CGES (Commissioner General for Essential Services) (2005) *Tsunami Circular*, 8 March.

CHA (Consortium of Humanitarian Agencies) (2002) *Annual Report* (Colombo: CHA).

Chalinder, A. (1998) *Temporary Human Settlement Planning for Displaced Populations in*

Emergencies, Good Practice Review, 6 (London: ODI).

Chambers, R. (1969) *Settlement Schemes in Tropical Africa: A Study of Organizations and Development* (New York: Routledge and Kegan Paul).

— (1970) *The Social Consequences of Resettlement* (London: Pall Mall Press).

— (ed.) (1971) *The Volta Resettlement Experience* (London: Paul Mall Press).

— (1979) 'What the Eye Does Not See', *Disasters*, 3(4): 381–92.

— (1986) 'Hidden Losers? The Impact of Rural Refugees and Programmes on Poorer Hosts', *International Migration Review*, 20: 245–63.

— and D. Butcher (1969) *The Volta Resettlement Experience* (New York: Praeger).

Chandraprema, C. (1991) *Sri Lanka: The Years of Terror: The JVP Insurrection, 1987–1989* (Colombo: Lake House Bookshop).

Chandraratne, D. (2003) *Making Social Policy in Modern Sri Lanka* (Colombo: Vijitha Yapa Publications).

Chandrasekharan, S. (1993) 'Sri Lanka: The Issue of High Security Zones', *South Asian Analysis Group*; www.saag.org/notes2/note174 (accessed January 2006).

Chandrasiri, J. K. (1996) *Final Evaluation Report on Model Villages for Integrated Rural Development Projects (MVRD) in Sri Lanka* (Colombo: HARTI).

Checkel, J. (1999) 'Why Comply? Constructivism, Social Norms and the Study of International Institutions', Arena Working Papers 24.

Chimni, B. (1998) 'The Geo-politics of Refugee Studies: A View from the South', *Journal of Refugee Studies*, 11(4): 350–74.

— (1999) 'From Resettlement to Involuntary Repatriation: Towards a Critical History of Durable Solutions to Refugee Problems', New Issues in Refugee Research, Working Paper 2.

Christensen, H. (1982) *Survival Strategies for and by Camp Refugees* (Geneva: UNRISD).

Clarence, W. (2001) 'Open Relief Centres: A Pragmatic Response to Relief and Monitoring During Conflict in a Country of Origin', mimeo, April.

Clifford, H. (1927) 'Some Reflections on the Ceylon Land Question', *Tropical Agriculturist*, 68: 290–2.

Cohen, R. (1996) 'Protecting the Internally Displaced', *World Refugee Survey* (New York: United States Committee for Refugees).

— (2001) *Exodus within Borders: The Global Crisis of Internal Displacement*, Sofia, Bulgaria; www.unhcr.bg/lecture/roberta_cohen.htm (accessed November 2006).

— (2004) 'The Guiding Principles on Internal Displacement: An Innovation in International Standard Setting', *Global Governance*, 10: 459–80.

— and F. Deng (eds) (1998a) *Masses in Flight* (Washington, DC: Brookings Institution).

— (1998b) *The Forsaken People: Case Studies of the Internally Displaced* (Washington, DC: Brookings Institution).

COHRE (Centre on Housing Rights and Evictions) (2006a) *Applying the Pinheiro Principles in Sri Lanka* (Colombo: COHRE).

— (2006b) *The Rights to Return, Resettlement and Restitution After the Tsunami Disaster: Applicable International Legal Standards* (Colombo: COHRE).

— (2007) 'The Rights to Housing and

Property Restitution in Sri Lanka', *COHRE News*, January.

Collier, H. (1984) *Developing Electric Power: Thirty Years of World Bank Experience* (Baltimore, MD: Johns Hopkins University Press).

Collier, P. and A. Hoeffler (2000) 'Greed and Grievance in Civil War', Policy Research Working Paper 2355 (Washington, DC: World Bank).

Colombo Page (2007) 'Sri Lanka to Initiate Another Major Development Project Under Accelerated Mahaweli Development Project', www.colombopage.com/ archive_07/January833515SL.html (accessed 7 January 2007).

Colson, E. (1971) *The Social Consequences of Resettlement: The Impact of the Kariba Resettlement Upon the Gwembe Tonga* (Manchester: Manchester University Press).

— (2003) 'Forced Migration and the Anthropological Response', *Journal of Refugee Studies*, 16(1): 1–18.

Committee on International Disaster Assistance (1979) *Assessing International Disaster Needs* (Washington, DC: National Academy of Sciences).

Cordiner, J. (1807) *A Description of Ceylon* (London: Longhurst and Reed).

CPA (Centre for Policy Alternatives) (1998) *Human Rights Violations of Internally Displaced Persons and Government Policies* (Colombo: Human Rights Commission and CPA)

— (2003) *Land and Property Rights of Internally Displaced Persons* (Colombo: CPA).

— (2005) *Land Issues Arising from Ethnic Conflict and the Tsunami Disaster: A Memorandum* (Colombo: CPA).

CPP (Council for Public Policy) (2006) *Proceedings of the Panel Discussion on Humanitarian Issues of Internally Displaced Persons* (Colombo: CPP and East-West Institute).

Crisp, J. (1999) 'Who Has Counted the Refugees: UNHCR and the Politics of Numbers?', *New Issues in Refugee Research*, 12 (Geneva: UNHCR).

— (2001) 'Mind the Gap! UNHCR, Humanitarian Assistance and the Development Process', *International Migration Review*, 35(1): 168–91.

— (2002) 'No Solutions in Sight: The Problem of Protracted Refugee Situations in Africa', Paper for the Conference on Forced Migration (San Diego: Centre for Comparative Immigration Studies).

Cuny, F. (1983) *Disasters and Development* (New York: Oxford University Press).

Cutts, M. (2000) 'Surviving in Refugee Camps', in *Forum: War, Money and Survival* (Geneva: ICRC), pp. 62–7.

— (2003) 'The Need for Material and Human Resources Alleviating Human Suffering: What are the Costs?', *Refugee Survey Quarterly*, 22: 35–40

Davis, J. (1992) 'The Anthropology of Suffering', *Journal of Refugee Studies*, 5(2): 149–61.

Davis, M. and S. Seitz (1982) 'Disasters and Governments', *Journal of Conflict Resolution*, 26(3): 547–68.

de Jong, E. and B. van Eesel (1970) *Review of Youth Settlement Projects and the Report on Youth Schemes* (Colombo: Land Commissioner's Department).

de Silva, D. (1982) 'Women and Social Adaptation in a Pioneer Mahaweli Settlement', unpublished manuscript.

de Silva, K. M. (ed.) (1970) *The History of Ceylon* (Delhi: Oxford University Press).

— (1981) *A History of Sri Lanka* (Delhi: Oxford University Press).

— (1986) *Managing Ethnic Tensions in Multiethnic Societies: Sri Lanka 1880–1985* (London: Lantham Books).

— and H. Wriggins (1994) *J. R. Jayewardene of Sri Lanka. A Political Biography*. Vol. 2: *From 1956 to His Retirement (1989)* (London: Leo Cooper).

de Silva, P. (1984) *Final Report of the Special Task Force on the Development and Settlement of System B Accelerated Mahaweli Programme* (Colombo).

de Silva, R. (2005) *Tsunami in Sri Lanka: Genesis, Impact and Response* (Kandy: University of Peradeniya).

de Wet, C. (2000a) *Improving Policy Outcomes and Protecting Human Rights in Resettlement Projects* (Oxford: RSC and DfID).

— (2000b) 'The Experience with Dams and Resettlement in Africa', in L. Bartolome, C. de Wet and V. Nagaraj (eds), *Thematic Review I.3: Displacement, Resettlement, Rehabilitation, Reparation and Development* (Cape Town: Rhodes University).

DEC (Disaster Emergency Committee) (2006) 'Independent Evaluation of the DEC Tsunami Crisis Response', Report to the Board of the Disaster Emergency Committee (DEC), January.

Demusz, K. (2000) 'Listening to the Displaced: Action Research in the Conflict Zones of Sri Lanka', Oxfam Working Papers (Oxford: Oxfam).

Deng, F. (1993) *Protecting the Dispossessed: A Challenge for the International Community* (Washington, DC: Brookings Institution).

— (2005) 'The Plight of the Internally Displaced: A Challenge to the International Community', mimeo; www.unglobalsecurity.org/pdf/deng.pdf (accessed January 2007).

— (2007) 'The Guiding Principles on Internal Displacement and the Development of International Norms', in T. Biersteker, P. Spiro, C. Sriram and V. Raffo (eds), *International Law and International Relations: Bridging Theory and Practice* (London: Routledge).

Denham, E. (1912) *Ceylon at the Census of 1911: Review of the Results of the Census of 1911* (Colombo: HC Cottle Government Printer).

Dickman, R. (1881) *Civil Service Manual* (Colombo, local printer).

Divisional Secretary (Trincomalee) (2001) Letter to Divisional Secretary Kuchaveli from Divisional Secretary Trincomalee, March 2001.

Dorcey, T. (ed.) (1997) *Large Dams: Learning from the Past, Looking at the Future* (Washington, DC: IUCN, World Bank).

Downing, T. (2002) 'Creating Poverty: The Flawed Economic Logic of the World Bank's Revised Involuntary Resettlement Policy', *Forced Migration Review*, 12: 11–12.

Drabek, T. (1970) 'Methodology of Studying Disasters: Past Patterns and Future Possibilities' *American Behavioral Scientist*, 13(33): 1–43.

— (1986) *Human System Response to Disaster: An Inventory of Sociological Findings* (London: Springer-Verlag).

— and K. Boggs (1968) 'Families in Disaster: Reactions and Relatives', *Journal of Marriage and the Family*, 30: 443–51.

Dubernet, C. (2001) *The International Containment of Displaced Persons: Humanitarian Spaces without Exit* (Aldershot: Ashgate).

Duffield, J. (2007) 'What are International Institutions?', *International Studies Review*, 9(1): 1–22.

Duffield, M. (1994) 'The Political Economy of Internal War: Asset Transfer, Complex Emergencies and International Aid', in J. Macrae and A. Zwi (eds), *War and Hunger: Rethinking International Responses to Complex Emergencies* (London: Zed Books), pp. 50–69.

— (2001) *Global Governance and the New Wars: The Merging of Development and Security* (London: Zed Books).

Dunham, D. (1982) 'Politics and Land Settlement Schemes: The Case of Sri Lanka', *Development and Change,* 13(2): 43–61.

— (1983) 'Interpreting the Politics of Settlement Policy: A Background to the Mahaweli Development Scheme', Institute for Social Studies Working Paper 11.

— and S. Kelegama (1995) *Stabilization and Liberalization: A Closer Look at the Sri Lankan Experience 1977–93* (Colombo: Institute of Policy Studies).

Durieux, J. (1997) 'Note for the File: Guiding Principles on Internally Displaced Persons – Meeting of Legal Experts Advising Mr. F. Deng', UNHCR (confidential), 13 June.

Dwivedi, R. (2002) 'Models and Methods in Development-Induced Displacement', *Development and Change*, 33(4): 709–32.

East-West Center (2005) *After the Tsunami: Human Rights of Vulnerable Populations* (Berkley: University of California).

Eckstein, H. (1975) 'Case Study and Theory in Political Science', in F. Greenstein and N. Polsby (eds), *Handbook of Political Science* (Reading, MA: Addison-Wesley).

Economist, The (2007) 'That Empty-Nest Feeling', 8–14 September, pp. 57–8.

El-Hinnawi, E. (1985) *Environmental Refugees* (Nairobi: UNEP).

Ellis, S. and S. Barakat (1996) 'From Relief to Development: The Long-Term Effects of Temporary Accommodation of Refugees and Displaced Persons in the Republic of Croatia', *Disasters*, 20: 111–24.

Ellman, A. (1975) *Management of New Settlement Schemes in Sri Lanka* (Kandy: Modern Ceylon Studies, Peradeniya University).

— and D. Ranaweera (1974) *New Settlement Schemes in Sri Lanka* (Colombo: University of Colombo).

Equator Principles (2003) *The Equator Principles*; www.equator-principles.com (accessed December 2006).

Eriksen, J. (1999) 'Comparing the Economic Planning for Voluntary and Involuntary Resettlement', in M. Cernea (ed.), *The Economics of Involuntary Resettlement*.

Esman, A. and R. Herring (eds) (2001) *Carrots, Sticks and Ethnic Conflict: Rethinking Ethnic Conflict* (Ann Arbour: Michigan University Press).

Evans, G. (2007) 'The Limits of State Sovereignty: The Responsibility to Protect in the 21st Century', Eighth Neelam Tiruchelvam Memorial Lecture (Colombo: International Centre for Ethnic Studies [ICES], Colombo, 29 July).

Evans, P. (1996) 'Government Action, Social Capital and Development: Reviewing the Evidence on Synergy', *World Development*, 24(6): 1119–32.

FAO (Food and Agriculture Organisation) (1975) *Water Management for Irrigated Agriculture (Gal Oya Irrigation Scheme)*, Sri Lanka: Project Findings and Recommendations (Rome: FAO).

Fardanesh, G. and B. Walker (2002) 'Dignified Village Life for the Displaced', *Forced Migration Review*, 12: 22–4.

Farmer, B. (1957) *Pioneer Peasant Colonisation in Ceylon* (Oxford: Oxford University Press).

— (ed.) (1977) *Green Revolution? Technology and Change in Rice-Growing Areas of Tamil Nadu and Sri Lanka* (London: Macmillan).

Ferguson, J. (1990) *The Anti-Politics Machine: 'Development', Depoliticization and Bureaucratic Power in Lesotho* (Cambridge: Cambridge University Press).

Fernando, A. (2006) 'Peace Process and Security Issues', in K. Rupesinghe, *Negotiating Peace in Sri Lanka*, vol. 2.

Finnemore, F. (2003) *The Purpose of Intervention: Changing Beliefs About the Use of Force* (Ithaca, NY: Cornell University Press).

— and K. Sikkink (1998) 'International Norm Dynamics and Political Change', *International Organization*, 52(4): 887–917.

Florini, A. (1996) 'The Evolution of International Norms', *International Studies Quarterly*, 40: 363–89.

Forbes, J. (1840) *Eleven Years in Ceylon* (London: Mahore Forbes).

Forbes, S. (1992) 'The Inhospitable Earth', *Refugees* 89: 12–15.

Forced Migration Review (2003) 'When Does Internal Displacement End?', editorial, *Forced Migration Review*, 17: 4–7.

Fraser, G. (2005) 'Can Old Foes Set Aside Strife?', *Toronto Star*, 12 October.

Fraser, I. (2005) 'Small Fish Trampled in Post-Tsunami Stampede', *Forced Migration Review*, 14, Special Tsunami Edition: 39–40.

Frelick, B. (2001) 'Solutions for Internally Displaced Persons', *Exodus within Borders: The Global Crisis of Internal Displacement* (Skopje, Conference by the Center for Refugees and Forced Migration Studies, 31 May–2 June).

Freund, P. and K. Kalumba (1985) 'Spontaneously Settled Refugees in Northwestern Province, Zambia', *International Migration Review*, 20(1): 299–312.

Frontline (1985) 'Sri Lanka: A Time of Troubles', *Frontline Magazine*, 2(6), March–April; www.hinduonnet.com/fline/.

Gamaathige, A. (2007) 'Development and Implementation of National Involuntary Resettlement Policy – Sri Lanka Experience', ADB Workshop, Colombo, 14 June.

Garikipati, S. (2005) 'Consulting the Development-Displaced Regarding Their Resettlement: Is There a Way?', *Journal of Refugee Studies*, 18(3): 340–61.

Gebre, Y. (2002) 'Contextual Determination of Migration Behaviours: The Ethiopian Resettlement in Light of Conceptual Constructs', *Journal of Refugee Studies*, 15(3): 265–82.

Geiger, W. (1964) *The Mahavamasa* (Berlin: MH Bode).

Geissler, N. (1999) 'The International Protection of Internally Displaced Persons', *International Journal of Refuge Law*, 11(3): 451–78.

Ghosh, B. (ed.) (2000) *Managing Migration: Time for a New International Regime?* (Oxford: Oxford University Press).

Gibney, M. (1999) 'Liberal Democratic States and Responsibilities to Refugees', *American Political Science Review*, 93(1): 169–81.

Gibson, D. (1993) 'The Politics of Involuntary Resettlement: World Bank Supported Projects in Asia', Ph.D. Thesis, Duke University.

— (2001) 'The World Bank and Displacement: The Challenge of Heterogeneity', in A. Esman and R. Herring (eds), *Carrots, Sticks and Ethnic Conflict*.

Gill, I. (2005) *Refugees of Sri Lanka Conflict are Back in Camp After Tsunami* (Manila: ADB).

Glantz, M. (ed.) (1976) *The Politics of Natural Disaster: The Case of the Sahel Drought* (New York: Praeger).

Glaser, B. (1992) *Emergence vs Forcing: Basics of Grounded Theory Analysis* (Mill Valley: Sociology Press).

Gleditsch, N. (1997) *Conflict and the Environment* (Dordrecht: Kluwer Academic).

Goetz, G. and P. Diehl (1992) 'Toward a Theory of International Norms. Some Conceptual and Measurement Issues', *Journal of Conflict Resolution*, 36(4): 55–78.

Goetz, N. (2001) 'Humanitarian Issues in the Biafra Conflict', *New Issues in Refugee Research Working Paper 36*.

Goldsmith, E. and N. Hildyard (1984) 'Dams and Society: The Problems of Resettlement', in *The Social and Environmental Effects of Large Dams*, vol. 1 (Cornwall: Wadebridge Ecological Centre).

Gombrich, R. and G. Obeyesekere (1988) *Buddhism Transformed: Religious Change in Sri Lanka* (Princeton, NJ: Princeton University Press).

Gomez, M. (1996) *The People in Between: Sri Lankans Face Long-Term Displacement as Conflict Escalates* (Washington, DC: US Committee for Refugees).

— (2002) 'National Human Rights Commissions and Internally Displaced Persons Illustrated by the Sri Lankan Experience', Brookings Institution, SAIS Project on Internal Displacement Occasional Paper.

Goodhand, J. (2000) 'Research in Conflict Zones: Ethics and Accountability', *Forced Migration Review*, 8(4): 12–16.

— (2001) 'Aid, Conflict and Peace Building in Sri Lanka', Conflict Assessments, Security and Development Group (London: University of London).

— and N. Lewer (1999) 'Sri Lanka: NGOs and Peace-Building in Complex Political Emergencies', *Third World Quarterly*, 20(1): 634–64.

Goodwin-Gill, G. (2000) 'UNHCR and Internal Displacement: Stepping into a Legal and Political Minefield', *USCR World Refugee Survey 2000* (Washington, DC: USCR).

— (2006) 'International Protection and Assistance for Refugees and the Displaced: Institutional Challenges and United Nations Reform', Paper presented at the Refugee Studies Centre Workshop on Refugee Protection in International Law: Contemporary Challenges, Oxford, 24 April.

Gorman, R. (1993) *Refugee Aid and Development* (Oxford: Oxford University Press).

Government Agent (Batticaloa) (1983) Letter to His Excellency the President from Government Agent for Batticaloa, M. Anthonimuthu, 4 September.

— (Trincomalee) (1996) Circular 02/10/96.

— (Trincomalee) (2005) confidential memo to author, August 2005.

Grabska, K. and L. Mehta (eds) (2008) *Problematizing Rights and Policies in Forced Displacement: Whose Needs are Right?* (London: Palgrave Macmillan).

Grundy-Warr, C. and E. Wong Siew Yin (2002) 'Geographies of Displacement: The Karenni and the Shan Across the Myanmar–Thailand Border', *Singapore Journal of Tropical Geography*, 23(1): 93–122.

Guggenheim, S. (1994) 'Involuntary Resettlement: An Annotated Reference Bibliography for Development Research', Environment Working Paper, 64 (Washington, DC: World Bank).

Gunaratne, M. H. (1980) *Social Infrastructure and the Proposed New Settlement System Structure for the Forward Areas* (Colombo: Mahaweli Development Board).

— (1998) [1985] *For a Sovereign State: A True Story on Sri Lanka's Separatist War* (Colombo: Sarvodaya Press).

— (2004) *A Tortured Island* (Colombo: Sarvodaya Vishwalekha Publishers).

Gunaratne, R. (1990) *Sri Lanka, a Lost Revolution? The Inside Story of the JVP* (Kandy: Institute of Fundamental Studies).

Gunasekera, S. (1996) 'Tigers, Moderates and Pandora's Package'; www.sinhaya.com/tigers_moderates_1.html (accessed December 2006).

Gunawardana, R. (1990) 'The People of the Lion: The Sinhala Identity and Ideology in History and Historiography', in R. Spencer (ed.), *Sri Lanka: History and Roots of Conflict* (London: Routledge).

Gupte, S. (1984) 'Ominous Presence in Tamil Nadu', *India Today*, 9, 31 March.

Haas, P. (1989) 'Do Regimes Matter?' *International Organization*, 43-4: 377–404.

— (1992) 'Introduction: Epistemic Communities and International Policy Coordination', *International Organisation*, 46(1): 1–35.

Habermas, J. (1987) *The Theory of Communicative Action*. Vol. 2: *Lifeworld and System: A Critique of Functionalist Reason* (London: Heinemann).

Haggard, S. and B. Simmons (1987) 'Theories of International Regimes' *International Organization*, 41(3): 491–517.

Hall, A. (2005) 'Widening Horizons? Social Development and Social Policy in the World Bank', Presentation for the ESRC Seminar, London, 2–3 June.

Hansard, Record of Proceedings of the Legislative Council (up to 1931), State Council (1931–47), Parliament (1947–72, 1978–81), National State Assembly (1972–78) (Colombo: Government Press).

Hansen, A. (1981) 'Refugee Dynamics: Angolans in Zambia 1966–72', *International Migration Review*, 15(1): 175–94.

— (1991) 'Dependency and the Dependency Syndrome', Meeting of the International Research and Advisory Panel on Refugees and Other Displaced Persons, Oxford, 2–6 January.

— and A. Oliver-Smith (eds) (1982) *Involuntary Migration and Resettlement: The Problems and Responses of Dislocated People* (Boulder, CO: Westview Press).

Hargrove, E. (1994) *Prisoners of Myth: The Leadership of the Tennessee Valley Authority, 1933–90* (Princeton, NJ: Princeton University Press).

Harrell-Bond, B. (1982) 'Towards Self-Sufficiency in Planned

Rural Refugee Settlements', unpublished paper for the Khartoum Refugee Seminar, September, mimeo.

— (1986) *Imposing Aid: Emergency Assistance to Refugees* (Oxford: Oxford University Press).

— (1998) 'Camps: Literature Review', *Forced Migration Review*, 12: 22–3.

Harris, S. (2005) 'Livelihoods in Post-Tsunami Sri Lanka', *Forced Migration Review*, 14, Special Tsunami Edition: 34–5.

Hartoungh, J. (1968) *An Appraisal of the Colonisation Schemes in Ceylon* (Rome: FAO).

Harvey, P. and J. Lind (2005) 'Dependency and Humanitarian Relief: A Critical Analysis', HPG Report 19 (London: ODI).

Hasbullah, S. (1999) 'Internal Displacement in Sri Lanka: Causes and Consequences', unpublished report.

Hasenclever, A., P. Mayer and B. Rittberger (1997) *Theories of International Regimes* (Cambridge: Cambridge University Press).

Hathaway, J. (1995) 'New Directions to Avoid Hard Problems: The Distortion of the Palliative Role of Refugee Protection', *Journal of Refugee Studies*, 8(3): 288–94.

— (2005) *The Rights of Refugees Under International Law* (Cambridge: Cambridge University Press).

— (2006) 'Forced Migration Studies: Could We Agree Just to "Date"?', Program in Refugee and Asylum Law, University of Michigan.

Hedman, L. (2005) 'The Politics of Tsunami Response', *Forced Migration Review*, 14, Special Tsunami Edition: 4–5.

Heilbroner, R. (1962) *The Making of Economic Society* (Englewood Cliffs, NJ: Prentice-Hall).

Helmann-Rajanayagam, D. (1986) 'The Tamil "Tigers" in Northern Sri Lanka: Origins, Factions, Programmes', *Internationales Asienforum*, 17: 62–85.

Henkel, H. and R. Stirrat (2001) 'Participation as Spiritual Duty: Empowerment as Secular Subjection', in B. Cooke and U. Kothari (eds), *Particiation: The New Tyranny?* (London: Zed), pp. 168–84.

Herring, R. (2001) 'Making Ethnic Conflict: The Civil War in Sri Lanka', in A. Esman and R. Herring (eds), *Carrots, Sticks and Ethnic Conflict*, pp. 140–74.

Hewitt, K. (1983) *Interpretations of Calamity* (Winchester, MA: Allen & Unwin).

Hindu, The (2004) 'India, Sri Lanka Urged to Ensure Return of Refugees', 11 July.

Hoffman, S. and A. Oliver-Smith (eds) (2002) *Catastrophe and Culture: The Anthropology of Disaster* (Oxford: James Currey).

Holsti, K. (1996) *The State, War and the State of War* (Cambridge: Cambridge University Press).

Homer-Dixon, T. (1994) 'Environmental Scarcities and Violent Conflict: Evidence from Cases', *International Security*, 19(1): 5–40.

— (2000) *Environment, Scarcity, and Violence* (Princeton, NJ: Princeton University Press).

— (2006) *The Upside of Down: Catastrophe, Creativity, and the Renewal of Civilization* (Toronto: Knopf).

Hulme, D. (1988) 'Land Settlement Schemes and Rural Development', *Sociologia Ruralis*, 28(1): 42–60.

Human Rights Watch (2006) *World Report 2006: Sri Lanka* (New York: Human Rights Watch).

Hunting Technical Services (1979) *System B Mahaweli Development*

Project. *Feasibility Study: Sociology and Organisation and Management*, vol. 4 (London: Ministry of Overseas Development).

— (1980) *Establishment and Operation of a Central Monitoring and Progress Control Unit,* Colombo.

Hurrell, A. (2002) 'Norms and Ethics in International Relations', in W. Carlnaes, T. Risse and B. Simmons (eds), *Handbook of International Relations* (London: Sage Publications), pp. 137–54.

Hyndman, J. (2000) *Managing Displacement: Refugees and the Politics of Humanitarianism* (Minnesota: University of Minnesota Press).

— (2003) 'Preventive, Palliative or Punitive: Safe Spaces in Bosnia-Herzegovina, Somalia and Sri Lanka', Paper for the International Association for Forced Migration Conference, 5–9 January.

— (2007) 'The Securitization of Fear in Post-Tsunami Sri Lanka', *Annals of the Association of American Geographers*, 97(2): 361–72.

— and M. de Alwis (2000) 'Capacity Building, Accountability and Humanitarianism in Sri Lanka', *Forced Migration Review*, 8; www.fmreview.org/text/FMR/08/05.htm (accessed June 2008).

IADB (Inter-American Development Bank) (1998) *Resettlement Guidelines: OP710* (Washington, DC: Inter-American Development Bank).

— (1999) *Involuntary Resettlement in IADB Projects: Principles and Guidelines* (Washington, DC: IADB).

IASC (Inter-Agency Standing Committee) (2005) 'Internally Displaced Persons: Strengthening UN Agency Accountability in Crises of Internal Displacement', Background Paper (Geneva: IASC).

— (2006a) 'Benchmarks for When Displacement Ends', mimeo, October.

— (2006b) *Protecting Persons Affected by Natural Disasters: IASC Operational Guidelines on Human Rights and Natural Disasters* (New York: IASC).

IBRD (International Bank for Reconstruction and Development) (1988) General Conditions Applicable to Loan and Guarantee Agreements, 1 January, 1985–87, Section 10.01.

ICIHI (Independent Commission on International Humanitarian Issues) (1986) *Refugees: Dynamics of Displacement: A Report for the Independent Commission on International Humanitarian Issues* (London: Zed Books).

ICISS (International Commission on Intervention and State Sovereignty) (2001) 'The Responsibility to Protect'; www.iciss.ca/report2-en.asp (accessed November 2006).

ICRC (International Committee of the Red Cross) (2000) 'Internally Displaced Persons: The Mandate and Role of the International Committee of the Red Cross', *International Review of the Red Cross*, 838, 30 June; www.icrc.org/web/eng/siteeng0.nsf/html/57JQHR (accessed June 2008).

IDMC (IDP Monitoring Centre) (2002, 2003, 2004, 2006); www.db.idproject.org (accessed various years).

IFRC (International Federation of the Red Cross) (2008) *World Disasters Report* (Geneva: IFRC); www.ifrc.org/publicat/wdr2003/index.asp (accessed July 2008).

Inter-Agency IDP Working Group (2002) 'Durable Solutions

Progress Report No. 8', *Bulletin of the United Nations Inter-Agency IDP Working Group*, November.

Iriyagolle, G. (1978) *The Truth About the Mahaweli* (Colombo: self-published).

Ismail, E. (1995) *Early Settlements in Northern Sri Lanka* (New Delhi: Navrang Publishing).

Jacobs, J. (1961) *The Death and Life of Great American Cities* (New York: Random House).

Jacobsen, K. (1997) 'Refugees' Environmental Impact: The Effects of Patterns of Settlement', *Journal of Refugee Studies*, 10(1): 19–36.

— (2001) 'The Forgotten Solution: Local Integration for Refugees in Developing Countries', UNHCR Working Paper 45.

— and L. Landau (2003) 'The Dual Imperative in Refugee Research: Some Methodological and Ethical Considerations in Social Science Research on Forced Migration', *Journal of Disaster Studies, Policy and Management*, 27(3): 185–206.

Jagtiani, S. (2006) 'Focus on Tsunami Overlooks Sri Lanka's War Refugees', *Christian Science Monitor*, 4 January.

Jamal, A. (2003) 'Camps and Freedoms: Long-Term Refugee Situations in Africa', *Forced Migration Review*, 16: 4–6.

Jayasekera, B. (2003) 'High Security Zones: Who Started the Fire?', *The Island*, 7 January.

Jayasena W. and M. Senanayaka (1999) 'Land Alienation Statistics for the Presidential Task Force on National Land Utilization and Distribution', Occasional Paper (Colombo: HARTI).

Jayasinghe, M. (2005) 'Rehabilitation and Reconstruction Activities in North and East Provinces', mimeo (Colombo: Ministry of Relief, Rehabilitation and Reconstruction).

Jayatilaka, D. and R. Muggah (2004) 'Where There is No Information: IDP Vulnerability Assessments Sri Lanka's Borderlands', *Forced Migration Review*, 20: 39–41.

Jayawardena, K. (1979) 'Economic and Political Factors in the 1915 Riots', *Journal of Asian Studies*, 29: 223–33.

— (1983) 'Aspects of Class and Ethnic Consciousness in Sri Lanka', *Development and Change*, 14: 1–18.

Jayawardene, R. (2008) 'Involuntary Resettlement: Can Disruption be Turned into Development by Compensation Alone? The South Asian Experience', in M. Cernea and H. Mathur (eds), *Can Compensation Prevent Impoverishment?*, pp. 233–59.

Jayawickrama, N (2002) *The Judicial Application of Human Rights: National, Regional and International Jurisprudence* (Oxford: Oxford University Press).

Jeffels, L. (2005) 'Six Months On: Facing Fears', *Forced Migration Review*, 14, Special Tsunami Edition: 36–7.

Jiggens, J. (1979) *Caste and Family in the Politics of the Sinhalese: 1947–1976* (Cambridge: Cambridge University Press).

Jones, M. (2000) 'The Ceylon Malaria Epidemic of 1934–35: A Case Study in Colonial Medicine', *Social History of Medicine*, 13(1): 87–110.

Kaldor, M. (1999) *New and Old Wars: Organised Violence in a Global Era* (Cambridge: Polity Press).

Kälin, W. (2000) 'Guiding Principles on Internal Displacement', *Annotations*, American Society of International Law and Brookings

Institution Project on Internal Displacement (Washington, DC: Brookings Institution).

— (2005a) 'Natural Disasters and IDP Rights', *Forced Migration Review*, 14, Special Tsunami Edition: 10–11.

— (2005b) 'Keynote Address', Regional Workshop: Capacity Building for Resettlement Risk Management (Manila: ADB).

Kamirthalingam, A. and R. Lakshman (forthcoming) 'Financing of Internal Displacement: Excerpts from the Sri Lankan Experience', *Disasters: The Journal of Disaster Studies, Policy and Management*.

Karunatillake, T. (1983a) *Examination of Certain Aspects of the Mahaweli Development Programme in Its Exercise to Harness Natural Resources for Development* (Kandy: University of Peradeniya).

— (1983b) 'Encroachments by Tamils and Stateless People in the Mullaitivu District', mimeo.

Kearney, R. (1967) *Communalism and Language in the Politics of Ceylon* (Durham, NC: Duke University Press).

— (1985) 'Ethnic Conflict and the Tamil Separatist Movement in Sri Lanka', *Asian Survey*, 25(9): 898–917.

— (1987) 'Territorial Elements of Tamil Separatism in Sri Lanka', *Pacific Affairs*, 60(4): 561–77.

— and B. Miller (1997) *Internal Migration in Sri Lanka and Its Social Consequences* (Boulder, CO: Westview Press).

Keegan, J. (1993) *A History of Warfare* (London: Hutchinson).

Keely, C. (1996) 'How Nations States Create and Respond to Refugee Flows', *International Migration*, 30(4): 1046–66.

Keen, D. (1998) 'The Economic Functions of Violence in Civil Wars', *Adelphi Paper 320* (London: International Institute of Strategic Studies).

Kelsen, H. (1960) 'Sovereignty and International Law', *Georgetown Law Journal*, 47(4): 627–40.

Kendle, A. (1998) 'Protecting Whom? The UNHCR in Sri Lanka, 1987–1997', *Round Table*, 348: 521–41.

Kendra, J. (2004) *Geography's Contribution to Understanding Hazards and Disasters* (Denton: University of North Texas).

Keohane, R. (1984) *After Hegemony: Cooperation and Discord in the World Political Economy* (Princeton, NJ: Princeton University Press).

— (1993) 'The Analysis of International Regimes: Towards a European-American Research Programme', in V. Rittberger (ed.), *Regime Theory and International Relations* (Oxford: Oxford University Press).

Kibreab G. (1989) 'Local Settlements in Africa: A Misconceived Option?', *Journal of Refugee Studies*, 2(4): 468–90.

— (1996a) *People on the Edge in the Horn* (Oxford: James Currey).

— (1996b) 'The Myth of Dependency among Camp Refugees in Somalia 1979–89', *Journal of Refugee Studies*, 6(4): 321–49.

— (2000) 'Displacement, Host Government Policies and Constraints on the Reconstruction of Sustainable Livelihoods', in M. Cernea and C. McDowell (eds), *Risks and Reconstruction*, pp. 184–201.

— (2003) 'Displacement, Host Governments' Policies, and Constraints on Construction of Sustainable Livelihoods',

International Social Science Journal, 175: 61–71.

Kilroy-Silk, R. and S. Roger (1985) 'Sri Lanka: A Nation Dividing', Report of a visit to Sri Lanka on behalf of the Parliamentary Human Rights Group London (London: House of Commons/Parliamentary Human Rights Group, February).

King, G. and C. Murray (2002) 'Rethinking Human Security', Political Science Quarterly, 116(4), Winter.

Kingsley-Nyinah, M. (1999) 'What May be Borrowed: What is New?', Forced Migration Review, 4: 32–3.

Kinsey, B. and H. Binswanger (1993) 'Characteristics and Performance of Settlement Programmes', World Bank Working Paper 1207 (Washington, DC: World Bank).

Klein, N. (2007) The Shock Doctrine: the Rise of Disaster Capitalism (New York: Metropolitan Books).

Kleinman, A. (1998) Social Suffering (New Delhi: Oxford University Press).

Klotz, A. (1995) Norms in International Relations: The Struggle Against Apartheid (Ithaca, NY: Cornell University Press).

Koenig, D. (2001) 'Toward Local Development and Mitigating Impoverishment in Development-Induced Displacement and Resettlement', Final Report for ESCOR R7644 (Oxford: RSC).

Kollgaard, E. B., W. L. Chadwick and J. Cooke (eds) (1988) Development of Dam Engineering in the United States (New York: Pergamon Press).

Korf, B. (2003) 'Control Over Land: Competing Claims and Fuzzy Property Rights in the Northeast of Sri Lanka', Draft Paper (Bonn: Center for Development Research/ ZEF).

Krasner, S. (1982) 'Structural Causes and Regime Consequences: Regimes as Intervening Variables', International Organization, 36(2): 185–206.

— (1998) 'Sovereignty: An Institutional Perspective', Comparative Political Studies, 21(1): 66–94.

Kratochwil, F. (1989) Rules, Norms and Decisions: On the Conditions of Practical and Legal Reasoning in International Relations and Domestic Affairs (Cambridge: Cambridge University Press).

— and J. Ruggie (1986) 'International Organisation: A State of the Art and the Art of the State', International Organisation, 40(4): 753–75.

Kreps, G. and S. Bosworth (1993) 'Disaster, Organizing and Role Enactment: A Structural Approach', American Journal of Sociology, 99(2): 428–63.

Kumar, A. and M. Vasanthan (2006) 'Protesting Sri Lanka Tsunami Refugees Occupy Government Building', World Socialist Website, 9 March.

Kumar, K. M. (2003) 'Dimensions of Poverty Among New Generation of Land Settlers in Mahaweli Villages', PASI Working Paper 6 (Colombo: IMCAP).

Kunder, J. and B. Nylund (1998) Mission to Sri Lanka with a View to Develop Best Practices to Internal Displacement (New York: UNICEF).

Land Commission (1929) Sessional Paper 18 of 1929. J. R. Jayawardena Cultural Centre in Colombo, Sri Lanka.

Lankaneson, T. (2000) Report on Institutional Framework for Relief, Rehabilitation and Reconciliation (Colombo: Government of Sri Lanka, 20 May).

Lassailly-Jacob, V. (1996) 'Land-Based Strategies in Dam-Related Resettlement Programmes in Africa', in C. McDowell (ed.), *Understanding Impoverishment*.

Lavoyer, J. (1995) 'Refugees and Internally Displaced Persons: International Humanitarian Law and the Role of the ICRC', *International Review of the Red Cross*, 305.

Lazarus, S. (2004) 'The Equator Principles: A Milestone or Just Good PR?', *Global Agenda*, 26 January; www.equator-principles.com/ga1. shtml (accessed June 2008).

Le Billion, P. (2000) 'The Political Economy of War: An Annotated Bibliography', HPG Report 1 (London: Overseas Development Institute).

— and A. Waizenegger (2007) 'Peace in the Wake of Disaster? Secessionist Conflicts and the 2004 Indian Ocean Tsunami', *Transactions of the Institute of British Geographers*, 32(3): 411–27.

Leach, M. and J. Fairhead (2000) 'Challenging Neo-Malthusian Deforestation Analysis in West Africa's Dynamic Forest Landscapes', *Population and Development Review*, 26(1): 17–43.

Leaning, J. (2001) 'Ethics of Research in Refugee Populations', *Lancet*, 357(9266): 1432–43.

Leary, V. (1981) 'Ethnic Conflict and Violence in Sri Lanka', Report of the Mission to Sri Lanka on Behalf of the International Commission of Jurists, Colombo.

Leckie, S. (2005) 'The Great Land Theft', *Forced Migration Review*, 25: 15–16.

— (2000) 'Housing and Property Issues for Refugees and Internally Displaced Persons in the Context of Return', *Refugee Survey Quarterly*, 19(3): 52–63.

Leiderman, S. (1996) 'Learning to Recognise Environmental Refugees', Annual Meeting of the American Association for the Advancement of Science, February. Unpublished document.

Lewis, C. (2005) 'UNHCR's Contribution to the Development of International Refugee Law: Its Foundations and Evolution', *International Journal of Refugee Law*, 17(1): 67–90.

Liu Centre (2005) *The Human Security Report* (Oxford: Oxford University Press).

Ljungman, C. (2004) 'Applying a Rights-Based Approach to Development: Concepts and Principles', Conference Paper, Winners and Losers from Rights-Based Approaches to Development, Manchester. Unpublished document.

Loescher, G. (1993) *Beyond Charity: International Cooperation and the Global Refugee Crisis* (Oxford: Oxford University Press).

— (2000) 'Forced Migration in the Post-Cold War Era: The Need for a Comprehensive Approach', in B. Ghosh (ed.), *Managing Migration*.

— and J. Milner (2005) 'Protracted Refugee Situations: Domestic and International Security Implications', *Adelphi Paper* no. 375.

LST (Law and Society Trust) (2000) *State of Human Rights Report 2000* (Colombo: LST).

Lubbers, R. (2004) Opening Statement by Mr Ruud Lubbers, United Nations High Commissioner for Refugees, at the Fifty-Fifth Session of the Executive Committee of the High Commissioner's Programme (UNHCR: Geneva).

McDowell, C. (ed.) (1996a) *Understanding Impoverishment: The Consequences of Development-*

induced Displacement (London: Berghahn Books).

— (1996b) *A Tamil Asylum Diaspora: Sri Lankan Migration, Settlement and Politics in Switzerland* (London: Berghahn Books).

MacFadden, G. (1954) 'The Gal Oya Valley: Ceylon's Little Tennessee Valley Authority', *Geographical Review*, 44: 271–81.

McGilvray, D. (2001) 'A History of Ethnic Conflict in Sri Lanka: Reintegration and Reconciliation', *Marga Monograph Series*, 24 (Colombo: Marga Institute).

Madeley, J. (1983) 'Leaks and Landslide Loom in Sri Lanka', *New Scientist*, 7 April, p. 8.

Mahakanadaawa, R. (1979) *A Study of Five Settlement Schemes Prior to Irrigation Modernization* (Colombo: ARTI).

Mahaweli Authority (1981) 'Draft Implementation Plan Left Bank – System B', mimeo (Colombo: Mahaweli Authority of Sri Lanka).

— (1984) *Appendices to the Final Report of the Special Task Force on the Development and Settlement of System B Accelerated Mahaweli Programme* (Colombo: PMU).

— (1987) 'Selected Material from Report on the Right Bank of the Maduru Oya', mimeo (Colombo: Mahaweli Authority of Sri Lanka).

— (1992) *Report of the Task Force on System B Right Bank of the Mahaweli Project* (Colombo: Ministry of Lands, Irrigation and Mahaweli Development).

— (1993) *System-B: The PMU-MARD Baseline Socio-Economic Survey 1991/92 Cultivation Year* (Colombo: Planning and Monitoring Unit of the Mahaweli Authority).

— (1994) *Irrigation and Social Infrastructure in System L (revised)* (Colombo: Mahaweli Authority of Sri Lanka).

— (2000) *Mahaweli Statistical Handbook* (Colombo: Planning and Monitoring Unit).

— (2004) 'Settlement Progress'; www.mahaweli.gov.lk (accessed November 2004).

— (2006) 'Mahaweli Settlements'; www.mahaweli.gov.lk (accessed November 2006).

Mahaweli Development Board (1974) *Kala Oya Left Bank Socio-Economic Survey Report on Blocks 301-308* (Colombo: Settlement Planning and Development Division).

— (1979) *Human Settlement in the Systems Under the Accelerated Programme* (Colombo: MDB).

Malkki, L. (1995) *Purity and Exile: Village, Memory and Rational Cosmology among Hutu Refugees in Tanzania* (Chicago, IL: University of Chicago Press).

Manogaran, C. (1994) 'Colonisation as Politics: Political Use of Space in Sri Lanka's Ethnic Conflict', in C. Manogaran and B. Pfaffenberger (eds), *The Sri Lankan Tamils: Ethnicity and Identity* (Boulder, CO: Westview Press), pp. 84–125.

— (1996) 'Sinhalese–Tamil Relations and the Prospects for Peace with Justice in Sri Lanka', Presentation to the Conference on Development, Social Justice and Peace (Brookland, Washington, DC: Catholic University of America), July.

Manor, J. (ed.) (1984) *Sri Lanka in Change and Crisis* (London: Croom Helm).

Mantuga, R. (2005) 'Tsunami Housing Reconstruction: A Major Challenge', *Daily News*, 11 October.

Marga Institute (1978) *Some Aspects of Population and Employment*

Related to the Mahaweli Programme (Colombo: Marga Sri Lanka Centre for Development Studies).

Martin, D. (1995) 'Refugees and Migration', in O. Schachter and C. Joyner (eds), *United Nations Legal Order*, vol. 1 (Cambridge: Cambridge University Press), pp. 155–80.

Martin, S. (2000) 'Forced Migration and the Evolving Humanitarian Regime', New Issues in Refugee Research Working Paper 20.

— (2004) 'Making the UN Work: Forced Migration and Institutional Reform', *Journal of Refugee Studies*, 17(3): 301–18.

— and E. Mooney (2007) 'Criteria for Determining the End of Displacement: Three Options for Consideration', unpublished paper for the Brookings Institution, Washington, DC.

Mason, D. (2004) *Qualitative Researching* (London: Sage).

Mathur, H. (2000) 'Involuntary Resettlement and Voluntary Organisations: A View from India', mimeo.

Meemeduma, A. (1994) *Feasibility of Continued Development of System L: Weli Oya* (Colombo: PMU).

Mehta, L. (2000) 'Risks, Safeguards and Reconstruction: A Model for Population Displacement and Resettlement', in M. Cernea and C. McDowell, *Risks and Reconstruction*.

Mellor, J. (1976) *The New Economics of Growth* (Ithaca, NY: Cornell University Press).

Mendie, N. (1973) 'The Planning Implications of the Mahaweli Development Project in Sri Lanka', mimeo (Colombo: University of Colombo).

Millennium Report (2000) 'Millennium Report of the Secretary General'; www.un.org/millennium/sg/report/, New York: UN (accessed December 2006).

Ministry of Development, Rehabilitation, Reconstruction of the East and Rural Housing Development (2001) Rehabilitation and Reconstruction Programme (Trincomalee: GA Statistics).

Ministry of Environment (1980, 1988) National Environmental Act No. 56 (Colombo: Mahaweli Authority archive).

Ministry of Irrigation (1979) Mahaweli Authority of Sri Lanka Act No. 23 (Colombo: Mahaweli Authority archive).

Ministry of Lands (1990) *National Land Use Policy of Sri Lanka* (Colombo: Land Use Policy Planning Division).

Ministry of Lands, Irrigation and Mahaweli Development (1991) *System L: An Action Plan to Develop 1,600 Hectares of Lowland Paddy in Weli Oya* (Colombo).

Ministry of Lands and Land Development (1985) *Landmarks in Sri Lanka's Land Policy: Some Selected Speeches and Papers* (Colombo: Ministry of Lands and Land Development).

Ministry of Mahaweli Development (1987) *Mahaweli Projects and Programmes* (Colombo: Ministry of Mahaweli Development).

Ministry of Reconstruction, Rehabilitation and Social Welfare (1987) 'Memorandum of Understanding Among the Government of the Socialist Republic of Sri Lanka and the Office of the United Nations High Commissioner for Refugees Relating to the Repatriation of Sri Lankan Refugees and Displaced Persons' (Colombo, 1 February).

Ministry of Rehabilitation, Resettlement and Refugees (2004) Letter to Government Agents in Trincomalee, Batticaloa and Ampara. MRRR/08/03.

Ministry of Resettlement (2006) 'Discussion on Internally Displaced People and Humanitarian Issues', Presentation by Ministry of Resettlement (Colombo: CPP).

Ministry of Shipping, Ports, Rehabilitation and Reconstruction (1995) 'Guidelines on Resettlement and Relocation' (MRR/7/RE/95/01, 24 February memorandum).

Monitor (2002) 'Supreme Court Declares Pass System Illegal', September; brcslproject.gn.apc. org/slmonitor/Sept2002/supre. html (accessed September 2003).

Mooney, E. (1995) 'Presence Ergo Protection? UNPROFOR, UNHCR, and ICRC in Croatia and Bosnia-Herzegovina', *Journal of Refugee Law*, 7(3): 407–35.

— (2002a) 'Exploring the Issue of When Internal Displacement Ends', Discussion Paper for CUNY/Brookings (Washington, DC: Brookings Institution).

— (2002b) 'An IDP No More? Exploring the Issue of When Internal Displacement Ends', Discussion Paper for City University of New York (Washington, DC: CUNY/ Brookings).

— (2004) 'Realizing National Responsibility for Internally Displaced Persons', Roundtable on the Protection of Internally Displaced Persons (Washington, DC: Brookings-SAIS Project on Internal Displacement).

— (2005) 'The Concept of Internal Displacement and the Case for Internally Displaced Persons as a Category of Concern', *Refugee Survey Quarterly*, 24(3): 9–26.

Moore, M. (1983) 'Space and the Generation of Socio-Economic Inequality in Sri Lanka's Irrigation Schemes', *Marga*, 7(1): 1–133.

— (1985) *The State and Peasant Policies in Sri Lanka* (London: Cambridge University Press).

— (1989) 'The Ideological History of the Sri Lankan Peasantry', *Modern Asian Studies*, 23(3): 179–207.

— (1990) 'Economic Liberalisation Versus Political Pluralism in Sri Lanka', *Modern Asian Studies*, 24(2): 341–83.

— (1992) 'The Ideological History of the Sri Lankan Peasantry', in J. Brow and J. Weeramunda (eds), *Agrarian Changes in Sri Lanka* (New Delhi: Sage Publications).

Muggah, R. (2000a) 'Through the Developmentalists Looking Glass: Conflict-Induced Displacement and Involuntary Resettlement in Colombia', *Journal of Refugee Studies*, 13(2): 133–64.

— (2000b) 'Conflict-Induced Displacement and Involuntary Resettlement in Colombia: Putting Cernea's IRLR Model to the Test', *Journal of Disaster Studies, Policy and Management*, 24(3): 198–216.

— (2003) 'Two Solitudes: Comparing Conflict and Development-Induced Displacement and Resettlement', *Journal of International Migration*, 41(5): 5–31.

— (2005a) *Listening for a Change* (Geneva: UN Department for Disarmament Research).

— (2005b) 'Distinguishing Means and Ends: The Counterintuitive Effects of UNHCR's Community Development Approach in Nepal', *Journal of Refugee Studies*, 18(2): 151–64.

— (ed.) (2006) *No Refuge: The Crisis of Refugee Militarization in Africa* (London: Zed Books).

— (2007a) 'How the World Fails

Internally Displaced People: The Sri Lankan Case', *Ottawa Citizen*, 7 July.

— (2007b) 'The Death-Knell of 4R?', *Humanitarian Practice Network Exchange*, 36: 25–7.

— (2007c) 'A Negotiated Darfur Settlement is Out of Reach', *Globe and Mail*, 16 November.

— (2007d) 'A Surefire Way to Reduce the Violence: No More Arms to Sudan', *Globe and Mail*, 24 August.

— (ed.) (2008a) *Security and Post-Conflict Reconstruction: Dealing with Fighters in the Aftermath of War* (New York: Routledge).

— (2008b) 'A Country Spins Out of Control', *Toronto Star*, 24 February.

— and K. Krause (2007) 'The True Measure of Success: The Discourse and Practice of Human Security', in S. MacLean, D. Black and T. Shaw (eds), *A Decade of Human Security Global Governance and New Multilateralisms* (London: Ashgate).

— and M. Samanayake, M. (2004) *Participatory Research in the South Pacific: A Methodological Guide* (New York/Suva: UNIFEM).

Müller, H. and Hettige, S. (2004) 'Mahaweli: The Blurring of a Vision. The International Research Institute for Climate and Society', mimeo.

Myers, N. (1997) 'Environmental Refugees', *Population and Environment*, 19(2): 167–82.

Nafziger, E. W., F. Stewart and R. Vayrynen (eds) (1999) *The Origins of Humanitarian Emergencies: War and Displacement in Developing Countries* (Oxford: Oxford University Press).

Narman, A. and U. Vidanapathirana (2005) 'Transiting from Prolonged Conflict to Post-Conflict Development: Locating the Case of

Trincomalee District of Sri Lanka', *Peace and Democracy in South Asia*, 1(1): 1–21.

Navaratnam, V. (1995) *The Fall and Rise of the Tamil Nation* (London: Tamilian Library).

NECORD (2005a) *UAS Work Plan* (Trincomalee: NECORD, August).

— (2005b) *Payment of Livelihood Assistance* (Trincomalee: NECORD, July).

NEDECO (Netherlands Engineering Consultants) (1979) *Mahaweli Ganga Development Programme: Implementation Strategy Study*, 8 vols, September.

— (1983) *Micro Model Studies: Progress Report 4*, Colombo.

Neff, S. (2005) *War and the Law of Nations: A General History* (Cambridge: Cambridge University Press).

Neldner, B. (1979) 'Settlement of Rural Refugees in Africa', *Journal of Disaster Studies, Policy and Management*, 3(4): 393–402.

NEPC (North East Provincial Council) (2003) *Circular No. NEERP/UAS/01* (revised), 24 February.

Newland, K and D. Papdemetriou (1998) 'Managing International Migration: Tracking the Emergence of a New International Regime', *UCLA Journal of International Law and Foreign Affairs*, 3 (Fall/Winter): 1–20.

Newsweek (1983) 'Bloodshed in Sri Lanka', *Newsweek Indian edition*, 8 August.

Nicholas, C. and S. Paranavitana (1961) *A Concise History of Ceylon: From the Earliest Times to the Arrival of the Portuguese in 1505* (Colombo: University of Ceylon Press Board).

Nissan, E. (1996) *Sri Lanka: A Bitter Harvest* (London: Minority Rights Group).

— and R. Stirrat (1990) 'The Generation of Communal Identities', in J. Spencer (ed.), *Sri Lanka: History and Roots of Conflict*.

Nithiyanandam, V. (2000) 'Ethnic Politics and Third World Development: Some Lessons from Sri Lanka's Experience', *Third World Quarterly*, 21(2): 283–311.

Niyangoda, S. (1979) *Basic Socio-Economic Data of Madura Oya* (Colombo: Settlement Planning and Development Division, Mahaweli Development Board).

Nustad, K. (2001) 'Development: The Devil We Know?', *Third World Quarterly*, 22(4): 479–89.

Obeyesekere, G. (1984) 'The Origins and Institutionalisation of Political Violence', in J. Manor (ed.), *Sri Lanka in Change and Crisis*.

OCHA (UN Office for the Coordination of Humanitarian Affairs) (2000) *Crises of Internal Displacement: Status of the International Response Through the Inter-Agency Standing Committee and Their Member Agencies* (Geneva: Policy Development Unit).

— (2002) *The Situation of IDPs in Sri Lanka: Report of a Mission by the Internal Displacement Unit* (Geneva: OCHA).

— (2003) *No Refuge: The Challenge of Internal Displacement* (Geneva: OCHA).

— (2005) 'Tsunami Coordination Arrangements for Reconstruction in Sri Lanka', mimeo, Colombo.

— (2006) 'Benchmarks for When Displacement Ends', mimeo.

— and IDD (2006) 'Benchmarks of Durable Solutions for IDPs: Flowchart', mimeo.

OECD (1991) *Guidelines for Aid Agencies on Involuntary Displacement and Resettlement in Development Projects* OECD/GD (91)201 (Paris: OECD).

Ofstad, A. (2002) 'Countries in Violent Conflict and Aid Strategies: The Case of Sri Lanka', *World Development*, 30(2): 165–80.

Oliver-Smith, A. (1979) 'Post Disaster-Consensus and Conflict in a Traditional Society: The 1970 Avalanche of Yungay, Peru', *Mass Emergencies*, 4: 39–52.

— (1986) 'Disaster Context and Causation: An Overview of Changing Perspective in Disaster Research', in V. Sutlive (ed.), *Natural Disasters and Cultural Responses* (Williamsburg, SC: Department of Anthropology).

— (1991) 'Involuntary Resettlement, Resistance and Political Empowerment', *Journal of Refugee Studies*, 45(2): 132–49.

— (1996) 'Anthropological Research on Hazards and Disasters', *Annual Review of Anthropology*, 25: 303–28.

— (2002) 'Theorizing Disasters: Nature, Culture, Power', in S. Hoffman and A. Oliver-Smith (eds), *Culture and Catastrophe: The Anthropology of Disaster* (Santa Fe, NM: School of American Research Press).

— (2004) 'Disasters and Forced Migration in the 21st Century'; www.understandingkatrina.ssrc.org (accessed January 2006).

— (2005) 'Communities After Catastrophe: Reconstructing the Material, Reconstituting the Social', in S. Hyland (ed.), *Community Building in the Twenty-First Century* (Santa Fe, NM: School of American Research Press).

— (2006) 'Disasters and Forced Migration in the 21st Century', SSRC Article; www.

understandingkatrina.ssrc.org/
Oliver-Smith/ (accessed July 2008).

— and G. Button (2005) 'Forced
Migration as an Index of Vulner-
ability in Hurricane Katrina',
Preliminary Draft for the 6th Open
Meeting of the Human Dimen-
sions of Global Environmental
Change Research Meeting, Expert
Working Group on Vulnerability
(Bonn, October).

— and S. Hoffman (1999) *The Angry
Earth: Disaster in Anthropological
Perspective* (New York: Routledge).

Orchard, P. (2005) 'Refugees and
the International Sovereign
State System: The Need for a
Relief Valve', Paper presented
at the Annual Conference of the
Canadian Political Science Association (London, Canada, 4 June).

Ostrom, E. (1986) 'An Agenda for
the Study of Institutions', *Public
Choice*, 58: 3–25.

— (1990) *Governing the Commons:
The Evolution of Institutions for
Collective Action* (Cambridge:
Cambridge University Press).

O'Sullivan, M. (1997) 'Household
Entitlements During Wartime:
The Experience of Sri Lanka',
*Oxford Journal of Development
Studies*, 25(1): 95–121.

Otrovsky, V. (1990) *By Way of Decep-
tion* (New York: St Martins Press).

Pain, A. (1986) 'Agricultural Research
in Sri Lanka: An Historical
Account', *Journal of Modern Asian
Studies*, 20(4): 755–78.

Palmer, G. (1974) 'The Ecology of
Resettlement Schemes', *Human
Organisation*, 33(3): 239–50.

Pankhurst, A. (1992) *Resettlement and
Famine in Ethiopia: The Villager's
Experience* (Manchester: Man-
chester University Press).

Parakrama, A. (2006) *The Impact of
the Tsunami Response on Local and
National Capacities* (Colombo:
Tsunami Evaluation Coalition).

Partridge, B. (1993) 'Successful
Involuntary Resettlement', in
M. Cernea and S. Guggenheim
(eds), *Anthropological Approaches
to Resettlement*.

Pedersen, M. (2003) 'Between Homes:
Post-War Return, Emplacement
and the Negotiation of Belonging
in Lebanon', *New Issues in Refugee
Research Working Paper 79*.

Peebles, P. (1990) 'Colonisation and
Ethnic Conflict in Sri Lanka',
Journal of Asian Studies, 40(1):
30–55.

Peiris, G. H. (1996) *Development and
Change in Sri Lanka: Geographical
Perspectives* (Colombo and Kandy:
International Centre for Ethnic
Studies).

— (2001) *Poverty and Entitlement
Dimensions of Political Conflict in
Sri Lanka: Bibliographic Survey*
(The Hague: Netherlands Institute
of International Relations).

Peiris, G. L. (1985) 'An Appraisal
of the Concept of a Traditional
Homeland', National Workshop
on the Economic Dimensions of
the Ethnic Conflict in Sri Lanka
(Kandy: ICES).

— (1999) 'An Appraisal of the
Concept of a Traditional Tamil
Homeland in Sri Lanka', *Ethnic
Studies Report*, 9(1).

Penz, P. (2003) 'Development, Dis-
placement, Coercion and Harm: A
Theoretical Treatment', Paper for
IASFM (Bangkok, 5–9 January).

Perera, A. (2005) 'Tsunami Impact:
Politics Narrows Coastal Buffer
Zone', *IPS*, October 28.

Perera, J. (1992) 'Political Development and Ethnic Conflict in Sri
Lanka', *Journal of Refugee Studies*,
5(2): 136–48.

Perera, N. (1985) 'Reference Models

for Mahaweli Rural Settlements: A Study Prepared During Special Sessions at MIT', mimeo (Cambridge, MA).

Pfaffenberger, B. (1990) 'The Harsh Facts of Hydraulics: Technology and Society in Sri Lanka's Colonisation Schemes', *Technology and Culture*, 31: 3.

Philpott, D. (2001) *Revolutions in Sovereignty: How Ideas Shaped Modern International Relations* (Princeton, NJ: Princeton University Press).

Phuong, C. (2005) *The International Protection of Internally Displaced Persons*, Cambridge Studies in International and Comparative Law, 38 (Cambridge: Cambridge University Press).

Picciotto, R., W. van Wicklin and E. Rice (eds) (2001) *Involuntary Resettlement: Comparative Perspectives* (New Jersey: Transaction Publishing).

Pinto-Jayawardena, K. (2006) 'Desperate Problems of the Internationally Displaced in Sri Lanka', *Sunday Times,* 2 April.

Pitterman, S. (1997) 'Resettlement: An Instrument of Protection and a Durable Solution', *International Journal of Refugee Law*, 9(4): 666–73.

Plender, R. (1994) 'The Legal Basis of International Jurisdiction to Act with Regard to the Internally Displaced', *International Journal of Refugee Law*, 6(3): 345–61.

Ponnambalam, S. (1983) *Sri Lanka: National Conflict and the Tamil Liberation Struggle* (London: Zed Books).

Premaratne, E. (2002) *Current Status of Land and Property of the Internally Displaced Persons in North of Sri Lanka*. Unpublished paper.

Price, S. (2003) 'National Standards on Involuntary Resettlement: Are They Achievable?', Paper presented to the XI International Congress of Anthropological and Ethnographical Sciences (Florence, Italy).

Pridham, C. (1849) *Ceylon and its Dependencies* (London: T. and W. Boone).

Puchala, D. and Hopkins, R. (1982) 'International Regimes: Lessons from Inductive Analysis', *International Organization*, 36(2): 245–75.

Pugh, M., N. Cooper and J. Goodhand (2004) *War Economies in a Regional Context: The Challenge of Transformation* (Boulder, CO: Lynne Rienner).

Qadri, I. (2005) *Abiding by Sri Lanka: On Peace, Place, and Postcoloniality* (Minneapolis: Minnesota University Press).

Quarantelli, E. (ed.) (1978) *Disasters: Theory and Research* (Beverley Hills, CA: Sage).

— and R. Dynes (1977) 'Response to Social Crisis and Disaster', *Annual Review of Sociology*, 3: 23–49.

RADA (Reconstruction and Development Agency) (2006a) 'Donor and Owner-Driven Housing Site Progress Reports (District/ Division/Site)'; www.rada.gov.lk (accessed June 2006).

— (2006b) *Mid-Year Review: Post-Tsunami Recovery and Reconstruction* (Colombo: RADA)

— (2006c) 'New Housing Policy Launched: Govt. Aims to Complete Tsunami Housing Reconstruction by End 2006'; www.rada. gov.lk (accessed November 2006).

Rajasingam, A. (1999) 'Displacement and Refugees: North-East Sri Lanka as a Case Study', in I. Ahmed (ed.), *South Asian Refugee Watch*, 1: 2 (Dhaka:

Centre for Alternatives; Colombo: Consortium of Humanitarian Agencies).

Rajasingham, K. (2001) 'Sri Lanka: the Untold Story', *Asia Times*, 11 November.

Rajasingham-Senanayake, D. (2006) 'The International Aid Architecture and Tsunami', *Polity: Special Issue on the Tsunami*, 3(2) (Colombo: Social Scientists' Association); www.ssalanka.org/polity.html (accessed June 2008).

Ram, K. (1968) *Agricultural Economics*, vol. 8 (Colombo: FAO and the Irrigation Department of Ceylon).

Ramsbotham, M. and T. Woodhouse (1996) *Humanitarian Intervention in Contemporary Conflict: A Re-conceptualisation* (Cambridge: Polity Press).

Ratnaweera, D. (1979) *First Settlements of Mahaweli* (Berlin: Konrad-Adenauer-Stiftung).

Ratnayake, R. (2000) *Country Case Study: Sri Lanka* (Washington, DC and Colombo: World Bank).

RDC (Resources Development Consultants) (2004) *North East Housing Reconstruction Programme: Report on the Land Survey* (Colombo: Commissioned Study).

Read, M. and D. Marsh (2002) 'Combining Quantitative and Qualitative Methods', in D. Marsh and G. Stoker (eds), *Theory and Methods in Political Science* (Basingstoke: Palgrave).

Refugee Council-UK (2003) *Internally Displaced Persons and Safe Returns* (London: Refugee Council-UK).

Refugee International (2000) 'Sri Lanka: Muslim Victims of Ethnic Cleansing Require Special Attention'; www.refugeesinternational.org/content/article/detail/765/?PHPSESSID=5cfliegen3C (accessed June 2004).

Reliefweb (2006) 'Sri Lanka-Muttur Massacre: Action against Hunger takes note of the SLMM declarations – Press Conference'; www.reliefweb.int/rw/RWB.NSF/db900SID/KHII-6T743L?OpenDocument (accessed January 2007).

Reuters (2005) 'Sri Lanka Tsunami Aid Becomes Geopolitical Game', 3 January.

Rew, A. (1996) 'Policy Implications of the Involuntary Ownership of Resettlement Negotiations', in C. McDowell (ed.) *Understanding Impoverishment*.

Richardson, J. (2005) *Paradise Poisoned: Learning About Conflict, Terrorism and Development from Sri Lanka's Civil Wars* (Kandy: International Center for Ethnic Studies).

Richmond, A. (1993) 'The Environment and Refugees: Theoretical and Policy Issues', Revised paper presented at International Union for the Scientific Study of Population, Montreal.

— (1994) *Global Apartheid* (Oxford: Oxford University Press).

Riggberger, V. (ed.) (1993) *Regime Theory and International Relations* (Oxford: Oxford University Press).

Risse, T., S. Ropp and K. Sikkink (eds) (1999) *The Power of Human Rights: International Norms and Domestic Change* (Cambridge: Cambridge University Press).

— and K. Sikkink (1999) 'The Socialization of International Human Rights Norms into Domestic Practices', in T. Risse, S. Ropp and K. Sikkink, *The Power of Human Rights*.

Rittberger, V. and P. Mayer (1993) *Regime Theory and International Relations* (Oxford: Oxford University Press).

Riviresa (1983) 'Sri Lanka's Dilemma', 14 August.

Roberts, A. (1998) 'More Refugees, Less Asylum: A Regime in Transformation', *Journal of Refugee Studies*, 11(4): 375–95.

Roberts, M. (1979) 'Elite Formations and Elites: 1832–1931', in *Collective Identities, Nationalisms and Protest in Modern Sri Lanka* (Colombo: Marga Institute).

— (2001) 'Sinhala-ness and Sinhala Nationalism'. *A History of Ethnic Conflict*, Sri Lanka Monograph Series 4 (Colombo: Marga Institute).

— (2004) 'Narrating Tamil Nationalism: Subjectivities and Issues' *Journal of South Asian Studies*, 27(1): 87–108.

Robinson, W. (2003) 'Risks and Rights: The Causes, Consequences and Challenges of Development-Induced Displacement and Resettlement Projects', Paper for Brookings Institution-SAIS Project on Internal Displacement (Washington, DC: Brookings Institution).

Rogers, J. (1987) 'Social Mobility, Popular Ideology and Collective Violence in Modern Sri Lanka', *Journal of Asian Studies*, 46(3): 583–602.

Rogge, J. (1980) 'Africa's Resettlement Strategies', *International Migration Review*, 15(1): 195–212.

Romer, K. (2006) 'Environmental Refugees?', *Forced Migration Review*, 24: 61.

Rosenau, J. (2001) 'Stability, Stasis, and Change: A *Fragmegrating* World', in R. Kugler and E. Frost (eds), *The Global Century: Globalization and National Security*, vol. 1. (Washington, DC: National Defence University), pp. 127–53.

— (2002) 'Governance in a New Global Order', in D. Held and A. McGrew (eds), *Governing Globalization: Power, Authority and Global Governance* (Cambridge: Polity Press).

RRAN (Resettlement and Rehabilitation Authority of the North) (1996) *Resettlement and Rehabilitation Programme for the Jaffna Peninsula* (Colombo: Resettlement and Rehabilitation Authority of the North).

— (1997) 'Compensation Scheme', Board Paper no. 31 (Colombo: RRAN).

Rupesinghe, K. (ed.) (2006) *Negotiating Peace in Sri Lanka: Efforts, Failures and Lessons*, vols 1 and 2 (Colombo: Foundation for Co-existence).

Rutinwa, B. (1999) 'How Tense is the Tension Between the Refugee Concept and the IDP Debate?', *Forced Migration Review*, 4: 29–31.

Sachs, J. (2005) *The End of Poverty: Economic Possibilities for Our Time* (New York: Penguin Books).

Sachs, W. (1992) *The Development Dictionary: A Guide to Knowledge as Power* (London: Zed Books).

SAHR (South Asians for Human Rights) (2007) *Report of the Mission to the North and East to Assess the State of Displaced Persons* (Colombo: SAHR).

Samarasinghe, A. (1982) 'Sri Lanka in 1982: A Year of Elections', *Asian Survey*, 23(2): 158–64.

— and H. Aunasekera (1980) *Pimburettewa: A Study of an Existing Settlement Scheme in System B of the Mahaweli Development Programme* (Colombo: Mahaweli Development Board).

Samaraweera, B. (1970) 'Land Policy and Peasant Colonisation, 1914–1948', *University of Ceylon History of Ceylon*, vol. 3 (Colombo: University of Colombo).

Sambandan, V. (2005) 'LTTE Leader Lashes Out at "Sinhala Forces"', *The Hindu,* 28 November.

Sanchez-Garzoli, G. (2001) *Selected Bibliography of the Global Crisis of Internal Displacement* (Washington, DC: Brookings Institution).

Sarfaty, G. (2005) 'The World Bank and the Internalization of Indigenous Rights Norms', *Yale Journal of Law,* 11(4); www.yalelawjournal.org/pdf/114-7/Sarfaty.pdf (accessed November 2006).

Sarvanathan, M. (2005) 'Post-Tsunami Sri Lanka: Swindlers Hold Sway', *Economic and Political Weekly,* 36(19): 1683–7.

Satchithanandan, K. (2000) 'Sinhala Colonisation in the Hereditary Tamil Regions of the Island of Sri Lanka', Submission by the Tamil Centre for Human Rights to the 56th UN Commission on Human Rights, March/April.

Satkunanathan, A. and C. Rainford (2008) *The Politics of Interim Arrangements in Sri Lanka* (Colombo: Berghoff).

Savolainen, J. (1994) 'The Rationality of Drawing Big Conclusions Based on Small Samples: In Defence of Mill's Methods', *Social Forces,* 72: 1217–23.

Schack, B. (2000) 'Integrating Protection and Assistance Working with Internally Displaced Persons in Sri Lanka', *Refugee Survey Quarterly,* 19(2): 101–9.

Schickle, R. (1969) *Toward a Progressive Theory of Land Tenure* (New York: Agricultural Development Council).

— (1970) *The Mahaweli Scheme: Success or Failure?* (Colombo: University of Colombo).

Schmidt, A. (2003) *Thematic Guide: Camps Versus Settlements,* Forced Migration-Online; www.forcedmigration.org/guides/fmo021/fmo021.pdf (accessed July 2008).

Schrijvery, J. (1999) 'Fighters, Victims and Survivors: Constructions of Ethnicity, Gender and Refugeeness among Tamils in Sri Lanka', *Journal of Refugee Studies,* 12(3): 307–33.

Scott, J. (1998) *Seeing Like a State: How Certain Schemes to Improve the Human Condition Have Failed* (New Haven, CT: Yale University Press).

Scudder, T. (1973) 'The Human Ecology of Big Projects: River Basin Development and Resettlement', in B. Siegel (ed.), *Annual Review of Anthropology* (Palo Alto, CA: Annual Reviews), pp. 45–55.

— (1980) *Sri Lankans, Tourists and National Parks* (Colombo: Data Registry, Planning and Monitoring Unit).

— (1983) 'The Relocation Component in Connection with the Sardar Sarovar (Narmada) Project', *World Bank Consultant Report.* Unpublished report.

— (1990) 'Victims of Development Revisited: The Political Crisis of River Basin Development', *Development Anthropology Network: Bulletin of the Institute for Development Anthropology,* 8(1).

— (1991) 'A Sociological Framework for the Analysis of New Land Settlements', in M. Cernea (ed.), *Putting People First,* pp. 148–87.

— (1992) 'Constraints to the Development of Settler Incomes and Production-Oriented Participatory Organisations in Large-Scale Government-Sponsored Projects: The Mahaweli Case', Paper presented at the Irrigation Society in the Context of Mahaweli, Sri Lanka (Ticino).

— (1996) 'Development-Induced Impoverishment, Resistance and River-Basin Development', in C. McDowell (ed.), *Understanding Impoverishment*, pp. 49–76.

— (2001) 'A Comparative Survey of Dam-Induced Resettlement in 50 Cases', unpublished annex to *The Future of Large Dams: Dealing with Social, Environment, Institutional and Political Costs.*

— and E. Colson (1979) 'Long-Term Research in the Gwembe Valley, Zambia', in G. Forster, T. Scudder, E. Colson and R. Kemper (eds), *Long-Term Field Research in Social Anthropology* (New York: Academic Press), pp. 227–54.

— and E. Colson (1982) 'From Welfare to Development: A Conceptual Framework for the Analysis of Dislocated People', in A. Hansen and A. Oliver-Smith (eds), *Involuntary Migration and Resettlement*, pp. 267–87.

— and K. Vimaladharma (1985) 'The Accelerated Mahaweli Programme (AMP) and Dry Zone Development', *Report 5* (Pasadena, CA).

— (1989) 'The Accelerated Mahaweli Programme (AMP) and Dry Zone Development', *Report 7* (Pasadena, CA).

Selznick, P. (1964) [1949] *TVA and the Grass Roots: A Study in the Sociology of Formal Organizations* (New York: Harper and Row).

Sen, A. (1999) *Development as Freedom* (Oxford: Oxford University Press).

Senanayake, D. S. (1935a) *Agriculture and Patriotism* (Colombo: Cave).

— (1935b) 'In Defence of Our Land and Agricultural Policy', *Ceylon Economic Journal*, 7: 3–5.

Senanayake, R. (2006) *The Tsunami in Sri Lanka: Geographical Perspectives* (Kandy: University of Peradeniya).

Sending, O. and I. Neumann (2006) 'Governance to Governability: Analysing States, NGOs and Power', *International Studies Quarterly*, 50: 651–72.

Seneratne, J. (1997) 'The Tamil Secessionist Insurrection, Political Violence', in *Sri Lanka: 1977–1990: Riots, Insurrections, Counter-Insurgencies, and Foreign Intervention* (Amsterdam: VU University Press).

— (1998) *Political Violence in Sri Lanka, 1977–1990: Riots, Insurrections, Counter-Insurgencies, Foreign Intervention* (Amsterdam: VU University Press).

— (2003) 'The Security Establishment in Sri Lanka: A Case for Reform', in G. Cawthra and R. Luckham (eds), *Governing Insecurity: Democratic Control of Military and Security Establishments in Transitional Societies* (London: Zed Books), pp. 181–204.

Seneviratne, H. and M. Stavropoulou (1998) 'Sri Lanka's Vicious Circle of Displacement', in R. Cohen and F. Deng (eds), *The Forsaken People*, pp. 359–98.

Seteney, S. (1994) *Population Displacement and Resettlement: Development and Conflict in the Middle East* (New York: Center for Migration Studies).

Shacknove, A. (1985) 'Who is a Refugee?', *Ethics*, 95: 274–84.

Shanmugaratnam, N. (1985) 'Some Aspects of the Evolution and Implementation of the Policy of Peasant Resettlement in the Dry Zone of Sri Lanka', in C. Abeysekera (ed.), *Capital and Peasant Production.*

— (2000) 'Forced Migration and Changing Local Political Economies: A Study from North-Western Sri Lanka', Noragric

Working Paper 22 (Aas, Norway: Department of International Environment and Development Studies).

Shell International (2004) *Resettlement: Managing Physical and Economic Displacement of People*, Guidance Note, Social Performance Management Unit.

Shihata, I. (1993) 'Legal Aspects of Involuntary Population Resettlement', in M. Cernea and S. Guggenheim (eds), *Anthropological Approaches to Resettlement*, pp. 39–54.

Shurke, A. (2003) 'Reflections on Regime Change', *Researching Displacement: State of the Art*, Trondheim Conference, 7–8 February.

Simmance, A. (1991) *Review of the UNHCR Programme of Immediate Relief Assistance to Returnees and Displaced Persons in Sri Lanka* (Geneva: Central Evaluation Unit).

Sivard, R. (1996) *World Military and Social Expenditures* (New York: Institute for World Order).

Skinner, J. (2005) 'The People In-Between: IDPs, Space, and (Dis)Placement in Sri Lanka', *Sussex Migration Working Paper* 25 (Brighton: University of Sussex).

Smith, C. (2002) 'In the Shadow of a Ceasefire: Armed Violence in Sri Lanka', *Occasional Paper 8* (Geneva: Small Arms Survey).

Smythe, M. and G. Robinson (2001) *Researching Violently Divided Societies: Ethical and Methodological Issues* (London: Pluto Press).

Snodgrass, D. (1999) 'The Economic Development of Sri Lanka: A Tale of Missed Opportunities', in R. Rotberg (ed.), *Creating Peace in Sri Lanka: Civil War and Reconciliation* (Washington, DC: Brookings Institution Press), pp. 89–107.

Sørensen, B. (1996) *Relocated Lives: Displacement and Resettlement within the Mahaweli Project, Sri Lanka* (Amsterdam: VU University Press).

— (1997) 'The Experience of Displacement: Reconstructing Places and Identities in Sri Lanka', in K. Olwig and K. Hastrop (eds), *Siting Culture* (London: Routledge), pp. 223–53.

— (2001) 'Sri Lanka: Developing New Livelihoods in the Shadow of War', in M. Vincent and B. Sørensen (eds), *Caught Between Borders: Response Strategies of the Internally Displaced* (London: Pluto Press), pp. 172–202.

Spencer, J. (ed.) (1990a) *Sri Lanka: History and Roots of Conflict* (London: Routledge).

— (1990b) 'Collective Violence and Everyday Practice in Sri Lanka', *Modern Asian Studies*, 24(3): 603–23.

Sphere (2004) 'Sphere Handbook'; www.sphereproject.org/handbook/index.htm (accessed November 2005).

Sri Lanka (1947) *Public Security Ordinance No. 25* (Colombo).

— (1951) *Census of Ceylon, 1946*, vol. 1 (Colombo: Government Press).

— (1972) *Constitution of the Democratic Republic of Sri Lanka* (Certified 4 August, Colombo).

— (1978) *Constitution of the Democratic Republic of Sri Lanka* (Certified 31 August, Colombo).

— (1979a) *Mahaweli Authority Bill, 2 March CO 1216-1364* (Colombo).

— (1979b) *Appropriations Bill 1980: Accelerated Mahaweli Development, 14 November CO 331-334* (Colombo).

— (1979c) *Administration Districts Act: Resolution, 3 July CO 1029-1091* (Colombo).

— (1979d) *Oral Answers: Accelerated Mahaweli Programme – NEDCO Report, 8 November CO 1512-1520* (Colombo).

— (1979e) *Prevention of Terrorism (Temporary Provisions) Act No. 48* (Certified on 20 July, Colombo).

— (1979f) *Mahaweli Authority of Sri Lanka Act No. 23* (Certified on 19 April, Colombo).

— (1981) *Census of Population and Housing* (Colombo: Census Department)

— (1985) *Mobilisation and Supplementary Forces Act 1985* (Colombo).

— (1987a) *Thirteenth Amendment to the Constitution* (Certified on 14 November (Colombo).

— (1987b) *Provincial Councils Act No. 42* (Colombo).

— (1989) *Emergency (Miscellaneous Provisions and Powers) Regulations No. 1* (Colombo)

— (1991) *Emergency (Restriction on Transport of Articles) Regulations No. 1* (Colombo).

— (1994) 'Emergency (Miscellaneous Provisions and Powers) Regulations No. 4', *Gazette of the Democratic Socialist Republic of Sri Lanka*, No. 843112, November (Colombo)

— (1997) 'Issue of Dry Ration/Cash and WFP Assistance 30/06/1997', Ministry of Shipping, Ports, Rehabilitation and Reconstruction (Colombo).

— (1998) *Presidential Task Force on Human Disaster Management* (Colombo: President's Office).

— (1999) 'Particulars of Resettled Families: 1995-1999', mimeo (Trincomalee: Government Agent).

— (2000a) *Framework for Relief, Rehabilitation and Reconciliation*, Progress Report (Colombo).

— (2000b) 'Part 1: Section (1): Government Notifications MD/L1/114/E7', *Gazette of the Democratic Social Republic of Sri Lanka* (Colombo).

— (2001a) *National Involuntary Resettlement Guidelines* (Colombo: Ministry of Irrigation).

— (2001b) *Census of Population and Housing* (Colombo: Department of Census and Statistics).

— (2001c) 'Total Number of Families to be Resettled', mimeo (Batticaloa: Land Kacheri).

— (2002a) 'National Framework for Relief, Rehabilitation and Reconciliation in Sri Lanka', at www.brookings.edu/fp/projects/idp/Sri-Lanka_NationalFramework2002.pdf (accessed December 2006).

— (2002b) 'De-escalation Plan proposed by Security Forces Commander, Jaffna Peninsula, Maj. Gen. Sarath Fonseka, to Enable Re-settlement of Civilians in High Security Zones'; www.satp.org (accessed December 2006).

— (2002c) *Statistical Abstract 2002* (Colombo: Department of Statistics).

— (2002d) 'Agreement on a Ceasefire Between the Government of the Democratic Socialist Republic of Sri Lanka and the Liberation Tigers of Tamil Eelam'; www.peaceinsrilanka.org/insidepages/Agreement/agceasefire.asp (accessed November 2005).

— (2003a) *Sri Lanka Demographic and Health Survey* (Colombo: Department of Health).

— (2003b) 'Regaining Sri Lanka: Vision and Strategy for Accelerated Development'; www.peaceinsrilank.org (accessed December 2006).

— (2005) *Sri Lanka: Post-Tsunami Recovery and Reconstruction. A Joint Report of the Government of Sri Lanka and Development Partners* (Colombo: Ministry of Finance and Planning, December).

— (2006a) *Jathika Saviya Authority/ Resettlement Authority, Bill 207*, Parliament of the Democratic Socialist Republic of Sri Lanka, 20 November.

— (2006b) 'Plan for Resettlement of Internally Displaced Families', mimeo (Colombo: Ministry of Finance and Planning).

— (2007) *Resettlement Authority Act No. 09*, Parliament of the Democratic Socialist Republic of Sri Lanka, 23 March.

Sri Nissanka, J. (2005) 'Buffer Zone Hampers Tsunami Reconstruction', *Sunday Observer*, 18 December.

Sriskandarajah, D. (2003) *The Returns of Peace in Sri Lanka: The Development Cart Before the Resolution Horse?* (Colombo: Centre for Ethnic Studies).

Stedman, S. and F. Tanner (eds) (2003) *Refugee Manipulation: War, Politics, and the Abuse of Human Suffering* (Washington, DC: Brookings Institution Press).

Stepputat, F. and N. Sørensen (2002) 'IDPs and Mobile Livelihoods', *Forced Migration Review*, 14: 36–7.

Stewart, F. and V. Fitzgerald (2001) *War and Underdevelopment*, vol. 1 (Oxford: Oxford University Press).

— F. Humphreys and N. Lea (1997) 'Civil Conflict in Developing Countries Over the Last Quarter Century: An Empirical Overview of the Economic and Social Consequences', *Oxford Development Studies*, 25(1): 11–42.

Stirrat, R. (1984) 'The Riots and the Roman Catholic Church in Histor-ical Perspective', in J. Manor (ed.), *Sri Lanka in Change and Crisis*.

Stokke, K. (1988) 'Sinhalese and Tamil Nationalism as Post-Colonial Projects from Above 1948–1983', *Political Geography*, 17(1): 83–113.

Strange, S. (1983) 'Cave! Hic Dragones: A Critique of Regime Analysis', *International Organization*, 36(2): 479–96.

— (1988) *States and Markets* (London: Pinter).

Strauss, A. (1987) *Qualitative Analysis for Social Scientists* (Cambridge: Cambridge University Press).

Sumith, D. (2007) 'When a Landslide Brought Them Down', *Groundviews*, 1(3), May–June.

Sutton, K. (1977) 'Population Resettlement: Traumatic Upheavals and the Algerian Experience', *Journal of Modern African Studies*, 15(2): 279–300.

Swamy, R. (2003) *Inside an Elusive Mind: Prabhakaran – The First Profile of the World's Most Ruthless Guerrilla Leader* (Delhi: Konark Publishing).

TAFREN (Task Force to Rebuild the Nation) (2005a) *Housing and Township Development: Assistance Policy and Implementation Guidelines* (Colombo: TAFREN).

— (2005b) *Post-Tsunami Recovery and Reconstruction: A Joint Report of the Government of Sri Lanka and Its Development Partners*, December.

Tambiah, R. (1958) 'Some Sociological Problems of Colonisation on a Peasant Framework', *Ceylon Economist*, 4(2): 453–5.

Tambiah, S. J. (1986) *Sri Lanka: Ethnic Fratricide and the Dismantling of Democracy* (Chicago, IL: University of Chicago Press).

— (1990) *Sri Lanka: History and*

the Roots of Conflict (London: Routledge).

Tamilnet (1998) 'Veeramunai's Perpetual Fear'; www.tamilnet.com (accessed January 2006).

— (2003a) 'Balasingham Opposes Resettlement Plan'; www.tamilnet.com (accessed January 2006).

— (2003b) 'Defunct' SDN is Shut Down', www.tamilnet.com (accessed January 2006).

— (2005) 'Sri Lanka 2006 Defense Expenditure to Increase by 30 Per Cent'; www.tamilnet.com/art.html?catid=13&artid=16290 (accessed February 2007).

TAMS (Tippets, Abbet, McCarthy and Stratten) (1980) Environmental Assessment of the Accelerated Mahaweli Programme (Submitted to the Sri Lankan Government).

TEC (Tsunami Evaluation Coalition) (2006) Links Between Relief, Rehabilitation and Development in the Tsunami Response: Sri Lanka Case Study (Belgium: Channel Research).

Tennekoon, M. (1982) A Critical Assessment of Thayer Scudder's Evaluatory Report on Mission to Sri Lanka Settlement Projects: A Discussion of Some Basic Issues (May 1979) (Colombo: PMU).

Tennekoon, S. (1988) 'Rituals of Development: The Accelerated Mahavali Development Programme of Sri Lanka', American Ethnologist, 15(1): 295–310.

Tennent, J. (ed.) (1977) [1859] Ceylon: An Account of the Island; Physical, Historical and Topographical (repr. Colombo: Tisara Prakasakayo).

Thangarajah, Y. (2003) 'Ethnicization of Devolution Debate and Militarization of Civil Society', in M. Mayer, D. Rajasingham-Senanayake and Y. Thangarajah (eds), Building Local Capacities for Peace: Rethinking Conflict and Development in Sri Lanka (New Delhi: Macmillan Press).

Thangavelu, V. (1998) 'At Mala Aru (Weli Oya) Who in Fact Ethnically Cleansed Whom'; www.tamilnet.org. (accessed November 2005).

Thornton, P. and R. Nihthiyananthan (2001) Sri Lanka: Island of Terror (Colombo: Wasala Publications for UTHR).

Tropical Agriculturist (1932), editorial (Peradeniya: H.W. Cave), p. 87.

Turner, B. (1978) Man-Made Disasters (London: Wykeham Press).

Turner, L. (1923) Census Publications, Ceylon, 1921: Town and Village Statistics, vol. 2 (Colombo: H. R. Cottle Government Printer).

Turton, D. (1996) 'Migrants and Refugees', in T. Allen (ed.), In Search of Cool Ground: War, Flight and Homecoming in Northeast Africa (Oxford: James Currey).

— (2003) 'Refugees and Other Forced Migrants', Working Paper Series 13 (Oxford: Queen Elizabeth House, RSC).

Twigg, J. (2004) Disaster Risk Reduction: Mitigation and Preparedness in Development and Emergency Programming, Good Practice Review, 9 (London: ODI).

UDA (Urban Development Authority) (2005) 'Public Notice, Ministry of Urban Development and Water Supply', Daily News, 1 January.

— (2006) Lands Identified for Resettlement; www.uda.lk (accessed December 2006).

Udall, L. (1999) The World Bank Inspection Panel: A Three Year Review of Involuntary Resettlement: Questions and Challenges (Washington, DC: World Bank).

UN (United Nations) (1972) ECOSOC Resolution 1705 (LIII), 27 July.

— (1991) *Resolution S/RES/0688*, 5 April.
— (1994a) 'Internally Displaced Persons', *Report of the 45th Session: A/AC.96/839*.
— (1994b) *Report of the Representative of the Secretary-General – F. Deng: Profiles in Displacement: Sri Lanka, E/CN.4/1994/44/Add.1*, January.
— (1997a) *Report of the Intergovernmental Working Group of Experts on IDPs*, UN Commission on Human Rights (Geneva: UNCHR).
— (1997b) *Renewing the United Nations: A Programme for Reform*, A/51/950, 14 July.
— (1998) *Guiding Principles on Internal Displacement. Compilation and Analysis of Legal Norms, E/CN.4/1996/52/Add.2*.
— (2001) *Note by the Secretary General: Internally Displaced Persons, A/56/168*, 24 April
— (2005a) *Mass Exoduses and Displaced Persons Addendum: Framework for National Responsibility, E/CN.4/2006/71/Add.1*, 23 December.
— (2005b) *World Summit, A/60/L.1*; www.un.org/ga/documents/overview2005summit.pdf (accessed January 2008).
— (2006) 'Sri Lanka – United Nations Condemns Indiscriminate Use of Force', Press Release; www.un.org/children/conflict/pr/2006-11 09srilankaunitedna129.html (accessed December 2006).
UN Chronicle (1985) *When Disaster Strikes: The United Nations Response to Natural Disasters* (Geneva: UNDRO).
— (1991) *UNDRO: Coping with Disaster … A Fine Line: Office of the United Nations Disaster Relief Coordinator* (Geneva: UNDRO).
UN ECOSOC (United Nations Economic and Social Council)

— (2002) *The Return of Refugee's or Displaced Person's Property, E/CN.4/Sub.2/202/17*, 12 June.
— (2005) *Specific Groups and Individuals: Mass Exoduses and Displaced Persons: Framework for National Responsibility, Commission on Human Rights E/CN.4/2006/71/Add.1*, 23 December.
UN Inter-Agency IDP Unit (2003) *Working Group in Sri Lanka: Durable Solutions Progress Reports* (New York: IASC).
UNDP (United Nations Development Programme) (1998) *Development Cooperation Sri Lanka: 1996–1997* (Colombo: UNDP).
— (1994) *Human Development Report* (Oxford: Oxford University Press).
— (2004) *Reducing Disaster Risk: A Challenge for Development* (New York: UNDP).
— (2005) *The Report on People's Consultations on Post Tsunami Relief, Reconstruction, and Rehabilitation in Sri Lanka* (Colombo: UNDP and Colombo University Community Extension Centre).
— and FAO (1968) *Mahaweli Ganga Irrigation and Hydro-Power Survey (Ceylon), Final Report*, vols 2 and 3 (Colombo and Rome: UNDP/FAO).
— (1969) *Mahaweli Ganga Irrigation and Hydropower Survey: Final Report. General Report*, vol. 1 (Colombo and Rome: UNDP/FAO).
UNGA (United Nations General Assembly) (1972) *Resolution 2958 (XXVIII)*, 12 December.
— (1975) *Resolution 428 (V)*, 14 December.
— (1991) *Resolution 46/182*, 19 December.
— (1992) *Resolution 47/195*, 16 December.
— (1995) *Resolution A/RES/49/19*, 15 December.
— (1993a) Office of the United

Nations High Commissioner for Refugees, *Resolution 48/116*, 20 December.

— (1993b) *Strengthening the Co-ordination of Emergency Humanitarian Assistance of the United Nations, UN Doc A/RES/48/57*, 14 December.

— (1993c) *Vienna Declaration and Programme of Action: World Conference on Human Rights, A/CONF.157/2*, 12 July.

— (2004) *Resolution A/RES/58/177*, 22 December.

— (2005a) *Resolution A/RES/60/124*, 15 December.

— (2005b) *Resolution A/RES/60/128*, 16 December.

UNHCR (United Nations High Commissioner for Refugees) (1950) *Statute of the Office of the United Nations High Commissioner for Refugees, 428 (V)*, 14 December.

— (1967) 'Notes of a Confidential UNHCR Meeting with Mr. Udo Affia, Commissioner for Health of Breakaway Eastern Nigeria "Biafra" of 9 November'. 6/1/NIG [3-1964/3-1970]: Fonds 11: *Records of the Central Registry*. Sub-Fonds 1: Classified Subject Files: 1951–1970, UNHCR Archives (Colombo).

— (1980) *Executive Committee Conclusion No. 18*, August.

— (1985) *Executive Committee Conclusion No. 40*, August.

— (1987a) 'Aide Memoire: Agreement Between the Government of Sri Lanka and UNHCR', October.

— (1987b) *Overview of UNHCR Activities 1986–87 (A/AC.96/696)*, 3 August.

— (1990a) 'Mission Report from the UNHCR Deputy Director of International Protection', mimeo, 9 August.

— (1990b) 'Note for the File: High Level Meetings on Sri Lanka', Internal Memo (C. J. Carpenter), Geneva-UNHCR office, 21 November.

— (1992) 'Mission to India and Sri Lanka: 8–15 March, 1992', Confidential UNHCR memo (from Moussalli to Chetty).

— (1993) *UNHCR's Role with Internally Displaced Persons, IOM/FOM/33/93*, April.

— (1994a) *Executive Committee Conclusion No. 75*, August.

— (1994b) 'Protection Aspects of UNHCR Activities on Behalf of Internally Displaced Persons', *EC/1994/SCP/CRO.2*, 4 May.

— (1996a) *International Legal Standards Applicable to the Protection of Internally Displaced Persons: A Reference Manual for UNHCR Staff* (Geneva: UNHCR).

— (1996b) *UNHCR 1997–1999 Country Operations Plan Sri Lanka* (Colombo: UNHCR).

— (1997a) *The State of the Worlds Refugees* (Oxford: Oxford University Press).

— (1997b) *Statement of the Director of International Protection to the 48th UNHCR Executive Committee* (Geneva: 16 October).

— (1997c) *IOM/FOM 87/91* (2 December).

— (1997d) *Inter-Office Memorandum No. 87/97*, from MacNamara D., 2 December.

— (1998a) *UNHCR's Operational Framework for Repatriation and Reintegration Activities in Post-Conflict Situations* (Geneva, December).

— (1998b) 'Confidential: Guidelines and Discussion Note on UNHCR's Protection Role with IDPs in Sri Lanka' Internal Memo (B. Schack), Colombo-UNHCR office, February 26.

— (1998c) 'UNHCR's Operational Role with Internally Displaced Persons: Information Note', mimeo.

— (1999a) 'Outline of the Capacities of Different Organisations with Regard to the Protection of Internally Displaced Persons', IASC XXII Meeting: Protection of Internally Displaced Persons (New York, December).

— (1999b) *Executive Committee Conclusion No. 87* (Geneva: UNHCR).

— (2000a) *State of the World's Refugees* (Oxford: Oxford University Press).

— (2000b) 'Internal Flight or Relocation Alternative within the Context of Article 1A (2) of the 1951 Convention and or 1967 Protocol Relating to the Status of Refugees' (Geneva: UNHCR position paper).

— (2000c) *Internally Displaced Persons: The Role of the United Nations High Commissioner for Refugees* (Colombo, March).

— (2000d) *Internally Displaced Persons in Government Welfare Centres in Sri Lanka: Workshop Results and Proposals for Action* (Colombo: CHA and UNHCR).

— (2000e) *Internal Displacement in Sri Lanka* (Colombo Branch Office, November).

— (2000f) *Country Strategy for Sri Lanka* (Colombo: UNHCR).

— (2000g) *Welfare Centre Survey* (Trincomalee: UNHCR, confidential).

— (2000h) *Statistical Yearbook* (Geneva: UNHCR).

— (2001a) 'UNHCR Inter-Office Memorandum No. 77/2001: Operational Guidelines for UNHCR's Involvement with Internally Displaced Persons' (Geneva: UNHCR, September 24).

— (2001b) *UNHCR Workshop: Durable Solutions for Displaced Persons in Trincomalee*, 27–28 November.

— (2001c) 'UNHCR Situation Report', Confidential Memo (Colombo) 11 March.

— (2001d) *Reintegration: A Progress Report. Executive Committee EC/51/SC/CPR.5.*

— (2001e) *Note for the File: Visit to Batticaloa and Ampara 9–11 March* (Trincomalee sub-office: UNHCR).

— (2001f) *Note for the File: Update Batticaloa 17–18 July* (Trincomalee sub-office: UNHCR).

— (2001g) 'Operational Guidelines for the Implementation of UNHCR's Policy on IDPs', confidential draft.

— (2002a) *The State of the World's Refugees* (Oxford: Oxford University Press).

— (2002b) 'UNHCR Programme for Internally Displaced Persons in Sri Lanka', *Report of a Joint Appraisal Mission by the UK Department for International Development and UNHCR* (Geneva: UNHCR Evaluation and Policy Analysis Unit).

— (2002c) 'Initial Report of Protection Review: Vavuniya and Mannar 8–13 March' (Colombo: UNHCR).

— (2003a) 'Land, Housing and Property: Proposals to the Parties for Comprehensively Addressing Land, Housing, and Property Rights in the Context of Refugee and IDP Return within and to Sri Lanka', *Report Submitted to the UNHCR and the Human Rights Commission of Sri Lanka* (Colombo, April).

— (2003b) *SIHRN*, power-point presentation (Colombo).

— (2003c) *Guidelines on International Protection: Cessation of Refugee Status Under Article 1C(5) and (6) of the 1951 Convention Relating to the Status of Refugees, HCR/ GIP/03/03.*

— (2004a) *Executive Committee Resolution on Protracted Refugee Situations, EC/54/SC/CRP*, 14 June.

— (2004b) *UNHCR Circular* (Trincomalee sub-office).

— (2004c) *Poverty Reduction Strategy Papers: A Displacement Perspective* (Geneva: UNHCR).

— (2004d) *Statistical Yearbook* (Geneva: UNHCR).

— (2005a) 'UNHCR Engagement Towards Internally Displaced Persons within the Collaborative Approach', Personal Reflections from Antonio Guterres.

— (2005b) *Consistent and Predictable Responses to IDPs. A Review of UNHCR's Decision-Making Processes* (Geneva: EPAU).

— (2005c) *Transitional Shelter Strategy*, version 6, section 1.

— (2005d) *Statistical Yearbook* (Geneva: UNHCR).

— (2006a) *Sri Lanka: Country Consolidated Appeal* (Geneva: UNHCR).

— (2006b) *Statistical Yearbook* (Geneva: UNHCR).

— (2006c) 'Rethinking Durable Solutions: Targeting Development Assistance', *The State of the World's Refugees 2006* (Oxford: Oxford University Press).

— (2007a) *Policy Framework and Corporate Strategy: January* (Geneva: UNHCR).

— (2007b) 'Guidelines on Confidence Building and Stabilization Measures for IDPs in the North and East', mimeo.

UNICEF (United Nations Children's Fund) (1984) 'Plan of Action (1984–88): Mahaweli System "B". Proposal to the Mahaweli Authority' (Colombo: UNICEF).

UNSC (United Nations Security Council) (1967) *Resolution 242*, November 22.

Uphoff, N. (1996) *Learning from Gal Oya: Possibilities for Participatory Development and Post-Newtonian Social Science* (London: Intermediate Technology Group).

— (2001) 'Ethnic Cooperation in Sri Lanka: Through the Keyhole of a USAID Project', in A. Esman and R. Herring (eds), *Carrots, Sticks and Ethnic Conflict*.

US State Department (2005) 'Report on Human Rights Practices'; www.state.gov/g/drl/rls/ hrrpt/2005/61711 (accessed June 2008).

USCR (US Committee for Refugees) (1991) *Refugee Focus: Sri Lanka* (Washington, DC: USCR).

— (1994–2004) *USCR Annual Statistics* (Washington, DC: USCR).

UTHR (University Teachers for Human Rights) (1993) 'From Manal Aaru to Weli Oya and the Spirit of July 1983', Special Report 5; www.uthr.org/SpecialReports/ spreport5.htm (accessed November 2004).

— (1995) 'Children in the North-East War: 1985–1995', Briefing Report 2, www.uthr.org/Briefings/ Briefing2.htm (accessed November 2004).

— (1997) 'Land, Human Rights and the Eastern Predicament', Report 11; www.uthr.org/Reports/ Report11/Report11.htm (accessed November 2004).

Uyangoda, J. (2005) 'Ethnic Conflict, the Sri Lankan State and the Tsunami Disaster in Sri Lanka', *Forced Migration Review*, 14, Special Tsunami Edition: 30–1.

Vamadevan, M. (2007) 'Towards a National Policy for Housing and Property Restitution', Workshop by COHRE, 15 March, Colombo.

van Damme, W. (1995) 'Do Refugees Belong in Camps? Experiences from Goma and Guinea', *The Lancet*, 346: 8971.

van Hear, N. (1998) *New Diasporas* (London: UCL Press).

— and D. Rajasingham-Senanayake (2006) 'From Complex Displacement to Fragile Peace in Sri Lanka', in N. van Hear and C. McDowell (eds), *Catching Fire: Containing Forced Migration in a Volatile World* (New York: Lexington Books).

Vedavalli, V. (1994) *Socio-Economic Profile of Sri Lankan Repatriates in Kotagiri* (New Delhi: Konark).

Venugopal, R. (2003) 'The Global Dimensions of Conflict in Sri Lanka', *Working Paper 99* (Oxford: QEH).

Verdirame, G. and B. Harrell-Bond (with Z. Lomo and H. Garry) (2005) 'Rights in Exile: Janus-Faced Humanitarianism', *Studies in Forced Migration*, 17 (Oxford: Berghahn Books).

Vernant, J. (1953) *The Refugee in the Post-war World* (London: Allen & Unwin).

Vimaladharma, K. (1982) *Land Settlement Experiences in Sri Lanka* (Colombo: USAID and Ministry of Lands and Land Development Seminar).

Vincent, M. and B. Sørensen (2001) *Caught Between Borders: Response Strategies of the Internally Displaced* (London: Pluto Press).

Vittachi, T. (1980) *Emergency '58: The Story of the Ceylon Race Riots* (London and Berlin: Andre Deutsch).

Von Clausewitz, C. (1989) *On War* (Princeton, NJ: Princeton University Press).

Voutira, E. (1997) 'Refugees, Migrants, Oustees, Displacees and Returnees: A Conceptual Framework for Understanding Varieties of Displacement', Paper for the International Workshop on Narrating Mobility, Boundaries and Citizenship (Mangleas, 30 August–1 September).

— and B. Harrell-Bond (2000) 'Successful Refugee Settlement: Are Post Experiences Relevant?' in M. Cernea and C. McDowell (eds), *Risks and Reconstruction*, pp. 56–76.

Walkiewicz, R. and K. Brockman (2004) 'Ethnic Conflict and the Impact on the Dry Zone of Sri Lanka', *ICES Report 123* (Colombo: ICES).

Wallensteen, P. (2005) 'Armed Conflict and Its International Dimensions 1946-2004', *Journal of Peace Research*, 42(5).

Wanigaratne, R. (1979) 'The Minipe Colonisation Scheme – an Appraisal', *Research Study 29* (Colombo: ARTI).

— (1987) 'Intra-Regional Disintegrating Effects of Frontier Land Settlement – Sri Lanka', mimeo.

— and M. Samad (1980) 'Land Alienation Under Recent Land Reforms', ARTI Occasional Publication 19.

Warren, M. (ed.) (1968) *Dams in Africa: An Inter-Disciplinary Study of Man-Made Lakes in Africa* (London: Frank Cass).

Weeramunde, A. (1982) 'Transforming Peasants: Social Change in a Dry Zone Settlement Scheme', *Research Paper Series* (1) (Colombo: University of Colombo).

Weerawardena, S. (1951) *Government and Politics in Ceylon: 1931–46* (Colombo: ICES Archives).

Weerawardna, I. (2007) 'Development of the NIRP for Sri Lanka – Overview of the Background and the

Process', ADB Conference Presentation, Colombo, 14 June.

Weiner, M (ed.) (1993) *International Migration and Security* (Boulder, CO: Westview Press).

— (1995) *The Global Migration Crisis: Challenges to States and to Human Rights* (New York: HarperCollins).

Weiss, R. and D. Korn (2006) *Internal Displacement: Conceptualization and Its Consequences* (New York: Routledge).

Weist, K. (1995) 'Development Refugees: Africans, Indians and the Big Dams', *Journal of Refugee Studies*, 8(2): 163–84.

Welch, S. (1975) 'Sampling by Referral in a Dispersed Population', *Public Opinion Quarterly*, 39(2): 237–45.

Wendt, A. (1992) 'Anarchy is What States Makes of It: The Social Construction of Power Politics', *International Organization*, 46(2): 391–425.

— (1994) 'Collective Identity Formation and the International State', *American Political Science Review*, 88: 384–96.

WFP (World Food Programme) (1999) 'Sri Lanka: Displacement in the North and East', mimeo.

— (2001) Projects for Executive Board Approval. Agenda Item 9. WFP/EB.3/2001/9-B/1.

White, G. (1994) 'Civil Society, Democratization and Development (I): Clearing the Analytical Ground', *Democratization*, 1(3): 375–90.

White, G. F. (1945) *Human Adjustment to Floods: A Geographical Approach to the Flood Problem in the United States* (Chicago, IL: Department of Geography, University of Chicago).

— (1964) *Adjustment to Floods* (Chicago: University of Illinois Press).

— (1973) *Natural Hazards Research*, in R. Chorley (ed.), *Directions in Geography* (London: Methuen), pp. 193–216.

— and J. Haas (1975) *Assessment of Research on Natural Hazards* (Cambridge, MA: MIT Press).

WHO (World Health Organization) (2000) *Internally Displaced Persons, Health and WHO* (New York: ECOSOC, 19–20 July).

Wickramasekera, P. (1985) 'The Mahaweli Development Programme, Agrarian Changes and the Peasantry', in C. Abeysekera (ed.), *Capital and Peasant Production: Studies in the Continuity and Discontinuity of Agrarian Structures in Sri Lanka* (Colombo: Social Scientists Association).

Wigley, B. (2002) 'Between Homes, Between Paradigms: Refugee Camp Experience and Development Policy Dilemmas', Paper for the IASFM Conference (Bangkok, January).

Wilson, A. (1988) *The Break-up of Sri Lanka* (London: Hurst and Co.).

— (2000) *Sri Lankan Tamil Nationalism: Its Origins and Development in the 19th and 20th Centuries* (London: Hurst and Co.).

Winslow, W. and W. Woost (eds) (2004) *Economy, Culture, and Civil War in Sri Lanka* (Bloomington and Indianapolis: Indiana University Press).

Wisner, B., P. Blaikie., T. Cannon and I. Davis (2004) *At Risk: Natural Hazards, People's Vulnerability and Disasters* (London: Routledge).

Wolde-Selassie, A. (2000) 'Social Re-articulation After Resettlement: Observing the Belles Valley in Ethiopia', in M. Cernea and C. McDowell (eds), *Risks and Reconstruction*.

Wood, G. (ed.) (1985) *Labelling in Development Policy* (London: Sage).

Woost, M. (1990) 'Rural Awakenings: Grassroots Development and the Cultivation of a National Past in Rural Sri Lanka', in J. Spencer, *Sri Lanka: History and Roots of Conflict*, pp. 164–83.

— (1993) 'Nationalising the Local Past in Sri Lanka: Histories of Nation and Development in a Sinhalese Village', *American Ethnologist*, 20(3): 502–21.

World Commission on Dams (2000) *Dams and Development: A New Framework for Decision-Making* (London: Earthscan Publishing).

World Bank (1980) *Operation Guidelines 4.30 for Resettlement* (Washington, DC: World Bank).

— (1984) *Staff Appraisal Report: Sri Lanka Mahaweli Ganga Development Project IV*, Report 4885-CE (Washington, DC: World Bank).

— (1986) *Involuntary Resettlement in Bank Operations: a Review of the Application of Bank Policies and Procedures FY79–85 Projects* (Washington, DC: World Bank AGR; Michael Cernea).

— (1993) *Early Experience with Involuntary Resettlement: Overview* (Washington, DC: Operations Evaluation Department).

— (1994) *Resettlement and Development: The Bank-Wide Review of Projects Involving Involuntary Resettlement: 1986–93* (Washington, DC: Environment Department).

— (1996) *World Bank Lending for Large Dams: A Preliminary Review of Impacts* (Washington, DC: Operations Evaluation Department).

— (1998) *Recent Experience with Involuntary Resettlement: Overview* (Washington, DC: Operations Evaluation Department).

— (2000) *Resettlement Monitoring Through the World Bank Inspection Panel* (Washington, DC: World Bank).

— (2004a) *Operational Policy 4.12* (Washington, DC: World Bank).

— (2004b) 'Project Appraisal Document on a Proposed Credit in the Amount of SDR 51.1 Million to the Democratic Socialist Republic of Sri Lanka for a North East Housing Reconstruction Programme', 20436-LK (Washington, DC: World Bank).

— (2004c) *Conflict and Structural Adjustment in Sri Lanka: Internal Evaluations Department* (Washington, DC: World Bank).

— (2004d) *Project Performance Reassessment Report: Sri Lanka Third Mahaweli Ganga Development Project* (Credit 1166-CE) (Washington, DC: Operations Evaluation Department).

— (2005) 'Post-Tsunami Recovery and Reconstruction Strategy', mimeo (Colombo).

Yeld, R. (1968) 'The Resettlement of Refugees', in R. Apthorpe (ed.), *Land Settlement and Rural Development in East Africa*, pp. 33–7.

Yiftachel, O. and A. Ghanem (2005) 'Understanding Ethnocratic Regimes: The Politics of Seizing Contested Territories', *Political Geography*, 23(4): 647–76.

Young, O. (1980) 'International Regimes: Problems of Concept Formation', *World Politics*, 32: 331–56.

— (1989) 'The Politics of International Regime Formation: Managing Natural Resources and the Environment', *International Organisation*, 45(3): 349–75.

Zeender, G. (2005) 'Engaging Armed

Non-State Actors on Internally Displaced Persons Protection', *Refugee Survey Quarterly*, 24(3): 96–111.

Zetter, R. (1991) 'Labelling Refugees: Forming and Transforming a Bureaucratic Identity', *Journal of Refugee Studies*, 4(1): 39–62.

— (2007) 'More Labels, Fewer Refugees: Remaking the Refugee Label in an Era of Globalization', *Journal of Refugee Studies*, 20(2): 173–92.

Zolberg, A., A. Suhrke and S. Aguayo (1989) *Escape from Violence: Conflict and the Refugee Crisis in the Developing World* (Oxford: Oxford University Press).

Newspapers

Saturday Review, 2 December 1984.
Saturday Review, 8 September 1984.
Sunday Island, 1 August 1998.
Sunday Leader, 15 August 2004.
Sunday Observer, 22 February 1998.
Sunday Times, 12 September 1983.

Index